SECOND WORDS:
Selected Critical Prose

Margaret Atwood

SECOND WORDS
Selected Critical Prose

Beacon Press   Boston

Copyright © 1982 by O.W. Toad Limited
First published in 1984 by Beacon Press

Beacon Press books are published under the auspices
of the Unitarian Universalist Association of
Congregations in North America,
25 Beacon Street, Boston, Massachusetts 02108

Printed in the United States of America

(hardcover) 9 8 7 6 5 4 3 2 1
(paperback) 9 8 7 6 5 4 3 2 1

Portrait of Margaret Atwood by Charles Pachter, acrylic on canvas, 1980.
From the collection of Lorraine Monk.

Cover design: Laurel Angeloff

Library of Congress Cataloging in Publication Data

Atwood, Margaret Eleanor, 1939–
 Second words.

 Includes index.
 1. Canadian literature–20th century–History and
criticism–Addresses, essays, lectures. 2. Literature,
Modern–20th century–History and criticism–Addresses,
essays, lectures. I. Title.
PR9184.6.A89   1984   810'.9'971   83-71983
ISBN 0-8070-6358-4
ISBN 0-8070-6359-2 (pbk.)

SECOND WORDS

Contents

Introduction   11

Part I: 1960-1971   17

1. Some Sun for this Winter   21
2. Narcissus: Double Entendre   24
3. Apocalyptic Squawk from a Splendid Auk   27
4. Kangaroo and Beaver: *Tradition in Exile* by J. P. Matthews   30
5. F. D. Reeve: *Aleksandr Blok*   33
6. Superwoman Drawn and Quartered: The Early Forms of *She*   35
7. Four Poets from Canada: Jones, Jonas, Mandel and Purdy   55
8. Some Old, some *New*, some Boring, some *Blew*, and some Picture Books   63
9. MacEwen's Muse   67
10. The Messianic Stance: *West Coast Seen*   79
11. Nationalism, Limbo and the Canadian Club   83
12. Eleven Years of *Alphabet*   90
13. Al Purdy: *Love in a Burning Building*   97

Part II: 1972-1976   103

14. Travels Back   107
15. How do I get out of Here:
     The Poetry of John Newlove   114
16. Mathews and Misrepresentation   129
17. Reaney Collected   151
18. Adrienne Rich: *Diving Into the Wreck*   160
19. Audrey Thomas: *Blown Figures*   164
20. Erica Jong: *Half-Lives*   167
21. What's so Funny? Notes on Canadian Humour   175
22. On Being a Woman Writer:
     Paradoxes and Dilemmas   190
23. Adrienne Rich: *Poems, Selected and New*   205
24. Kate Millett: *Flying*   210
25. The Curse of Eve—
     Or, What I Learned in School   215
26. Canadian Monsters: Some Aspects of the
     Supernatural in Canadian Fiction   229
27. Adrienne Rich: *Of Woman Born*   254
28. Marie-Claire Blais: *St. Lawrence Blues*   259
29. Audrey Thomas: *Ten Green Bottles,
     Ladies & Escorts*   268
30. Marge Piercy: *Woman on the Edge of Time,
     Living in the Open*   272

Part III: 1977-1982   279
31. *A Harvest Yet to Reap:*
     A History of Prairie Women   283
32. *Anne Sexton: A Self-Portrait in Letters*   287
33. Timothy Findley: *The Wars*   290
34. Diary Down Under   296
35. Last Testaments: Pat Lowther
     and John Thompson   307
36. Tillie Olsen: *Silences*   313
37. Sylvia Plath:
     Johnny Panic and the Bible of Dreams   316
38. Valgardsonland   320
39. E. L. Doctorow: *Loon Lake*   325
40. Witches   329
41. An End to Audience?   334
42. *Midnight Birds: Stories of Contemporary*
     Black Women Writers   358
43. Nadine Gordimer: *July's People*   363
44. Ann Beattie: *Falling in Place*   366
45. An Introduction to *The Edible Woman*   369
46. Canadian-American Relations:
     Surviving the Eighties   371
47. Amnesty International: An Address   393
48. Northrop Frye Observed   398
49. Jay Macpherson: *Poems Twice Told*   407
50. Writing the Male Character   412
Acknowledgements   433
Index   437

Introduction

This book is called *Second Words* for two reasons. The first is that I am not primarily a critic but a poet and novelist, and therefore my critical activities, such as they are, necessarily come second for me, although for a writer who is essentially a critic they would of course come first. The other reason is based on precedence: that is, a writer has to write something before a critic can criticize it. This is in no way to imply that words spoken first are always better than the critical fabrics raised upon them. It is only to state what seems to be the obvious; that is, you can't have a thought about a stone without first seeing a stone. (Which leaves us in a curious position *vis à vis* unicorns.)

So much for introductory doodling. The real truth is that I don't like writing the kinds of things that are brought together in this volume nearly as much as I like writing other kinds of things. It's all too much like homework, which I never used to get done on time either, being, as most poets and novelists are, much fonder of looking out the window. Scrabbling through the bottoms of cardboard boxes and the backs of filing cabinets, trying to locate things I suspected I'd written but had carelessly mislaid, finding other things I had no knowledge of but which were unmistakably in my handwriting, raking over, in other words, the sins of the past, both of omission and commission, brought it all back to me: the promises extracted from me, as juice is extracted from lemons, usually over the phone (I'm better at *No* in letters), the procrastination, the approach-avoidance reactions, the cold sweat at the approach of the inevitable deadline, the late nights up with the typewriter and the cups of half-drunk cold tea and the stapler and the box of Kleenex (for the never-fail psychosomatic cold), and, sometimes, the apologies and guilt when, despite all this, the item in question just didn't get produced. The memories are not fond.

Why do I find it so painful? And why then do I do it all? The kinds of pain, and the reasons for doing it, vary from *genre* to *genre*, but I suppose you could sum up both under the general heading of that old Victorian chestnut, A Sense Of Duty. I still believe, despite the Me Generation, that there can be reasons for doing a thing other than the fact that you may find it pleasurable or self-fulfilling. Book reviews seem to me one of the dues you pay for being a writer, especially in Canada. When I began writing and first discovered that there were other people writing in Canada, it was fairly clear that unless some writers reviewed Canadian books, some of the time, they wouldn't get reviewed at all. That has changed a great deal, but some of the feeling lingers on. Occasionally I may review a book, still, just to get it reviewed, or, because I feel it's been badly treated or misunderstood. For instance, my first Canadian review of Adrienne Rich was done because the book review editor I was speaking with didn't know who she was, and my review of Timothy Findley's *The Wars* was done because the book had been very unfairly reviewed in an influential paper. (However, if one devoted one's life to this kind of rescue operation one would have time for nothing else.) Sometimes I review out of enthusiasm, which is a variation on the above; the same holds true for introductions. I don't review books I can't at all respect or like, although people have tried to set me up with things they knew I'd hate. In cases like this, I assume I'm the wrong reader but that a right reader may possibly exist.

Book reviews I think are the most difficult form for me. It's easy in them to be flip and dismissive, to make jokes at the book's expense, to sneer at the author; some papers think of this as being "controversial" or "readable." But if you're an author yourself you know how much time and effort has gone into a book, even a bad book, and you can't take it so lightly. A reviewer has a responsibility to the public, but she also has a responsibility to the book; you have to try to see and say what is actually there.

Longer critical essays are less painful. For one thing, you know they aren't going to damage sales and affect someone's livelihood, because they are usually *post facto* and printed in little magazines or academic journals. They also allow more room, for judicious reconsideration, for more complex evaluation than is usually possible in (for instance) *The Globe and Mail*, and for that luxuriant weed of academe, the footnote. If the book review leans a little towards Consumer Reports, the critical essay is perhaps more like talking to yourself. It's a way, too, of finding out what you really think.

Then there are speeches, or as they are sometimes in my case euphemistically called, "lectures." The reasons for giving those are even more Victorian; they go all the way back to John Stuart Mill on the subjugation of women. Even in the 1980's I am still being approached by groups who say I just have to do it because this or that august body has never had a woman before (as they're fond of putting it) and if I won't do it and they can't get Barbara Frum, whatever will become of them? (Sometimes it isn't a woman. Sometimes it's a writer, and sometimes, even and especially in Canada, it's a Canadian. Sometimes its all three. So there you are, addressing an audience half of which fought tooth and nail to get you there and the other half of which wishes you were at the bottom of Lake Ontario instead. Being an ice-breaker isn't all that much fun, but as they used to say in those war movies I watched as an adolescent, someone has to do it.) The other reason for making a speech is that there are things that ought to be said, at that time, to that audience; but it often boils down to the same thing. For the speeches, I've indicated the audience and the occasion in the source list at the back, so the reader will be able to tell when "here" means Waterloo, Ontario, and when it means Cambridge, Massachusetts. What gets said, when you're making a speech, depends a lot on whom you're saying it to.

I've divided this book into three parts, which correspond to three periods of my life. The first, or Rooming House, runs from 1960 to 1971, during which I moved about fifteen times, always to places with a lot of stairs to climb and inadequate heat. It was during this time that I was developing some of the ideas set forth in *Survival.* The second, or Dugout, period runs from 1972 (or publication of *Survival*) to 1976, and covers a time when I was being attacked a lot; much of what I wrote then was in response to some of these attacks, the more intellectually serious ones, I think. (People who attack me for having curly hair, breast feeding and making public appearances I can't do much about.) It also corresponds to the peak of cultural nationalism and the popularization of feminism.

The third period, which has no name yet, runs from 1976, in which I published *Lady Oracle* and had a baby, thus becoming instantly warm and maternal and temporarily less attacked, to the present. It covers my growing involvement with human rights issues, which for me are not separate from writing. When you begin to write, you deal with your immediate surroundings; as you grow, your immediate surroundings become larger. There's no contradiction.

When you begin to write you're in love with the language, with the act of creation, with yourself partly; but as you go on, the writing—if you follow it—will take you places you never intended to go and show you things you would never otherwise have seen. I began as a profoundly apolitical writer, but then I began to do what all novelists and some poets do: I began to describe the world around me. This book is part of that description.

—Margaret Atwood   1982

PART I
1960-1971

Part I: 1960-1971

I began reviewing books and writing about writing where many people do: at college, in my case for *Acta Victoriana*, the literary magazine of Victoria College, University of Toronto. To say that there wasn't a long lineup for editorial positions would be an understatement. It was 1960 and cashmere sweaters and pearl-button earrings were still in, except among the few interested in the arts, for whom they were definitely out. Black was in.

So a handful of us, all in black, not only edited the magazine but practically wrote the whole thing, under pseudonyms and otherwise. I've spared you my pseudonymous parodies of Layton and Frye....

I notice that I was reviewing Canadian books exclusively, even though, I recall, none of us thought it was really possible to be a genuine writer and remain in Canada. The appearance of books by young writers like Marie-Claire Blais was, for us, a beginning.

Between 1961 and 1971, fate and the need for jobs took me to Harvard, back to Toronto, to Váncouver, back to Harvard, where I was working on material connected with the Superwoman essay here included, to Montreal, to Edmonton, to England, France and Italy, and finally back to Toronto in 1971, where I joined the Board of Directors of Anansi Press and, in 1972, wrote and published *Survival*. In the meantime I had of course published a number of books, but my reviewing activities were limited; I did some things for people who asked, mainly George Woodcock of *Canadian Literature* and James Reaney of *Alphabet* and Daryl Hine of *Poetry*. By 1967 Coach House Press and House of Anansi had been established, and the rapid growth of Canadian publishing that characterized the late '60's and early '70's was underway.

My reviewing activities weren't unconnected with my own writing at this time, which included, for instance, *Susanna Moodie* and *Power Politics*, and, in 1970-71, *Surfacing*, which must have been started (or re-started, since I actually began it in 1965) shortly after I'd written "Nationalism, Limbo and the Canadian Club"; which itself marks a transition, since it was my first piece in anything meant for an audience which was not primarily literary.

1
Some Sun for this Winter

(1961)

Winter Sun is an appropriate title for the first book of collected poems by Margaret Avison, a Canadian poet of already considerable standing. The title, like so many of the poems themselves, is not merely what it seems. One might, at first glance, take it as a hint about the prevailing mood of the contents, and it does indeed evoke the bleak sombre bareness of the Toronto watery-sunlight winters that provide material for much in the book. But although Miss Avison's light is a winter light, it is still the sun: a particular sun which is capable of rendering immediate appearance transparent as the glass of a lens.

One always runs the danger, when speaking of a poet's "reality beyond the finite," of branding the poet as a floaty-footed and cloudy-headed mystic whose vision, although it may be directed upwards, tends to encounter nothing but fog. (In Toronto, of course, the fog has at least some relation to actual experience.) To identify Miss Avison with this cliché would be sticking the label on the wrong bottle. She has her feet firmly on the ground (usually the "cinder mash" or "cool tar" of the city poems); her vision is always focused to, and through, specific concrete reality rather than past it. Again, if one praises a poet's descriptive powers, one risks conveying the image of a housewife cooking up a poem (of the Oh Beautiful Sunset or Hooray For Autumn variety) by applying adjectives to an object like icing to a cake, with the same result: if one swallows much of it, one feels a little ill. But Miss Avison never slathers her poems. Her use of descriptive words is not only precise and striking, but so precise and striking that the words do not just describe the object but *are* the object: there are other tennis players in both art and life, but *her* tennis players, "albinos bonded in their flick and flow," are the only ones of their kind.

She pares her works to the core, and throws out all extraneous and diluting verbal peelings. The result of this critical cutting and sorting is a highly condensed poetic texture which demands a lot of conscious concentration on the part of the reader. For example:

> ... The even-bread
> Of earth smokes rainbows. Blind stars and swallows parade
>   the windy sky of streets
>   and cheering beats
> down faintly, to leaves in sticks, insects in pleats
>   and pouches hidden
>   and micro-garden....

Winter Sun is not a chocolate-covered poetic pill, guaranteed to taste nice, go down easily, and eliminate all need for effort. Such sweetness would be useless in its universe:

> Nobody stuffs the world in at your eyes.
> The optic heart must venture: a jail-break
> And re-creation.

Miss Avison portrays consciousness as an attempt to encounter and to form a relationship with the external; the ultimate locus of such an encounter is the individual human mind, which makes its ordered cosmos out of a chaos which includes bits of society, scraps of sense perception, snips of science, moments of history, chips of myth, and the elbowings of the insistent self, as well as the phenomena of the natural universe. Her ordered structure is built of various poetic forms, among them simple lyric stanzas, unconventional sonnets, blank verse, and highly disciplined irregular lines which avoid the free and all-too-easy idiom of the contemporary common denominator. Her verbal wit is considerable, but never coy; her humour subtle, sometimes ironic, but always wise; her human warmth (a warmth which is connected with a strong sense of nostalgia) is most evident in the last, longest, and most definitely not least poem, "The Agnes Cleves Papers."

In the last analysis, the poetic eye sees its own world, a world which both reflects and transcends the formlessness of the finite world outside, and reality becomes internal:

> ... Gentle and just pleasure
> It is, being human, to have won from space
> This unchill, habitable interior
> Which mirrors quietly the light
> Of the snow, and the new year.

Winter Sun is a book not to be read, on any account, just once.

2
Narcissus:
Double Entendre

(1961)

Alphabet, a new semi-annual edited by James Reaney, is indicative of a growing tendency to regard the individual piece of writing neither as an isolated phenomenon nor as a part of its author's total outlook or output but as a work whose real context is provided by literature as a whole. Thus, the structure is thematic rather than haphazard (as it would be in a review); and one is well advised to begin at the beginning and end at the end. (Presumably, the absence of a table of contents is intended to discourage browsing.) Such an arrangement is designed both to relate the various works to each other and to a central figure—Narcissus this issue—and to place them along an axis whose poles are Art and Life. Just about everything fits, from the poetry, (by James Reaney, Jay Macpherson, and Daryl Hine, among others), to Jay Macpherson's pertinent article "Narcissus: Some Uncertain Reflections," to Hope Arnott Lee's autobiographical account of the difficulties of twinship, to John Peter's book review which presents a "billboard image" of Irving Layton as a phallus-waving self-absorbed mirror-gazer.

There are dangers in this sort of selection: for instance, one feels that some of the pieces have to be stretched a little to fit the bed on which Mr. Reaney would have them lie. Also, in reading *Alphabet: A Semiannual Devoted to the Iconography of the Imagination*, and Reaney's editorial, one must be careful not to confuse the terms *symbol, myth,* and *icon,* which are tossed around quite freely. One of the main pitfalls of "iconographic" writing is over-stylization, or the development of stereotypes; so far, *Alphabet* has avoided it successfully.

A word must be said in defence of the format, which should not really need any. There seems to be some feeling that *Alphabet,* being an experimental magazine, should have printed the titles sideways or indulged in some other pseudo-artsy puerility to make itself *look* experimental, instead of adopting its rather conservative design. Considering that it was handset by Reaney himself (which accounts for the educational spelling mistakes and the wobbly lines) and that the emphasis in any literary magazine should be on content rather than appearance, one feels that the editor was well advised to keep things simple.

In conclusion, it should be made clear that *Alphabet* is not just another "little" magazine. It is, in a very lively sense, a "way of looking at things." "Besides which," (to quote the editor again) "it's a hell of a lot of fun."

If Reaney were looking for support of his view that symbolism is "a fact of our cultural life," he need look no farther than *Mad Shadows.* This is the English title of *La Belle Bête,* a novel by the young French-Canadian writer Marie-Claire Blais. It is a book that will perturb the reader who is committed to the doctrine of "realism," in the sense of "naturalism" or "social realism," in fiction. If one looks for any but the most fleeting reflections of the contemporary French-Canadian scene, one will be looking for the wrong thing. The most fitting context for *Mad Shadows* is a mythological one: the most fitting myth, Narcissus.

Practically all the characters in the book are, in some way, Narcissus-figures; practically all are, in addition, either physically or spiritually warped. The central figure, Patrice, is a Beautiful Beast who is in love with his own image. His jealous sister Isabelle-Marie is clever, sadistic, and ugly. Their mother, Louise, dotes on Patrice as the image of herself and refuses to admit that he is an idiot. (She spends so much time mirror-gazing that one keeps expecting, "Mirror mirror on the wall. . . . ") Lanz, her lover, is also her double—elegant, sensual and hollow. Both their beauties are deceptive: Louise's face is eventually destroyed by disease, and Lanz is a paste-up composed of a false beard and wig and a gold cane.

The handling of the characters is direct and forceful. The reader is often told about them rather than left to infer, much as a folk-legend *tells* that a princess is good and a step-mother wicked. The technique has its drawbacks; for instance, when Isabelle-Marie is rather incongruously described as "a creature of innate purity," or when Patrice asks, after his sister has disfigured him by pushing his head into boiling water, "Mother, why didn't you tell me that I was an idiot?" The plot is treated in the same forthright manner. Time goes forward in a straight narrative line (no flashbacks); again, much in the style of the folk-myth. The action is violent, as are all the deaths; and emotions throughout are of the extremest nature.

Mad Shadows might be accused of melodrama, were it not for its saving graces. Because the book is completely self-sustaining and self-contained, small defects may easily be passed over and exaggerations accepted. The world of Miss Blais is not that of so-called "real life." It is a world of the imagination, of myth, somehow *more* real for its exclusion of sociological paraphernalia. It possesses almost ritual under-tones, and is able to create strangely evocative images out of strangely intense relationships. It gets down to the primal, and sacrifices naturalism and subtlety in the process; but the sacrifice is justified in a work so rewardingly original.

The total effect is overpowering; one almost needs a page of Henry James as an antidote.

3
Apocalyptic Squawk from a Splendid Auk

(1959)

The Cruising Auk, like its namesake, is a member of a rare and all-but-extinct species: the book of humorous verse which somehow manages to be also a book of poetry. George Johnston achieves this hybrid result by refusing to take himself, or any of his other subjects, seriously—but by taking the demands of his form and language seriously enough to do them admirable justice.

Mr Johnston's subjects are delightfully trivial—and almost always small. His universe is a backyard pond—somewhat puddly and muddy, but teeming with lively bits and pieces of life and half-life. The blithe spirits which Mr Johnston calls from this vasty deep include neighbourhood notables like Boom, the pompous sufferer, who knows

> what is and what
> In spiritual things is not,

and Goom, who sips at Life, but doesn't know

> Whether it's really good or bad
> Its sweetest moments sour so;

Mr Murple, his "underslung long dog," and his gin-
drinking mother; a sprinkling of timorous virgins (virginal
with a truly Canadian practicality), and several other
youngish ladies whose very abandon has a sort of grim
determination. There are also poor nervous Edward:

> In the short sharp winter twilight
> When the beans are in to cook
> Edward under the trilight
> Reads a detective book;

various other cowed males, and a formidable caste of wormy
aunts and assorted old ladies. All, like the "sweetish aunt,
Beleek," are slightly rotten—and their progeny all empath-
ize with Eliot's Mrs Porter, either in thought or in deed. The
bird's-eye of Mr Johnston's Auk focuses on more than the
worms, however. His children are exuberantly innocent (for
instance, Andrew in "Kind Offices") or painfully tender:

> The wind blows, and with a little broom
> She sweeps across the cold clumsy sky.

His sketches of the city are lightly done, but with
affection and a train-whistle kind of nostalgia:

> One hears a sink
> And low voices, rustling feet;
> Clocks in the town put by the night,
> Hour by hour, ticked and right.

He reveals the small well-meaning suburbanite, living
life with a quieter than usual desperation:

> I've got time in my clocks
> And beer in my cellar and spiders in my windows;
> I can't spend time nor drink all the beer
> And I feel in the spread web the spider's small eye.

The really remarkable thing about *The Cruising Auk* is not,
however, the subjects themselves, but the author's treatment
of them. The poems are surprisingly simple in form and
image. Their ironic and often hilarious effect comes from

the aptness of the choice of words and, above all, from the timing. A simple comic-verse rhythm and a punchline sequence tend to become tedious after the first five minutes (as anyone who has read too much Robert W. Service or Rudyard Kipling at a time will know); but Johnston, because he uses his rather exacting forms with a great deal of variety, never bores. Several poems fail in total effect—surely "A Little Light" and "Yeats' Ghost" are below the usual standard—but they are interesting failures, at least.

Throughout the book, Mr Johnston preserves an objectivity that allows his verses to be humour rather than invective. Even when jabbing a favourite dusty aunt he is amused and amusing rather than spiteful. Like the splendid Auk, he remains detached:

> Surely his eye belittles our despair
> Our unheroic mornings, afternoons
> Disconsolate in the echo-laden air . . .

The product of his peripatetic musings is a collection poetic enough to delight even the most literate of the *literati*, and hilarious enough to soothe the most book-shy quarterback to a charming diffidence.

4
Kangaroo & Beaver:
Tradition in Exile
by J. P. Matthews

(1962)

The subtitle of this book, "A Comparative Study of Social Influences on the Development of Australian and Canadian Poetry in the Nineteenth Century," indicates the highly amorphous nature of the material. Any author who attempts to grapple this subject is threatened by engulfment, as if by a giant amoeba, and Dr Matthews is to be congratulated on the degree to which he imposes form on such a sprawling mass of tenuously related data. It is perhaps not his fault that he has had to snip and stretch a little to fit the past neatly into his Procrustean structure.

Comparative studies have a way of becoming invidious, and this one is no exception. Dr Matthews establishes two opposed sets of categories. "Colonialism" is seen in two aspects: one ignores the indigenous and strives to emulate the mother country, the other reacts against its parent and turns in upon itself. There are two corresponding kinds of poetry: the Academic and the Popular. These contrasts are acceptable, but they are made to imply doubtful value judgements: Popular Nationalism *per se* is a Good Thing;

Australia has always had, for historical, social, and geographical reasons, more of it; therefore Australian poetry is potentially "better" than Canadian poetry, which has always attempted to lean on its English heritage and to deal with universals rather than particulars. Dr Matthews' attitude is best illustrated by a metaphor: "...those who would avoid the growing pains and the unsightly pimples of adolescence by trying to jump prematurely to precocious maturity must pay some price for their action." He sees Nineteenth Century Australia as a healthy normal growing boy and Canada as a miniature mimicking adult; but better pimples than overgroomed priggishness. The image of the Bushman, virile, lawless, unwashed and above all virile, composing four-line ballad verses with irrepressible gusto, is set up against a pale straw-man of a nail-gnawing Canadian intellectual, smothered in Englishness, bleating and effete.

A Canadian reader is apt to be puzzled by some of this. Why is the Academic, as represented, for instance, by Lampman, necessarily worse than a Robert W. Service Popularity? "Aha!" Dr Matthews would snort. "You see, that's just the kind of question an Academic Canadian *would* ask!" Still, he doesn't really answer the question. The undesirability of all the qualities he lumps under "Academicism" is, for him, axiomatic rather than hypothetical.

Such an approach has its drawbacks. Confined by his rigid *a priori* two-category system, Dr Matthews sometimes has difficulty finding pigeonholes that fit the particular clay pigeons he singles out for potting. Thus, "Souster, Dudek, and Layton have denounced Academic poetry in Canada, but they have not become, in any sense, Popular poets. Theirs is a cerebral poetry, intellectual in conception and not concerned with reaching a mass audience." (The picture of Irving Layton coyly retiring into an ivory tower is, to say the least, naive.)

However, apart from its suppressed flag-waving, *Tradition in Exile* is informed, thoroughly documented, and comprehensive. Dr Matthews' skeleton-in-the-closet clutching the somewhat flaccid vitals of modern Canadian poetry is overdrawn but nonetheless relevant: Canadians need to be reminded from time to time that their poetry did not spring fully-formed from the head of A. J. M. Smith. The book is well-organized though inclined to be repetitious; the prose smacks of Ph. D. thesisisms but manages to make itself palatable; and the many quotations, often from little-known sources, are of considerable value. Whatever else it does, and despite the my-daddy's-better-than-your-daddy attitude, *Tradition in Exile* ought to encourage Canadian interest in Australian literature.

5

F. D. Reeve:

Aleksandr Blok

(1963)

Aleksandr Blok, the important almost-modern Russian Symbolist poet, has hitherto been unduly neglected in the West. F. D. Reeve's book is an evaluation of his work in its relation both to the literary and political activities of Blok's contemporaries and to the somewhat New-Critical microscope of the modern scholar. Any English-language "effort to make Blok's work known in the terms with which we have come to regard poetry during the last forty years" would be in danger of wrecking itself on the language-barrier if it took a too-textural approach; but Reeve avoids this peril by supplying translations literal enough to render his comments understandable (though, inevitably, form and mood are often lost), and by drawing in enough historical, biographical, and theoretical material to make his close analysis of the poems meaningful for a non-Russian-speaking reader.

Of course that many-headed hydra Symbolism rears its perplexing heads. Reeve takes a few passing swipes at them in the first chapter and stirs up a tangled nest of question-marks. This chapter may owe its comparative turgidity both to the necessity of dealing with a large subject in a small space and to the Peer-Gynt's-Onionism of which the whole Symbolist movement is suspiciously redolent. That, in evoking "transcendental reality," the Symbolists often skirted the edges of a spurious cultism, is especially evident in the passages of prose theory quoted. Even if the Symbolists themselves knew what they were talking about, we never will: the vaguely-religious central Mystery was poetically useful for them only as long as it remained arcane.

But the Russian Symbolist movement was only a background for Blok. He himself disliked the label and preferred to be regarded as an individual, which is largely how Reeve treats him. The staccato biographical sections outline the events in his personal life that lay behind his poetic career. The critical portions trace his early emergence as a celebrator of the "Beautiful Lady" (a static mystical symbol analogous to Yeats' early "Rose"), of whom Belyi remarked, "The Beautiful Lady turned out to be the most venomous caterpillar, later decaying into a whore and an imaginary quantity something like the square root of minus one," and the rapid development of his poetry in much more vital and inclusive directions as he searched for a means of bridging the gap between external actuality and his subjective "transcendental" world.

Reeve's stress on the affinities of Blok's lyric poems with dramatic forms, an emphasis natural for any critic familiar with Yeats' theory of masks, is particularly helpful in his brilliant analysis of "The Twelve," which, quoting Medvedev, he sees as " 'an original modification of the old romantic plot several times before used by Blok—Columbine-Pierrot-Harlequin.' " He denies that it is a Communist manifesto: "Its political associations are not so much intentional as merely coincidental. Its design is apolitical. It is a poem about revelation." His excerpts from Blok's diary support his interpretation: Blok's attitude was obviously that of a dramatist rather than a dogmatist.

Reeve's book is probably the best and most comprehensive study of Blok written in English. Despite its occasional murkiness, it is stimulating reading for anyone concerned with the history of modern poetry.

6

Superwoman Drawn and Quartered:
The Early Forms of *She*

(1965)

> *"You are a whale at parables and allegories and one thing reflecting another."*
> —Rudyard Kipling, in a letter to Rider Haggard.

Rider Haggard is a writer whom it is difficult to approach with straight face and serious intent. Though he wrote most of his early novels in an attitude of the most extreme High Seriousness, the reader tends to treat them as though they were comic books, and read them, if at all, on the sly. He had great success, both popular and critical, during the last decades of the nineteenth century and was ranked with Kipling and Stevenson, yet to-day his particular combination of high-flown rhetoric and bathos brings a wince to the sensitive nostril of the stylistic analyst, while those willing to go further than the flawed surfaces of his prose in search of significant archetypes may well founder in a morass of half-grasped symbols, promising but dead-end literary references, and only semi-mythic plots. The usual judgements made are of two kinds: The Adventure Yarn stance in which *King Solomon's Mines, Allan Quatermain*, and the later adventure stories are praised for their internal coherence, excitement of plot, and fidelity to exotic detail and claimed as cognates of Kipling and Stevenson and direct antecedents of Edgar Rice Burroughs, the muscle-flexing hard-hunting male mags, and (ultimately, with an effort) of Hemingway; and the Burning Imagination approach which places Haggard's romances with such late-flowering allegorical fantasies as George Macdonald's *Lilith* and W. H. Hudson's *A Crystal Age* and singles out *She* for special praise. The latter approach habitually includes a tribute from Henry Miller (note the dust-jacket on any modern edition) and leads to such statements as, "The story . . . has bewitching power, the sort one is accustomed to meet only in superior works of art such as 'Christabel' and some of Poe's masterpieces." Those eager for more literary parallels may see the mysterious central figure of *She* as someone who ought to have been included in Mario Praz's *The Romantic Agony*: another appearance of the Fatal Woman, a literary sister of Pater's Mona Lisa and of Swinburne's various vampire Venuses. Such peripheral connections abound, but the difficulty remains, and seems to be one which is inseparable from the study of any interesting but second-rate writer: many comments are possible but none seem necessary.

Haggard said of *She*, "There is what I shall be remembered by," and one might be content to read, remember accordingly, and leave it at that. The motives for going further are similar to those that connect themselves with jigsaw puzzles: curiosity, an assumption that the pieces can be fitted together somehow, and a desire to see what the total picture looks like: for *She* remained a puzzle to Haggard, unsolved, unresolved, throughout his life. He did not consider the novel finished, and wrote three sequels to it which he thought of as approaches towards ultimate Truth but which only succeed in thickening the metaphysical mists which cloud the first novel. He was obsessed with the personality of Ayesha, the central figure in *She*, and offers various lame hints of her "meaning" in letters to his friends; for instance, "Of course the whole thing is an effort to trace the probable effects of immortality upon the mortal unregenerate. *She*'s awful end is also in some sense a parable—for what are Science and Learning and the consciousness of Knowledge and Power in the face of Omnipotence? The same event happened to them all—and like *She* in all her loneliness they are liable to be resolved 'with laughter and hideous mockery' into what they really are. At least that is what I want to convey;" but the reader tends to share the perplexity of the "Editor" when he says, in the introduction to *She*, "At first I was inclined to believe that this history of a woman, clothed in the majesty of her almost endless years, on whom the shadow of Eternity itself lay like the dark wing of Night, was some gigantic allegory of which I could not catch the meaning."

She does indeed bear some resemblance to a "gigantic allegory," but it reads like a *Faerie Queene* from which the supporting theological and political substructures have been removed: the emblematic topography and the stylized figures are present but they have no specific referents. A search for this missing factor, the book's ideological structure, leads backwards toward its possible sources. *She* was written in six weeks, and Haggard himself says of its genesis, "I remember that when I sat down to the task my ideas as to its development were of the vaguest. The only clear notion that I had in my head was that of an immortal woman inspired by an immortal love. All the rest shaped itself round this figure. And it came—it came faster than my poor aching hand could set it down." One biographer concludes that Haggard was "writing deep, as though hypnotized," and proceeds to connect *She* with the world of the psychological unconscious and with scraps of past experience such as Haggard's childhood fear of an ugly rag doll "of particularly hideous aspect" which came to be named "She-Who-Must-Be-Obeyed," his early discovery of the terror of death, his interest in antiquity and myth, and his adventures in Africa. These associations are doubtless valid as far as they go; however, they relate only to some of the incidental detail and can explain neither the unresolved plot nor the ambiguous central personalities of *She*.

A more directly productive territory for pattern-hunters is available, in the five works of fiction that Haggard wrote during the three years before he wrote *She*. Two of these are the "Adventure Yarns" already mentioned; two are usually dismissed as bad Gothic Romances in which "the people he creates are caricatures illustrating maxims;" and the fifth is classed as a realistic novel which expresses the bitterness Haggard felt over the ceding of the Transvaal to the Boers. Yet these five books, when examined, are found to contain, not only unmistakable suggestions of every thematic element that makes *She* an unusual book, but also the gradual development of the personality of Ayesha, She herself. Haggard may have been writing "deep, as though hypnotized;" but if so the unconscious experience he was drawing upon was the creation of his previous books. The problematical themes and the patterns of *She* had been present in his work since the writing of his first work of fiction.

Before attempting to catalogue the pertinent elements of character and imagery in the earlier works it would be well to outline the main features of *She*. The plot turns upon an assumption of cyclical reincarnation. Although the story takes place in the nineteenth century, its events were set in motion two thousand years before, when Ayesha killed Kallikrates, the man she loved, through jealousy of his wife, an Egyptian princess named Amenartas for whom he had broken his vows as a priest of Isis. Ayesha, having obtained virtual immortality by bathing in the fires of the Place of Life, a cavern in the heart of a mountain, has spent the intervening centuries brooding over the preserved body of her lover and waiting for his next incarnation. Amenartas fled from Africa and gave birth to a son, through whom her story has passed along a line of descendents to Leo Vincey, an Englishman who decides to explore the mystery with his guardian Horace Holly. They reach Kor after a perilous journey across the ocean, through vast fever-ridden swamps and through a maze of tunnels in Kor's surrounding mountains. Leo is almost killed three times: once during a storm on the ocean, once by the Amahaggar, the cannibalistic matrilineal tribes who are under the government of She-Who-Must-Be-Obeyed, and once by swamp-fever; however he is preserved the first time by Holly, the second by Ustane, a native girl who has attached herself to him as a wife, and finally by She herself.

Ayesha, or She, makes her appearance halfway through the book. From the first she is a split personality, or so she appears to the story's narrator, Holly. With her immortality she has gained an irresistible superhuman beauty, "a rich and imperial shape, instinct with a life that was more than life, and with a certain serpent-like grace which was more than human;" she is described in terms of divinity, her expression one of "a godlike stamp of softened power, which shone upon that radiant countenance like a living halo." But her beauty is sinister: "I have heard of the beauty of celestial beings, now I saw it; only this beauty, with all its awful loveliness and purity, was *evil*—or rather, at the time it impressed me as evil. . . . Never before had I guessed what beauty made sublime could be—and yet, the sublimity was a dark one—the glory was not all of heaven. . . . It bore stamped upon it a seal of unutterable experience, and of deep acquaintance with grief and passion."

The ambiguity of Ayesha's moral nature is reflected in two opposed groups of associations. The sinister ones suggest the power and evil of witchcraft. In the chapter entitled "A Soul in Hell," she is described as a "white sorceress," a "modern Circe;" she curses her dead rival Amenartas with "an appalling malevolence" and an "awful vindictiveness." With her immortality she has also acquired supernatural intelligence and supernatural power; she can kill by the force of her will alone, and it is thus that she destroys Ustane, who, the reader is led to believe, is a reincarnation of Amenartas. She is a mistress of illusion, a mindreader with the ability to see events at a distance (though she herself says, "There is no such thing as magic, though there is knowledge of the hidden ways of Nature"), and to enchant and mesmerize, as she mesmerizes Leo over the corpse of Ustane, compelling him to yield to her, much against his better nature.

On the positive side, she is connected with a statue that stands in the ruins of Kor, a winged female figure representing Truth, "perhaps the grandest allegorical work of Art that the genius of her children has ever given the world." The inscription reads, in part, "Behold! Virgin art thou, and Virgin thou shalt go till time be done. There is no man born of woman who may draw thy veil and live, nor shall be. By Death only can thy veil be drawn, O Truth." Ayesha's earlier comparison of herself with the goddess Artemis whose unveiling meant death for Actaeon—"I too, O Holly, am a Virgin goddess"—underlines the identification, as does Holly's rather obvious comment: "As usual, Ayesha was veiled like the marble Truth, and it struck me then that she might have taken the idea of covering up her beauty from the statue." When she is seen as the embodiment of this ideal of ultimate Truth, she is "more perfect—and in a way more spiritual—than ever woman was before her."

That her double nature is split also into eternal youth and extreme age is first divined by Holly in his dream of a Nightmare Life-in-Death: "Then in the background of the vision a draped form hovered continually which, from time to time, seemed to draw the coverings from its body, revealing now the perfect shape of a lovely blooming woman, and again the white bones of a grinning skeleton, which, as it veiled and unveiled, uttered an apparently meaningless sentence: 'That which is alive hath known death and that which is dead yet can never die, for in the circle of the Spirit life is naught and death is naught. Yea all things live forever, though at times they sleep and are forgotten." Holly first sees Ayesha as a "swathed mummy-like form," and is then astounded by the freshness of her beauty when she unveils; but her skeleton aspect overtakes her in the Place of Life, where she has led Holly and Leo in order to let them become as immortal as herself. She passes through the fire again in order to demonstrate its effects for Leo, but somehow its powers are reversed: suddenly the weight of her great age falls upon her and she shrivels into a monkeylike figure "no larger than a big ape," and dies. Holly exclaims with horror over this withered embyro, "And yet—it was the *same* woman," and the unification of opposites—ugliness and beauty, youth and age, the desirable and the sinister—is complete in the Place of Life, now identical with the Place of Death.

Yet the symmetry of the pattern, and even its effectiveness as a parable of the nature of Nature (which seems to be one of the meanings Haggard thought he intended) is disturbed by the presence of Ustane. Ayesha's true moral nature is inevitably connected with the justice of her murder of Ustane. Ayesha herself says, "her sin is that she stands between me and my desire," but this is hardly an adequate excuse. Ustane is portrayed throughout with great sympathy: she saves Leo's life at the risk of her own, nurses him during his critical fever with absolute devotion, and defies Ayesha with what Holly calls "moral courage and intrepidity." At no time is it suggested that Ustane is evil: rather it is Ayesha whose "sin" is constantly emphasized and whom Leo calls a "fiend and murderess" for her deed. But Leo must judge between the two, and he eventually chooses Ayesha. As in most nineteenth-century romances in which the hero must decide between two women, the choice is of great importance: he is choosing a fate, a soul, and, ultimately, an ideology. Although it is clear by the end of the book that Leo considers his choice of Ayesha to have been the right or good choice, and that the murder of the innocent Ustane is thereby condoned (Holly even writes a footnote rationalizing it), it is never made clear what Ustane is supposed to represent, and therefore what two sets of values Leo is really choosing between. She might be considered an occasion for one more demonstration of Ayesha's power and her defiance of conventional morality, were it not for the hints that identify her with Amenartas and the predictions that future reincarnations will somehow involve a struggle between Ayesha and the "other woman" for the control of Leo's soul.

Other versions of the same battle take place in the earlier books. Since all six books, including *She*, tend to have a common vocabulary of images and symbols, it is possible to trace the character-types as the moral values assigned to them shift from book to book. The hero himself tends to be static: he is always an English Gentleman, and, in the love triangles and rectangles, always displays the passivity of a bone being disputed among dogs. From the beginning of his writing career the heroines seem to be Haggard's major interest. The first novel, *Dawn*, written in 1883, has been called "a shapeless anthology of two-dimensional actors, vague symbolism, ... and blood-curdling horror-stories," but although the plot is somewhat involved, the relationships among the female figures are almost diagrammatic. There are three central women—one good, one bad, and one either both or neither—with hair to match, in the traditions of the nineteenth-century romance convention (blonde, black, and chestnut). The good woman is Angela, after whom the first version of the book was named (Haggard re-wrote it on the advice of a publisher). She is a pale blonde Ideal, chiefly associated with great intelligence, and a spiritual beauty. "But how it is possible to describe on paper a presence at once so full of grace and dignity, of the soft loveliness of woman, and of a higher and more spiritual beauty?" the author asks, and proceeds to devote a page to such description, scattering references to saints, "the harps of Heaven," and Angela's "spirit look" with lyric fervour. Like Ayesha she is a "marble goddess," but her symbolic statue is not Truth but a marble Andromeda that adorns the villain's study and is the only thing saved from the fire that eventually consumes his house. Each of the three women in *Dawn* has a "philosophy," and Angela's is a pure belief in individual immortality. She says to the hero, Arthur Heigham (who is obsessed by death, and of course chooses a graveyard by moonlight as the setting for his proposal), "I am sure that when our trembling hands have drawn the veil from Death, we shall find his features, passionless indeed, but very beautiful." Towards the end of the book, when she thinks she has lost Arthur, she writes him a long letter expressing the belief that their fates are linked eternally and that she will join him after death. It is of interest that in the first version of the novel Angela was doomed to an early death, presumably leaving Arthur to be semi-consoled by the chestnut-haired lady, Mildred Carr.

Mildred is a doll-like widow who falls in love with Arthur when he has been exiled to Madeira for a year through the plottings of Angela's cousin George, the villain of the book. Mildred, who possesses a certain amount of worldly wisdom, quickly realizes that Arthur loves another woman; nevertheless she makes herself omnipresent in his life on Madeira, and hopes to become indispensable to him. Arthur develops a brotherly affection for her but does not discover the true state of her feelings until shortly before the year of his exile is up. He leaves Mildred and returns to England to marry Angela, only to discover that the latter, deceived by a false report of his death, has undergone a marriage ceremony with her cousin George. Arthur flees to Mildred, who receives him tenderly, takes him on a yacht cruise, and tries to replace the memory of Angela. Like Angela, Mildred represents a "philosophy:" her faith is placed in "neither death nor immortality, but . . . the full, happy, pulsing existence of the hour, and . . . the beautiful world that pessimists like yourself and mystics like Angela think so poorly of, but which is really so glorious and so rich in joy . . . as for life after death, it is a faint, vague thing, more likely to be horrible than happy. This world is our only reality, the only thing that we can grasp; here alone we *know* that we can enjoy." Mildred is not an evil woman: she is kind, tender and devoted; but as the embodiment of a *carpe diem* philosophy she can only be a dangerous temptation on the allegorical journey. She plays "Calypso" to Arthur's Ulysses, is a "hothouse flower" on the lush "lotus-eating" island of Madeira. Thinking that she may be able to salvage something from his ruined life, Arthur asks her to marry him, but she refuses him because she realizes she can never gain his full love. When the evil George has been neatly disposed of by Arthur's bulldog and Angela has recovered from the insanity caused by her mock-marriage and the knowledge that she has been deceived, the two lovers are reunited and Mildred is left brokenhearted, an example of "the vanity of passions which suck their strength from earth alone."

The third member of the female triad is Anne Bellamy. She is George's confidante, and the prime contriver of the plot to sell Angela to George at the price of some family estates which will be returned to Angela's avaricious father by the marriage. Throughout the book she is presented as an evil but intriguing Egyptian "Sphinx," an enigma. She is first seen through the eyes of Philip, Angela's father, who is "at a loss to know whether this woman, so bizarrely beautiful," fascinated or repelled him: "The head was set squarely on the shoulders, the hair was cut short, and clustering in ringlets over the broad brow; whilst the clearly carved Egyptian features and the square chin gave the whole face a curious expression of resoluteness and power." A conversation between Angela and Arthur pinpoints her emblematic identity:

"What does Lady Bellamy remind you of?" Angela asked Arthur.

"Of an Egyptian sorceress, I think. Look at the low, broad forehead, the curling hair, the full lips, and the inscrutable look of the face."

"To my mind she is an ideal of the Spirit of Power. I am very much afraid of her."

Her position on the allegorical map is made even clearer when the author calls her "Princess of Evil," and when she says, speaking of Angela's nature, that it is "in its way ... greater even than my own, representing the principle of good, as I represent the principle of evil." Her philosophy is one of power, and she attempts to practise it through her manipulation of her ineffectual husband, her plot to sacrifice Angela, and her dabblings in occult science by which she hopes to gain "power over Nature." That she is both prophetess and sorceress is suggested by Arthur's reaction to her; "she looked oracular. Her dark face and inscrutable eyes, the stamp of power upon her brow, all suggested that she was a mistress of the black arts. Her words, too, were mysterious, and fraught with a bitter wisdom and a deep knowledge distilled from the poisonous weeds of life." However, her Faustian aspirations lead her to a sticky end. When threatened with exposure by her husband, who has obtained the compromising letters that reveal her past relationship with George, she decides to commit suicide, hoping thus to probe the mysteries of Death; but the potion she drinks does not kill her, and she awakes to find herself paralyzed, doomed to a "living death."

Arranged according to their ages and functions, the three women in *Dawn* form a Robert-Graves-White-Goddess trinity, with Angela as Maiden, Mildred as Nymph, and Lady Bellamy as Crone. In terms of the moral values they represent, Angela is at the Good end of the spectrum and

Lady Bellamy at the Evil one, with Mildred in between. But another arrangement is possible. Lady Bellamy, who was once a minister's wife but was led into evil paths by George, is a fallen Angela, a great intellect that has been distorted. In an interview between the two at the end of the book Lady Bellamy wishes to atone for the harm she has done by making Angela her protégé in the study of the secrets of Nature; but Angela chooses to devote herself to Arthur instead. At the same time there is some suggestion that Lady Bellamy may eventually be redeemed through Angela's saving spiritual vision. Mildred, also, has affinities with Lady Bellamy. They meet on Madeira and Lady Bellamy offers to help Mildred in her attempt to win Arthur. Although Mildred refuses aid, the two women "interest" each other. The recurring image of Lady Bellamy as an "Egyptian sorceress" links her with Mildred's museum, a tomb-like structure called the Hall of the Dead which houses a collection of mummies and Egyptian curiosities and which is the scene of Mildred's final heartbreak. Arthur, pondering on Lady Bellamy's "expression of quiet power, of conscious superiority and calm command ... tried to think what it reminded him of, and remembered that the same look was to be seen on the stone features of some of the Egyptian statues in Mildred's museum." In this arrangement, then, Lady Bellamy becomes the middle term. She is seen not only as Angela's opposite but also as her complement, the intellectual and aspiring mystic turning her powers to evil instead of good; while Mildred is associated with the Egyptian-sorceress aspect and with her ultimate defeat and mummy-like living death.

The pattern of *Dawn* is repeated, with significant variations, in Haggard's next novel, *The Witch's Head* (completed in 1884). The figure that corresponds to Angela is Eva Ceswick, a woman "beautiful as an angel" who is compared to a "swan" and "the light of a star." She is the novel's Ideal, but, as the hero's friend Mr Alston remarks, "Something gone wrong with 'the Ideal,' I should say...that is the way with ideals;" for poor Eva is weak-willed and "not finely strung." The hero, Ernest Kershaw, falls in love with her and becomes engaged to her, echoing Angela's words to Arthur, "You are my fate, my other self," with "You are my fate, my other part" but, having killed his cousin in a duel, he is exiled from England, and Eva is left to become a prey to fate in the form of her sister Florence, "strong as Fate and unrelenting as Time."

Florence is the Lady Bellamy of this book; but, unlike the latter, she is in love with the hero. She reveals her love when Ernest, before his first meeting with Eva, kisses her lightheartedly. At this time Florence says menacingly that she has a "heart as deep as the sea," and that she has the power to both love and hate intensely; whereupon Ernest reflects that "he was not in the smallest degree in love with Florence Ceswick; indeed, his predominant emotion towards her was one of fear." When Florence realizes that Ernest loves Eva, she dedicates herself to revenge, and finally accomplishes it by forcing the weak-willed Eva to renounce Ernest and marry the sinister Mr Plowden, a clergyman with a varicose-vein cross on his forehead. The descriptions of Florence constantly recall those of Lady Bellamy. When first encountered she remarks that it is her intention to "exhaust every emotion," and as she speaks her expression is remarkable for its "power and unchanging purpose." She is the possessor of a "strength of purpose and rigidity of will that few of her sex ever attain to at any period of their lives," but she dedicates her talents to "conscious wickedness" because her love has been thwarted. Like Lady Bellamy she manipulates the fate of the Ideal; but she is able to succeed, whereas Lady Bellamy ultimately fails.

The emblematic identities of Eva and Florence are partially defined by three pictures which Florence draws while she is meditating Eva's destruction: one of Eva as a doe being chased by a hound that looks like Mr Plowden, another of Eva as a statue-like Andromeda chained to a rock while a serpent with the head of Mr Plowden rises from the water, and a third, drawn after the marriage has taken place, of herself as a dark winged shape, its face hidden, brooding over a scene in which Ernest drowns while Eva looks on, horrified. Florence is more completely defined by her identification with a strange but beautiful mummified head (after which the book is named) that is discovered by Eva in a crumbling graveyard. The head, with its "malicious" and "mocking" smile is "awfully fascinating." "Those who had seen it once would always long to see it again." The dark rippling hair is the same colour and texture as Florence's, and the features, "the beautiful teeth and the fixed hard smile," are like hers: "The dead face was more lovely indeed, but the woman of the Saxon era and the living girl of the nineteenth century might have been sisters, or mother and daughter." Florence herself realizes that there is some bond between herself and the dead woman, and comments ominously, "I think she must have been a witch." Although the head is introduced as a major factor in the plot it soon disappears from the story almost completely; its only real purpose is to establish Florence's identity as immortal sorceress. Florence herself vanishes from the book after Eva's marriage, reappearing only once at Ernest's wedding as a mysterious veiled lady: "She raised her thick veil and fixed her keen brown eyes upon the two who stood before the altar, and, as she did so the lips of this shadowy lady trembled a little, and a mist of trouble rose from the unhealthy marshes of her mind and clouded her fine-cut features . . . Then she rose, did this shadowy, lonely-looking lady, and glided from the church, bearing away with her the haunting burden of her sin."

The woman that finally captures Ernest is Dorothy Jones, whom he has known from childhood; she is the ward of his uncle and the sister of his lumbering friend Jeremy, who also loves Eva Ceswick and who plays an unintellectual version of Horace Holly to the "Grecian statue" Ernest's Leo Vincey. Dorothy, or "Doll" as she is called, is a sweet housewifely woman whom Ernest thinks of at first as a "sister" but who loves him secretly (recalling Arthur's relationship with Mildred). After Ernest has lost Eva to Mr Plowden the book concerns itself with the conflict between the devotion of Dorothy and Ernest's idealized memory of Eva. When Ernest returns from Africa, blinded by lightning, Dorothy is waiting to care for him and to "weave herself into the substance of his life," attempting (like Mildred) to take the place of his lost beloved. Ernest cannot forget Eva, though he refers to her as the "evil destiny" that has destroyed his life. When he proposes to Dorothy it is in words that anticipate one of the major themes of *She*: "It is somehow fixed in my mind that my fate and that woman's are intertwined. I believe that what we are now passing through is but a single phase of interwoven existence, that we have perhaps already passed through many stages, and that many higher stages and developments await us. Of course it may be fantasy, but at any rate I believe it. The question is, do you care to link your life with that of a man who holds such a belief?" Dorothy replies that, if there is such a future existence, she expects to share it with Ernest in some way that will not exclude Eva.

From the first two novels, then, a common triangle emerges. Each book contains an Ideal who is associated with the purity of marble statues and with a future immortal love; a sinful Dark Sorceress who is an "Ideal of Power" and is inscrutable, veiled, linked with images of antiquity: the Sphinx, the Egyptian sorceress, the mummified witch's head; and a Domestic Woman who can offer the hero little beyond her loyalty and the mundane and more earthly comforts. In each book the Dark Sorceress concerns herself with the destruction of the Ideal, but in each book the real battle for the hero's soul is between the Ideal and the Domestic Woman. In *Dawn* the Ideal wins (although she was originally to have died), the Dark Sorceress is rendered powerless and the Domestic Woman defeated, but in *The*

Witch's Head the outcome is not decisive: Florence merely vanishes, and neither Eva nor Dorothy manage to gain full possession of Ernest's heart.

In the next two novels, *King Solomon's Mines* and *Allan Quatermain*, (both 1885), the primary emphasis shifts from the female triangle to Haggard's version of the quest theme, which takes the form of an imaginative exploration of the African landscape, with the goals of an ancient forgotten treasure (in the first book) and an ancient forgotten civilization (in the second). The physical features of the journey—deserts, mountains, underground rivers, Coleridgian chasms—are treated, not as the abstract contents of a dreamvision (as they are in *Dawn*, where Arthur's search for Angela is prefigured by an allegorical dream of a walk through a forest, then along a wilderness path which ends at an "illimitable ocean"), nor as realistically-handled settings for the action (as in the African portions of *The Witch's Head*), but with the combination of solid detail and symbolic suggestiveness that makes the landscape of *She* an integral part of the story's force. The female figures in these two adventure stories are relatively undeveloped, but they deserve brief mention. *King Solomon's Mines* has a sorceress of the darkest dye in a most hideous phase: the witchfinder and prophetess Gagoola, known as "Mother of Evil," the keeper of the secret of the "Place of Death" (a grisly cave-tomb which conceals the treasure). The previous Sorceress figures have only suggestions of immense age, but it appears that Gagoola, a shrivelled monkey-like creature very much like Ayesha at the time of her death, must be actually several hundred years old at least. *King Solomon's Mines* was written as a boys' adventure yarn and "petticoats" were excluded from it on purpose; but in its sequel, *Allan Quatermain*, the battle for the hero's heart is resumed, though it does not occupy the centre of the stage. The two women involved, the twin sister-queens of the lost country of the Zu-Vendis, are much more recognizably the Fair Beautiful and the Dark Sublime of earlier nineteenth-century romantic convention from Scott's *Ivanhoe* on, but they have some habitual Haggard attributes also. Nyleptha, "The White Queen," "a woman of dazzling fairness," has her familiar allegorical statue ("... a draped female form of such white loveliness as to make the beholder's breath stand still. And as for the calm glory that shines upon her perfect face—well, I can never hope to describe it. But there it rests like the shadow of an angel's smile; and power, love, and divinity all have their part in it.") while Sorais, "The Lady of the Night," has the cruelty and passion of the Dark Sorceress type: "Somehow her face, quiet and even cold as it was, gave an idea of passion in repose, and caused me to wonder what its aspect would be if anything occured to break the calm. It reminded me of the deep sea, that even on the bluest days never loses its visible stamp of power." When she sings, her voice has "all the sorrow of the world and all the despair of the lost." The Domestic Woman is nowhere to be seen, perhaps because Nyleptha assumes her functions at the end of the book, after Sorais has committed suicide. The impression that the sister-queens are divided halves of a single personality is very strong.

In Haggard's next novel, *Jess*, which he completed a month before he started to write *She*, a rearrangement of types and a consequent shift of moral values has taken place. The book's heroine, Jess Croft, is called "the soul of it all," and although the story is ostensibly a treatment of the Boer rebellion in the Transvaal it is her personality that is the centre of interest. In terms of the earlier triangle, Jess is a peculiar combination of the Ideal and the Sorceress. She has exceptional intellect and a will stronger than that of the hero, whom she "mesmerizes" at a critical moment much as Sorais holds Curtis spellbound and Ayesha mesmerizes Leo Vincey. She combines the coldness of a "Virgin Goddess," a marble maiden, with the emotional intensity of Lady Bellamy, Florence, and Sorais: she is "very cold—cold as stone—but when she does care for anybody it is enough to frighten one." Above all she is "uncanny," "a riddle," "an Egyptian Sphinx," and an inscrutable veiled woman: "For here and there there is a human heart from which it is not wise to draw the veil — a heart in which many things slumber as undreamed dreams in the brain of the sleeper. Draw not the veil, whisper not the word of life in the silence where all things sleep, lest in that kindling breath of love and pain dim shapes arise, take form, and fright thee."

Jess's sister Bessie is the epitome of the Domestic Woman: "housewifely," a picture of "healthy, happy womanhood," a good practical woman not overburdened with intelligence. The hero, John Neil, an ex-army English Gentleman who comes to work on the farm where the two sisters live with their uncle, finds himself attracted to both sisters, and both secretly love him; but Jess sacrifices her love for Bessie's sake and leaves the farm to visit Pretoria, and John proposes to Bessie. Then the Boer rebellion breaks out and John goes to Pretoria to fetch Jess, where he discovers that he has made the wrong choice: it is Jess and not Bessie who is, in Haggard's terms, his "fate." However, both he and Jess consider his engagement to Bessie binding, even after they have escaped from Pretoria together and sworn eternal love while facing death at the hands of the book's villain, a rival for the hand of Bessie. Jess rapidly becomes more and more ethereal: ("Her face was more like that of a spirit than of a human being, and it almost frightened him to see it."); she dies at the end of the book after committing a murder to save her sister from a forced marriage to the villain, and John marries Bessie while continuing to hope for the reunion that Jess has promised him after death.

Reconsidered against the background of the novels written before it, *She* is seen as an amplification of earlier patterns. In it Haggard combined the larger-than-life landscapes of *King Solomon's Mines* and *Allan Quatermain* with the larger-than-life personalities of *Dawn, The Witch's Head,* and *Jess,* and the sphinx-like female who is not quite believable as a genteel Englishwoman or even as the niece of an ostrich-farmer in Africa is able to become a character who creates her own decorum and who moves in a setting that mirrors the precipices, tombs, and unhealthy marshes of her own Gothic mind. Ayesha's double nature parallels that of Jess: she is a combination of the Ideal and the Dark Sorceress types: but whereas in Jess the Ideal predominates, Ayesha is at first more notable for her sinister qualities. The question of Ustane's function in the "gigantic allegory" is, by analogy, partially answered: she is a camouflaged version of the Domestic Woman, offering the fleshly, the earthly, the daily, as opposed to Ayesha's virginal inaccessibility, semi-divinity, and immortality; but Ustane too is immortal and will be re-incarnated whenever Ayesha reappears, as the sequel to *She* implies; for their opposition is eternal.

It is perhaps making one of Haggard's own mistakes, that of attempting to pile more weight on his "allegory" than its flimsy fabric will bear, to attempt to suggest further significances. However, those interested in literary patterns may note that Haggard, consciously or unconsciously, was working within the conventions of nineteenth-century fiction, re-creating the split heroine, the tension between domestic and exotic, in yet other forms. Whereas Rowena's victory is almost unequivocal and remains decisive throughout such duets, or duels, as those between Hawthorne's Priscilla and Zenobia, Dickens' Biddy and Estella (the former is seen, too late, as the right choice) and Meredith's Lucy and the temptress Bella, Haggard's re-vision is closer to the ambiguity of Melville's *Pierre* and Poe's *Ligeia*, with the final triumph, in *Ayesha; or The Return of She*, of the sublime over the merely beautiful. Predictably, as Ayesha moves from withered mummy to beautiful woman to divine spirit, almost a reversal of her progress in *She*, Asene, the reincarnation of Amenartas and Ustane, takes over many of Ayesha's original evil qualities, and Ayesha as Hes, the Nature-Goddess, becomes not double but triple; her allegorical statue is not a virginal marble truth but a divine Mother carrying a human child (a parody of the

Virgin-and-Christ-Child). The hero perishes, none the less, through his disregard for her deathly aspect; in his attempt to marry her before he himself has become immortal, he is "withered" by her kiss. Haggard's great popular success might lead the cultural trend-tracer to conclude that he was dramatizing some of the central conflicts of his society, and to find a connection between the rise of feminism towards the end of the century and the development of Haggard's power-hungry Superwoman (with a passing glance at the impassioned plea for women's rights in *The Witch's Head*), or between the growing disillusionment with the efficacy of material progress as a panacea for England's ills, and the movement of Haggard's hero away from English domesticity towards the African wilderness in yet another attempt to return to something more primitive and more essential. His books are full of passages deprecating the shallow veneer of European civilization and praising "Nature," but it is a Nature inscrutable, powerful and death-ridden. Haggard's hero can never quite decide whether Nature-Red-In-Tooth-And-Claw and Behind-the-Veil may not, after all, turn out to be the same thing. In Haggard's vaguely allegorical world, which is really a world of inverted romanticism carried to its extreme, the English Gentleman does not have as clearly defined a choice towards the end of the century as he had at the beginning. Ultimately any choice that leads to earthly happiness becomes impossible: the true enemy of the hero's salvation and spiritual fulfillment proves to be The Angel In The House; the only good woman is a dead woman, preferably swathed in the graves-clothes of mystery; and, in Butler's paraphrase of Tennyson, "it is better to have loved and lost than never to have lost at all."

7
Four Poets from Canada:
Jones, Jonas, Mandel, and Purdy

(1969)

These poets differ widely enough in technique to indicate that eclecticism still flourishes healthily in Canada, yet it would be hard to mistake any one of them for an English or even an American poet. Why? There's no single answer, but it has something to do with space, sensed as vast, open, unconfining, and oppressive.

The feeling for space permeates the work of D. G. Jones. His last book, *The Sun Is Axeman*, was dominated by summer and by celebrations of the fulness and self-sufficiency of nature, of the space within things. In *Phrases From Orpheus* he turns to the space between things. This is a winter book, in many senses: the most frequently-recurring images are of snow, barren fields, stones; the verse line is stripped down, the phrasing defoliated; in place of the earlier presiding sun-god is Death, the "brutal lord." But the arrangement of the poems suggests a journey through winter and out again. In the initial poem "The mind is not / Its own place / Except in Hell," and in the next few poems Jones' trust in the outside universe is affirmed. However this universe ceases to support as the poet's own world falls apart, and the meditating self is forced back upon whatever resources can be dredged up in the face of separation, the disintegration of personal relationships, and deaths: "At first you can't think straight. Stillness, / Deprivation and the empty bed / Are a derangement, every valve / Closes, light / Is an abstraction...." The soul works out, not its own salvation exactly, but at least some possible tactics for survival in its attempt "To find words for what we suffer, / To enjoy what we must suffer— / Not to be dumb beasts." In the long complex title poem the poet descends into a Hell where the mind *is* its own place, confronts the past, the dead and the horror of existing, and manages to emerge into the saving world of real objects, "the dawn upon the winter hills / the quiet lake." The Orpheus-voice maintains that Eurydice is not, in fact, down here but out there. The last poems point tentatively toward rebirth from desolation, a "ghostly spring," and accept "the certain ground that is no / ground;" they accept also the goddess who, in various guises, has been a lost Eurydice or an absent or sinister Persephone throughout the book but who returns at the end as a tangible human Eve.

Jones is a convincing and responsible poet, but he is sometimes "difficult," and not always in laudable ways. The title poem suffers from over-allusiveness, a circling round rather than an articulation, perhaps because its subjects are so agonizing that the poet must hold them at a distance. The reader may question a sometimes irrelevant use of classical myth (as in "At The Edge Of The Garden" and the second last stanza of "En Guise d'Orphee;" "Your mouth, like great Achilles' bow / Drawn to Troy, your long / Neck drawn / Like Leda's, boldly to the skies..."). The occasional fiddlings with fashionableness (the capitalizations in "Animals," for instance) are uneasy in this book, as is the poem "For Robert Duncan;" it's unsettling to find an example of this over-played parlour game in work so generally serious. Jones is best when apparently simplest, in such poems as "On A Picture Of Your House," "Poem," "The Path," "Putting On

The Storms," and "The Stream Exposed With All Its Stones,"
which follows:

> The stream exposed with all its stones
> Flung on a raw field
> Is covered, once again,
>
> With snow
> It is not hidden. It
> Still flows.
>
> The houses in the valley, standing
> Motionless below,
> Seem wrapped in sunlight like a snow
>
> And are deceptive. Even stones
> Deceive us.
>
> The creator goes
> Rampaging through our lives: winter
> Is a masquerade.
>
> I tell you
> Nakedness is a disguise: the white
> Is dark below.
>
> This silence is the water's cry.
>
> I tell you in those silent houses girls
> Are dancing like the stones.

In *The Absolute Smile*, a first book by a Hungarian who
came to Canada in 1957, the spaces are between people.
George Jonas' usual subject is himself, but he moves from an
individual self with private histories to the self as representative urbanite, furtive inhabitant of a patrolled and quietly
repressive society, to the self as the very society under
attack: "I am fair, peaceful and wise; my smooth voice / Is
never raised; I forgive and forget. / My grey navies sit in
heavy waters, / My compassionate guns are trained at the
world." These are political poems only insofar as politics is
part of the texture of life "In Any City." They lack stridency
because they lack self-righteousness: the poet identifies

with the ordinary-faced killers he describes as well as with the victims: "I do not know what to make of inhumanity / Beyond sharing and understanding it, / Inflicting it and having it inflicted upon me / Every day usually before noon."

There is little sense of place here: all cities are alike in that they become battlegrounds, and weather, that pervasive Canadian subject, is not of much importance to the indoors *isolato*. Even solid objects detach themselves from any coherent background and float in a surreal space, or take on a nasty life of their own. Women too become objects, seen as assemblages of interchangeable parts. The poet sidesteps the suspicion that he too may be an assemblage through negative affirmation: "I cannot be shown / I cannot be shared / No one can learn me. / . . . Mirrors do not reflect me / Sound waves do not bounce off me/ I am not revealed in my dreams. . . . " Finally, nothing can be known or possessed by him, least of all himself.

Jonas' poems are deftly-handled and remorseless, though they tend to sound the same note. If some of them, especially the "love" poems, read like light-versified extracts from *Games People Play*, no one is more aware of it than the author. The urbane hopelessness and gallant, self-mocking despair are faintly Byronic; Jonas hits hardest when he turns from making faces in the mirror to contemplating the view from his "metal tower," in such fine poems as "Peace," "Portrait: The Freedom Fighter," and "On A State Funeral."

Eli Mandel's third collection is a trip to inner space, the consciousness cut adrift in its own void. Gwendolyn Mac-Ewen once wrote, "I do not fear that I will go mad / but that I may not," and this kind of fear informs the dialectic of *An Idiot Joy*. Insanity is the possession of, or by, a version of reality not shared by one's society, and in the context of poetry-denying "politics, political men and government," insanity is also a fit (and post-Romantic) metaphor for poetry. Thus the writing of poetry becomes both a desirable

madness and an exorcism of society's "real" madness. On
another level, the dilemma is that of McLuhan's print man—
McLuhan himself appears in "Galaxy"—squashed between
the pages (the first half of the book is packed with images
such as "print," "script," "writing," "book," "newspapers,"
"mss.," "texts," and "libraries") and repelled by the brute
physical universe, yet trying desperately to get out of
the realm of words, words, words, like the escape artist
Houdini, for whom "manacles, cells, handcuffs" are words,
and who struggles to free himself from "those binding
words, wrapped around him / like that mannered style, his
formal suit." For cerebral printman such an escape offers
itself in the form of violence, rage, mimed murder, and
contact with the physical, and is signalled by silence: halfway through the book Mandel's universe, which has been a
scripture or a horrible talking machine, finally shuts up,
and the poet exhorts, "think only of the unwritten / all / a
shrine / of possible / silences." The escape artist is freed to
confront history, betrayal, the personal past, and love, and to
concentrate on the thing said rather than the act of saying.
But articulate speech is itself a betrayal of the divine
madness, and the book ends with the poet's desire to transform himself into an object ("The Apology") and an ultimate,
doubtful attempt to synthesize the verbal and the physical
("Cosmos," III, a), though the reader suspects that the
struggle with the binding word will be, like Houdini's, a
repeated one.

The prosodic strategy is an expansion of the open-
endedness and fragmentation of Mandel's first book, *Fuseli
Poems*, though some of the most successful single poems
("Agamemnon's Return," the extraordinary "House of
Candy," "Houdini," "Signatures") are in the more structured
manner of *Black and Secret Man*. If the use of mythology is
more persuasive than D. G. Jones', it is perhaps because
Mandel provides an abstract listing of components or a sort
of emulsion rather than a particular environment. Thus he
can title a poem "Agamemnon's Return" or "Joseph" without

raising the question of what these figures are doing in a Canadian landscape. That there *is* no "real" landscape is part of the theme; it's also part of the problem, both for poet and reader.

A. W. Purdy is among Canada's most versatile and prolific poets: *North of Summer* is his eighth book, *Wild Grape Wine* his ninth, and he shows no signs of slacking. But haste has its price, and in these books poems are included to plump out the volumes, images and even incidents get repeated, and there aren't many signs of the excising scalpel. In addition Purdy can be banal, silly, cute, overly-rhetorical, irrelevant and corny. What then makes him one of Canada's finest, as he is?

One thing is his trick of including his opposites. There are many overlapping self-created versions of Purdy, but three strains can be isolated: A. W., intellectual, amateur archeologist, amateur historian, not above references to philosophy, mythology, and what-have-you; Alfred Wellington, a sentimentalist with a big soggy heart who indulges in "globs of LOVE" and fantasies of being a mother robin; and plain Al, who sneers at A. W.'s pretensions, questions Alfred Wellington's motives, and puts down the reader when either of the others has sucked him in. Which is the real one? They all are, and when two or more are gathered together the result is a dazzling display of psychological fancy footwork, as in "Shoeshine Boys on the Avenida Juarez." One of Purdy's specialties is catching himself in the act, and at these moments his honesty and his wire-cutter toughness are never in doubt.

These qualities come in handy in *North of Summer*, a collection of poems written during, and about, a trip taken to Baffin Island in the summer of 1965. In the prose piece at the back Purdy says he wants the reader to use the poems as "an extension of his or her own eyes and mind," a "pair of binoculars" for viewing the Arctic. But there's not much chance of that: no-one else's eyes and mind are like Purdy's, and at the centre of his "optic glass" is the figure of Purdy himself, soliloquizing over dead seals, not understanding Eskimo, pissing from a boat, loafing, and (madly, heroically) clutching his pants and a roll of "violet toilet tissue" while husky dogs attack him from the rear. The book has the virtues and flaws of a diary: things are there because they were there, and for the most part the author is "a kind of witness / but not exactly a reporter," producing a variety of literary journalism.

Insofar as the book has a shape (as Purdy hints it has), it's the shape of a journey back: back in history, back to a more primitive life, back before Paradise to the "chaos" evoked in the first poem; and of a corresponding personal journey, the poet in this alien environment becoming a "grey-haired child" rediscovering the language (though what he finds is his own inability to communicate) and himself (though at the end it's all a puzzle, and "the point I'd hoped to separate / from all these factual things stubbornly / resists me and I walk home slowly feeling stupid.... ").

One of the recurrent devices in these poems is the "civilizing" of the Arctic through sometimes preposterous similes applied to natural things: icebergs are like bowling alleys, hamburgers, Maple Leaf Gardens, the seed pods of the ground willow are "like delicate grey earrings." This annoys—it's as though Purdy won't let these things be themselves—but then, like Crusoe on the island, he's pre-programmed. Sometimes it works, as in the poignant "What Do The Birds Think?" where birds are "perched on rubbery muskeg / like blue teacups / or lost brown mittens." This poem, "Listening," and "Tent Rings" would be my choices for a Purdy anthology.

Wild Grape Wine is a more satisfying book, partly because Purdy is operating from his home ground in rural Ontario (though with excursions to Cuba, Ottawa and New-foundland). He explores this territory in depth, viewing its time as space, digging into its past through history and his own memories, as in "Elegy for a Grandfather," or recreating it through his imagination, as in "Private Property," "Wilderness Gothic," and "Roblin Mills," in which the past is held eerily under water: "The black millpond / holds them / movings and reachings and fragments / the gear and tackle of living / under the water eye / all things laid aside / discarded / forgotten / but they had their being once / and left a place to stand on." This is a fourth Purdy: no wisecracks, no sentimentality, no adjective embroidery, the lines quite simply right. These poems go beyond Purdy's interest in people and incidents to the process of human life within the larger process of nature; they create, not a personality and a speaking voice (that's the achievement of the first three Purdys) but a landscape with figures, both alive and dead. It's this Purdy rather than the political commentator or the bum-pincher or the town wit that remains with the reader: a lonely, defiant, almost anonymous man, dwarfed by rocks, trees and time but making a commitment, finally, to his own place, "where failed farms sink back into the earth" and grim ancestors reach up from the ground to claim him.

8

Some Old, some *New*, some Boring, some *Blew*, and some Picture Books

(1966)

Your estimate of any little magazine will depend on what you think little magazines should be doing. Should they simply exist as open-ended receptacles for the work of whatever writers happen along, or should they be publishing the writers of a city or region? Should they be actively fostering a poetic or political ideology? These are all useful functions. Of perhaps less obvious value are the magazines set up by university English Departments to furnish prestige of a sort, and the magazines which exist primarily to express a bloated editorial ego.

The Far Point (No. 1) is an example of the university engdept type, and it illustrates the pitfalls. Apart from a desire to play it safe and turn out something that looks pro there seems to be no editorial policy. In spite of the attractive Kanadian eskimo-print cover, a chauvinistic count found American contributors outnumbering Canadians two to one. (Maybe the cover's symbolic: it shows a huge toothy bear about to devour a small clueless-looking seal.) There's some good poetry and a few interesting articles, but no particular reason why it should all be gathered together in this place.

Hyphid (No. 3) has a beautiful name (aphid? creature from another planet?) but apart from that it's thin: this issue contains the work of only five poets, though a couple of the poems are longish. No editorial, no regional slant, the poetry ranging from John Newlove's condensed starkness to Bill Bissett's incantatory lyricism. Most little mags need money and better distribution, but *Hyphid's* need is greater: then they'd be able to turn out something longer than sixteen pages for seventy-five cents.

New: American and Canadian Poetry (No. 7, No. 8) gives you lots of mimeo pages, the occasional picture, and a promise to go into offset next issue. It does indeed publish Canadian poetry, sometimes, and its alert review section even covers books by Canadian poets, though with an occasional tut-tut at "Kiplingesque provincialism," or Canadians being distressingly outspoken about being Canadian. (Well, O. K., it may be a bore to you, *New*, but back in 1830 Americans were doing the same thing vis-à-vis the English and getting similarly put down for it; anyway what else do you do in the face of cultural imperialism?) *New's* taste in poetry leans towards the Kayakian, though judging from only two issues it's slightly more eclectic.

Intercourse (No. 9) does a lot more horsing around. *The Far Point, Hyphid* and *New* share an earnest, not to say solid attitude towards the presentation of poetry to the reader, but *Intercourse* makes it clear that one of its aims is the insertion of a jocular thumb in the Establishment bum. This issue takes potshots at such familiar sitting ducks as *Playboy* and Irving Layton. It offers also some competent though not evisceratingly-original poetry, a professionally-handled prose vignette, and some guest appearances: Alden Nowlan, Al Purdy feeling silly about writing about himself at 25 but doing it anyway. For 35¢ it's a bargain.

Copperfield (No. 1) has a mailing address that makes it look university-linked, but actually it's an independent venture. It also goes straight for this reader's jugular; no matter what the quality of the work inside (and it's irregular) I *have* to like it as a magazine, because it's dedicated to this country's "mythos," specifically that of the North. Any magazine conceived in the Temagami Provincial Forest Reserve has to have its heart in the right place. *Copperfield* offers not only poetry, but short fiction (in this issue, a strange Milton Acorn short story), reviews (of, for instance, Sig Olson, a writer familiar to conservationists if not to poets), and excerpts from early Canadian writers. In addition, it's well-printed, and illustrated, too (the photo of Joseph Pickering, looking like everyone's murderous ancestor, is alone well worth the price). Reservations: will quality be sacrificed to subject-matter concerns? will the vein here being mined prove easily exhaustible? I hope neither of these things happens.

Blew Ointment (Vol. 5, No. 2) has been around for a while, and it's gotten bigger and better. It expresses its own region and its own point of view while managing an astonishing range and flexibility. It can print poetry so awful you'd have to be high to appreciate it, and poems so good they create their own high, like Margaret Avison's "All Out or Oblation." *B. O.* is the creation of polyinspirational Bill Bissett, and some of the contributions, both pictorial and poetic, are neobissettesque, but this merely emphasizes Bissett's own originality: if you don't share Bissett's magical approach to language, "th" and "luv" and "yu" don't carry you very far, and a flowered nipple doesn't equal the translucent quality of a Bissett line drawing. This *B. O.* also has some loose pinups, the most joyful of which is Phyllis Gotlieb's "A Wall of Graffitti." Altogether *B. O.* is a stimulating grab-bag, though there's a certain amount of used newspaper in with the goodies.

grOnk shares *B. O.*'s interest in pictorial-verbal values and combinations. It's the Concrete Poetry magazine and that's what it publishes. No.'s 1 and 2 of Series 2 suggest either that the genre has rather narrow limits or that its practitioners still have a lot of exploring ahead of them. But it may be a production problem: concrete poetry must above all be visible, and the mimeo process doesn't help. (Certainly the poem-objects in bp nichol's *Journeyings and the Return* package were more exciting. Maybe *grOnk* shouldn't be a magazine with pages at all, but a box full of things?) However if you're interested in the movement, this is what you should be reading.

Which leads to the picture books. David Aylward's *Typescapes* is unique, a book of elegant structures made with letters and given titles, some comic ("the inlain crocodile"), some mythic ("the cactus god," "the forest of knives"). No one will ever do this better; in fact, no one else will probably ever do it at all, since Aylward has exploited the form to its margins already.

If *Typescapes* is classical, Keewatin Dewdney's *The Maltese Cross Movement* is decidedly romantic, as its merge-and-takeoff last page poem emphasises. According to *Alphabet 15*, it's based on an underground movie of the same name, but those who haven't seen the movie can react only to the book as book. Dewdney uses a collage technique, linking pictures with an organic-looking matrix of tiny hieroglyphics which may or may not be decipherable into English. There are a few recognizable words, and two symbols, a maltese cross and a moon, which weave through the pictures, sometimes together, sometimes apart. The oversize fingers, ears and eyes coupled with machines, etc. suggest a McLuhan extended-senses theme, but a linear-sequential interpretive approach doesn't work (unless there's some Rosetta Stone I missed). What *The Maltese Cross Movement* does is to provide the reader with a lush field of images from which he can improvise his own poems ("make a world," as the first collage says). It raises scrapbooking, that thing you did with old magazines and a pair of scissors while recovering from the measles, to an art.

9

MacEwen's Muse

(1970)

Now you comprehend your first and final lover
in the dark receding planets of his eyes,
and this is the hour when you know moreover
that the god you have loved always
will descend and lie with you in paradise.

—MacEwen, "The Hour of the Singer"
(unpublished, 1969).

In reading Gwendolyn MacEwen's poetry it is a temptation
to become preoccupied with the original and brilliant verbal
surfaces she creates, at the expense of the depths beneath
them. But it is occasionally instructive to give at least
passing attention to what poets themselves say about their
work, and MacEwen has been insisting for some time that it
is "the thing beyond the poem,"[1] the "raw material"[2] of
literature, that above all concerns her. There is, of course,
more than one thing beyond the poems, but there is one
figure whose existence is hinted at throughout her work and
who acts as a key to much of it. This is the Muse, often
invoked and described but never named; and in MacEwen's

poetry the Muse, the inspirer of language and the formative power in Nature, is male. Ignore him or misinterpret him and her "muse" poems may be mistaken for "religious"[3] ones or reduced to veiled sexuality. Acknowledge him, and he will perform one of the functions MacEwen ascribes to him: the creation of order out of chaos.

The twentieth-century authority on the poetic Muse is, of course, Robert Graves. In his *White Goddess*,[4] he asserts that the Muse is always female, and if it isn't it should be. Poets who have the bad luck to be women should write either as priestesses of the Goddess, singing her praises or uttering her oracles, or as the Goddess herself. That some female poets have recalcitrantly invoked a Muse of the opposite sex would be viewed by Graves as new-woman perversity; but then, he labours under the same difficulty as does Freud when he tries to discuss female psychology and Jung when he deals with the *animus* archetype: he's a man. There are several male Muses about, even in Canadian poetry;[5] often when the reader comes across an unnamed "you," he would be better employed searching for the Muse than for someone with a birth certificate and a known address. But no one has invoked the male Muse with such frequency and devotion as has Gwendolyn MacEwen.

MacEwen is a poet whose interests and central images have been present from the time of her early publications, though her ability to elaborate them, clarify them, transform them and approach them from different angles has developed over the years. Thus her first small pamphlet, *Selah* (1961), contains two images which are later viewed more specifically as incarnations of the Muse: the God-figure and the winged man. The God of the first poem is spoken of as having "fathered" the hills and as being "the guardian / of the substance of light,"[6] but he is remote; he encloses the individual human life but remains unknown by it ("we ... do not even ... hint You"). This distant God reappears in MacEwen's later work as the "almost anonymous" God of

"The Two Themes of the Dance"[7] and the electrical First Cause of "Tesla."[8] Although he is the ultimate source of all power, including the power of language (as early as "Selah" he is spoken of as one who "writes," and "sound and light" flow from his "tongue" in "Tesla"), he cannot be conversed with. This may explain the rareness of his appearances: MacEwen much prefers a Muse who may be addressed or who may provide the other voice in a dialogue.

The image of the winged man does not begin as an incarnation of the Muse. In "Icarus" (*Selah*), the parallel developed is that between Daedalus and Icarus, and the Muse, addressed as "you," and the poet, with the wings—instruments of flight—being quite explicitly the poet's pen, and the flight of Icarus, ending in destruction, being the writing of a poem which is later burnt. Here the Muse stands in the relation of quasi-father to the poet,[9] as is usually the case when MacEwen employs the words "legacy," "heritage," and "inherit."[10] But having once used the Icarus image, MacEwen takes it through a whole series of transformations. Always the man-bird is a creature halfway between human being and supernatural power. When he is ascending, he is a human being aspiring towards godhead;[11] when he is descending, he is the divine Muse in the act of becoming incarnate.

In the first "Icarus" poem, in which Icarus becomes a "combustion of brief feathers," the idea of burning is connected with the winged man, and it reappears almost every time the figure itself does. For the god-man the fire is divine; for the man-god it is either destructive or regenerative, the fire that precedes a phoenix-like rebirth. The man who flies but dies is readily available for sexual metaphor, as witness "Black and White" and "The Phoenix."[12] In the first poem the Muse is descending, becoming incarnate; in the second he is an individual man becoming Muse ("beyond you, the image rising from the shoulders / is greater than you . . . "). In *A Breakfast For Barbarians* the flaming birdman

makes an ironic appearance as a "motorcycle Icarus," "without
wings, but burning anyway," a profane version of the divine
Muse who "cannot distinguish between sex and nicotine."[13]
Instead of the Muse's descent into the flesh or even Icarus'
descent into the sea, the poet imagines a splashdown into
Niagara Falls. But the flying Muse is back again full-fledged
in *The Shadow Maker*. In the book's first poem, "The Red
Bird You Wait For,"[14] he appears, now more bird than man,
as poetic inspiration itself, the Muse in its Holy Ghost form
which rises phoenix-like from its own ashes only to descend
once more "uninvited:"

> Its shape is a cast-off velvet cape,
> Its eyes are the eyes of your most forbidden lover
> And its claws, I tell you its claws are gloved in fire.

That the image of the descending Muse caught in mid-flight
is far from exhausted for MacEwen is made evident in the
recent unpublished poem, "The Hour of the Singer."

Having become incarnate, the Muse may both disguise
and reveal himself in many forms. There are a number of
poems in *The Rising Fire* and *A Breakfast For Barbarians* which
praise men in action: the athletes, the escape artist, the
surgeon who is "an Indian, and beautiful, and holy,"[15] the
several magicians, are all men but a bit more than men,
possessed at the sacramental instant by a power greater than
their own, the power of their craft, skill or performance.[16] In
these poems the poet places herself at a distance; she watches
the act but does not participate directly. Instead she trans-
forms the act into a metaphor for the poetic process; in "The
Magician," for instance, the magician's "fingers' genius / wave
out what my poems have said."[17] This kind of male figure is
thus both Muse or inspirer and one who is himself inspired.
Though these figures are partial masks assumed temporarily
by the Muse, they are never total revelations.[18]

All of the above figures are taken from "real" life:
some of the poems in which they appear are dedicated to
actual people, others (such as "The Athletes," set in an

explicitly Canadian park) are located in a world which may be identified, more or less, with the objective external one. But there are two other forms of the Muse which belong to his own proper realm, that of the imagination. These are the king and the singer-dancer, the Muse at his most static as sacramental object and at his most dynamic as sacramental creator/actor. Song and dance, princes and kings are used as images in the early pamphlets, and "The Two Themes of the Dance" and "The Absolute Dance"[19] are tentative explorations of the relationships among dance, poetry and the divinity of the Muse; but not until *A Breakfast For Barbarians* are Muse, dance and kingship synthesized.

The poems most important in this respect[20] are "Black Alchemy," "Finally Left in the Landscape," "Subliminal," and "The Aristocracies." "Black Alchemy" and "Finally Left in the Landscape" complement each other. In the first, the emergence of the elemental Muse from formless water and his taking shape as "the prince of laughter" "cancels the cosmos:" the world disintegrates, turns fluid, to be recreated by his word which is a dance:

> ... in his dance
> worlds expire like tides, in his flaming
> dance the nameless cosmos
> must await its naming.[21]

But in "Finally Left in the Landscape," it is the Muse, not the world, which has disappeared. Here the poet invokes the "dancer" who is also a "deity." He is both present and absent: the poet seeks him, but finds only possible fragments of him. Her task is to gather him together (*vide* Isis and Osiris), to see him as a whole, and her poetry is part of the attempt to recreate him; though her "lines can only / plagiarize his dance,"[22] since, though absent, he remains the originator of both language and world.

"Subliminal" and "The Aristocracies" deal with the relationship betwen Muse and poet, and with their mutual involvement in time. In "Subliminal," the poet, having achieved a state of mind in which "there is no time... but co-presents, a static recurrence,"[23] is able to hold the Muse still for an instant in order to contemplate him: "... in that substratum I hold, / unfold you at random." He is seen as both dynamic and static: "... you do not move / but are always moving." But such a state cannot persist: both must re-enter the world of time, in which movement forward is the only possibility:

> I rise to see you planted
> in an earth outside me
> moving through time
> through the terms of it,
> moving through time again
> along its shattered latitudes.

"The Aristocracies" is placed at the end of *A Breakfast For Barbarians*, and pulls together a number of its motifs. The figure addressed is the Muse, incarnate as lover but also as a "natural" king; the tension in the poem is created as the poet's vision moves from the Muse as man to the Muse as a supernatural power ("The body of God and the body of you / dance through the same diagonal instant / of my vision... "[24]), a movement which both traps the human element in the man, turning him into a "crowned and captive dancer," and makes him eternal:

> You must dance forever beneath this heavy crown
> in an aristocratic landscape, a bas-relief of living bone.
> And I will altogether cease to speak
> as you do a brilliant arabesque within the bas-relief,
> your body bent like the first letter
> of an unknown, flawless alphabet.

The Muse exists both inside and outside time, and like the letters on a page he is static yet in movement. Bodies as alphabets occur earlier in *A Breakfast For Barbarians*, and, again, word-thing metaphors date back to *Selah*; the importance of this body-letter lies in the fact that it is the first letter and the alphabet to which it belongs is unknown. The Muse is always *about* to be interpreted: he can never be completely deciphered.

Two attributes of MacEwen's Muse worth noting are his preference for a certain sort of landscape and the cyclical nature of his appearances. Before *The Shadow Maker*, the Muse's landscape tends to be identified with actual, reachable landscapes: those of the south and east rather than those of the north and west, exotic Palestinian, Arabian or Greek locales as opposed to bleak Canadian ones. The landscape of the Muse is also the landscape of the imagination, and there is often a sense of the grim "altogether Kanadian" reality of metal cities, snow, breakfasts of "unsacred bacon"[25] and the mechanical clock-time present pulling against a different kind of reality, that of the ornate, hierarchical landscapes and the ancient stone city-scapes of the Middle East, or of the bell-time or blood-time[26] of a more organic past. In *The Shadow Maker*, the poet is clearer about the relationship between self and Muse. Here she takes "the roads that lead inward . . . the roads that lead downward,"[27] and although the south-eastern landscapes are still present,[28] the Muse's most authentic landscape is identified more positively with the inner landscape of dream and fantasy. "Song for a Stranger" has Muse and poet meeting in a mutual dream to "plot / the birth of a more accurate world" in a setting of "pavilions" and "pools."[29] In the two songs from the "Fifth Earth," the meeting takes place in a kind of science-fiction otherworld. Towards the end of *The Shadow Maker*, the Muse is seen more as a potential force than as an actual or incarnate being: the "chosen abyss" of the title poem[30] has replaced the chosen landscape"[31] of *A Breakfast for Barbarians*.

The encounter between Muse and poet is an increasingly dominant theme in MacEwen's poetry. Through their meeting each actualizes the other, and together they are able to enter the Muse's landscape, he as a returning exile, she more often as an alien discoverer or explorer rather than a native. Together, also, they form the divine or cosmic couple which is a recurring image in the poetry. This couple may be either the original (and rather vegetable) Adam-Eve, the "man and woman naked and green with rain"[32] of "Eden, Eden" (who reappear, for instance, in the pastoral, innocent, season-linked couple of "We Are Sitting on a High Green Hill"[33]); or it may be an earth-sky couple like that in "Seeds and Stars."[34] It is interesting to juxtapose the early "couple" poem, "Tiamut,"[35] in which the female figure is "Chaos," "the earth . . . sans form"[36] and the male figure is the shaper, the divider, the former of Cosmos, with the later poem "The Name of the Place," in a sense its other half. In the later poem, the god and goddess responsible for the divided world momentarily glimpse a regained unity: "All things are plotting to make us whole / All things conspire to make us one."[37] There is a strong pull in MacEwen's poetry towards completion, synthesis: if the divine couple could ever permanently join, the universe which has emanated from their division would be drawn back into them and all things would indeed be truly one, a sky-earth, flesh-spirit, spirit-flesh landscape which would also be the homeless "adam"[38] returned from exile[39] and a dance containing its own extremity."[40] Time and space would be abolished.

But the union of the Muse and poet is limited by the flesh, and even when it takes place in dream or fantasy it is bound by the strictures of time and, in poetry, by the length of the poem. Hence the emphasis on the cyclical nature of the Muse's appearances. Again, the wheel or cycle is an image used frequently by MacEwen. The revolving wheel is an organizing symbol in *Julian the Magician*, and in "The Ferris Wheel"[41] it is made a "wheel of lyric" connected with the writing of poetry as well as with the movement of life around the "still middle, the / point of absolute inquiry." Wheel, circle and still centre occur as images again in "The Cyclist in Aphelion."[42] But the moving wheel becomes the shape of time itself in three poet-Muse poems in *A Breakfast For Barbarians*: "She,"[43] which draws on Rider Haggard's tale of the reincarnations of a pair of lovers; "Green with Sleep,"[44] in which the "great unspeakable wheel," which is both diurnal time and the mythical time of recurrences, renews the lovers; and "Cartaphilus,"[45] in which the two lovers encounter each other repeatedly: "Whoever you love it is me beneath you / over and over...." In *The Shadow Maker* the wheel image is connected not only with the poet's own circular movement,[46] but also with the circularity of time and the recurrences of the Muse. "First Song from the Fifth Earth" is even more positive than is "Cartaphilus" about the underlying identity of all the incarnations of the Muse: "I say all worlds, all times, all loves are one...."[47] "The Return," in addition to illustrating the theme of recurrence, is one of the clearest "Muse" poems MacEwen has written, and is worth quoting in its entirety:

The Return

I gave you many names and masks
And longed for you in a hundred forms
And I was warned the masks would fall
And the forms would lose their fame
And I would be left with an empty name

(For that was the way the world went,
For that was the way it had to be,
To grow, and in growing lose you utterly)

But grown, I inherit you, and you
Renew your first and final form in me,
And though some masks have fallen
And many names have vanished back into my pen
Your face bears the birth-marks I recognize in time,
You stand before me now, unchanged

(For this is the way it has to be;
To perceive you is an act of faith
Though it is you who have inherited me)[48]

Who has created whom? Is the male Muse as Marduk shaping the female chaos of the poet into an order or defining her by contrast (as in "The Shadow Maker"), or is the poet putting the Muse together out of words, as she sometimes suspects?[49] Is the Muse outside the poet, or is he inside, a fragment of the self? Does he exist outside time, or can he be apprehended only through time and through the senses? These are questions the poems ask; the answers to them are never final, since another turn of the wheel may invalidate all answers. The poet wrestles with the angel, but to win finally, to learn the true name of the angel, would be to stop the wheel, an event which she fears.[50] The last poem in *The Shadow Maker*, "The Wings," is a series of questions; in it the Muse, despite his many names, languages and landscapes, is again nameless. He has created, destroyed and restored innumerable worlds and several phases of the poet herself, and through the poet's invocation is about to begin the process again.

"I want to construct a myth," Gwendolyn MacEwen has written, and she has indeed constructed one. MacEwen is not a poet interested in turning her life into myth; rather, she is concerned with translating her myth into life, and into the poetry which is a part of it. The informing myth, developed gradually but with increasing clarity in her poetry, is that of the Muse, author and inspirer of language and therefore of the ordered verbal cosmos, the poet's universe. In MacEwen's myth the Muse exists eternally beyond sense, but descends periodically as winged man, becomes incarnate for a time as magician, priest-king, lover or all of these, then dies or disappears, only to be replaced by another version of himself. Though the process is cyclical, he never reappears in exactly the same form. Each time he brings with him a different landscape and language, and consequently a different set of inspirations, though beneath these guises he keeps the same attributes. He is a dancer and a singer; his dance and his song are the Word made flesh, and both contain and create order and reality. The poet's function is to dedicate her life to the search for the Muse,[52] and the poetry itself is both a record of the search and an attempt to reproduce and describe those portions of the song-dance which she has been able to witness. The Muse is both "good" and "evil," both gentle and violent, both creative and destructive; like language itself, he subsumes all opposites. Since he is infinite, the number of his incarnations is potentially infinite also. Though the final poem in *The Shadow Maker* may look like a last word, each of MacEwen's previous collections has an ending which is really a beginning: the "growing" of *The Rising Fire*, the "unknown" alphabet of *A Breakfast For Barbarians*. Here the final word is "floods," chaos come anew, a chaos which invites the creation of a fresh cosmos. There is little doubt that the Muse will rise again from his ashes in yet another form.[53]

NOTES

TRF: *The Rising Fire* (1963)

BB: *A Breakfast for Barbarians* (1966)

SM: *The Shadow Maker* (1969)

1 "The Double Horse," TRF, 18.

2 Introduction, BB.

3 A. Schroeder in *The Vancouver Province*, July 25, 1969.

4 With which MacEwen is familiar: see "Thou Jacob," BB, 27.

5 Where however the Muse, male or female, is more typically a place rather than a person. But see e.g. Jay Macpherson's Angel and some of the male figures in Dorothy Livesay's *Plainsongs*.

6 "Selah," *Selah* (1961).

7 TRF, 41.

8 BB, 19.

9 cf. Graves, for whom the Muse is, among other things, a Mother.

10 cf. e.g. "The Return, " SM, 81. Nor is it strange to find the "boy" as parallel for the poet: this is elsewhere the case in MacEwen's poetry; see e.g. "Dream Three: The Child," SM, 56.

11 cf. the astronauts of "The Cosmic Brothers" (TRF) and "The Astronauts" (BB); cf. also the poet as a child, attempting to fly with the help of the magic word Shazam, as humorously recounted in "Fragments of a Childhood" (*Alphabet*, No. 15, December 1968, 10).

12 TRF, 19, 57.

13 "Poem Improvised Around a First Line," BB, 16.

14 SM, 2.

15 "Appendectomy," BB, 42.

16 cf. also Julian in *Julian the Magician* (1963).

17 BB, 36.

18 MacEwen's interest in Christ is connected with his role as divine priest-king-physician incarnate; he is not the original or archetypal Muse, but another of the Muse's earthly incarnations.

19 TRF, 41, 43.

20 Though see also "Thou Jacob," the "Arcanum" series, and the cosmic dance at the electron level in "Tesla."

21 BB, 40.

22 BB, 52.

23 BB, 31.

24 BB, 53.

25 "The Last Breakfast," BB, 35.

26 See for instance "The Drunken Clock," the last poem in the pamphlet of that name.

27 "The Wings," SM, 82.

28 As in, for instance, such poems as "One Arab Flute" and "The Fortress of Saladin."

29 SM, 53.

30 "The Shadow Maker," SM, 80.

31 "Finally Left in the Landscape," BB, 52.

32 *The Drunken Clock* (1961).

33 SM, 58.

34 SM, 71.

35 TRF, 5.

36 cf. other woman-as-earth images: e.g. in the verse play *Terror and Erebus*, in "Poet vs. The Land" (*Selah*), and in "The Discovery" (SM, 31).

37 SM, 16.

38 "The Catalogues of Memory," TRF, 66.

39 cf. also "The Caravan," BB, 51.

40 "The Absolute Dance," TRF, 43.

41 TRF, 49.

42 BB, 7.

43 BB, 9.

44 BB, 28.

45 BB, 46.

46 See "Dream Three: The Child," SM, 56.

47 SM, 68.

48 SM, 81.

49 See e.g. "The Face," BB, 9.

50 See e.g. "Fragments of a Childhood," in which the pronouncing of the "Final Formula" would stop everything.

51 BB, Introduction.

52 cf. again Graves; though for MacEwen the Muse is less Nature than creating Word or Logos.

53 See, for instance, the recent poem "Credo" (*Quarry*, Vol. 19, No. 1, Fall 1969, 5), in which the poet says, "no one can tell me that / the Dancer in my blood is / dead ...."

10

The Messianic Stance:

West Coast Seen

(1971)

The Messianic stance has long been indigenous to the West Coast, and *West Coast Seen* does not fail to adopt it. The anthology opens with a sermonistic piece by Jim Brown in which dogmatically-formulated snatches of antidogma are interspersed with hymns of praise (to Vancouver as a "source of energy," to *Tish Magazine*) and with mystic quotations from *Words* and elsewhere. After being told that we are "moving through the mystery," though, it's a slight letdown to turn the page and find the editors going on about money, publishing and Canada Council grants just as though they were Torontonians.

Despite the naiveté of this juxtaposition, the introduction does make some valid points. Vancouver is, as Brown claims, an open city, which may account for the collection's extreme diversity. Phillips is quite right in stating that the book's relevance is "immediate:" he seems to fear that these poems won't stay representative of what's going on in Vancouver for very long, and indeed several of the poets are already elsewhere. All anthologies are necessarily retrospective, but this one is a little more so than, for instance, *T. O. Now* or *Canada First*: the poems date roughly from 1965 to 1969. They're no doubt a reasonably fair cross-section of what was being done in those years among new (though not always young) poets, if one chooses to skip the customary quibbles (if X, why not Y, if Hulcoop and Jungic, why not Yates, where are Jamie Reid, Daphne Marlatt, etc?). On this point Brown defends himself in advance:

> Our conception that the scene here has not been easily defined since the early days of Tish is even more true today. There are so many people writing here now that it would be impossible to say that this is a complete and absolute statement of the WC thing/scene in Canada.

This comment underlines one of *West Coast Seen*'s problems: its attempt to contain a sort of poetic urban sprawl. Vancouver is a city that poets go to rather than come from; the result is a book that can either be praised for its range and inclusiveness or reprimanded for its lack of focus. Stylistically, *WCS* has something for everyone: for an editor whose "whole conception of publishing is centred around the personal aspect," Brown's taste is surprisingly eclectic. But he seems aware of this too, and the shifts in typeface are perhaps intended as a comment rather than simply as a decorative device.

West Coast Seen's variety makes it unsatisfactory for trend-spotting purposes, but a reviewer is honour-bound to make the attempt. The cover provides a clue of sorts: on the back is an alphabet with some of the letters replaced by images (a clock, people walking); on the front is something that looks like a geological strata diagram (reflecting perhaps the editor's intention of presenting simply what has happened, with critical judgement kept to a minimum) until it is turned sideways, when it becomes a series of thin pictures: trees, houses, telephone poles. Here then are two concerns important to West Coast poets (though not altogether unknown elsewhere); the concern with image as physical object stripped of rhetoric, and the concern with language as visual and aural medium, stripped of what Brown calls "intellectual meaning."

The first direction was taken some years ago by, for instance, George Bowering, Lionel Kearns, and some of the other early *Tish* poets, and (less programmatically but some-

times more profoundly) by John Newlove. It is followed here
most notably by Ken Belford, Pat Lane and Barry McKinnon. Belford is a delight: he has his language well under
control, and such poems as "Carrier Indians," "Stove" and
"Omega" read with the kind of inevitability of image and
rhythm that makes other poets grit their teeth with envy
once they have recovered from the poem. Pat Lane is finally
discovering his own voice; some of the selections here lack
the austerity and condensation of the best work in his recent
collection, *Separations*, but one outstanding poem, "Last
Night in Darkness," appears in both. Barry McKinnon's most
impressive poem here is the roughly-finished but powerful
"Letter II: for my wife."

The second direction is rapidly gaining adherents, but
the local source of energy is undoubtedly still Bill Bissett. At
their best, his poems transcend the technical peculiarities
and conventions of much "sound" poetry—phonetic spelling, distortion or abolition of syntax, serial repetition, and a
childlike preoccupation with sounds for their own sakes and
with the fact that two words of different meanings can be
pronounced alike (producing what would be known in other
circles as "puns"). Such poems as "the tempul firing" are
invocations, conjuring (as opposed to descriptions) of the
ecstatic vision, and Bissett does them better than anyone.
Siebun, Tan Trey, Mayne (sometimes) and Phillips (in a
much cooler way) are somewhere in the vicinity of the same
wave-length. "Image" poems usually concentrate on the
outer world, describing things (and the poet's reaction to
them) as they are; "sound" poetry leans toward the magical,
the inner, toward the evocation of a world transfigured. The
difference is illustrated by the work of Brown himself, which
moves from the earlier "image" poems such as "Poem to my
father" to later "sound" ones such as "th breath."

But these two kinds of poem-making are not the only
ones going on in *West Coast Seen*. Some poets, such as Stephen
Scobie, are exploring the visual type of concrete poetry,

though this area is not adequately represented. Others, such as Pat Lowther, are happily unclassifiable: they are simply writing good poems. Others are either very versatile or still searching for a personal style. Another group, if group they be, are trending towards neo-surrealism; among these are Andreas Schroeder, the interesting Zoran Jungic, and Pierre Coupey—a more ambitious poet than many in this collection.

Is Vancouver special? Is it really, as the introductory letter of David Phillips implies, that much different from Montreal or Toronto as a place to write poems, that much better? Does *West Coast Seen* have a distinctive flavour not found in, for instance, *T. O. Now*? There is certainly a difference in editorial attitude: anthologizers further east at least pretend that they are cool, semi-professional and semi-objective; they are more willing to comment, less willing to preach. The isolation of Vancouver and its consequent cultishness result in a gleeful do-it-yourself attitude towards publishing—a kind of "I'm doing this for me, my friends and the rest of the converted, but you can watch if you like" posture. It's as much of a pretense as the other one, but it does produce a different kind of grab-bag. If cultivated maturity results in quality control and a certain uniformity and dullness (like a convention of Iowa Writing School old boys), cultivated youthful enthusiasm obviously results in sloppiness. *West Coast Seen* is too long and too undiscriminating: it includes a number of pretentious, silly and trivial poems as well as a number of good ones. But children, though sometimes tedious and aggravating (to others: never to themselves) are also refreshing and delightful, and the Vancouver poets seem more willing to take the more obvious risks, to branch out, to experiment and fail, than their more cautious eastern counterparts. On the other hand, wit seems to flourish better in the East: the *WCS* poets, though they play wordgames, do not as a rule turn phrases. However, making final judgements about poets, cities or regions on the basis of an anthology is always dangerous: anthologies are mirages created, finally, by their editors.

11
Nationalism, Limbo and the Canadian Club

(1971)

Washington questioner: An English writer who recently moved to the States said England was very nice, very calm, but he felt he had to leave England in order to live through the agonies in the United States... Do you feel you ought to leave Canada for the same reasons?

Self: We have a few agonies of our own at the moment.

Time's man in London: Would you say there was anything, any dimension, growing up as a Canadian gave you that you wouldn't have got, say, growing up in the United States?

Self: I guess one of the main things is that south of you you have Mexico and south of us we have you.

—October, 1970.

"So Robert Fulford has finally come round," I said, putting down the recent copy of *Saturday Night*. "It took him long enough."

"What do you mean?" asked my young friend. "He was one of the first to get the New Nationalism going."

"That's not what *he* says," I replied, "and I remember those early *Star* columns, the ones that assumed everyone knew the Yanks always did it better."

There followed a heated argument concerning the merits and demerits of the Fulford psyche. What I was thinking about, though, was what it had been like for me, what I and my so-called generation had been up to when Fulford was grooving on imported jazz. Were we so much better? Did I even *have* a generation? I doubted it through high school and university, where most of my contemporaries wanted nothing more from life than to be engineers or chartered accountants if male or married to them if female. But as I tally up now the writers of roughly my own age, I realize that in contrast to many members of the "generations" before them who sprinted for London or New York as soon as they could, convinced they could never create anything of value in dull, restrictive Canada (see Mordecai Richler, *passim*), all of them have either remained in Canada or returned to it, not from necessity but by choice. When they leave now it's not because they find Canada too bland; it's because they find it overstimulating and they need a rest.

Something changed, then, during the early 1960s. Canada ceased to be a kind of limbo you were stuck in if unlucky or not smart enough and became a real place. Whatever worked the change, it had little to do with the official educational experience, if mine was any example. In public school I remember singing Rule Britannia and drawing pictures of the Union Jack under the eyes of teachers who still believed in the Empire; but they wore bloomers in winter, they were a dying race. The truth about the universe was contained in comic books traded and re-traded till their covers fell off: Batman, Blackhawk, The Human Torch, Plastic Man, Captain Marvel. We knew these comic books were American, because occasionally a grey and white Canadian imitation of inferior quality would turn up. Canada for us was not-America, the place where popsicle bag offers didn't apply and everything was ten cents extra; the comics were news bulletins of the action going on across the border which we could watch but not join.

In school, under the inaccurate heading of Social Studies, we were learning the Kings of England and the Explorers. The Kings were fun because they were red, blue and purple, but the Explorers, once they hit Canada and got into the woods, were tedious: they were mostly brown, with green trees or white snow. There was The Battle of the Plains of Abraham, of course, but whichever way you cut it Wolfe came off as sneaky and Montcalm as stupid; none of us could get too worked up over their deaths.

By the time we reached high school it was the mid-1950s. America came to us in the form of *Life* magazine and seemed to be populated by drum majorettes and spaniels. McCarthy was down there, it was true, but he wasn't real to us: he and his caricature in *Pogo* were identical. Indoors we studied the Ancient Egyptians, the Greeks and Romans, Mediaeval Europe, the Elizabethan Age, the American Civil War. One year we got around to Canada and touched on such engrossing subjects as Wheat, The Beaver and Transportation Routes. The exciting parts were the World Wars, the most memorable experience a propaganda film about Fascism made to be shown to U.S. forces. We emerged knowing quite a lot about Pyramids, Henry VIII, Hitler, serfs, Winston Churchill, the Cotton Gin, and F. D. R.; something about The Beaver; very little about Louis Riel, W. L. Mackenzie and Quebec, except that they all lost; and not much about Ontario except The Family Compact, which I visualized as a large bowl of face powder, and the fact that copper refining produces slag, which I knew already.

Of the things I later discovered I wanted to know we were told next to nothing. Among these were the disadvantages of being a colony, political or economic, and the even greater disadvantages of being an Indian. On the cultural end, poetry was at first chiefly narrative; later it became

chiefly nineteenth century. The general impression was that
to be a poet you had to be English and dead. You could also
be American and dead but this was less frequent. There was,
to be sure, E. J. Pratt, who was Canadian and at the time
still alive, but I despaired of ever being able to write
long poems about shipwrecks; consequently my first poems
all sounded like Byron or (even less happily) Edgar Allan
Poe. Novels by Canadians were almost unheard of, for once
a faithful reflection on the part of the high school curric-
ulum of conditions in the outside world.

When I reached college I found out that these things
had been kept from me. Again, the revelation did not take
place through official channels: I was Specializing (you still
did, then) and somehow there wasn't any room in Eng. Lang.
and Lit. for Canadian Literature. But there was a small
Periodicals Room in the library, and after I had stumbled
upon it I spent many arcane hours reverently grubbying the
pages of the handful of Little Magazines then in existence:
Fiddlehead, *Queen's Quarterly*, *Delta* and *Canadian Forum*, and
the radiant *Tamarack Review*. The awe in which I held these
oracles may seem strange, but they were the only ones.
However, I did not think of them as especially "Canadian":
only as more accessible to me than their English or American
counterparts. This was true also of the individual poets they
led me to read: Reaney, Page, Macpherson, Avison, Klein,
Mandel, Souster. It was not the Canadianness but the fact
that actual published books were possible, here and now or
rather there and then, that was exhilarating.

It wasn't until I went as a graduate student to the United
States that I started thinking much about Canada at all.
Before, it was just an unexamined condition, like air; one
lived in it but paid no attention to it. Suddenly, though,
America was proving to be not what I had thought. It wasn't
full of Supermen, drum majorettes or even kindly F. D. R.'s,
and I and the other Canadians that soon gathered in tiny
exiled groups found ourselves engaged in an unhappy
scramble for our own identities. Our background had given

us such negligible amounts of help that we were often absurd in our search for differences. "Their subways are messier," we would report to one another; "They call back bacon 'Canadian Bacon.'" One of us, returning from the men's washroom, confided in the furtive tone of an espionage agent, "They have dirtier graffitti." We could move amongst them, questioning, examining, listening in, mistaken for one of Them unless we ourselves made the disclosure, in which case their reaction was good-natured (we were no threat): "I've always thought of Canada as, I mean, sort of a *grey* country." (Americans said, "I mean," Canadians said, "you know;" though that too has changed.)

Our final, horrible discovery was that they *thought* differently. They weren't groping for their identities; they had gone through all that, I found, back in the post-revolutionary decades, with symptoms very much like ours—the short-run, little-read magazines, the petty literary squabbles, the adulation of foreign writers, the conflict between "native" and "cosmopolitan" schools, the worry over cultural imperialism (don't buy British fashions, why is there no great American writer, etc.). But they had identity now with a vengeance; it caused its own problems. My roommate was studying art history; she was terrified to learn that she was expected to have some knowledge of Europe and the Renaissance. Although her education had provided her with a ponderous amount of detail concerning her home state and a thorough grounding in American history at large, she had only the sketchiest notions about any of the rest of the world, past or present. Being from the South, she was somewhat atypical; but still, par for the high school course for Them was one year of American history, one year of World history which went swiftly from Mesopotamia to now, hitting the high points, and two years of "Civics" or "Citizenship:" local government and How To Be An American, though in practice it sometimes deteriorated into visits to the waterworks. "They" had been taught that they were the centre of the universe, a huge, healthy apple pie, with other countries and cultures sprinkled round the outside, like raisins. "We" on the other hand had been taught that we were one of the raisins, in fact, *the* raisin, and that the other parts of the universe were invariably larger and more interesting than we were. A distortion of the truth in both cases, let us hope.

There were several disturbing corollaries. One was that we knew more about them, much more, than they knew about us; another was that they knew a lot more about themselves than we knew about ourselves. Another, related to our growing consciousness of economic domination, was that we had let ourselves come under the control of a people who neither knew nor cared to know anything about us. The most disturbing of all was the realization that they were blundering around in the rest of the world with the same power, the same staggering lack of knowledge and the same lack of concern: the best thing for the raisins, in their opinion, was to be absorbed into the apple pie.

It's of interest that many of the outspoken Canadian nationalists of the moment have done time, as it were, in the States. But a lot of those who went south to study never returned. In my second year I was contacted by an acquaintance then attending the Harvard Business School. (In Canada he had prided himself on being a right-wing conservative; to his dismay, he now found himself branded as a Socialist Pinko.) At the Business School there was an institution known as The Canadian Club; it threw parties at which amounts of Canadian Club mixed with Canada Dry were consumed and, on good nights, record players were hurled from the windows. To one of these parties I was duly taken. Mistaken by everyone for a nurse—they all went out with nurses—I quizzed and eavesdropped my way through the evening. What I wanted to find out was what they were going to *do* about it; they were the ones with the economic know-how. But the big topic was whether or not to "go back:" most of them wanted to stay in the States, where they could make more money. A few thought of going to Alberta, where there was money in oil. The only one displaying much patriotism was a short red-head from Newfoundland who kept trying to sing the Newfoundland National Anthem.

Towards the end, when most of the bottles of Canadian Club were gone, one of the members wobbled over to the record player, put on The Star Spangled Banner, and turned the volume up full blast. This roused the latent chauvinism in several of the onlookers. They tried to remove the record, but he kept replacing it, sadly, doggedly. Finally one of them said, "Cut that out, you bloody Yank." This made him angry. "I'm not a Yank, I'm a Canadian!" he shouted, several times. Then he started the record over again from the beginning.

What was he trying to tell us? Probably nothing; or maybe that you can't win, the Yanks do it better, and you have to admit The Star Spangled Banner is more successful as a piece of music—I mean, you know, all provincialism aside and on strictly objective cultural terms—than O Canada, now, don't you? *Pace* my high school history courses; those early Fulford columns were not written by a villain but by a symptom. It was our own choices, our own judgements, that were defeating us.

12
Eleven Years of *Alphabet*

(1971)

Now the young intellectual living in this country, having gone perhaps to a Wordsworth high school and a T. S. Eliot college, quite often ends up thinking he lives in a waste of surplus USA technology, a muskeg of indifference spotted with colonies of inherited, somehow stale, tradition. What our poets should be doing is to show us how to identify our society out of this depressing situation.

—*James Reaney, "Editorial," Alphabet* #8.

Searchers for a Canadian identity have failed to realize that you can only have identification with something you can see or recognize. You need, if nothing else, an image in a mirror. No other country cares enough about us to give us back an image of ourselves that we can even resent. And apparently we can't do it for ourselves, because so far our attempts to do so have resembled those of the three blind men to describe the elephant. Some of the descriptions have been worth something, but what they add up to is fragmented, indecipherable. With what are we to identify ourselves?

—Germaine Warkentin, *"An Image in a Mirror,"*
Alphabet #8.

All this is connected together, by the way.

—James Reaney, *"Editorial,"* Alphabet #16.

With the appearance this year of its combined eighteenth and nineteenth issues, *Alphabet* will be over, and its small but faithful audience can only mourn and collect back issues.[1] While it lasted, it was perhaps the most remarkable little magazine Canada has yet produced. Many literary magazines are group or movement oriented: they publish certain people or certain styles. Others, if they have "professional" pretensions, are greyish collections of goodish writing. *Alphabet* was different; its editorial decisions were based not on last names or idiosyncracies of punctuation, or even on "literary" standards, but on a set of premises about literature—or rather art of any kind—and therefore about life that was in application all-inclusive.

The premises themselves were set forth in the initial issues. The first *Alphabet* was subtitled "A semiannual devoted

to the iconography of the imagination." Each issue was
to concern itself with a "myth," the first being Narcissus, the
second the child Dionysos, the third Prometheus, and so
forth. To those unfamiliar with *Alphabet*'s actual methods,
the terms "iconography" and "myth" may suggest rigidity
and a tendency to collect and categorize. But the editor's
faith in the correspondences between everyday reality (life,
or what *Alphabet* calls "documentary") and man-made symbolic patterns (art, or what *Alphabet* calls "myth") was so
strong that in practice he left interpretation and pattern-
finding to the reader. He merely gathered the pieces of
writing, both "literary" and "non-literary," and other subjects (an article on Narcissus, a real-life account of what it
was like to be a twin, the Tarot card of the Fool) and let the
echoes speak for themselves; coincidences were there, he
insisted, not because he put them there but because they
occur. The "myth" provided for each issue was only a kind of
key:

> ... Actually the same thing happens if you take the face
> cards out of a card deck; then put a circular piece of
> cardboard near them. Curves and circles appear even in
> the Queen of Diamonds and the Knave of Spades. But
> place a triangular shape close by and the eye picks up
> corners and angularities in even the Queen of Clubs. What
> every issue of *Alphabet* involves, then, is the placing of a
> definite geometric shape near some face cards.[2]

The reader never knew when he picked up an issue of
Alphabet what would be inside. It might be anything, and
the announced "myth" for the issue was not always an
obvious clue. In eleven years and nineteen issues *Alphabet*
published or mentioned, among other things, an article on
Aztec poetry, a list of the Kings of England reaching back to
the Old Testament, Indian rock paintings, an article on
Christabel which identified Geraldine as Wordsworth, James
McIntyre the Mammoth Cheese poet, the Nihilist Spasm
Band, an early review by Bill Bissett in the form of a poem,

the music of the Doukhobors, schoolboy slang and hand puppetry, the Black Donnellys, and a cantata about Jonah. Academic and pop, "traditional" and "modern," verbal and visual, "local" and "international:" *Alphabet* had no snobberies.

Because Reaney cheerfully acknowledged an interest in Frye, hasty codifiers stuck him in a Myth School of their own creation and accused him of the sin of "being influenced," without pausing to consider that for an artist as original as Reaney "influence" is taking what you need because it corresponds to something already within you. Others, who preferred a glossier, more Cream-of-Wheat-like "professional" consistency of texture in their magazines, found it easy to sneer at *Alphabet* for being one man's magazine (which it was), eccentric and eclectic (which it also was), and provincial, which it wasn't. Surely it's much more provincial to turn out second-rate copies of the art forms of another culture (what price a TV variety show with Canadian tap dancers instead of American ones), than it is to create an indigenous form, and *Alphabet* had something much more important than "Canadian Content;" though it was catholic in content, it was Canadian in *form*, in how the magazine was put together.

What follows is hypothetical generalization, but it is of such that national identities are composed. Saying that *Alphabet* is Canadian in form leads one also to say that there seem to be important differences between the way Canadians think—about literature, or anything—and the way Englishmen and Americans do. The English habit of mind, with its preoccupation with precedent and the system, might be called empirical; reality for it is the social hierarchy and its dominant literary forms are evaluative criticism and the social novel. It values "taste." The American habit of mind, with its background of intricate Puritan theologizing, French Enlightenment political theory and German scholarship and its foreground of technology, is abstract and analytical;

it values "technique," and for it reality is how things work. The dominant mode of criticism for some years has been "New Criticism," picking works of art apart into component wheels and springs; its "novel" is quite different from the English novel, which leans heavily towards comedy of manners and a dwindled George Eliot realism; the American novel, closer to the Romance, plays to a greater extent with symbolic characters and allegorical patterns. The Canadian habit of mind, for whatever reason—perhaps a history and a social geography which both seem to lack coherent shape—is synthetic. "Taste" and "technique" are both of less concern to it than is the ever-failing but ever-renewed attempt to pull all the pieces together, to discover the whole of which one can only trust one is a part. The most central Canadian literary products, then, tend to be large-scope works like the *Anatomy of Criticism* and *The Gutenberg Galaxy* which propose all-embracing systems within which any particular piece of data may be placed. Give the same poem to a model American, a model English and a model Canadian critic: the American will say "This is how it works;" the Englishman "How good, how true to Life" (or, "How boring, tasteless and trite"); the Canadian will say "This is where it fits into the entire universe." It is in its love for synthesis that *Alphabet* shows itself peculiarly Canadian.

"Let us make a form out of this," Reaney says in the *Alphabet* #1 Editoral. "Documentary on one side and myth on the other: Life & Art. In this form we can put anything and the magnet we have set up will arrange it for us." The "documentary" aspects of *Alphabet* are as important as the "myth" ones, and equally Canadian. Canadian preoccupation with and sometimes excellence in documentaries of all kinds—film, TV, radio, poetic—is well known. *Alphabet* was addicted to publishing transcriptions from life: accounts of dreams, conversations overheard in buses, Curnoe's Coke Book, a collage of letters from poets, known and unknown across the country. The documentarist's (and *Alphabet*'s) stance towards such raw material, and thus towards everyday life, is that it is intrinsically meaningful but the meaning is hidden; it will only manifest itself if the observer makes the effort to connect. Give our model Englishman a hamburger and he will tell amusing anecdotes about it (his great aunt once tripped over a hamburger, hamburgers remind him of Winston Churchill); the American will make it into a symbol by encasing it in plastic or sculpting it in plaster. The Canadian will be puzzled by it. For a while he will say nothing. Then he will say: "I don't know what this hamburger means or what it's doing in this particular place—where is this, anyway?—but if I concentrate on it long enough the meaning of the hamburger, which is not *in* the hamburger exactly, nor in the hamburger's history, nor in the mind of the onlooker, but in the exchange between the observing and the observed—the meaning of the hamburger will reveal itself to me." The Canadian, one notes, is less sure of himself, and more verbose about it than the other two, but he is also more interested in the actual hamburger.

Such theories, like all theories, are questionable, but the joys and graces of *Alphabet*, luckily, are not: its variety, its enthusiasms, the innocent delight it took in almost everything. Above all, one is amazed by its uncanny ability to anticipate, sometimes by five or ten years, trends which will later become fashionable, Canadian cultural nationalism among them. "Who would have thought seven years ago," says Reaney in *Alphabet* #14 (1967) "that pop culture would catch up to *Alphabet*?"

The reasons for *Alphabet*'s demise are partly personal— "In ten years," comments Reaney, "you say what you have to say"—and partly financial. The first ten issues were handset by the editor who taught himself typesetting for this purpose; the last five needed grants to help pay the spiralling printing costs. But it's ironic that *Alphabet*, never in any way commercial, should fold just when a potential market for it is appearing in the form of large Canadian Literature classes at universities. If every serious student of Canlit acquires (as he should) a set, *Alphabet*, like beavers and outlaws, may soon be worth more dead than alive. Searchers for the great Canadian identity might do well to divert time from studying what also occurs here, like Ford motor cars, and pay some attention to what, like *Alphabet*, occurs *only* here. *Alphabet*'s light is done; we can only hope that someone else with an equally powerful third eye, coupled with the desire to start a little magazine, will happen along soon.

NOTES

[1] Back issues and facsimiles: Walter Johnson Reprint Company, 111 Fifth Avenue, New York 10003, New York, U.S.A.

[2] *Alphabet* #2.

13
Al Purdy:
Love in a Burning Building

(1971)

At first sight I was prepared to dislike this book. Perhaps it was the presentation: on the cover some pleasant photos of two teenies embracing (a middle-aged man and a scowling woman hitting each other with brooms or tied together with lengths of barbed wire or staring out a window in opposite directions would fit the contents better); or the nine pages of flame drawings before we get to the poetry (design is design, but nine pages?); or the peek-behind-the-scenes-at-McClelland-&-Stewart author's introduction. Or the title (meant to suggest a context of social desperation, riots, wars, The Bomb and such? But Purdy's desperations, here at any rate, are domestic and cosmic rather than social). Or the fact that few of the poems are new: though most of the old ones have been revised, it's like eating leftovers—they've been warmed up but you know you've had them before.

Buried under all the floss, though, there's a real book with real poems in it and some very valid reasons for existing. As always, one has to swallow Purdy whole, take the horsing around and the hyperbole along with the painfully-arrived-at honesties and the moments of transcendently good poetry. Purdy writes like a cross between Shakespeare and a vaudeville comedian (so did Shakespeare) and that's not such a flip remark as it may seem: note those Shakespearean double "and"-linked adjectives ("my faint and yapping cry," "the sad and much emancipated world," "the unctuous and uneasy self I glimpse"), the way iambic pentameter keeps creeping in; and on the vaudeville end the patter acts, sad clown laughing at us laughing at him, telling awful jokes while knowing full well how awful they are. Purdy too is inherently dramatic; assumed by all his poems are a human speaking voice or voices and a responding audience, and his sense of timing is often superb. But these poems have been chosen according to subject— "sexual love and its mental counterpart," says Purdy—and it's matter rather than manner that deserves attention here.

In his introduction, Purdy recounts an incident in which he's told his poems aren't "romantic" but are instead "hard-boiled:" a slightly archaic adjective, redolent of rock-jowled, mush-hearted 'thirties newspapermen and Humphrey Bogart private detectives. "Hard-boiled" and "romantic" are not mutually exclusive, and Purdy is both; certainly he's a semi-Romantic. He can hardly write Love without writing Death on the same page; his brand of immortality (see his introduction and "Archeology of Snow") is reminiscent of Shelley's; Byronic swashbuckle and Don Juanesque undercutting of one's own heroics, both are there. He's filled with yearnings for the ideal, the absolute, the eternal, with no unshakeable conviction they exist and with a consequent awareness of loss, transience and imperfection. What may have been meant is that Purdy's poems aren't pretty or foggy-eyed: the women in them are often, to Purdy's credit, solid flesh and blood, with a good deal of the latter. They do things the Blessed Damozel wouldn't: they sweat under the arms, menstruate, argue, sulk, have miscarriages, V.D., operations and orgasms (though not babies, oddly enough).

They move in accurately observed surroundings full of what in a woman writer would be classed as typically female domestic imagery: Purdy is not above having insights in kitchens. They get bedraggled in the rain and have colds, and Purdy can be generous enough to comment, "When you sniff the acoustics of your nose are delightful." But Purdy has little trouble recognizing both his realism and his romanticism for what they are: "I can be two men if I have to," he says, and is.

Purdy's love poems demonstrate the self divided against itself to perhaps an even greater extent than do his poems on other subjects. Here the freedom-loving adventurer pulls against the husband, that "greyish drunkish largeish anguished man," and the female landscape (Purdy's metaphor) separates itself into corresponding territories of Others and Wife. From Wife-country, viewed sometimes as a prison and sometimes as a place of refuge, Purdy makes brief excursions into Otherland, alluring but also threatening: he'd leave for good, he claims in "Song of the Impermanent Husband," if he weren't afraid to. The Others, whether memories of youth, exotic fantasies of "brown girls" or "white and lily girls," a low-comedy "waggling fanny" pursued through a supermarket or a young girl in a poignant hotel-room interlude, are escapes or weapons to be used against Wife. Like Odysseus or a boomerang Purdy always returns, because Wife is where the action is and the action is not a tourist-trip but a battle.

It is this interaction which is central to the book, a constant unavoidable even when it is being denied and attacked. Like all crucial relationships it involves a number of emotions: Purdy, faced with the stubborn actuality of Wife, reacts with lust, anger, false pride, grudging admiration, claustrophobia, sadism, laughter, alienation, joy, fear of growing older and dying, and even a love "that can never be freedom exactly." But he doesn't make many guesses about the possible reciprocal feelings of Wife: either he doesn't know, thinks he can't know, or doesn't want to know. Thus the celebrated skirmish in "Home Made Beer"— "Whereupon my wife appeared from the bathroom / where she had been brooding for days / over the injustice of being a woman and / attacked me with a broom"—is made to seem both unprovoked (either being a woman isn't an injustice, or it is but why blame Purdy?) and funny, a sort of Edwardian seaside-postcard surly-wife gag; though an in-depth interview conducted on the other side of the bathroom door would doubtless have been revealing. Wife, however, except for occasional mutterings of "you bastard," remains silent, and is ultimately ungraspable, inscrutable, "neutral as nature." From this war-torn relationship emerge two of the consistently best poems in the book: "Love Poem," totally brutal and totally convincing, in which the poet identifies himself with the knife used to perform a painful and possibly fatal operation, and "Poem:"

> You are ill and so I lead you away
> and put you to sleep in the dark room
> —you lie breathing softly and I hold your hand
> feeling the fingertips relax as sleep comes
>
> You will not sleep more than a few hours
> and the illness is less serious than my anger or cruelty
> and the dark bedroom is like a foretaste of other darknesses
> to come later which all of us must endure alone
> but here I am permitted to be with you
>
> After a while in sleep your fingers clutch tightly
> and I know that whatever may be happening
> the fear coiled in dreams or the bright trespass of pain
> there is nothing at all I can do except hold your hand
> and not go away

This is simple and so good.

It's also about as close as Purdy gets to tenderness, and it's perhaps noteworthy that it chronicles a sickness: Purdy is more likely to express this kind of love in connection with the woman's possible or fantasized death than in

her here-and-now, awake and healthy presence. (See also
"Necropsy of Love" and "The Widower," even the poem in
which he says "so / hell it must be love I guess" is titled
"Engraved on a Tomb." Sex is another thing though, as
Purdy well knows. Some of his metaphors for it evoke war
and aggression: "I ... / hold my separate madness like a
sword / and plunge it in your body all night long;" "the
exaggerated zone / and bombbursting place that / fucking
is ... " Others change humans to animals; the wonderful
"werewolf metamorphosis" passage at the end of "For Norma
in Lieu of an Orgasm," for instance, and the slapstick
"vulgar elephant" equation in "Love at Roblin Lake." But
Purdy's verbal orgies are counterpointed by a certain amount
of hysteria. His interest in sex tends to be metaphysical
rather than sensual: sexual attraction may be a "comic
disease" (" ... this chemical / formula is emotional / cancer
even guinea pigs can't stand"), love may be "ambiguous" and
sex "a bully," but still he can use it to convince himself he's
alive and vital and (perhaps) to keep himself from dissolving
into the cosmic soup, the flux of nature or the outerspace
landscape that so repeatedly invades his bedrooms. Many
times we find him recalling or memorializing old episodes
and indulging in new ones in an attempt to banish his real
enemies, pain, sorrow and — especially — time. "That you are
here at all," he says in "Idiot's Song," "delays my own
death / an instant longer." It is the fear of death and vanishing, we realize, that underlies a lot of the Victory Burlesque
joke-man routines ("The Muse has thighs of moonlight and
silver / her cunt is frozen gold / and that is why if any mortal
woman need ask / my hands are always cold"): as in war, the
wisecracks sustain the illusion of sanity in the face of an
otherwise intolerable anxiety. Purdy does indeed "take
women serious," but he needs his laughter at times to keep
himself from screaming.

   Love in a burning building raises a lot of extra-poetic,
even extra-Purdy questions. Is it possible for men and

women to stop mythologizing, manipulating and attacking one another? Do all men divide women into Wife and Others, do they all share Purdy's tendency to think of women in terms of separate anatomical features—for Purdy usually ass and breasts, he's not much of a leg man and there's only one fully-described face in the book—like cut-up chickens? Is Purdy's attitude towards women that of his sex, his country, his generation (in which case *Love* can be a handy guide for women who want to know what really goes on in the male skull, the Canadian male skull, etc.) or is it strictly personal?

Personal it certainly is. It may be more, but it's also one man's reflections, experiences and emotions, recorded so honestly that even the lies, the cruelties, the bathos and the trivialities are included.

PART II
1972-1976

PART II
1972-76

The publication of *Survival* caused a certain flurry. Although *Surfacing* put me on the literary map in places like New York and London, it was *Survival* that put me on the rubber-chicken map in places like The Empire Club, Toronto. Canadians have traditionally been rather queasy about words such as "literature" and "art;" they would much rather talk *about* them than actually come to grips with them, though in defence of Canadians let me say at once that their *per capita* readership is very high, higher than that of the States and England. Maybe it's businessmen I mean, rather than Canadians. They'd rather have a speech than a novel. Having written an expository work *about* Canadian literature, I was suddenly called upon to produce yet more expositions of my exposition. Which recalls the first Canadian joke I ever heard: the road to Heaven forks. The right branch has a sign on it that says *To Heaven*. The left branch has a sign that says *Panel Discussion on Heaven*. All the Canadians go to the left.

Survival was fun to attack. In fact, it still is; most self-respecting professors of Canlit begin their courses, I'm told, with a short ritual sneer at it. It's true that it has no footnotes: the intended audience was not the footnote crowd, and it reached its intended audience, which was all those

people whose highschool English teachers told them they
weren't studying Canadian literature because there wasn't
any. Responses to *Survival* are summed up in "Mathews and
Misrepresentation." "What's So Funny" and "Canadian
Monsters" contain material I would have included in
Survival, had I thought of it at the time. "Canadian Monsters"
also continues my interest in fantasy literature, which was to
have been the subject of my temporarily unfinished PhD
thesis.

This was also a period in which I was asked to review a
number of books by women, and to speak and write about
the same subject. I had of course reviewed books by women
before, and written about women authors and female protagonists in books, but "women" had now become a *subject*. I
began to get worried about the possibility of a new ghetto:
women's books reviewed only by women, men's books reviewed only by men, with a corresponding split in the
readership. It wasn't what one had in mind as a desirable
future for the species.

It's in this period too that I began to get requests for
reviews from publications other than Canadian ones. They
too often wanted me to review women, but not always
Canadian women. So a certain amount of cross-fertilization
took place, and I found myself reviewing Canadians for
Americans and Americans for Canadians and sometimes
Canadians for English and English for Canadians. . . . Could
this be internationalism?

14
Travels Back

(1973)

Three hours past midnight, Highway 17 between Ottawa and North Bay, November, I'm looking out the Greyhound bus window at the almost nothing I can see. Coffee taste still with me from the Ottawa station, where I was marooned four hours because someone in Toronto mixed up the schedules; I sat writing letters and trying not to watch as the waitresses disposed of a tiny wizened drunk. "I been all over the world, girlie," he told them as they forced his coat on him, "I been places you never seen."

The headlights pick out asphalt, snow-salted road borders, dark trees as we lean round the frequent bends. What I picture is that we'll pass the motel, which they said was on the highway outside Renfrew—but *which* side?—and I'll have to walk, a mile maybe carrying the two suitcases full of my own books I'm lugging around because there may not be any bookstores, who in Toronto knows? A passing truck, Canadian Content squashed all over the road, later the police wondering what I was doing there anyway, as I am myself at this moment. Tomorrow at nine (nine!) I'm supposed to be giving a poetry reading in the Renfrew high school. Have fun in Renfrew, my friends in Toronto said with, I guess, irony before I left.

I'm thinking of summer, a swimming pool in France, an acquaintance of mine floating on his back and explaining why bank managers in Canada shouldn't be allowed to hang Group of Seven pictures on their walls—it's a false image, all nature, no people—while a clutch of assorted Europeans and Americans listen incredulously.

"I mean, *Canada*," one of them drawls. "I think they should give it to the United States, then it would be good. All except Quebec, they should give that to France. You should come and live here. I mean, you don't really live *there* any more."

We get to Renfrew finally and I step off the bus into six inches of early snow. He was wrong, this if anywhere is where I live. Highway 17 was my first highway, I travelled along it six months after I was born, from Ottawa to North Bay and then to Temiskaming, and from there over a one-track dirt road into the bush. After that, twice a year, north when the ice went out, south when the snow came, the time between spent in tents; or in the cabin built by my father on a granite point a mile by water from a Quebec village so remote that the road went in only two years before I was born. The towns I've passed and will pass—Arnprior, Renfrew, Pembroke, Chalk River, Mattawa, the old gingerbread mansions in each of them built on lumber money and the assumption that the forest would never give out—they were landmarks, way stations. That was 30 years ago though and they've improved the highway, now there are motels. To me nothing but the darkness of the trees is familiar.

I didn't spend a full year in school until I was 11. Americans usually find this account of my childhood—woodsy, isolated, nomadic—less surprising than do Canadians: after all, it's what the glossy magazine ads say Canada is supposed to be like. They're disappointed when they hear I've never lived in an igloo and my father doesn't say "On, huskies!" like Sergeant Preston on the defunct (American) radio program, but other than that they find me plausible enough. It's Canadians who raise eyebrows. Or rather the Torontonians. It's as though I'm a part of their own past they find disreputable or fake or just can't believe ever happened.

I've never read at a high school before. At first I'm terrified, I chew Tums while the teacher introduces me, remembering the kinds of things we used to do to visiting dignitaries when I was in high school: rude whispers, noises, elastic bands and paper clips if we could get away with it. Surely they've never heard of me and won't be interested: we had no Canadian poetry in high school and not much of anything else Canadian. In the first four years we studied the Greeks and Romans and the Ancient Egyptians and the Kings of England, and in the fifth we got Canada in a dull blue book that was mostly about wheat. Once a year a frail old man would turn up and read a poem about a crow; afterward he would sell his own books (as I'm about to do), autographing them in his thin spidery handwriting. That was Canadian poetry. I wonder if I look like him, vulnerable, misplaced and redundant. Isn't the real action—the *real* action—their football game this afternoon?

Question period: Do you have a message? Is your hair really like that, or do you get it done? Where do you get the ideas? How long does it take? What does it *mean*? Does it bother you, reading your poems out loud like that? It would bother me. What is the Canadian identity? Where can I send my poems? To get them published.

They are all questions with answers, some short, some long. What astonishes me is that they ask them at all, that they want to talk: at my high school you didn't ask questions. And they *write*, some of them. Inconceivable. It wasn't like that, I think, feeling very old, in my day.

In Deep River I stay with my second cousin, a scientist with the blue inhuman eyes, craggy domed forehead and hawk nose of my maternal Nova Scotian relatives. He takes me through the Atomic Research Plant, where he works; we wear white coats and socks to keep from being contaminated and watch a metal claw moving innocent-looking lethal items—pencils, a tin can, a Kleenex—behind a 14-inch leaded glass window. "Three minutes in there," he says, "will kill you." The fascination of invisible force.

After that we examine beaver damage on his property and he tells me stories about my grandfather, before there were cars and radios. I like these stories, I collect them from all my relatives, they give my a link, however tenuous, with the past and with a culture made up of people and their relationships and their ancestors rather than objects in a landscape. This trip I learn a new story: my grandfather's disastrous muskrat farm. It consisted of a fence built carefully around a swamp, the idea being that it would be easier to gather in the muskrats that way; though my cousin says he trapped more muskrat outside the fence than my grandfather ever did inside it. The enterprise failed when a farmer dumped out some of his apple spray upstream and the muskrats were extinguished; but the Depression hit and the bottom fell out of the muskrat market anyway. The fence is still there.

Most of the stories about my grandfather are success stories, but I add this one to my collection: when totems are hard to come by, failure stories have their place. "Do you know," I say to my cousin, repeating a piece of lore recently gleaned from my grandmother, "that one of our ancestresses was doused as a witch?" That was in New England; whether she sank and was innocent or swam and was guilty isn't recorded.

Out his living-room window, across the Ottawa River, solid trees, is my place. More or less.

Freezing rain overnight; I make it to the next poetry reading pulling my suitcases on a toboggan two miles over thin ice.

I reach North Bay, an hour late because of the sleet. That evening I read at the Oddfellows' Hall, in the basement. The academics who have organized the reading are nervous, they think no one will come, there's never been a poetry reading in North Bay before. In a town where everyone's seen the movie, I tell them, you don't have to worry, and in fact they spent the first fifteen minutes bringing in extra chairs. These aren't students, there are all kinds of people, old ones, young ones, a friend of my mother's who used to stay with us in Quebec, a man whose uncle ran the fishing camp at the end of the lake...

In the afternoon I was interviewed for the local TV station by a stiff-spined man in a tight suit. "What's this," he said, dangling one of my books nonchalantly by the corner to show the viewers that poetry isn't his thing, he's virile really, "a children's book?" I suggested that if he wanted to know what was inside it he might try reading it. He became enraged and said he had never been so insulted, and Jack McClelland hadn't been mean like that when *he* was in North Bay. In place of the interview they ran a feature on green noodles.

Later, 30 poetry readings later. Reading a poem in New York that has an outhouse in it and having to define outhouse (and having the two or three people come up furtively afterwards and say that they, too, once...). Meeting a man who has never seen a cow; who has never, in fact, been outside the city of New York. Talking then about whether there is indeed a difference between Canada and the U.S. (I been places you never seen...) Trying to explain, in Detroit, that in Canada for some strange reason it isn't just other poets who come to poetry readings. ("You mean ...people like *our mothers* read poetry?") Having someone tell me that maybe what accounts for the "strength" of my work is its fetching "regional" qualities—"you know, like Faulkner . . . "

In London Ontario, the last poetry reading of the year and perhaps, I'm thinking, for ever, I'm begining to feel like a phonograph. A lady: "I've never felt less like a Canadian since all this nationalism came along." Another lady, very old, with astonishing sharp eyes: "Do you think in metaphor?" Someone else: "What is the Canadian identity?" That seems to be on people's minds.

How to keep all this together in your head, my head. Because where I live is where everyone lives: it isn't just a place or a region, though it is also that (and I could have put in Vancouver and Montreal, where I lived for a year each, and Edmonton where I lived for two, and Lake Superior and Toronto . . .). It's a space composed of images, experiences, the weather, your own past and your ancestors', what people say and what they look like and how they react to what you're doing, important events and trivial ones, the connections among them not always obvious. The images come from outside, they are *there*, they are the things we live with and must deal with. But the judgements and the connections (what does it *mean?*) have to be made inside your head and they are made with words: good, bad, like, dislike, whether to go, whether to stay, whether to live there any more. For me that's partly what writing is: an exploration of where in reality I live.

I think Canada, more than most countries, is a place you choose to live in. It's easy for us to leave, and many of us have. There's the U.S. and England, we've been taught more about their histories than our own, we can blend in, become permanent tourists. There's been a kind of standing invitation here to refuse authenticity to your actual experience, to think life can be meaningful or important only in "real " places like New York or London or Paris. And it's a temptation: the swimming pool in France is nothing if not detached. The question is always, Why stay? and you have to answer that over and over.

I don't think Canada is "better" than any other place, any more than I think Canadian literature is "better"; I live in one and read the other for a simple reason: they are mine, with all the sense of territory that implies. Refusing to acknowledge where you come from—and that must include the noodle man and his hostilities, the anti-nationalist lady and her doubts—is an act of amputation: you may become free floating, a citizen of the world (and in what other country is that an ambition?) but only at the cost of arms, legs or heart. By discovering your place you discover yourself.

But there's another image, fact, coming from the outside that I have to fit in. This territory, this thing I have called "mine," may not be mine much longer. Part of the much-sought Canadian identity is that few nationals have done a more enthusiastic job of selling their country than have Canadians. Of course there are buyers willing to exploit, as they say, our resources; there always are. It is our eagerness to sell that needs attention. Exploiting resources and developing potential are two different things: one is done from without by money, the other from within, by something I hesitate only for a moment to call love.

15
How Do I Get Out Of Here:
The Poetry of John Newlove

(1973)

> Black night window—
> rain running down
> the fogged glass,
>
> a blanched leaf
> hanging outside
> on a dead twig,
>
> the moon dead,
> the wind dying
> in the trees,
>
> in this valley,
> in this recession[1]

John Newlove is one of the most important young poets to emerge in English Canada during the 1960's. He was born in Regina in 1938. He grew up in rural Saskatchewan, and managed somehow to survive that and become a poet; from the evidence in the books one gathers that each of these events was a near impossibility and both together constitute something like a miracle. His first major collection, *Moving In Alone*, appeared with Contact Press in 1965. It was followed by *Black Night Window* in 1968 and *The Cave* in 1970. A fourth volume, *Lies*, will be published shortly.

I could say a lot about Newlove's "technique" or "craftsmanship"—the way he puts poems together—for he is indeed a master builder. His versatility is impressive: he's in control of his words, he can move easily and convincingly from clipped, terse epigrams to flowing lyricism to something like a grand manner, his work is often a demonstration model of how it should be done. But that isn't my primary interest. I would rather talk about corners; what they are, what you do in them and how you get out of them. Because that seems to me what Newlove's poetry is obsessed with, and for him it's a life-and-death obsession.

The corner Newlove so persistently writes about is the world he lives in, or, rather, his sense of the world he is stuck in. That sense may be defined by its negative qualities. Newlove's "usual" world or starting point is, first, one in which external nature is something to be disliked or feared. Its typical locales are swamps and seas, in which scenes of petty and mindless carnage repeat themselves like the bad dreams that often reflect them:

> . . . . Frogs touch
> insects with their long tongues, the cannibal fish and
> the stabbing birds
>
> wait[2]

Further inland, in forests for example, "even the deer" are "dangerous;"[3] the poet's habitual response to the natural environment is to feel threatened by it:

> I dream of the animals
> that may sulk there,
> deer snake and bear
> dangerous and inviolable
> as I am not inviolable.[4]

If an animal is not threatening it is likely to be dead. Various carcasses litter the poems, sometimes singly, sometimes in slaughterhouse profusion, as in "A Circus Went Berserk Here,"[5] which contains not only the dreamed slaying of an entire menagerie but the memory of an actual massacre of wild dogs. With animals which are dead and therefore not frightening the poet may identify as fellow-victim; or he may allow himself to feel guilt for not identifying as much as he might:

> The dead beast, turned up
> (brown fur on back and white
> on the belly), lay on the roadway,
> its paws extended in the air—
> worn-out attitude of prayer.
>
> It was beautiful on the well-travelled roadway
> with its dead black lips: God help me,
> I did not even know what it was.
> I had been walking into the city then,
> early, with my own name in mind.[6]

But most of the time Nature is cannibal fish and stabbing birds, a darkness in which you can't see what's going on but suspect it is not only nasty but likely to happen to you also if you stay outside too long. An English critic might identify this sort of thing as the hallucination of a feverish post-Darwinian; a Canadian one spots it instantly as purely and simply Canadian.

But the human universe in Newlove's work is scarcely to be preferred. On a panoramic scale, men and women are seen as leading the same kinds of meaningless and mutually destructive lives as the cannibal fish and stabbing birds, and in a similar environment:

> In the cities men wait to be told. They sit between the
> locomotive and the fish. The flat sea and the prairie
> that was a sea contain them. Images float before their eyes,
>
> men and women acting,

entertaining, rigorously dancing with fractured minds
contorted to a joyless pleasure, time sold from life.[7]

From this perspective all human action and the desire that
shapes action is seen as a relentless piece of machinery:

.... People sleep with mechanical dreams, the sea
hums with rain, the locomotive shines black, fish wait under
the surface of a pinked pool.

Frogs shiver in the cold. The land waits, black, dreaming.
Men lie dry in their beds.

History, history!

Under the closed lids their eyes flick back and forth as they
try to follow the frightening shapes of their desires.[8]

The epitome of this viewpoint is found in "The Last Event,"
in which natural and animal life and human life and history
are speeded up and mashed together into a kind of horrible
seething porridge:

Great heaps of captivating skulls, stretched tents of our
human skin, filling the dark plain with mementoes, objects
of historical curiosity only, an avoidance ....

. . . .

Black chaos is below, the convulsed world swarming with
flesh, the fleshly trees, fluid animals, skin over flexing bone,
relapsed humanity
flowing in rivers over the earth of water, rock sand and black
dirt, unsteady mouths, hands carefully searching for the
slack lax vaccine of warring love.[9]

What kind of life is possible for the individual—as man,
lover, poet—in such a universe? Not, as you might guess, a
very enjoyable one. Newlove's most typical stances in the
single-voice or "I" poems are revulsion, guilt, fright and
paralysis. Significantly often we find him saying things like
"I cannot move,"[10] being "unable to move,"[11] sitting locked
in a minor catatonic trance surrounded by objects, tables,

cups, walls, which threaten him because they refuse to respond to or mirror what he is feeling. Sometimes he recites catalogues of the subjects he possesses—shoes, shirts, paper, pencils, boxes[12]—in an attempt to anchor or locate himself in the physical world; but the act of cataloguing is in itself a demonstration of its own futility. When he is not trapped and rigid, caged in a world of unanswering *things*, he is a man running away, watching himself running away.[13] The goal is escape, the method perpetual motion:

> On that black highway,
> where are you going?—
>
> it is in Alberta
> among the trees
>
> where the road sweeps
> left and right
>
> in great concrete arcs
> at the famous resort—
>
> there you stood on
> the road in the wind,
>
> the cold wind going
> through you and you
>
> going through the country
> to no end, only
>
> to turn again at one sea
> and begin it again,
>
> feeling safe with strangers
> in a moving car.[14]

This kind of escape is ultimately impossible, since what the "hitchhiker" persona seeks to escape from is himself: more than once we find him by the roadside or in the forest between lifts, brain churning, "caught in all I have done, afraid / and unable to escape, formulating / one more ruinous way to safety."[15] There is more than a suggestion that the position of isolation, exile, failure and despair is chosen and even at times indulged in for pleasure, that the early "delight at making / myself feel sad" chronicled in "Kamsack"[16] has become an unshakeable habit, that he fucks it up because he likes it:

> In self
> exile again,
> having bungled
>
> everything, living
> in other people's
> houses, seeing
>
> all the clean snow,
> styrofoam, about,
> the wind
>
> swirling, people
> strangers, hours
> blank, prospects
>
> gone, self
> in exile again,
> content
> in adversity.[17]

He rules out the possibility of change and is able to depise himself for that very reason:

> .... There's pride
> even in my despising,
> my inability
> to change, which I call
>
> stubbornness and praise
> in myself and strum
> like a dirty old
> one-string guitar .... [18]

In fact, to be successful at anything is a position he must almost by definition—self-definition—reject.[19] He is a loser and his proper study is loss.

Alone he's a paralytic or a transient, with others he sees himself more often than not as a treacherous friend[20] and a lover who is incapable of love. In relationships with women he can express nausea or terror,[21] caused by his own visions as much as by reality:

> But what I really dream
> is those women suffocating me
> their dead flesh denser than cold syrup to swim in
> Slowing me down slowing me down
>
> Dreams of the thick women turning
> Turning and turning their gross bellies on me
> wrapping their gelatin thighs and mottled breasts
> Graving me deeper than winter mud Choking
> with their red-grease kisses my airy mouth[22]

More typically though he is wistful and rejected,[23] or, and especially, a deceitful fool and bungler, messing up love for himself the way he messes up the other areas of his life. Again he is quite aware of the self-defeating nature of his behaviour. "It is a greedy man who acts as you," he tells himself, "one who cannot have enough of loving / and always plans his leavings."[24] He sums up the sterility of his position in two lines of "Away, or Far:" "I live / to be loved, but love I cannot give."[25]

It is in this area that the poet's obsessive and truly desperate concern with lies and with truth-telling—the inevitability of the former and the hope for the latter—finds one of its most significant focuses. But this concern extends beyond love, beyond the personal. Negatively it is expressed through self-hatred, hatred of his own lies:

> . . . . Why
> do I lie? Why do I?
>
> It is that the confession
> hopes to be the cure, the lie
> to engender the truth.[26]

"I describe the holes in me / as if truth were a virtue," he says in "This Is The Song I Sing;"[27] but for him truth *is* a virtue, the primary one. As the title of his forthcoming book may indicate, the concept of truth, the truth, is perhaps the only piece of firm ground he has to build on.

Possibly it is this belief, this faith, that is at the root of Newlove's enormous distrust of words, a distrust amounting at times to a contempt which extends to poetry and to himself in his role as poet. Sometimes the act of writing itself appears to him as a piece of trickery, the supreme lie. "Everything must be faked,"[28] it seems, in poetry as in love, and from time to time he succumbs to his own suspicion and takes the easy way: "one remembers," he says, "how warm the falsity was."[29] But usually he opts for truth, improbable though it may seem to him that he can ever tell it. Again and again this motif surfaces; again and again "the words do not suffice,"[30] speaking is evil[31] or simply inadequate, reality is too complicated to be encompassed by mere words, "there is always so much more to be said than can be said."[32] "Words impart mystery, not sense," he says in "The Last Event,"[33] "preaching is an art, oratory, / flashy flesh, slick ornamentative goings-on, but poems . . . . "

He doesn't complete the thought, although—or perhaps because—it is crucial to him. What about poems? Given this closed circle,[34] this corner that Newlove finds himself so repeatedly backed into—a corner in which the self exists isolated in a revolting body, dwarfed by a threatening and destructive universe where action is futile, love impossible and words fraudulent—why write poems at all? Why not stick one's head in the gas oven or the toilet, where according to this analysis it logically belongs? Such a conclusion has occurred certainly to Newlove himself; occasionally it is death, not truth, that seems the only reality:

> there are too many liars,
> myself among them:
> what is there to believe, the myths
> made to hold a small nation together
> that is not ours?

> love?
> that will not believe itself,
> ourselves, whom we do not love in truth,
> exultances
> which cannot be found?
>   the mind
> feuding with itself or the stumbling body,
> men debased to astonish gods?
>   The death,
> the death
> that surrounds us,
> believe that,
> but do not love it.[35]

If he could only see himself as an innocent victim picked on by fate, courageous and guiltless ... and it's a temptation,[36] but it won't do. "There are no innocent people in Vancouver,"[37] Newlove says, including himself. That's the worst of it: we ourselves are responsible for the negative qualities of the space we find ourselves in. "I see that we all make the world what we want," Newlove asserts; then, paradoxically, "Our disappointment lies in the world as it is."[38] This is the corner, the closed circle, the double bind: we are able to make the world and we have made a bad one.

But if that is the worst, it is also the beginning of the way out. The "here" that one must get out of or die in, "this valley," "this recession," is partly a state of mind: its undesirable qualities can perhaps be cancelled out or at least balanced if we can change our point of view, the direction from which we are seeing and therefore creating it. Easier said, as Newlove would be quick to point out, than done:

> it is imperfection
> that eyes see, it is
> impreciseness they deserve,
>
> but they desire so much more,
> what they desire, what they hope,
> what they invent,

is perfection, organizing
all things as they may not be,
it is what they strive for

unwillingly, against themselves,
to see a perfect order, ordained
reason —

and what they strive against
while they wish it, what they want
to see, closed, is what
they want, and will not be.[39]

Given the odds which he has stacked so overwhelmingly against himself, how can he even begin? What *is* there to believe, *how* can one affirm? In a way it is the desire for "perfection" that both renders the actual world so impossible for Newlove and makes him want to see it differently; but there are various ways of transforming the world, some real, some fake. In several brief, easily-missed poems there is a suggestion that the true process begins, on the most basic level, with the simple refusal to see anything that is not there, which can also be a refusal of metaphor and thus of "poetic" speech:

It is my refusal to make comparisons
this time that keeps me silent. There
is this snow, and me,

I saw on the dry snow, which was
grey, a bird sitting as if he would
eat bread or seeds.

And I saw an eaten melon: it was
this and it was that and red
with black seeds.

I spat them out. What keeps me silent
is not the bird on the dry snow,
but my continuous refusal.[40]

But out of "silence" and "refusal" Newlove has still made a poem, a structure of words — an act that affirms the value of such structures and of the words that compose them, even when the materials are so limited. From this ground one may go on to small acknowledgements: the desirability of survival even though difficult and absurd,[41] the desirability of awareness even though painful. "What hurts me," he says in "The Drinker,"[42] "is that I see it," a remark that might well be applied to most of his perceptions. With this bare minimum of affirmation love can be, if not a "perfection," at least a human and therefore fragile possibility:

> The wet sun shines a muddy spring,
> warm wind blows; I walk, content
> with the weather of our hands.
>
> What if the world does end,
> and we are only stained shadows
> the sidewalk photographed? Today
>
> I hold you and have a happiness
> that makes me human once again.[43]

Because the self and the corner are connected and possibly synonomous, the way out of the corner is the way out of the self. If everything outside the self, including other people, is postulated as negative or devoid of reality, one may as well stay in the self; it at least is known, which is some comfort, and one can have dreams and fantasies there. But if there is a "truth" to which words in some way correspond, then the encounter with the outside world through words, the externalization and transcendence of the self, becomes possible. Newlove has written several poems in which the function of the poet is seen as praise, though it must be a praise based on the truth. One of the most curious of these is "The Singing Head." The head belongs to the poet as martyr, the prototype for whom is of course Orpheus. In Newlove's version the head, which has been severed for a number of years, is not singing about its pain (for a change!) but about the goodness of the universe it finds itself in, which consists at the moment of a ditch:

... the head
in grass or just

tossed under any
bush or muddled in
a ditch ....

it carries on
to raise its breathless
voice, praise

the life that while it
lived was good, to praise
the grass
or muddy ditch,

that where it stays
is good.[44]

In another poem, he reverses his usual paranoia by finding himself able to praise even his fear:

.... What's lovely
is whatever makes the adrenalin run:
therefore I count terror and fear among
the greatest beauty. The greatest
beauty is to be alive, forgetting nothing, ... [45]

The naming of the details of external reality which is affirmation and praise—if words are valid this can happen, even when the reality so named is not beautiful or impressive, when the land and the cities in it are "isolate," "tentative," as in "East From the Mountains,"[46] or full of "emptiness" as in "Ride Off Any Horizon."[47] Or when the people who inhabit it are, as they so often are for Newlove, wounded, crippled, amputated, crazed, grotesque or dead. By describing them, entering into their lives, as he does so exceptionally well in such poems as "The Flowers,"[48] "For Judith,"[49] "Samuel Hearne in Wintertime,"[50] "Doukhobor,"[51] and the extraordinary "The Fat Man," [52] he reaches out of himself towards the actual, with its various shapes and flaws.

In a few poems—and it is significant that they are few—Newlove views the act of saying as not only affirmative and laudatory but redemptive. It is obvious from the previous descriptions of his "usual" universe that he regards the world and the self as somehow imperfect, in need of salvation, though he uses no formal religious structure to contain this intuition. Newlove seldom makes myths, but when he does they operate in the direction of pulling together all the elements that he more often sees as decaying, falling to pieces: himself, the land, history, time, identity. This synthesis takes place most notably in "The Pride,"[53] an almost epic long poem which traces the history of western Canada through the defeat and dispersal of the Indians and ends by seeing the current inhabitants—"we" or "us"—as their metaphorical descendants. For me, a poem that does a similar thing better (it also draws in Indian mythology, though it is more personal and less formally ambitious) is "Resources, Certain Earths."[54] It places the focus on the real desire, the real urgency, that appears to me to underlie most of Newlove's poems: the wish for salvation, a salvation that must come both through and despite words and from facing the truth:

> In my words, masked in my words,
> the realization of death! which
> will not come true for you, not here!
>
> The realization is stretched out,
> is seized, set up for me. Let me
> come forth, let me seize it,
> swallow it whole and understand!
> I am grappling, the realization of death
> is the realization of life, the spirit
> of that wind formidable. O by pondering
> on those other things we think them
> important and ourselves profound,
> Paracelsus, whom I address. But this, this....

To see, touch, eat a particle of it
means disaster, at once
every joint in the body is dislocated,
the head turns back, skin becomes stone;
but whole it imparts power!

Let me swallow it whole and be strong,
accept it whole and be strong!
Let me take it whole and be strong!

Let me know it well
and be strong and complete and be saved.

The realization of death is the realization of life. So we must believe if we are to read Newlove with any joy, for much of the poetry is death poetry. Its tension is the tension between despair and hope, between the corner, the black night window, that is always waiting there for him and the brief moments of transcendence from which he must return. Out of the tension comes the poems. As usual.

NOTES

MIA: *Moving In Alone*, Contact Press, 1965.
BNW: *Black Night Window*, McClelland and Stewart, 1968.
TC: *The Cave*, McClelland and Stewart, 1970.
Lies, McClelland and Stewart, forthcoming.

1 "Black Night Window," BNW, 11.
2 "The Engine and the Sea," TC, 10. See also "Dream," TC, 56, and "Dream," TC, 62.
3 "Two Letters From Austria," MIA, 66.
4 "The Forest," MIA, 54.
5 MIA, 33.
6 "The Well-travelled Roadway," MIA, 55. See also "It Just Lay There," TC, 32.
7 "The Engine and the Sea," TC, 9.

8 Ibid., 10.
9 TC, 38-39. For victimizing politics with America as exploiter and Canada as dupe, see "America," TC, 58. For the rejection of Canadian "patriotism," see "Canada," BNW, 74, and "Like a Canadian," BNW, 75; in the latter the poet feels "like a Canadian / only when kissing someone else's bum."
10 "She Reaches Out," MIA, 11.
11 "Seeing Me Dazed," MIA, 21.
12 These objects are from "Brass Box. Spring. Time." BNW, 46.
13 The phrase is from "Solitaire," BNW, 78.
14 "The Hitchhiker," BNW, 15.
15 "By the Church Wall," MIA, 56.
16 BNW, 61.
17 "Exile," TC, 28.

18 "Without Ceremony," BNW, 26.

19 See e.g. "It Was All There," BNW, 44. Sometimes his awareness of his own masochism results in a rather weak-chinned self-pity, but sometimes in tough, superbly put-together poems like "Revenge," TC, 44, in which the central figure is considering breaking his arm with a hammer to make others feel sorry for him.

20 See e.g. "Seattle," TC, 73.

21 See also "The First Time," MIA, 28.

22 "Succubi," MIA, 23. For an overwhelmingly Protestant disgust with the human body, see the hideously detailed "Public Library," BNW, 70; for sexual brutality and dominance-exploitation relationships between men and women, see "Alcazar," TC, 59, and the brilliant "What Do You Want?" BNW, 48.

23 See "The Funny Grey Man," TC, 18.

24 "Never Mind," TC, 21.

25 TC, 29.

26 "All My Friends," MIA, 20.

27 MIA, 17.

28 "Away, or Far," TC, 29.

29 "Strand by Strand," TC, 24.

30 "The Prairie," TC, 35.

31 "The Man," TC, 33.

32 "When I Heard of the Friend's Death," BNW, 63.

33 TC, 38.

34 The phrase is from "A Former Dream," TC, 32.

35 "Show Me A Man," BNW, 92. See also death as the "perfect moment" in "A Young Man," TC, 27.

36 See "You Cannot Step Twice," BNW, 22.

37 In the poem of the same name, BNW, 38.

38 "Remembering Christopher Smart," TC, 57.

39 "In This Reed," BNW, 82.

40 "At This Time," MIA, 68. See also "No Song," BNW, 25, and "The Flower," TC, 46.

41 See "If You Can," MIA, 65.

42 BNW, 69. See also "You Can See," MIA, 16.

43 "Warm Wind," TC, 15. See also TC, 16 and 17.

44 MIA, 48.

45 "The Double-Headed Snake," BNW, 42.

46 MIA, 50.

47 BNW, 34.

48 MIA, 40.

49 MIA, 34.

50 BNW, 84.

51 TC, 34.

52 TC, 78.

53 BNW, 105. A personal note: my enjoyment of and therefore belief in this poem is somewhat mitigated by the reflection that the dead Indians would derive scant joy from the statement that the white men who ousted them are their spiritual progeny. But the poem is central in Newlove's work.

54 MIA, 72.

16
Mathews and Misrepresentation

(1973)

When the editors of *This Magazine* told me that Robin Mathews had done a substantial review of my book *Survival: A Thematic Guide to Canadian Literature*, and asked me to reply to it, I readily agreed, although I had not yet seen the review. The editors felt that a "dialogue" might deepen our understanding of the problems facing all of us, and I myself welcomed the chance to engage in such a dialogue with someone who was known to take these problems seriously and to have an acquaintance with the subject. (Such was not the case with all reviewers.) But when the review arrived, my initial response was that I had made a mistake. The prospect of replying to a piece which seemed to me so incorrect in its assumptions about my own position, so riddled with warpings and misconstructions of what I had actually written, so pervaded with wishful thinking and so bestrewn with unsubstantiated claims about specific pieces of literature was disheartening to one who believes, as I do, that the minimum qualification for a critic should be the ability to read and write. It would be like trying to get through a church stuffed with bread dough: sanctimonious perimeter, amorphous content.

The review itself, then, was a disappointment, and the result of the intended dialogue is more likely to resemble two monologues, since it is obvious nothing will change Mathews' mind, and very little of the evidence he puts forward has succeeded in changing mine. Why then reply? The essential reason is this: although I don't find it of any importance whether Margaret Atwood or Robin Mathews as individual egos are "right," I do think it's of importance whether the view of Canadian literature and of Canada put forth in *Survival* is substantially accurate. For this reason I will attempt to treat the review with the seriousness it ought to have deserved. I believe that Mathews' differences of opinion with the book are fundamentally concerned with tactics, which in turn depend on an estimate of position; and this I believe to be worth discussing. The dialogue, insofar as there is one, is probably about where we are now, where we would like to go and how we can get there. As I will indicate, I find the present position a more difficult one than Mathews seems to, and consequently one requiring more remedial effort.

But first I would like to do two things, both of which are steps leading to these conclusions. I would like to discuss other responses to *Survival*; and I would like to skim briefly over the inaccuracies of Mathews' review. The first will give some indication of what position the reading public seems to feel it's in; the second will reveal the directions in which Mathews distorts, when he does distort, thus giving us some clues as to *his* position. It would have saved considerable time if he'd been more explicit about the latter; but maybe it isn't clear yet even to him.

Other Responses to Survival

Quite a lot of words and pieces of paper came my way in response to *Survival*. They took a number of forms: reviews, media commentary, letters from general readers, letters from established writers, letters from students and young writers, conversations. They ranged all the way from serious, concerned and informed to trivial (Barry Callaghan saying, for instance, that *Survival* was a bad thing because it would make highschool teachers lazy; which is an interesting view of highschool teachers). I'll try to indicate briefly the range and nature of the response.

Nobody felt splendid after reading the book. It wasn't a simple "upper" for anyone, though some found it amusing, others "uncannily cheerful." But a note sounded again and again—in letters from readers as well as reviews—was that the subject was news to *them*. They'd either never heard of Canadian literature, or never thought of it as an entity before, and most found the experience "liberating" in that it gave them a focus for thinking about themselves, their own experiences and attitudes, or individual things they'd read, in a way they hadn't done previously. Some went so far as to say they never realized before that they had a culture. Some young writers—and these were the spookiest letters—wrote to say I'd just described the novel (or poems) they were currently working on. Some Americans, and Americans-in-exile, wrote to say they hadn't realized how different "we" are, and why.

But beyond that: many writers wrote to say that though they didn't agree with everything in *Survival*, the central thesis gave them a shock of recognition about what they themselves had been up to. Some gave helpful suggestions, ranging from technicalities to what else might have been included. Having sifted out all the suggestions—from reviews as well as letters—and having thought further about the implications and variations of the themes, I've decided to try to write sections for inclusion in a second edition of *Survival* on a few other areas—Humour, War, Magic, Struggle (if I can find enough material), and something about the shapes of critical theories, which was to have been in *Survival* but which got too abstruse. I find these areas correlatives rather than contradictions of the *Survival* thesis; for instance, under Humour, try reading *Northern Blights, Laughing Stalks, The Blasted Pine, The Incomparable Atuk, Cocksure, Sunshine Sketches, Sarah Binks* and Lawrence Garber's *Circuit* in quick succession, throwing in Max Ferguson's Rawhide Little Theatre sketches for fun, and see what you find. Or for War, try Colin McDougall's *Execution*. Or for Magic, try reading *Fifth Business* and Gwen MacEwen's *Noman* and see if you notice anything they have in common.

Apart from technical corrections and possibilities for inclusion, serious criticism also focussed on the following:

i) *Surely what you've described is the post-war European literature of despair, and thus universal.*
No; "survival" is in a way the opposite of "despair." A "survival" hero clings to the edge of the cliff with his fingernails, determined to hang on. A "despair" hero hurls himself off the cliff out of sheer *malaise*. Strangely enough, literary suicides are rare in Canadian literature.

ii) *Other literatures have victims. It's a universal theme.* (Variation: "King Lear is a victim.") Other literatures *do* have "victims;" but we have to consider the relationship between victim and society. For instance, in *Hard Times*, the working class is a victim within an otherwise non-victim society; in American literature, those who fail do so by dropping out of a society where success is the norm. The thing about Canadian victims is that they tend to be representative of the society. In *As For Me and My House*, everyone else in the book is failing too. Victims the most like Canadian ones are to be found in the literature of other "emerging nations" or former and present colonies (or, as someone suggested, the literature of the Holocaust) and I think it would be useful to do a study on this. My main concern in *Survival* was to distinguish Canlit from Britlit and Amlit. But to see the theme as "universal" is to view it as a *constant* in human society—like saying "the poor you have always with you"—and therefore as an *unalterable* fact, like birth and death and the weather. It is to ignore the political and economic context of "victims." In fact, you have "victims" only where you have hierarchies. For instance, to my knowledge, the Kalihari Bushmen do not produce "victim" myths.

King Lear? Well, he has lots of power at the beginning of the play, but he gives it to the wrong bunch. I've yet to encounter a Canadian fictional hero who starts at the apex of the pyramid like that!

iii) *The real theme of Canadian literature is not victims, but "sense of community."* Great; I'd love to hear about it, in a 250 page book with ample illustrations which doesn't ignore Ross, Laurence, Buckler, Pratt, etc. There are certainly communities in Canadian literature; so are there in almost all other literatures. Perhaps one of the differences is that the Canadian community is *itself* seen as a "victim"— everyone on the Titanic, all the brethern of Brébeuf, all the occupants of Horizon, everyone in the Manawaka of the Thirties, etc. Nothing brings out "sense of community" like victimization! (Cf. ghettoes.) Are the "communities" happy?

iv) *X, Y and Z don't fit your thesis: therefore the thesis is wrong.* There may be indeed things that don't fit (though my model allows for considerable vertical and horizontal stretch) and in Physics this would indeed be a tragic flaw. But in describing biological populations and human cultures, one tries to describe the norm. For instance, brown rats are brown, and an albino doesn't disprove this general rule. Mutations are very important—from them come strains and variations that may later be necessary for survival; and perhaps I should have described a few more mutations (though see the end of each chapter). But a book all about mutations would hardly be useful as a description of a species.

v) *Your book shows Canadian literature as grim and awful and badly-written and boring; woe, what are we to do?* (Variation:

What *should* we be writing?) Far from finding Canadian literature boring and badly-written, I find it fascinating as a species, with many pieces that accomplish excellently what they've set out to do. I'd hardly spend all that blood on something I found a total drag. I myself would much rather read a piece about someone lost in the Arctic with only a pencil-sharpener for protection than one about someone winning the Miss Teen America contest; but that may be just my Canadian bias. I don't equate "Canadian" with "bad literature," as was for so many years the fashion; neither do I equate it with "good literature", as may become the fashion (which would be unfortunate). For what we are to do, see the last section of this article. For what we should be writing . . . no one can tell writers what to write, and they won't listen if you do tell them. They will just continue writing, as they always do. And critics will continue to comment. My own critical comments are in no way to be construed as a prescription for writers.

vi) *What about Spiritual Victories?* They're fine, but no substitute for the other kind. One of the possibly harmful psychological advantages of being a "victim" is that you can substitute moral righteousness for responsibility; that is, you can view yourself as innocent and your oppressor as totally evil, and because you define yourself as powerless, you can avoid doing anything about your situation. "Winning" is not always "good", obviously; but neither is losing.

vii) *Survival is too convincing. It may get turned into dogma.* I recognize this as a danger, and I'd be upset if it happened. I certainly didn't intend it to be The Bible; more like a working hypothesis, to be altered or discarded if one more in accord with literary reality comes along. It should be regarded as a stage in a dialogue.

Which brings us to:

The Mathews Monologue

My first step in this task was to read Mathews' review. After recovering from the haze thereby induced, I read it again, placing a checkmark beside every paragraph where I felt misrepresentation had occurred. This resulted in a lot of checkmarks, and when I tried to write about all of them I found I was producing a batch of niggles which resembled those domestic disputes about who left the cap off the toothpaste tube, as boring to engage in as they are to listen to.

So I will confiscate some of my minor responses, mentioning only in passing Mathews' lack of perception about what *Survival* is (he thinks it's a teachers' manual), his curious implication—or do I misread him?—that one has to be an academic to write a book like *Survival*, the rhetoric— "ploy," "it won't work," "game," "apology"—that implies I'm engaged in an activity at once frivolous and underhanded, his ascription of Guilt by Dedication (the dedicatees were chosen simply because they are the only other people I know of who have previously attempted this kind of critical work on Canadian literature, though possibly I should have included James Reaney or even Robin Mathews), his uninformed remarks about Anansi (I say uninformed because they display remarkable ignorance about who is publishing what in Canada, especially in paperback; try doing some title counting), his use of a quote from Scott's "Laurentian Shield" as an example of something I missed, that can in fact be found, same three lines, on page 236 of *Survival*, and his confusion, semantic only, I'm sure, of Dorothy Livesay and Nellie McClung, among others, with fictional characters.

These are minor points. More important is the way in which Mathews makes up a book he thinks I've written, based on what he takes to be my political principles (also invented by him), and then attacks it. In order to do this he has to distort considerably the actual content of *Survival*.

Thus he says: "Margaret Atwood's selections as I said are mainly from the other side: George Grant, Northrop Frye, Douglas LePan, D. G. Jones, Eli Mandel, Dennis Lee, George Bowering, Ann Hébert, St Denys Garneau."

This is a gross misrepresentation. Even supposing Mathews to be "right" about these writers, he does not mention those to whom I in fact give much more space. What about Alden Nowlan (6 references in the *Index*; not counting Epigraphs), John Newlove (3 pages), Margaret Laurence (11 references), Irving Layton (4), Charles G. D. Roberts (5), Al Purdy (5), Sinclair Ross (7), E. J. Pratt (10), Earle Birney (4 references, 6 pages), Alice Munro (6), E. T. Seton (8 references), Ernest Buckler (7), Gwen MacEwen (4), James Reaney (8), Leonard Cohen (3 references, 3 pages). My argument in fact rests much more on the work of people like Pratt, Ross, Buckler, Laurence, Birney and Purdy than it does on that of George Grant (a mere 3 references), LePan (3 references, 2 pages), Jones (a mere one reference), Mandel (2 references), Bowering (2 references). Does Mathews distort this way because he *wants* people like Pratt and Ross and Purdy to be "on his side" and can't face the fact they aren't?

Reading Mathews, you'd get the impression that my chapter on Québec includes no one but St Denys Garneau and Anne Hébert; in fact he says " . . . there is almost no mention of the poets of Quebec after St Denys Garneau, for instance who reject Garneau and his internal writhings in order to get on with the revolution." You'd never know from him that most of the chapter is about fiction, not poetry, (it's much easier to get in translation), that Préfontaine and Aquin are quoted in the Epigraphs, that the chapter spends considerable time on Roch Carrier—even on *Philibert*, which is nothing if not anti-capitalist—and that it concludes with a discussion of Aquin's *Prochaine Episode*, a revolutionary novel, and of Jacques Ferron, one of the first writers in Quebec to open up this area. Maybe Mathews doesn't want to face the fact that even when these writers do write about revolution they have trouble pinpointing the enemy, imaging the shape the revolution is to take and visualizing what is to come after it. (The same qualities characterize, by the way, Quebec revolutionary poetry, if examples in Glassco are to be taken as representative.)

Just as Mathews has to distort *Survival* to get out of it the straw book he wants, so must he distort works of Canadian literature themselves to get support for his position. He does this a lot, but nowhere more obviously than in his treatment of *Wacousta*. I refer the reader to his paragraph beginning "John Richardson's *Wacousta* for instance, is constantly misread (and is by Atwood)."

Now, the *only* thing I say about *Wacousta* is that it has a garrison in it similar to the one Brébeuf constructs: Europeans on the inside, hostile Indians on the outside. Since Mathews himself says this is true, I'm not sure to what extent this constitutes a "misreading." But when I read the rest of Mathews' paragraph my chin dropped like that of Marley's ghost (excuse the non-Canadian reference); could this be the same book I'd read? Could it be true, as Mathews claims, that "The Indian is seen as savage, dark, bestial when described by the British soldiers. But he is seen as quite other when described by Richardson?" Looking at *Wacousta* again, I found that *both* Richardson *and* the British officers—and these latter are the focal points of the story—describe the Indians as "devils," "demons," "savages," malicious, treacherous, "lazy" (when not on the warpath), and also lousy: this latter put with characteristic nineteenth century grace:

> Among the warriors were interspersed many women, some of whom might be seen supporting in their laps the heavy heads of their unconscious helpmates, while they occupied themselves by the firelight in parting the long black matted hair and maintaining a destructive warfare against the pigmy inhabitants of that dark region. (Ch. XVI)

The general orientations of *Wacousta* may be seen from these two paragraphs describing the fort at Michelimackinac:

Lakeward the view was scarcely less monotonous, but it was not, as in the rear, that monotony which is never occasionally broken in upon by some occurrence of interest. If the eye gazed long and anxiously for the white sail of the well known armed vessel, charged at stated intervals with letters and tidings of those whom time and distance and danger, far from estranging, rendered more dear to the memory and bound more closely to the heart, it was sure of being rewarded at last; and then there was no picture on which it could love to linger so well as that of the silver waves bearing that valued vessel in safety to its wonted anchorage in the offing. Moreover, the light swift bark canoes of the natives often danced joyously on its surface, and while the sight was offended at the savage skulking among the trees of the forest, like some dark spirit moving cautiously in its course of secret destruction, and watching the moment when he might pounce unnoticed upon his unprepared victim, it followed with momentary pleasure and excitement the activity and skill displayed by the harmless paddler in the swift and meteor-like race that set the troubled surface of the Huron in a sheet of hissing foam.

Nor was this all. When the eye turned woodward it fell heavily and without interest upon a dim and dusky point known to enter upon savage scenes and unexplored countries, whereas whenever it reposed upon the lake it was with an eagerness and energy that embraced the most vivid recollections of the past, and led the imagination buoyantly over every well-remembered scene that had previously been traversed, and which must be traversed again before the land of the European could be pressed once more. The forest, in a word, formed, as it were, the gloomy and impenetrable walls of the prison-house, and the bright lake that lay before it the only portal through which happiness and liberty could be again secured.

The French settlements (whose inhabitants are usually referred to by Richardson as "peasants") are not, at this time, threatened by Indians, it is true; but not because of superior merit or essential difference in way of life.

The garrisons now occupied by the British were, in fact, originally constructed by the French, and merely taken over by the British after the fall of Quebec (the story is set in 1763).

British and French are both after the same thing, as we learn from Pontiac himself: fur trade with the Indians. Pontiac is mad at the British not because of their evil capitalism but because of the bad influence of Wacousta— who, far from being "exploited by a competitive, power-seeking system," is mad at Colonel De Haldimar for having stolen his girl and getting him kicked out of the army: personal revenge reasons. Colonel De Haldimar is a meanie, all right, and Wacousta has become a monster, but there are lots of "good" Britishers in the book, and the better born, the nicer. Take Sir Everard, for instance, who has a black servant called Sambo who says "Massa:" "Under a semblance of affectation, and much assumed levity of manner —never, of course, personally offensive—he concealed a brave, generous, warm and manly heart, and talents becoming the rank he held in society...." There are a couple of "good" Indians, too; Pontiac is noble-looking, as befits a chief; Oucanasta and her brother both get points for helping the British. The story concludes with peace between Indians and British garrison, with nothing to indicate that Richardson thought this a bad thing for the Indians. (A footnote on Richardson: in his 1851 "Introduction," dated New York City, he mentions he wrote a sequel to *Wacousta* which he published in Canada rather than in England. "I might as well," he comments, "have done so in Kamchatka." Cf. Chapter 9, *Survival*.)

The difference between what I find in *Wacousta* and what Mathews finds there may be due to a difference of editions; mine is unabridged, author credit reading "Major Richardson," whereas the one most readily obtainable is the NCL abridged. But it is much more likely to be due to a tendency on Mathews' part to rewrite books in his head so

that they say what he wishes they had said. I'm under no
such compulsion; I see little reason why a book written
in 1832, thirty-five years before Confederation and when
Karl Marx was only fourteen, should reflect the concerns
Mathews wants it to. "We cannot afford to lie to each other,"
says Mathews, and I heartily agree; but let us begin, please,
by trying to tell the truth about the books we are reading.

This brings us to one of Mathews' major concerns; his
wish that there should exist, in Canada, a tradition of
'struggle.' After calling Godfrey's "Hard Headed Collector,"
Lee's *Civil Elegies* and Bissett's *Nobody Owns Th Earth* "works
of colonial stagnation"—he just applies the label, there's no
justification offered—Mathews says,

> Nor is there any significant use of major Canadian
> writers who have dealt deeply with our colonial condition,
> writers that are at home in the recognition of oppression
> and the struggle against it. Now is it possible to write a
> thematic guide to Canadian literature and neglect totally
> or almost totally people like D. C. Scott, F. R. Scott,
> Richardson, Livesay, Marriott, Lampman, MacLennan,
> Mitchell, Haliburton, Leacock?

In fact I looked long and hard for writers, and for pieces
of writing, that would do this; it's one of the few themes on
which I did extra research rather than relying on previous
reading. As much as Mathews does, I wanted this literature
to exist in the past so that those in the present would have a
tradition to turn to. What I was looking for were pieces
that combine recognition of Canada—not just some group
within Canada, but Canada as a whole—as an oppressed
entity, plus some constructive effort directed at overcoming
this condition, with chances of, if not success, at least not the
passive acceptance of defeat that Mathews seems to find so
attractive in his previous article for *This Magazine*. I didn't
find much of it (I'm still looking, by the way), and I think
there are very good reasons for this, one of them being that
Canada-as-colony-as-oppressed is, I think, fairly new as a

generally-visible concept. You can't fault the writers of the thirties for Internationale-ism: those were the terms of *their* struggle. But let's not confuse that with this. As for the writers Mathews mentions, none of them has the above combination. Certainly not Leacock with his condescension and portraits of quaint provincials; nor MacLennan, who chooses individual solutions to social problems every time; nor Richardson (see above). Who "wins" in Haliburton?

There are indeed poems of social concern, but as I say in *Survival*, the groups in question are usually entities *within* Canada, not the country as a whole. (In Livesay's *Collected Poems*, for instance, Canada is mentioned three times in 359 pages.) And when reading these "social concern" poems, we ought to pay quite a lot of attention not just to the presence of "concern" but to the way the work is resolved. Take a good look at the ends of *The Wind Our Enemy* and *Call My People Home* and tell me what you see. Had Milton Acorn's *More Poems for People* been published before *Survival* was written, it would have been more than useful; but that it appeared in 1973, not 1963 or 1953, says a lot for the changing Canadian climate.

More work needs to be done on this area; but again, let's be honest. It does no good to pick books as "heroes" when in fact they don't really do what you want them to.

Two other areas of concern in Mathews' review have to do with more specifically literary problems. One has to do with my critical method; the other with my stance on writing.

Mathews is alarmed by my statement that *Survival* is meant to be "nonevaluative." Here is what I actually say:

> It is not evaluative. I try to refrain from handing out merit badges, and no admiring reader should feel elated or put down because his favourite author is or isn't included. Though I try not to include any book I myself find tedious, it isn't "good writing" or "good style" or "literary excellence" I'm talking about here.

I make it clear also that I'm concerned with patterns, not authors, and I don't find this concern invalid. It's quite true that some literature written in Canada, which I happen to enjoy and find "good"—got left out; things like George Jonas' poetry, Michael Ondaatje's poetry, Malcolm Lowry's prose, a lot of Brian Moore; nor do I pay as much attention to Grove as some might like. Why? It seems to me dangerous to talk about "Canadian" patterns of sensibility in the work of people who entered and/or entered-and-left the country at a developmentally late stage of their lives. Other things—such as some of my favourite Margaret Avison poems—got left out because, much as I like them, their themes were universal and/or religious, and *Survival* isn't about metaphysics.

Apart from all this, Mathews and I have different opinions about what constitutes the bulk—or the "central tradition," if you like—of Canadian literature. He thinks that there are two "halves" to it, and that I've paid attention to the shape of only one of them. Even if you take the writers he says constitute the other "half" of the tradition, you haven't got a "half," not when you match it up with my "half." And when you then consider the extent to which he warps most of the writers in his "half" to fit his specifications, you've got something much less than a "half." The other mistake Mathews makes is that he ignores the allowance I've made *within each theme* for variations: he thinks what I'm saying is that Canlit is always and only Position Two.

Let me further clarify what I mean by "not evaluative." Benjamin Franklin's *Poor Richard's Almanac*, the Horatio Alger books, Henry James' *The Golden Bowl*, Fitzgerald's *The Great Gatsby*, and Nathaniel West's satires all have a theme in common: that virtue and wealth are coordinates of each other. Franklin and Alger treat it "straight," James raises it to a metaphysic, Fitzgerald treats it tragically—what happens to a man who *believes* it—and West uses it for satire; but all books inhabit the same imaginative landscape. Also:

English literature is obsessed with class, from Chaucer through Shakespeare through Dickens through Huxley, through P. G. Wodehouse. Chaucer and Shakespeare in general approve of the system, Dickens chronicles the evils it produces, Huxley, in *Brave New World*, uses it for the basis of a sinister Utopia, and Wodehouse plays with it. But it would be hard to find an English writer—lyric poets aside—whose work seems unaware of it.

Now: Alger and Wodehouse are hardly "great" literature. But they exemplify central cultural patterns just as much as writers more seriously thought of. It is in this sense that *Survival* is not evaluative: I don't feel I have to apply the adjective "great" to something in order to include it. In fact, it reminds me unpleasantly of the Chicago Great Books programme and of Ruskin's hierarchical efforts to arrange the plant kingdom according to nobility. I suppose I find "great" an adjective which, in addition to its vagueness of definition, tends to structure literature like a ladder, with "great" at the top and everything else disregarded; a capitalistic kind of adjective. Not so Mathews. He desires, *requires* that things he approves of be "great" or "major;" he is nothing if not evaluative, though one may question his values. D. C. Scott's "The Height of Land" as "one of the great poems of the last hundred years," for example.... (Incidentally, if Mathews wants models for the kind of thematic approach I'm attempting in *Survival*, he might take a look at *Tradition in Exile*, some of Reaney's editorials in *Alphabet*, *Love and Death in the American Novel*, *The Englishness of English Art*, (stylistic rather than thematic), and the literature section in *The Second Sex*, to name a few.)

Mathews' comments on my attitude towards writing as an act or process raise once more the whole question of the relationship between individual and society, between individual change and social change. I feel this territory is covered in *Survival*, but I'll run through it again. I don't like repeating myself, but when someone hasn't heard you the first time, due to deafness or inattention, your only choice if you wish to be understood is to say it again. Mathews says:

> And so is her assertion (ambiguous) that writers in the act of writing are in the position of ex-victims or of never having been victims. The implication is that the writer is somehow freed from the effects of the oppressed society ... (etc. to end of paragraph).

In *Survival* I suggest there are four basic positions a victim can take, whether the victim is a country, a group, or an individual:

1. to deny that you are a victim.

2. to acknowledge that you are a victim but explain this as an Act of Fate, the will of God, or any other large general powerful Idea.

3. to acknowledge that you are a victim, but refuse to accept the assumption that the role is inevitable.

4. to be a creative non-victim.

If he will look again at pp. 38-40, he will find both my definition of Position Four and my comments on the act of writing. It may help him if he makes a simple distinction between *activity* and *content of activity*. Thus I hold that writing fiction and poetry is a creative act: no one forces you to do it, it's an act of the imagination operating freely, etc., and I would maintain this even for acts of writing which I personally do not find too impressive, for instance the composition of *The Plink Savoir*. But the *content* of the writing may not be Position Four. And I say this in *Survival*: " ... though the subject of his book may be Position Two, and the energy for it may come from Position Three," etc. Far from thinking *the writer insofar as he is connected with his society* can have, at will, a Position Four content in a Position Two society, I go to some pains to deny this: again on p. 40, I say "if ... your society is in Position Two, perhaps you can't move through Position Three into Position Four except by repudiating your society ... " Mathews seems to think I find such repudiation desirable, or that I think "Position Four" content is preferable to any other kind; that is, that I equate it with "good" writing and "morally desirable" writing. This is simply distortion. If Mathews looks on p. 189, he will find more on this subject, in the discussion of the dilemma of the artist in a colonial society.

The key phrase above is "insofar as you are connected with your society." Let me translate it into Womens' Lib terms, just for fun. In a sexist society, a woman can:

1. Ignore her victimization, and sing songs like "I Enjoy Being A Girl."

2. Think it's the fault of Biology, or something, or you can't do anything about it; write literature on How Awful It Is, which may be a very useful activity up to a point.

3. Recognize the source of oppression; express anger; suggest ways for change. What she *can't* do is write as a *fully* liberated individual-as-woman-in-society. She can't do that, *as part of the society*, until the society is changed, though she may do it by abandoning the society; a choice I do not find morally commendable. Clear? Far from being an individualist position, this is one that insists on interdependence between individual and community. If you want Position Four Canadian literature, change the society. There will still be problems, but they won't be Canada-as-victim problems. (I'm glad Mathews admits, however, that the *content* of much Canadian writing inhabits "a complete imaginative world based on psychological colonialism." Just what *Survival* is saying!)

A lot of discussion could take place around questions which still, it seems to me, remain open, such as what we mean by "colony;" is Canada a colony? (Mathews seems to think it is, in which case I would ask him: How can the bulk of its literature *not* reflect this fact in some form or another?); what you do about roots or traditions which stem from oppression; that is, how do you retain your identity without also retaining the oppression; and whether it's indeed true, as Mathews maintains, that a castrated bourgeoisie is a good thing, or that the bourgeoisie is the only element of a society that gets "castrated" by colonialism. (To this last question my own answer would be a resounding No; take a look at the history of union takeovers and the American orientation of the Left during, especially, the mid and late sixties.)

But this would take us quite far outside the present topic. Returning to that, let me sum up briefly the directions in which Mathews distorts, and try to indicate why I think he does it and what might be done instead.

1. He sees *Survival* as more negative than it is. In order to do this, he grossly misrepresents the range of the writers and books dealt with, and pays a lot of attention to things like the dedication, George Grant, etc., distorting as he goes. He ignores "positive content," especially—and consistently—the ends of all the chapters.

2. He assumes another Canadian tradition, which he thinks of as the other "half" and which he sees as consisting of people like Richardson, Leacock, MacLennan, Lampman, Livesay, Marriott, Mitchell, Haliburton, Callaghan, etc.

Why does he do this? I think the tactical reasoning may go something like this:

Canada is in a bad position. (We both agree on this.)

We must change this position if we are to survive. (Also agreed.)

In order to do this we must take positive action. (Also agreed.)

To help us take positive action, we must find positive "role models"—people who make us feel good about ourselves.

We must not pay attention to negative "role models," that will make us feel bad. We must discard writers who are "pessimistic," describe "alienation, defeatism, victimization."

Here is where the disagreement lies. I would like to find positive role models too, and I looked—and am still

looking—for them. None of the writers Mathews puts forward
as candidates satisfies me. (I find it of interest, too, that of all
the ones he mentions, none are of his own generation or
younger—I wonder why?) In the course of my search, I
approached an authority on the Left who had been searching
for years. He too is convinced such a tradition must exist,
but he is far from certain where it lies. In the course
of the discussion, various names and titles came up (Peter
MacArthur, Joe Wallace, Gilbert Parker, *Joshua Doane*,
Fatherless Sons by Dyson Carter, Irene Baird). None of them
are in *Survival*; but neither are they on Mathews' lists. All
this demonstrates is that this kind of literature has been
rendered invisible, both to Mathews and to myself; that if
you want something a little more stringent than Stephen
Leacock, you have to go digging for it. What a society buries
is at least as revealing as what it preserves. I haven't read any
of this material yet, but I have a pile of it sitting on my desk.
I'll lend it to Mathews when I'm through, if he's interested.
But the *mainstream* of Canadian literature is essentially, I
believe, the one described in *Survival*.

To return to our fundamental disagreement: I feel that
in order to change any society, you have to have a fairly
general consciousness of what is wrong—or at least that
something is wrong—among the members of the society; call
it "consciousness-raising" if you like; and an examination of
the effects of the situation on the heads of those in the
society. Until you've done that, any efforts at change will be
futile, because the society itself will not admit that anything's
wrong, that it *should* be changed. In other words: to fight
the Monster, you have to know that there is a Monster, and
what it is like (both in its external and internalized manifestations). I feel that Canadian writing has mostly been
describing the Monster—and often describing it very
well—and that's a good thing. Mathews feels that we've had
enough descriptions of the Monster, and besides, by describing the Monster too much you make it seem overwhelmingly

large, impossible to defeat. He wants some descriptions of
the Hero and the Fight, even the Victory. Good, say I; let's
find them or produce them. But let's not distort things that
aren't this in order to pretend they are. And let's find the *real*
Monster (or Monsters), not substitute ones that only divert
energy. Another point of disagreement is that Mathews
thinks consciousness has been sufficiently raised already (*his*
has, we gather). He wants us to stop doing that and start
doing *his* thing, like those "liberated" women who wonder
what all the other women are grumbling about because
they have a good job. Mathews thinks the battle is well
on its way to being won, so it's time to cheer. I think it's
just beginning, and to waste your mouth foam on cheering is
a luxury we cannot yet afford. Examining the way we think
and react is still something that has to be done, because
very few in the society have done it, or have even paid
attention to those who have.

But our most major disagreement is over the relation
between writer and society, and the consequences as they
affect the interpretation of Position Four. Far from thinking
of writers as totally isolated individuals, I see them as
inescapably connected with their society. The nature of the
connection will vary—the writer may unconsciously reflect
the society, he may consciously examine it and project ways
of changing it; and the connection between writer and
society will increase in intensity as the society (rather than,
for instance, the writer's love-life or his meditations on
roses) becomes the "subject" of the writer.

Thus, if we are looking for *social* (rather than personal
or metaphysical) paradigms we are more likely to find them
in fiction and in narrative and dramatic poetry, than in, for
instance, lyric poetry. (Notice I'm not saying you shouldn't
write lyric poetry....)

The question is: How can a writer in a Position One,
Two or Three society (Mathews thinks it's Three, I think
it's One moving into Two, with stirrings of Three) write

authentically with a Position Four content? My answer is that he can't. He can write poetry with a Position Four "individual," "personal" or "universal" content—though even these will be influenced by the social surroundings—but *not* with a Position Four *social* content. In other words, to pretend the society is out from under when it isn't is just lying, though your own finances and sex life may be pretty good. I think for instance that some of the things Mathews holds up as shining Position Four examples are in fact Position One.

The problem facing all of us writers, insofar as we are concerned with this area of our experience, is: how to describe the Monster—in all its forms, including those in our heads—accurately and without being defeatist? I don't think minimizing the Monster, or castigating—as Mathews does—all those who have attempted the description, is the answer. I think the answers are only in the process of being found; I don't believe, as Mathews does, that they have been found already. Nor do I think saying "Boo to Colonialism" will make it go away; life isn't that magic. You won't get Position Four writing *about society* until you've changed society.

How do you change? Well, for starters—and I hope this doesn't sound too pious—beginning where you really are, using what you've got, sharing your experience with others and learning from them. That's a far cry from beginning where you wish you were, distorting what you've got to make it resemble what you'd like, and repudiating the experience of others unless it agrees with what you'd like yours to be. When Mathews writes *his* book on Canadian literature, as I suspect he's in the process of doing, I hope he'll give a little more time to accuracy than he's done in his review of *Survival.*

There are a number of things about Mathew's work, in this and other areas, that are truly admirable. No one could fault his motives or his courageous university campaign. And I admire the *intention* of his critical work, especially because he is trying to locate a tradition and an ideology with roots inside the country, rather than (like some of the hysterical Left) trying to cram Canada into some other country's ideological grid. But when it comes to dealing with the actual literature, as we must if we are to be literary critics, zeal often leads him astray. His critical behaviour both here and elsewhere suggests he's in danger of becoming a one-man garrison society, walled up in his own paranoia, scanning the critical and literary scene like a periscope and going Bang at anything that moves. For a fate like that to overtake him would be unfortunate, both for him and for us.

17
Reaney Collected

(1973)

Watching poets' critical reputations is a lot like watching the stock market. Some poets make slow but steady gains and end up safe but dull, like blue chips. Others are more like shady gold mines: they're overvalued initially, then plunge to oblivion. More often it's a combination of the two, with each high period being followed by a low of sneers and dismissals and an ultimate recovery engineered by a later squad of critics who rescue the poet's reputation, from a safe distance.

This is especially likely to be true of a poet who, like James Reaney, has been associated with a trend, group or movement which has either angered people or gone out of fashion. Judging from a sampling of recent critical commentary on his collected *Poems*, Reaney's reputation is in its slump phase; which is a shame. Any poet who has created an original body of work, especially one of such uniqueness, power, peculiarity and, sometimes, unprecedented weirdness as Reaney's deserves better treatment. A critic might begin by attempting to actually *read* the poems, as opposed to reading into them various philosophies and literary theories which the poet is assumed to have. If you start this way, with the actual poems, one of your first reactions will almost certainly be that there is nothing else *like* them.

I'd never before read most of the uncollected single poems—my reading of Reaney had been limited to *The Red Heart, A Suit of Nettles, Twelve Letters To a Small Town*, and *The Dance of Death in London, Ontario* (as well as the plays and the short story "The Bully") so I was most intrigued by sections I, III and V of this volume. I was especially struck by the early appearance of a number of Reaney images which crop up again and again, variously disguised, in his later work. The fascination with maps and diagrams ("Maps," 1945), the collections of objects ("The Antiquary," 1946), the sinister females, both mechanical ("Night Train," 1946) and biological ("Madame Moth," 1947), and that nightmare, the Orphanage, already present in "Playbox," 1945—all foreshadow later and more fully realized appearances.

But what became clear to me during a chronological reading of this book is that most commentators—including Reaney himself, and his editor and critics—are somewhat off-target about the much-discussed influence of Frye on his work. I have long entertained a private vision of Frye reading through Reaney while muttering "What have I wrought?" or "This is not what I meant, at all," and this collection confirms it. Reaney is to Frye as a Salem, Mass. 17th century tombstone is to an Italian Renaissance angel: Reaney and the tombstone may have been "influenced," but they are primitives (though later in time) and their models are sophisticates. The influence of Frye, however, was probably a catalyst for Reaney, rather than a new ingredient; let me do a little deductive speculation.

The world presented to us in the early poems, up to and including *The Red Heart* (1949), does not "work" for the poet on any level. The people in them are bored and trivial, like "Mrs Wentworth," or they are actual or potential orphans, loveless, lost or disinherited, like the speaker in "Playbox" or the one in "Whither do you wander?":

...I never find
What I should like to find;
For instance, a father and mother
Who loved me dearly...
Instead I must forever run
Down lanes of leafless trees
Beneath a Chinese-faced sun;
Must forsaken and forlorn go
Unwanted and stepmotherishly haunted
Beneath the moon as white as snow.

The reverse side of the melancholy state of being an orphan—hate for and disgust at the rest of the world and the desire for revenge—is explored in two other orphan poems, "The English Orphan's Monologue" and "The Orphanage," but in these the orphans are not touching and wistful children; they are repulsive, "With plain white / And cretinous faces," or filled with elemental destructiveness. Within a larger social context, the speakers are stifled by their society, like the speaker in "The Canadian," who longs to escape from a parlour haunted by his "grim Grandfather" and the Fathers of Confederation to "hot lands" and "heathen folks" (a theme treated more succinctly later in "The Upper Canadian"). In these "social" poems, Reaney does not analyze, he dramatizes; and, like a dramatist, he counterpoints. Thus to the smothered longing of the provincial in the "Canadian" poems he opposes the sneering of a cosmopolite who has escaped the Fathers of Confederation, is reading *Tristram Shandy* and Anais Nin, and who says to the "proletariat":

Your pinched white and grey faces
Peer in
Like small white tracts held off at a distance.
Well...is it not all very beautiful?
As you stand hungry in the rain
Just look to what heights you too may attain.

("The Ivory Steeple")

If this poem had been written by anyone else but Reaney, everyone would have called it savage socialist satire; in fact it's a good deal more savage and socialist than much that passes by that name.

In these early poems the objects—and the poems bulge with objects—create the effect of a kind of rummage sale, partly because the objects are lacking in all but personal significance:

> .. my spotted ring
> · And the wool blanket hemmed in red ...
> Also the corduroy suit
> And the scarf with the purple bars ...

("Playbox")

> The Cup had the outlines of a cup
> In a lantern-slide
> And it was filled with Congou tea
> What did it mean this cup of tea?

("Faces and the Drama in a Cup of Tea")

The speaker can rarely make "sense" of them by relating them to anything else; all he can do is record them, and the effect is a still-life, captured and rendered immobile, like the pictures Miss ffrench takes in "Kodak:"

> They have their camera.
> No one sits in its gloomy parlour
> Of pleated walls.
> No wind stirs or ghost stalks ...
> And all my garden stands suddenly imprisoned
> Within her pleated den.

In the early poems on "love"—and there are quite a few of them—the love is either unconsummated, as in "Platonic Love," or it turns into sex, which is as inextricably linked with death as it is in the poetry of Al Purdy. This is sex observed through a child's eyes, foreign and monstrous. At times Reaney manages a kind of queasy humour, as in "Grand Bend," which begins:

It is the rutting season
At Grand Bend
And the young men and the women
Explode in each others' arms
While no chaperones attend.

More often it is simple horror, mixed with revulsion, as in "The Orphanage:"

They that lie pasted together
In ditches by the railroad tracks
And seethe in round-shouldered cars
With the lusty belches of a Canadian spring.
Young men with permanent waves
Crawl over ghastly women
Whose cheeks are fat as buttocks...

"So love does often lead a filthy way to death" one poem ends, and another concludes, "It has always been that lust / Has always rhymed with dust."

Reaney's early world, then, is an unredeemed one, populated with orphans and spiritual exiles, littered with couples engaged in joyless, revolting and dangerous copulation, and crammed with objects devoid of significance. In it, babies are doomed as soon as conceived (as in "Dark Lagoon"), the "real world" is the one described at the end of "The School Globe," filled with "blood, pus, horror, stepmothers and lies," and the only escape is the temporary and unsatisfactory one of nostalgic daydreaming. If you believed you lived in such a world, you'd surely find the negative overwhelming. Anyone familiar with the techniques of brainwashing knows that all you have to do to convert almost anyone to almost anything is to subject him to a nearly intolerable pressure, then offer him a way out. The intolerable pressures rendered with such verbal richness in the earlier poems are those of the traditional Christian version of this earth, but with Christ (and escape to Heaven) removed; sin with no possibility of redemption, a fallen world with no divine counterpart.

Frye's literary theories—this is a guess—would surely
have offered Reaney his discredited childhood religion in a
different, more sophisticated, acceptable form: the Bible
might not be *literally* true, but under the aegis of Frye it
could be seen as metaphorically, psychically true. Frye's
"influence," then, is not a matter of the critic's hardedged
mind cutting out the poet's soul in its own shapes, like cookie
dough: "influence," then, for good poets, is surely in any
case just a matter of taking what you need or, in reality,
what you already have.

Frye made a difference (and again I'm guessing) not so
much to Reaney's choice of materials, or even his choice of
forms, but to the kinds of resolutions made available to him.
Horror remains and evil is still a presence, but a way past
the world, the flesh and the devil is now possible. The
redemptive agents are all invisible, internal: they are the
imagination, the memory, verbal magic (Reaney has several
poems about language, and many references to the magic
tongue) and—I'm thinking here of the short story "The Bully"
—dream. These elements are so important in Reaney's work
because the hideousness of existence can be redeemed *by
them alone*: it is the individual's inner vision, not the
external social order, that must change if anything is to
be salvaged.

It is this arrangement of priorities that surely accounts
not only for some of Reaney's themes, but also for some of his
characteristic structures, in the plays as well as the poems.
The pattern I'm thinking of is that of the sudden
conversion—a Protestant rather than a Catholic pattern. If
you think of the Divine Comedy with the Purgatorio left out
you'll see what I mean: we get the hellishness of the
"earthly" situation and the quick turnabout followed by a
transcendent vision, but we are never told how you get to the
vision—what process you undergo, what brings it about. No
indulgences sold here; it's Faith, not Works and you just
somehow have to "see." There are several Reaney plays (*The*

Sun and the Moon, The Kildeer) in which the evil witch figure is defeated simply by being perceived as a fraud; but in the lyric poetry, this structure can best be illustrated by that unsettling poem, "The Sparrow." It's a poem about grubby lechery in the most unappealing places—the underpass, the episcopal church—symbolized by obscene chalk drawings, and the fourth verse starts like this:

> Dirty, diseased, impish, unsettling, rapist
> Illegitimate, urban, southless, itching,
> Satyromaniac, of butcher string the harpist,
> The sparrows and their gods are everything.

Then comes the turn:

> I like to hear their lack of tune
> On a very cold winter snowy afternoon.
> They must be listened to and worshipped each—
> The shocking deities: ding dung is sacred
> So is filthiness, obscenity . . .

And the last stanza makes the point: *everything*, not just beauty, is in the eyes of the beholder:

> Christ and Gautama and Emily Brontë were
> Born in the midst of angelic whir
> In a dripping concrete den under,
> Under the alimentary trains: it is we
> Who see the angels as brown lechery
> And the sacred pair—Venus and Adonis
> As automatons coupled as a train is.
>   And so step down my chalky reader,
>   Why keep our festival here
>   In this crotch?
>   *Ding dung chirp chirp:*
>   *A sparrow sings if you but have an ear.*

In Reaney's work, the Songs of Innocence come *after* the Songs of Experience; in fact, you can take a number of figures or images from the earlier poems and follow them through the *corpus*, watching how the Lost Child gets found (most notably

in *Night-Blooming Cereus*), how the sinister Orphan gets
changed into the harmless comic-strip Little Orphan Annie,
how the baby doomed from before birth is allowed more
latitude (though he can be the Christ Child as parody dwarf,
he can also be the real Christ Child or magic baby; see "A
Sequence in Four Keys") and how the collection of random
objects is permitted (or perhaps forced) to have universal
significance (see, for instance, the pebble, the dewdrop, the
piece of string and the straw, in "Gifts").

The problems I have with Reaney's work are both
theoretical (I can't see certain pieces of evil, for instance
Hitler and the Vietnam war, as angelic visitations or even
unreal, no matter how hard I try; and I don't think that's a
flaw in my vision) and practical — that is, some of the poems
work admirably for me and others don't get off the ground at
all. Reaney's best poems come from a fusion of "personal"
and "mythic" or "universal;" when they lean too far towards
either side, you get obscurity or straight nostalgia at one end
or bloodless abstraction at the other. And at times, reading
his work, I feel the stirrings of that old Romantic distinction
between the Fancy and the Imagination, though I try hard to
suppress it; I even hear a voice murmuring "Whimsy," and it
murmurs loudest when I come across a concrete image
linked arbitrarily and with violence to a "universal" meaning.
If you can see a world in a grain of sand, well, good; but you
shouldn't stick one on just because you think it ought to be
there.

But this is a Collected rather than a Selected; it isn't
supposed to be Reaney's best poems, it's all of his poems, and
I can't think of any poet who produces uniformly splendid
work. It's by his best, however, that a writer should ultimately be judged; and Reaney's best has an unmistakable quality,
both stylistic and thematic, and a strength that is present
only when a poet is touching on something fundamental.
Certain of Reaney's poems do admirably what a number of
his others attempt less successfully; they articulate the

primitive forms of the human imagination, they flesh out the soul, they dramatize—like Blake's "Mental Traveller"—the stances of the self in relation to the universe. That sounds fairly heavy; what I mean is that Reaney gets down to the basics— love, hate, terror, joy—and gives them a shape that evokes them for the reader. This is conjuring, it's magic and spells rather than meditation, description or ruminating; Coleridge rather than Wordsworth, MacEwen rather than Souster. The trouble with being a magic poet is that when you fail, you fail more obviously than the meditative or descriptive poet: the rabbit simply refuses to emerge from the hat. But you take greater risks, and Reaney takes every risk in the bag, including a number of technical ones that few others would even consider attempting.

The physical appearance and presentation of a book such as this is really the least important part of it, but it never hurts a book to look good. Typeface and design—spare and antique, but somehow lush and eccentric—are in harmony with Reaney's world. The Introduction by Germaine Warkentin, informative about both poet and poems, represents only a small part of her editorial task; the major piece of work must have been the sifting, comparison and selection of the poems, some of which exist in a dismayingly large number of versions.

The most unattractive thing about this collection is its price. The ways of publishers are unfathomable, but I hope someone can convince New Press to bring Reaney's poems out in paperback soon so that more than a few people will have the chance to read what Reaney actually wrote rather than what he is popularly supposed to have written. The difference, it seems to me, is considerable.

18
Adrienne Rich:
Diving Into the Wreck

(1973)

This is Adrienne Rich's seventh book of poems, and it is an extraordinary one. When I first heard the author read from it, I felt as though the top of my head was being attacked, sometimes with an ice pick, sometimes with a blunter instrument: a hatchet or a hammer. The predominant emotions seemed to be anger and hatred, and these are certainly present; but when I read the poems later, they evoked a far more subtle reaction. *Diving Into the Wreck* is one of those rare books that forces you to decide not just what you think about it; but what you think about yourself. It is a book that takes risks, and it forces the reader to take them also.

If Adrienne Rich were not a good poet, it would be easy to classify her as just another vocal Women's Libber, substituting polemic for poetry, simplistic messages for complex meanings. But she is a good poet, and her book is not a manifesto, though it subsumes manifestoes; nor is it a proclamation, though it makes proclamations. It is instead a book of explorations, of travels. The wreck she is diving into, in the very strong title poem, is the wreck of obsolete myths, particularly myths about men and women. She is journeying to something that is already in the past, in order to discover for herself the reality behind the myth, "the wreck and not the story of the wreck / the thing itself and not the myth." What she finds is part treasure and part corpse, and she also finds that she herself is part of it, a "half-destroyed instrument." As explorer she is detached; she carries a knife to cut her way in, cut structures apart; a camera to record; and the book of myths itself, a book which has hitherto had no place for explorers like herself.

This quest—the quest for something beyond myths, for the truths about men and women, about the I and the You, the He and the She, or more generally (in the references to wars and persecutions of various kinds) about the powerless and the powerful—is presented throughout the book through a sharp, clear style and through metaphors which become their own myths. At their most successful the poems move like dreams, simultaneously revealing and alluding, disguising and concealing. The truth, it seems, is not just what you find when you open a door: it is itself a door, which the poet is always on the verge of going through.

The landscapes are diverse. The first poem, "Trying to Talk With a Man," occurs in a desert, a desert which is not only deprivation and sterility, the place where everything except the essentials has been discarded, but the place where bombs are tested. The "I" and the "You" have given up all frivolities of their previous lives, "suicide notes" as well as "love-letters," in order to undertake the risk of changing the desert; but it becomes clear that the "scenery" is already "condemned," that the bombs are not external threats but internal ones. The poet realizes they are deceiving themselves, "talking of the danger / as if it were not ourselves / as if we were testing anything else."

Like the wreck, the desert is already in the past, beyond salvation though not beyond understanding, as is the landscape of "Waking in the Dark:"

> The tragedy of sex
> lies around us, a woodlot
> the axes are sharpened for....
> Nothing will save this. I am alone,
>   kicking the last rotting logs
> with their strange smell of life,
>   not death
> wondering what on earth it all
>   might have become.

Given her view that the wreck, the desert, the woodlot cannot be redeemed; the task of the woman, the She, the powerless, is to concentrate not on fitting into the landscape but on redeeming herself, creating a new landscape, getting herself born:

> ...your mother dead and you
>   unborn
> your two hands grasping your head
> drawing it against the blade
>   of life
> your nerves the nerves of a midwife
>   learning her trade
>   —from "The Mirror in Which Two Are Seen as One"

The difficulty of doing this (the poet is after all, still surrounded by the old condemned landscape and "the evidence of damage" it has caused) is one of the major concerns of the book. Trying to see clearly and to record what has been seen—the rapes, the wars, the murders, the various kinds of violation and mutilation—is half of the poet's effort; for this she requires a third eye, an eye that can see pain with "clarity." The other half is to respond, and the response is anger; but it is a "visionary anger," which hopefully will precede the ability to love.

These poems convince me most often when they are true to themselves as structures of words and images, when they resist the temptation to sloganize, when they don't preach at me. "The words are purposes / the words are maps," Rich says, and I like them better when they are maps (though Rich would probably say the two depend on each other and I would probably agree). I respond less fully to poems like "Rape" and references to the Vietnam war—though their truth is undeniable—than I do to poems such as "From a Survivor," and "August" with its terrifying final image:

> His mind is too simple, I cannot go on
> sharing his nightmares
>
> My own are becoming clearer, they
> open
> into prehistory
> which looks like a village lit with
> blood
>
> where all the fathers are crying:
> *My son is mine!*

It is not enough to state the truth; it must be imaged, imagined, and when Rich does this she is irresistible. When she does this she is also most characteristically herself. You feel about her best images, her best myths, that nobody else writes quite like this.

19

Audrey Thomas:

Blown Figures

(1976)

Blown Figures is the fifth book by this already accomplished writer of fictions, and to date her most ambitious. In it Audrey Thomas approaches the height of her powers as a spinner of prose, a teller of surprising and engaging tales. With each of her books, the reader feels that the next will be not only better but different in some unimaginable way, and *Blown Figures* is unlike any of its predecessors, in technique at any rate.

The book returns to territory familiar to readers of *Mrs Blood* and *Songs My Mother Taught Me*, and like these it is a self-contained unit. The heroine again is Isobel, who lost her unborn child in Africa in *Mrs Blood* and whose hideous childhood is described in *Songs My Mother Taught Me*. In *Blown Figures*, Isobel returns to Africa alone, leaving her husband Jason and her two children behind, searching for the child she has lost—she's obsessed with her failure to find out what was done with the body—but searching also for expiation. She feels the death of the child was her fault, an absurd guilt left over from an earlier affair which ended in a traumatic abortion.

Such a synopsis barely indicates what *Blown Figures* is like, for the book's approach is not linear. The title is evocative. "Blown" suggests blown glass, explosions, the winds of Dante's Inferno with its wandering souls, inflation, or exhaustion, and as Thomas is a lover of puns and Isobel worries about the hidden meanings of words, all connotations are probably intended. *Blown Figures* is composed of fragments and contrasting textures: passages of narrative, flashbacks, fantasies, scraps from what may or may not be Isobel's notebook or the narrator's (bits of comic strips, quotations, *pensées*, dreams, African myths, ads from African newspapers; there are, perhaps, a few too many of these). AFRICA, Thomas informs us, was originally "MAFROKA, the broken, the divided land." The central character is multiple—"This curious child was very fond of pretending to be two people," the notebook quotes from *Alice*—and Isobel roams through Africa in the third person, interrupted, interpreted and possibly created by a voice calling itself "I", who in turn addresses a shadowy woman called "Miss Miller" (governess, teacher, keeper, superego?). The "I" feels sorry for Isobel at times; she also hates her, is contemptuous of her and threatens to destroy her.

In hands less skilful than Thomas', such devices could spell tedious experimentation for its own sake, self-indulgence or chaos. But Thomas is enormously skilful, and instead of being a defeating pile of confusions *Blown Figures* is amazingly easy to read. It leads the reader from clue to clue like a detective story, though it lacks a comforting resolution; and it fascinates, like Africa itself, by its richness and mystery. Thomas has a faultless ear for dialogue, for how people sound, even Dutchmen speaking English or Africans speaking French. And she has a camera eye for physical detail, so that the lands through which Isobel wanders on her quest shimmer on the page like mirages, sharp and charged with nameless fear, like hallucinations. Which perhaps they are, for Isobel is haunted: she sees visions of people with no

backs, hears voices and dreams of witches and the Devil and
of her vengeful dead child. A haunted person is one for whom
the past is more real than the present, and this is certainly
true of Isobel. Her husband and her living children are
mannequins, and it is her false lover and her dead child who
obsess her. Her muted Western culture has never allowed
her to grieve, to mourn, to expiate, but Africa is different:
"These people, with their elaborate rituals for birth and
death, their singing and dancing...their belief in the power
of another person's hatred as well as the power of a vulture's
foot, how right they were...." Africa supplies in abundance
the myths, ceremonies and magic which Isobel needs to give
a meaning to her experience of loss and death. In ancient
cultures and in modern Africa, women are seen as those who
give birth and also as those who mourn the dead. But for
Isobel, these functions have been thwarted and confused.
Birth has become death, and she sees herself as a witch, a
killer. "I ate the child in my womb," she says. "Since then I
have never been happy."

On one level, *Blown Figures* is about Isobel's attempts at
exorcism. On another it is about the exorcism of Isobel
herself. Isobel must be taken to the end of her journey, her
nightmare, so that the narrator can finally somehow get rid
of her, return to the present, stop creating her. Isobel is
haunted but she is also a pathetic and irritating ghost, fixed
in time and repeating herself endlessly. " 'Isobel doesn't live'
said Jason to a friend, 'she exits.' He had meant to say
'exists.' " "How to rescue Isobel ... without becoming oneself
an Isobel," muses the narrator. Perhaps *Blown Figures* is her
answer.

20
Erica Jong:
Half-Lives

(1974)

Erica Jong's first book of poems, *Fruits & Vegetables*, was one of those things rare in poetry: a new experience. I read these poems the way you watch a trapeze act, with held breath, marvelling at the agility, the lightness of touch, the brilliant demonstration of the difficult made to look easy. The poems were brief, swift, sure of themselves; they combined a cool eighteenth-century detached wit and a talent for epigram with a virtuoso handling of that favourite seventeenth-century figure of speech, the conceit, with body as fruit as body, poem as food as poem, man as Muse, Muse as man. They did not pose as straight-from-the-soul confessions; rather they posed as artefacts, beautifully *made*: china figurines which were really Iron Maidens, the spikes hidden beneath the painted foliage. They were literate without being literary. They toyed with the reader, refusing to reveal the extent of their seriousness, whether they *meant* it. Laughter may instruct but it may also conceal, defending the joker against anger and retaliation: a game is only a game. The "tongue ... stubbornly stuck in [the] cheek" may become in fact one of the "various subtle forms of lockjaw," to quote Jong.

In *Half-Lives* the tongue is out of the cheek, at least part of the time. This book's cover is not lush pink but stark black. The wit is still there, but it's less like a flirtation than a duel. There's less fun, more pain. That Lizzie Borden axe, disguised in *Fruits & Vegetables* as a pair of embroidery scissors, is out in the open and active. The difference in tone may be felt by comparing poems with similar themes. Try "Bitter Pills for the Dark Ladies" from *Fruits & Vegetables*, which treats male contempt for female poets as a burlesque of white attitudes toward blacks:

> Words bein' slippery & poetry bein'
> mos'ly a matter of balls
> men what gives in to the lilt and lift of words
> (o love o death o organ tones o Dickey!)
> is "Cosmic." You is "Sentimental."
> So dance in your Master's bed (or thesis) & shut
> yo' mouth. Ain't you happiest there?

Then read "Alcestis on the Poetry Circuit" from *Half-lives*, which begins:

> The best slave
> does not need to be beaten
> She beats herself....

she ends,

> If she's an artist
> and comes close to genius,
> the very fact of her gift
> should cause her such pain
> that she will take her own life
> rather than best us.
>
> & after she dies we will cry
> & make her a saint.

A mockery of contempt, itself contemptuous, has become a straight examination of self-contempt and its effects, the model that most self-sacrificing of wives, Alcestis, praised for dying to save her man. Or place the cool, musing "In Sylvia Plath Country" from the earlier book beside "The Critics" and "In the Skull." Neither of the later poems is as fully realized, but both are more engaged, and both offer a version of the poet as suicide which is more complex than the lyrical drowning Ophelia of the first poem, and in the later vision the poet is less imposed upon than imposing:

> Living in a death's head,
> peering at life through its eyeholes,
> she wondered why she could see only death ...

Or compare the very funny third section of "Arse Poetica" with the two equally funny but more scathing poems in *Half-Lives*, "Seventeen Warnings in Search of a Feminist Poem" and "Men." The poet is no longer jus' funnin', or pretending to.

The shift in tone corresponds with a shift in subject-matter, or rather a shift of emphasis: certain themes which were peripheral to the first book are central to the second. The games with fruits and vegetables which provided so much joy and whimsy in the first book are echoed, it is true, in the second ("The Eggplant Epithalamion," "The Woman Who Loved to Cook," "Chinese Food"), but the poet is no longer preoccupied with playing with her food. She has turned her attention instead to the Boneman, that Sexual Gothic figure who first appears in *Fruits & Vegetables*, materializing most fully in "The Man Under The Bed:"

> The man under the bed
> The man who has been there for years waiting
> The man who waits for my floating bare foot
>
> ...
> The man whose breathing I hear when I pick up the phone
> The man in the mirror whose breath blackens silver
> The boneman in closets who rattles the mothballs
> The man at the end of the end of the line....

He is Death, sinister and frightening, but he is also a lover
and attractive; he is the lure of suicide, and he is thus
created by the poet herself:

> I wrap myself around him in the darkness
> I breathe into his mouth
> & make him real.

The Boneman makes only brief or indirect appearances
in the first book, but he is everywhere in the second. There is
a fascination with death, one's own specifically, which moves
beyond the effective but two-dimensional horror-movie
images of "The Man Under the Bed" to an exploration of the
rationale of self-destruction. In the earlier part of the book
the Death figure is dual. Half of the Boneman is a punitive,
devouring, powerful male, as in "The Wives of Mafiosi,"
where the man is:

> ... the power
> of a dark suit lined with lead
> of a man with a platinum mouth and knuckles of brass
> of a bullet the colour of a Ferrari ...

or a kind of vampire, as in "Anniversary:"

> Every night for five years
> he chewed on her
> until her fingers were red & ragged
> until blue veins hung out of her legs ...

or a necrophiliac ghoul, as in "The Man Who Can Only
Paint Death" and "The Widower;" or just a destructive
impossible shit, as in "Seventeen Warnings in Search of a
Feminist Poem" and "Men." The other half of the Boneman is
the Maiden, cast as "I" in "The Man Under the Bed." She is
masochistic, interested in her own pain, as in "Paper Cuts,"
"Loving the way she hates herself / much too much / to stop,"
as in "The Send-Off," wallowing in "a dream of rejection," as
in "The Orphan."

The Boneman poems sometimes skirt the edges of
Sitting-duck Poetry, in which the object of verbal attack is

held to be totally guilty and allowed no way out, while the attacker goes scot-free; and the Maiden poems run the risk of turning into miniature soap-operas, in which the only activities possible are the wringing of hands and the shedding of tears. (Is suffering really a function simply of being female?) What rescues the poems from these potential pitfalls is Jong's seemingly inexhaustible verbal dexterity, plus her capacity for mockery, of self and other. Jong may be a romantic, but she's a romantic well aware of the absurdity of romantic excesses.

By the end of the book, though, both Boneman and Maiden are seen as what the poet has always suspected they were: incarnations of the poetic "I," the Boneman a dramatization of the fear of death, the Maiden of the desire for it. In "The Prisoner" the poet plays all the roles, including Hangman; and it is at this point, the point at which the prison is revealed as self-constructed, that the poems can transform themselves from poems about death and suicide to poems against them. In "The Lure of the Open Window," death is not a lover, but plain emptiness:

> At the bottom of the pit
> are alley cats and glass
> not truth.

The death of the timorous couple in "Thirteen Lines for a Childless Couple" is not romantic. "Waiting" begins, "It is boring, this waiting for death," and ends, "Where is the life you are so afraid to lose?" An obsession with death can be a refusal to live, and this is the final conclusion to the long and complicated dialogue with death.

The dance of Death and the Maiden has as its obverse, "the dance against death" ("The Send-Off"), which consists for Jong primarily of two pursuits: sex and writing. Both are active, as opposed to the passive suffering of the Maiden; both are conducted with a certain defiance, and are greeted, it appears, with a certain contempt. Jong's images habitually spill over into each other or reverse places, so these two activities become entwined in her poems, sometimes with semi-hilarious results: "Castration of the Pen," for instance, or "The Book with Four Backs." Other poems play with images of body-as-page, poet-turning-to-poem, love-as-writing ("I am binding up your legs with carbon ribbon. / I tie you to the bed with paper chains.")

A number of poems circle the problem—which Jong strives hard not to find a paradox—of the woman who is a writer who is also a woman, with the Siamese twins pulling uneasily against each other, the writer feeling suffocated by the woman, the woman rendered sterile by the writer, as in "The Send-Off:"

> I want to write about something other than women!
> I want to write about something other than men!
> I want stars in my open hand
> & a house round as a pumpkin
> & children's faces forming at the roots of trees.

The act of speaking can be a great release, though Jong also perceives it as a potentially dead end:

> I am fixed in my longing for speech,
> I am buried in the snowbank of my poems,
> I am here where you find me
>
> dead
>
> on the other side of the page.

The texture of the poetry itself has something of the still-life about it. It is a curiously urban poetry, not because it's filled with images of transit systems, factories and tall buildings—it isn't—but because nothing in it ever grows or changes, except surreally. Fruits and vegetables are spotted only after they've been picked and are lying on a table; an apple may magically transmute itself into a woman, but it never changes from a green apple on a tree to a ripe apple. Objects outnumber processes, and everything, including the "I" and her lovers, is a kind of hard-edged Dali visual metaphor,

clear, incredible, paralyzed, moving if at all in frightening
leaps and free-falls, like the flying chamber-pots and the
predatory giant feet in *The Monty Python Show*. It is a world
created from words. As usual, Jong is aware of the difficulty:
she has wanted writing to be more organic, "a tree with a
voice," but has found instead

> ... this emptiness.
> The hollow of the book resounding
> like an old well
> in a ruined city.

Or, stated another way,

> Sometimes the sentimentalist
> says to hell with words
> & longs to dig ditches,
> She writes of this longing, of course ...

Sex, "the dance / against death," is an antidote but no final
answer. The dialogue between the two halves, woman-writer
and writer-woman, is an argument about which will contain
and define the other, and at the end of the long prose-poem
"From The Country of Regrets" it is the writer who wins,
albeit with irony:

> And there in the corner, writing about
> everyone, trying to separate herself out of the
> scene, or be above it, or control it, or pretend
> she dreamed it—am I. I am the one with the open
> notebook, the one who lost her pornographic postcards,
> the one with thousands of mosquito bites behind
> each knee. Nothing bad can happen to me, I am
> only collecting material. I am making notes:
> on hell, on heaven.

There are two images which bracket the "writer" per-
sona in *Half-Lives*: one in the first poem and one in the last.
Both have to do with the writer's relationship to the reader.
In "The Evidence," the writer is a fool, but a fool who talks:

> My business is to always feel
> a little like a fool
> & speak of it.

In "To the Reader," the writer is a magician, pulling something out of nothing:

> ... that is where I begin,
> where I open my hand
> to the reader
> & shake out my cuffs,
> where I show my magician's hat
> & swear on my life
> it is empty.

Both images are double-bladed. A professional fool, or so tradition has it, included in his act not only jokes made at his own expense but jests against his audience, the straight-men of the court. The reader may be invited by Jong to laugh at her, but he can't get away without a wry look at his own reflection in the funhouse mirror. A magician, on the other hand, is a trickster rather than a jester; his business to fool the audience in a different way, to make us believe he can create and transmute. Jong's poetry is sometimes tricky, like a well-performed conjuring trick; the props show only occasionally. But a good magician's best trick is to leave some doubt in the minds of the audience: perhaps the magic is real, perhaps the magic *power* is real. And in Jong's best poems, it *is* real. We may find the fool more entertaining, but the magician is, finally, more impressive.

21
What's So Funny?
Notes on Canadian Humour

(1974)

Women do not tend to find sexist jokes funny, cripples don't respond well to "sick" jokes about cripples, Blacks don't like "nigger" jokes, and Jews aren't fond of anti-semitic jokes. There is no such thing as universal humour, a joke that everyone will find amusing all the time. The funnybone, like other personality traits, is related to class, sex, colour, nationality and even age, as well as to individual character. Without banishing the other variables to outer darkness for all time, I would like at this time to ask one simple question: *What do Canadians laugh at?*

Instead of using a theory that assumes a quality called "humour" intrinsic to a piece of writing, imperishable and universal, I'll propose a model which has to do with the triangular relationship between the person telling the joke, the person listening to it and the person laughed at. I'll call the first of these the "laugher," the second the "audience," and the third the "laughee." In any given piece of humour, what designs does the laugher have upon the audience? What response does he want? Just as importantly, *who does he assume the audience to be?* What do both laugher and audience think of the laughee, and—a question seldom asked—*what does he think of them?* If the joke is made at his expense, can we assume that he resents it? Is he in a position to display his resentment?

There are, of course, many kinds of laughter. There's the laughter of recognition and identity, in which the laugher's response is essentially, "I am like that." There's the laughter of derision and distancing, in which the laugher is laughing *at*, not *with*; his laughter makes him feel superior to the butt of the joke, and he can say to himself smugly, "That person is stupid, or crude, or absurd; I am not like that." There is also survival laughter, born from conditions so awful that you either have to laugh or stick your head in the oven: ghetto humour of many kinds, certain varieties of war and hospital humour, the hysterical laughter of women in the Depression-time kitchen in Margaret Laurence's *A Bird in the House*. And there is the laughter of satire, laughter used as a weapon, scathing and destructive, in which the laugher assumes that the object is not feeble and silly, but evil and dangerous: F. R. Scott's social satires, Milton Acorn's "old depression workman, jokes all the time, jokes loaded with hate," Klein's *Hitleriad:*

> "Let anger take me in its grasp, let hate,
> Hatred of evil prompt me, and dictate!"

Before turning to Canadian humour, I'd like to try this model on something distant in time and place.

If you thumb through the pages of the nineteenth century *Punch*, one of the first "humour" magazines, you'll be surprised at the parade of Fagin-like Jews, banjo-eyed Blacks in funny costumes, effete Frenchmen and, especially, Neanderthal-browed, dirty, drunken Irishmen (the Irish were more of a threat). Also the Cockneys with their improper accents, the garrulous and silly females, the *nouveaux riches* with their pretensions. What can we deduce about the writers and readers of *Punch*, apart from the fact that they were not Blacks, Irishmen, women or Jews or "lower-class?" The laugher and the audience apparently share the assumption that there is a "correct" way of being human, and that all other ways render one an object of ridicule. The "correct" way involves being white, English, male, and *of a certain class*, not financially (much scorn is reserved for those who have *only* money) but, somehow, spiritually. Laugher and audience are English gentlemen; they subscribe to a code of thought and behaviour which, though not necessarily linked to birth and breeding, simply rules out the lesser breeds without the law. Rich lords and ladies come in for a certain amount of joshing, but only when they render themselves absurd by somehow violating the code by being eccentric or affected or dumb. The code itself is not absurd. The laugher flatters the audience by taking it for granted that both laugher and audience are members of the elect. In reality, of course, they were not the elect at all: they were merely aspirants, "snobs," like Dickens' Veneerings, defining themselves as at least potential members of the elect by disparaging those who had no hope: "I am not like them." Gentlemen of the Tennysonian or even the Chaucerian variety would not have indulged in this type of joke, partly because they would not have needed to. One function of sex, class and race jokes is that they bolster the shakily held notions of superiority of laugher and audience alike.

What of the laughees? We do not know what the objects of *Punch*'s numerous sallies thought of them, as they did not have access to the means of retaliation or reply. In fact, many of them probably never saw the magazine, as they were poor or illiterate.

As contrast to what I propose to say about Canadian humour in English, I'd like to put forward a version of "typical" English humour and a version of "typical" American humour.

Our comments about *Punch* provide a key to English humour. Most English humour, like English writing in general from Chaucer and Spenser through Shakespeare to Dickens, Austen, Thackeray and Eliot, is inextricably connected with class consciousness of one kind or another. This is hardly escapable, since class was historically, and still is, such a determining factor in the life of the individual within society. Accent is of paramount importance; generally, the more "correct" the accent and manners the less funny the individual is held to be. Thus the Wife of Bath is funny, the Knight (who approaches the pattern of "gentleman") is not. The Gravedigger is intended to be funny, Hamlet is not. The Fool is comical and ironic, Lear is tragic. Shaw's *Pygmalion* makes the point perfectly. How many comic turns of the screw have been twisted out of that classic situation, master and mistress masquerading as servants and *vice versa?* All England loves a Lord, as the saying used to go; and even Bertie Wooster, that inept and languid upper-class creation of P. G. Wodehouse, is funny because he is played off against the pattern of what a gentleman *ought* to be.

Very generally, the laugher in English humour poses as one with the "correct" gentlemanly tastes and accent; he flatters the audience by implying that the audience, too, possesses these attributes. The *real* audience, however, is the snob within, and the real accomplishment of laughter is reassurance: "I am not like them. I am classier."

American humour is a different kettle of fish. Classically, it has been Tall Tale or Wooden Nutmeg humour. The three roles available are the con-man or sharpie, sucker or dupe, and audience, and the idea is for the sharpie to put one over on the dupe, with the audience admiring the con-man's superior cunning and laughing at the dupe's gullibility. In Tall Tale, the audience itself plays dupe until the tallness of the tale is finally revealed. A simple con-man story is Mark Twain's famous Jumping Frog tale; a more complicated rendition is the episode in Owen Wister's *Virginian*, where the cowboy hero wins his duel, not with pistols but by telling an absurd story and sucking the villain into believing it. The "audience" is both the reading audience and an audience of "cultivated" easterners who have gathered to listen. Both audiences are flattered by being able to perceive themselves as more astute than the dupe. Then there's the King and the Duke and their Royal Nonesuch in *Huckleberry Finn*, with the audience in the book playing dupe and the reading audience laughing; and the Connecticut Yankee, putting things over on the "gentlemen" of King Arthur's Court. "Gentlemen" get short shrift in American humour; in fact they are distrusted as generally as they are in the rest of American literature, and are likely to be exposed as fakes, pretenders, snobs or ninnies. Real admiration is reserved for the con-men, who are just as likely to have a "regional" accent and play their tricks on city slickers as they are to be travelling salesmen pulling a fast one on the farmer's daughter (a wonderful variation occurs in Flannery O'Connor's story of the Bible salesman who steals the crippled woman's wooden leg.) Faulkner's Compsons are Southern Gentlemen and have a kind of crumbling nobility, but it's the lowbrow Snopeses who make the sharp horse trades and end up with the money.

One of the charms of James Thurber is that he reverses the roles: in "Sitting in the Catbird Seat," the potential dupe turns the tables on the con-lady, and time and again the ineffectual Walter Mittys end up, if not top dog, at least unduped.

In American humour the desired pattern is not one of right, correct, "gentlemanly" behaviour; instead it is a pattern suited to a highly competitive, individualistic society: you have to be smart enough to take care of yourself and not let the other guy outsmart you. Better still, you should have the wit to do it to him.

What about Canadian humour? It would be possible to deny the existence of such a thing, as the existence of a Canadian literature distinct from European and American literature was denied for many years (and still is, in some quarters). To set up such a denial, all you'd have to do would be to talk a lot about "regionalism," considering Canada as a "region" of the U.S. or of England. You can find "gentleman" assumptions in Canadian humour, I'm sure, just as you can find con-men and dupes. Once you've denied that Canadian literature is in any way different, that it is merely an inferior kind of subspecies, you'll have a perfect excuse for ignoring it in favour of other, presumably more accomplished specimens. This strategy has worked for many years in high schools and colleges across the land.

I propose to demonstrate that Canadian humour is indeed different in kind from these other varieties; not necessarily in overt content or *genre*, but in the assumptions the laugher makes about the audience, and in the kinds of satisfaction or reassurance the audience is intended to derive.

I'd like to examine three different *genres* of written humour, the parody, the satire and the kind of writing usually described as "humour." My main examples will be Hiebert's *Sarah Binks*, Mordecai Richler's *The Incomparable Atuk* and *Cocksure*, and Stephen Leacock's *Sunshine Sketches of a Little Town*. To avoid misconceptions, I'll say at the outset that I have a good deal of affection for all the pieces; I am not attempting to diminish or demolish them, merely to examine them in the light of my model.

Sarah Binks is a literary parody.

I was first exposed to parody through the Rawhide Little Theatre's rendition of *Wuthering Heights* in which an obnoxious Heathcliff chanted,

> I must go out on the moors again
> To the lonely moors and the sky,
> And all I want is a sharp stick
> To poke in Edgar Linton's eye.

The poem itself is a parody (a take-off on a specific piece of writing, using the same rhythms but exploding the form by altering the content in the direction of the absurd). The entire playlet is a burlesque of the romantic novel and of Brontë in particular.

Parody habitually works in a double-edged way: by trivializing a specific work or style whose original has pretensions to profundity, it allows the audience an escape from the magical and mysterious in "art." Laugher and audience are not sucked in by the artist, they see through him, they refuse to be moved by high seriousness. But in trivializing the artist and his work, laugher and audience diminish themselves as well. They aren't up to the idealistic poses of Don Quixote; for them it's Sancho, practical and stolid. Contrast the following well-known parody with its original and you will see what I mean:

> The Working Class can kiss my ass,
> I've got the foreman's job at last.

Parody and burlesque are, it seems to me, inherently cynical, albeit in a mild way.

Thus *Sarah Binks*. Sarah herself is a fictitious poetess, the "Sweet Songstress of Saskatchewan." Hiebert's biography of her is itself a takeoff of those ponderous, doleful and ultra-serious literary biographies which proliferate like guppies on the fringes of the literary scene; and like such biographies, it quotes extensively from Sarah's own work, most of which proves to be parody of various nineteenth and twentieth century modes, styles and individual poems.

To get the full joy of Sarah it's necessary to have a fairly extensive literary education, which the laugher assumes the audience possesses. Sarah's translations of Heine take some of the wind out of the sails of German Romanticism, and her milking song quite properly diminishes Longfellow. But much of the humour in the biography itself is based on the assumption that there is something intrinsically unpoetic about Saskatchewan and especially about farms and Regina, ("the Athens of Saskatchewan"), and that a poet from Saskatchewan is a contradiction in terms. Laugher and audience are, we assume, from other, more cultured places.

> Sarah Binks has raised her home province of Saskatchewan to its highest prairie level. Unschooled, but unspoiled, this simple country girl has captured in her net of poesy the flatness of that great province.... No other poet has so expressed the Saskatchewan soul. No other poet has caught in deathless lines so much of its elusive spirit, the baldness of its prairies, the alkalinity of its soil, the richness of its insect life.

Throughout the book Saskatchewan (and by extension Canada: Sarah is a "great Canadian") is treated as funny *per se*. Time and again references to other, *real* cultural centres are juxtaposed with Sarah's milieu, with a diminishing effect on the latter. What is so funny about Saskatchewan? In a word, it is viewed as overwhelmingly provincial, prohibitively lacking in "culture." Sarah is the best Saskatchewan can do, the Wheat Pool Medal and an honourary degree from St. Midget's the highest honours bestowed on her. She is not only Saskatchewan's best poet; she is its *only* poet, and her tombstone bears the word ALONE.

Sarah Binks pokes fun at a number of things, but foremost among them is the mere idea of anything "cultural" coming out of Saskatchewan (and Canada; in passing, it may be noted that Sarah's poems take off just about every "Canadian" theme, including the depredations of Nature, the lives and deaths of animals, community life and effort, the Indian.) To return to my model, laugher and audience are assumed to be different from and superior to the denizens of Saskatchewan. Laugher and audience are educated, they are from somewhere else, they are not provincial. A reassuring thought, except, of course, for those in Saskatchewan. . . .

Satire, unlike parody, has traditionally had moral designs upon the reader. Humour is used as a weapon and directed at objects the laugher considers out of line with his ideas of reason and correct behaviour. The force of satire depends on laugher and audience holding roughly similar ideologies, and unlike the parodist, the satirist often wishes to arouse moral indignation with a view to reform. Thus Swift's *Modest Proposal*, which advocates selling and eating babies as a solution to the population problem, will not be perceived as effectively scathing if in fact you believe in cannibalism and don't care what happens to the surplus population.

Much Canadian political satire has been in verse form (see, for instance, *The Blasted Pine*, compiled by Smith and Scott), and much of it is severe indeed, so severe that a friend of mine who was compiling an anthology of Canadian humour decided to leave out poetry altogether because it was "too bitter." Its targets are usually abuses within the body politic, its aims to expose, rebuke and correct. Satires like F. R. Scott's imply that situations, however deplorable, can and should be remedied: Canada, although behaving badly at present, can do better. Satires like these take the country seriously.

The breakdown in generally-held moral values has made it more difficult to write traditional satire, and the term "black humour" has come into use, applied to that kind of writing which points out abuses by exaggerating and fantasizing but does not assume the possibility of correcting them. Mordecai Richlers's two prose satires, *The Incomparable Atuk* and *Cocksure*, fall somewhere between traditional satire and "black humour." On one hand, Richler has made it clear that he considers the writer to be a moralist; on the other, neither of his satires provide many clues for the reformation of the society attacked. Perhaps it is the reformation of the reader that is aimed at instead: go thou and do unlikewise. In any case, that these two books are satires rather than "novels" is evident from the beheading of the hero on a quiz show in the first, and the science-fiction "Star Maker" and artificial inflatable film stars in the second. This is Gulliver's Travelogue, not sense and sensibility.

The laughee in *Atuk* is the Canadian Community, with its cultural pretensions, its "Canada's Darling" swim-champion national heroine, its hypocritical media-men, its two-faced treatment of native peoples. Atuk himself is a con-man who ends up as a dupe, but the laugh isn't on him. Atuk, after he has been arrested for having eaten a U.S. Army colonel in the arctic, becomes the focus in a wave of anti-American feeling, inspired, we are led to understand, mainly by envy, disappointment and pique:

> A mechanic who had been fired by General Motors...a widow who had bought oil shares in a Texas swamp; another whose most unforgettable character had been rejected by the *Readers' Digest*...some who recall Senator McCarthy ...a politician who had never made the Canadian section of *Time*; and more, many more....

The nationalism of the intellectuals is perceived as equally fatuous:

> "This is not a banana republic," an important novelist said. A University of Toronto psychologist pointed out, "Atuk's act was one of symbolic revenge. Culturally, economically, the Americans are eating our whole country alive."

(Richler assumed that his audience would find these remarks as hilarious as he did, and in 1963 he was probably right.) Public outrage at Atuk's arrest is skilfully manipulated by tycoon Buck Twentyman for his own ends, and Atuk dies as the final touch in his efforts to undermine a rival American food chain. Twentyman is the real con-man and Canada is the dupe. What of the audience? If non-Canadian, its members can laugh at Canada's provinciality and stupidity. But if Canadian, their laughter will surely be less single-minded, more complex.

Complexity reigns in Richler's later satire *Cocksure*. On one level, its hero is an embodiment of Richler's oft-repeated contention that Canadians are the world's elected squares. Mortimer Griffen is Canadian, white, Anglo-Saxon, and Anglican, was educated at Upper Canada College, and reads *The Best of Leacock* in bed while his wife is reading *The Story of O*. He finds hockey games sexually stimulating, and used to take the *Boys' Own Paper*, from which he has memorized the motto: "Fear God, honour the crown, shoot straight and keep clean." He has been awarded a Victoria Cross. In swinging London he's everybody's scapegoat, because he still has old-fashioned "moral" attitudes.

Laugher and audience join with the swingers in mocking Mortimer, but they are also expected to laugh at the modernist inanities of the swingers. Mortimer is a sane man in a society of amoral cosmopolitan loonies, but his brand of sanity is old-fashioned, provincial.

Read as a Canadian fable-of-identity, *Cocksure* can be seen as Richler's map of the national inferiority complex. Mortimer is obsessed with what he considers the small size of his cock, and he swiftly becomes impotent. He is hounded by a Jewish editor who insists that Mortimer is really Jewish, and finally tells him why:

> "Griffen, the scapegoat. ... A Jew is an idea.
> Today you're my idea of a Jew."

Because of his moral principles, which he can't get rid of, he refuses to work for the Star Maker, a purveyor of plastic cinema images to the American public, and a wielder of enormous American capital power. The Star Maker, in addition to being immortal and a murderer, has become double-sexed and is pregnant by himself at the end of the book; he has absorbed Mortimer's missing sexuality. In the face of the omnipotent American mogul, Mortimer the Canadian "scapegoat" is powerless, and his fate is similar to Atuk's: he is to be killed as a publicity gimmick.

It's difficult at first to place the laugher's attitude to the audience. Presumably laugher and audience are detached enough from Mortimer's "Canadian" values to find them archaic, but detached also from the extremes of hip London and mad Hollywood-America. Laugher and audience exist somewhere in mid-Atlantic, and the laughter is uneasy partly because of a lack of moral focus. We can see all the things Richler the moralist thinks are wrong, but we aren't sure exactly what alternatives he is offering, what modes of behaviour he would approve.

Leacock's *Sunshine Sketches of a Little Town* is neither satire nor parody. It's usually classed as "humour," and intends to be funny without either literary parody (a Leacock specialty in other books, such as *Literary Lapses* and *Nonsense Novels*) or satirical attack. Nevertheless, the assumptions about the audience and the things held up for chuckles are similar to those in the Hiebert and Richler books.

Leacock makes it clear in his introduction that Mariposa is not just one small town. It is the representative Canadian small town: " . . . if you know Canada at all, you are probably acquainted with a dozen small towns just like it." Much of the humour is created by the contrasts between the inhabitants' point of view—for them, Mariposa is a large and important place—and that of the narrator, who has been somewhere else and takes it for granted that the reader has also:

> Of course if you come to the place fresh from New York, you are deceived. Your standard of vision is all astray. You do think the place is quiet. You do imagine that Mr Smith is asleep merely because he closes his eyes as he stands. But live in Mariposa for six months or a year and then you will begin to understand it better. . . .

One amusing thing about the inhabitants of Mariposa is that they think they are important. They take themselves seriously, and the narrator pretends to do so too. Leacock's method is to make mock-epics out of trivia, thus deflating both the epic manner and the trivial events. The typical Mariposa event is the anti-climax: the Mariposa Belle sinks while the excursionists are singing O CANADA, but unlike the Titanic it lands on a sandbank. Peter Pupkin plans to kill himself for love, but unlike Werther he can't work up to it. It is a place where pathos is possible but nothing really tragic is allowed to happen. It is silly, muddle-headed and harmless. Even politics, although taken seriously by the inhabitants, is a laughing matter for Leacock: Smith the con-man rigs the election by circulating the rumour that he has won, and Mariposa, ever sensitive to majority opinion, votes for him *en bloc*. The British connection is saved by chicanery. Not that Leacock cares much about the issues:

> Don't ask me what election it was, whether Dominion or Provincial or Imperial or Universal, for I scarcely know.... I only know that it was a huge election and that on it turned issues of the most tremendous importance, such as whether or not Mariposa should become part of the United States, and whether the flag that had waved over the school house at Tecumseh Township for ten centuries should be trampled under the hoof of an alien invader, and whether Britons should be slaves, and whether Canadians should be Britons, and whether the farming class would prove themselves Canadians, and tremendous questions of that kind.

Leacock makes his own position as laugher clearer than either Richler or Hiebert. Hiebert poses as a literary biographer, Richler does not address the audience directly. But Leacock is an ex-Mariposan who has gone on to more cosmopolitan haunts, and in the nostalgic Envoi he places the audience as a member of the same group. The Envoi is an imaginary train journey undertaken by a man who has left Mariposa to become successful in the big city. He recognizes the Mariposa people on the train by their quaintness: "... those people with the clothes that are perfectly all right and yet look odd in some way, the women with the peculiar hats and the—what do you say?—last year's fashions?" The object of fun in *Sunshine Sketches* is the same as that in the Richler and Hiebert books: provinciality. The reader, being Canadian, is invited to recognize part of himself and his background in the sketches, but only part. The laugher implies that the audience now knows better.

If laugher and audience in English humour are saying, "I am not like them, I am a gentleman," and if their American counterparts are saying, "I am not like them, I am not a dupe," Canadian laughers and audiences—or those examined here, at any rate—seem to be saying, "I am not like them. I am not provincial, I am cosmopolitan." But as provinciality is seen as something irrevocably connected with being Canadian, the audience can renounce its provinciality only by disavowing its Canadianism as well.

The concealed self-deprecation, even self-hatred, involved in such disavowal, the eagerness to embrace the values of classes and cultures held superior, the wish to conciliate the members of those other groups by deriding one's own— these are usually attitudes displayed by people from oppressed classes or ethnic groups who have managed to make their way out of the group, alienating themselves in the process. "Yes, *they* are awful," such jokes seem to be saying, "But look, I am laughing at them. I am no longer one of them." Much of Canadian humour is like an extended Newfie joke, told by a Newfie who has made it for the amusement of a number of other succesful Newfies, as well as for that of the external British and American audience. Current examples are the "Canadian" jokes in the *National Lampoon*, written, of course by Canadians.

Who then are these cosmopolitan Canadians, uneasily laughing at their country, their countrymen and to a lesser extent at themselves? Certainly a large number of them are members of the educated middle class, conditioned through many years of schooling to depreciate things Canadian. Is Canada really such a joke? Or is the absurdity in the eyes of the beholder?

22

On Being a "Woman Writer":
Paradoxes and Dilemmas

(1976)

I approach this article with a good deal of reluctance. Once having promised to do it, in fact, I've been procrastinating to such an extent that my own aversion is probably the first subject I should attempt to deal with. Some of my reservations have to do with the questionable value of writers, male or female, becoming directly involved in political movements of any sort: their involvement may be good for the movement, but it has yet to be demonstrated that it's good for the writer. The rest concern my sense of the enormous complexity not only of the relationships between Man and Woman, but also of those between those other abstract intangibles, Art and Life, Form and Content, Writer and Critic, etcetera.

Judging from conversations I've had with many other woman writers in this country, my qualms are not unique. I can think of only one writer I know who has any formal connection with any of the diverse organizations usually lumped together under the titles of Women's Liberation or the Women's Movement. There are several who have gone out of their way to disavow even any fellow-feeling; but the usual attitude is one of grudging admiration, tempered with envy: the younger generation, they feel, has it a hell of a lot better than they did. Most writers old enough to have a career of any length behind them grew up when it was still assumed that a woman's place was in the home and nowhere else, and that anyone who took time off for an individual selfish activity like writing was either neurotic or wicked or both, derelict in her duties to a man, child, aged relatives or whoever else was supposed to justify her existence on earth. I've heard stories of writers so consumed by guilt over what they had been taught to feel was their abnormality that they did their writing at night, secretly, so no one would accuse them of failing as housewives, as "women." These writers accomplished what they did by themselves, often at great personal expense; in order to write at all, they had to defy other women's as well as men's ideas of what was proper, and it's not finally all that comforting to have a phalanx of women—some younger and relatively unscathed, others from their own generation, the bunch that was collecting china, changing diapers and sneering at any female with intellectual pretensions twenty or even ten years ago—come breezing up now to tell them they were right all along. It's like being judged innocent after you've been hanged: the satisfaction, if any, is grim. There's a great temptation to say to Womens' Lib, "Where were you when I really needed you?" or "It's too late for me now." And you can see, too, that it would be fairly galling for these writers, if they have any respect for historical accuracy, which most do, to be hailed as products, spokeswomen, or advocates of the Women's Movement. When they were undergoing their often drastic formative years there *was* no Women's Movement. No matter that a lot of what they say can be taken by the theorists of the Movement as supporting evidence, useful analysis, and so forth: their own inspiration was not theoretical, it came from wherever all writing comes from.

Call it experience and imagination. These writers, if they are honest, don't want to be wrongly identified as the children of a movement that did not give birth to them. Being adopted is not the same as being born.

A third area of reservation is undoubtedly a fear of the development of a one-dimensional Feminist Criticism, a way of approaching literature produced by women that would award points according to conformity or non-conformity to an ideological position. A feminist criticism is, in fact, already emerging. I've read at least one review, and I'm sure there have been and will be more, in which a novelist was criticized for not having made her heroine's life different, even though that life was more typical of the average woman's life in this society than the reviewer's "liberated" version would have been. Perhaps Women's Lib reviewers will start demanding that heroines resolve their difficulties with husband, kids, or themselves by stomping out to join a consciousness raising group, which will be no more satisfactory from the point of view of literature than the legendary Socialist Realist romance with one's tractor. However, a feminist criticism need not necessarily be one-dimensional. And—small comfort—no matter how narrow, purblind and stupid such a criticism in its lowest manifestations may be, it cannot possibly be *more* narrow, purblind and stupid than some of the non-feminist critical attitudes and styles that have preceded it.

There's a fourth possible factor, a less noble one: the often observed phenomenon of the member of a despised social group who manages to transcend the limitations imposed on the group, at least enough to become "successful." For such a person the impulse—whether obeyed or not—is to disassociate him/herself from the group and to side with its implicit opponents. Thus the Black millionaire who deplores the Panthers, the rich *Québecois* who is anti-Separatist, the North American immigrant who changes his name to an "English" one; thus, alas, the Canadian writer who makes it, sort of, in New York, and spends many magazine pages decrying provincial dull Canadian writers; and thus the women with successful careers who say "*I've never had any problems, I don't know what they're talking about.*" Such a woman tends to regard herself, and to be treated by her male colleagues, as a sort of honorary man. It's the rest of them who are inept, brainless, tearful, self-defeating: not her. "You think like a man," she is told, with admiration and unconscious put-down. For both men and women, it's just too much of a strain to fit together the traditionally incompatible notions of "woman" and "good at something." And if you *are* good at something, why carry with you the stigma attached to that dismal category you've gone to such lengths to escape from? The only reason for rocking the boat is if you're still chained to the oars. Not everyone reacts like this, but this factor may explain some of the more hysterical opposition to Women's Lib on the part of a few woman writers, even though they may have benefitted from the Movement in the form of increased sales and more serious attention.

A couple of ironies remain; perhaps they are even paradoxes. One is that, in the development of modern Western civilization, writing was the first of the arts, before painting, music, composing, and sculpting, which it was possible for women to practice; and it was the fourth of the job categories, after prostitution, domestic service and the stage, and before wide-scale factory work, nursing, secretarial work, telephone operating and school teaching, at which it was possible for them to make any money. The reason for both is the same: writing as a physical activity is private. You do it by yourself, on your own time; no teachers or employers are involved, you don't have to apprentice in a studio or work with musicians. Your only business arrangements are with your publisher, and these can be conducted through the mails; your real "employers" can be deceived, if you choose, by the adoption of an assumed (male) name; witness the Brontës and George Eliot. But the private and individual nature of writing may also account for the low incidence of direct involvement by woman writers in the Movement now. If you are a writer, prejudice against women will affect you *as a writer* not directly but indirectly. You won't suffer from wage discrimination, because you aren't paid any wages; you won't be hired last and fired first, because you aren't hired or fired anyway. You have relatively little to complain of, and, absorbed in your own work as you are likely to be, you will find it quite easy to shut your eyes to what goes on at the spool factory, or even at the university. *Paradox:* reason for involvement then equals reason for non-involvement now.

Another paradox goes like this. As writers, woman writers are like other writers. They have the same professional concerns, they have to deal with the same contracts and publishing procedures, they have the same need for solitude to work and the same concern that their work be accurately evaluated by reviewers. There is nothing "male" or "female" about these conditions; they are just attributes of the activity known as writing. As biological specimens and as citizens, however, women are like other women: subject to the same discriminatory laws, encountering the same demeaning attitudes, burdened with the same good reasons for not walking through the park alone after dark. They too have bodies, the capacity to bear children; they eat, sleep and bleed, just like everyone else. In bookstores and publishers' offices and among groups of other writers, a woman writer may get the impression that she is "special;" but in the eyes of the law, in the loan office or bank, in the hospital and on the street she's just another woman. She doesn't get to wear a sign to the grocery store saying "Respect me, I'm a Woman Writer." No matter how good she may feel about herself, strangers who aren't aware of her shelf-full of nifty volumes with cover blurbs saying how gifted she is will still regard her as a nit.

We all have ways of filtering out aspects of our experience we would rather not think about. Woman writers can keep as much as possible to the "writing" end of their life, avoiding the less desirable aspects of the "woman" end. Or they can divide themselves in two, thinking of themselves as two different people: a "writer" and a "woman." Time after time, I've had interviewers talk to me about my writing for a while, then ask me, "As a woman, what do you think about—for instance—the Women's Movement," as if I could think two sets of thoughts about the same thing, one set as a writer or person, the other as a woman. But no one comes apart this easily; categories like Woman, White, Canadian, Writer are only ways of looking at a thing, and the thing itself is whole, entire and indivisible. *Paradox*: Woman and Writer are separate categories; but in any individual woman writer, they are inseparable.

One of the results of the paradox is that there are certain attitudes, some overt, some concealed, which women writers encounter *as* writers, but *because* they are women. I shall to try to deal with a few of these, as objectively as I can. After that, I'll attempt a limited personal statement.

A.   *Reviewing and the Absence of an Adequate Critical Vocabulary*

Cynthia Ozick, in the American magazine *Ms.*, says, "For many years, I had noticed that no book of poetry by a woman was ever reviewed without reference to the poet's sex. The curious thing was that, in the two decades of my scrutiny, there were *no* exceptions whatever. It did not matter whether the reviewer was a man or a woman; in every case, the question of the 'feminine sensibility' of the poet was at the centre of the reviewer's response. The maleness of male poets, on the other hand, hardly ever seemed to matter."

Things aren't this bad in Canada, possibly because we were never fully indoctrinated with the Holy Gospel according to the distorters of Freud. Many reviewers manage to get through a review without displaying the kind of bias

Ozick is talking about. But that it does occur was demon
strated to me by a project I was involved with at York
University in 1971-72.

One of my groups was attempting to study what we
called "sexual bias in reviewing," by which we meant not
unfavourable reviews, but points being added or subtracted
by the reviewer on the basis of the author's sex and supposedly associated characteristics rather than on the basis of the
work itself. Our study fell into two parts: i) a survey of
writers, half male, half female, conducted by letter: had they
ever experienced sexual bias directed against them in a
review? ii) the reading of a large number of reviews from a
wide range of periodicals and newspapers.

The results of the writers' survey were perhaps predictable. Of the men, none said Yes, a quarter said Maybe, and
three quarters said No. Half of the women said Yes, a
quarter said Maybe and a quarter said No. The women
replying Yes often wrote long, detailed letters, giving instances and discussing their own attitudes. All the men's
letters were short.

This proved only that women were more likely to *feel*
they had been discriminated against on the basis of sex.
When we got around to the reviews, we discovered that they
were sometimes justified. Here are the kinds of things we
found.

i) *Assignment of reviews*
Several of our letter writers mentioned this. Some felt books
by women tended to be passed over by book-page editors
assigning books for review; others that books by women
tended to get assigned to women reviewers. When we started
totting up reviews we found that most books in this society
are written by men, and so are most reviews. Disproportion-
ately often, books by women were assigned to women
reviewers, indicating that books by women fell in the minds
of those dishing out the reviews into some kind of "special"
category. Likewise, woman reviewers tended to be reviewing

books by women rather than by men (though because of the preponderance of male reviewers, there were quite a few male-written reviews of books by women).

ii) *The Quiller-Couch Syndrome*
The heading of this one refers to the turn-of-the-century essay by Quiller-Couch, defining "masculine" and "feminine" styles in writing. The "masculine" style is, of course, bold, forceful, clear, vigorous, etc.; the "feminine" style is vague, weak, tremulous, pastel, etc. In the list of pairs you can include "objective" and "subjective," "universal" or "accurate depiction of society" versus "confessional," "personal," or even "narcissistic" and "neurotic." It's roughly seventy years since Quiller-Couch's essay, but the "masculine" group of adjectives is still much more likely to be applied to the work of male writers; female writers are much more likely to get hit with some version of "the feminine style" or "feminine sensibility," whether their work merits it or not.

iii) *The Lady Painter, or She Writes Like A Man*
This is a pattern in which good equals male, and bad equals female. I call it the Lady Painter Syndrome because of a conversation I had about female painters with a male painter in 1960. "When she's good," he said, "we call her a painter; when she's bad, we call her a lady painter." "She writes like a man" is part of the same pattern; it's usually used by a male reviewer who is impressed by a female writer. It's meant as a compliment. See also "She thinks like a man," which means the author thinks, unlike most women, who are held to be incapable of objective thought (their province is "feeling"). Adjectives which often have similar connotations are ones such as "strong," "gutsy," "hard," "mean," etc. A hard-hitting piece of writing by a man is liable to be thought of as merely realistic; an equivalent piece by a woman is much more likely to be labelled "cruel" or "tough." The assumption is that women are by nature soft, weak and not very good, and that

if a woman writer happens to be good, she should be deprived of her identity as a female and provided with higher (male) status. Thus the woman writer has, in the minds of such reviewers, two choices. She can be bad but female, a carrier of the "feminine sensibility" virus; or she can be "good" in male-adjective terms, but sexless. Badness seems to be ascribed then to a surplus of female hormones, whereas badness in a male writer is usually ascribed to nothing but badness (though a "bad" male writer is sometimes held, by adjectives implying sterility or impotence, to be deficient in maleness). "Maleness" is exemplified by the "good" male writer; "femaleness," since it is seen by such reviewers as a handicap or deficiency, is held to be transcended or discarded by the "good" female one. In other words, there is no critical vocabulary for expressing the concept "good/female." Work by a male writer is often spoken of by critics admiring it as having "balls;" ever hear anyone speak admiringly of work by a woman as having "tits?"

Possible antidotes: Development of a "good/female" vocabulary ("Wow, has that ever got Womb . . ."); or, preferably, the development of a vocabulary that can treat structures made of words as though they are exactly that, not biological entities possessed of sexual organs.

iv)   *Domesticity*

One of our writers noted a (usually male) habit of concentrating on domestic themes in the work of a female writer, ignoring any other topic she might have dealt with, then patronizing her for an excessive interest in domestic themes. We found several instances of reviewers identifying an author as a "housewife" and consequently dismissing anything she has produced (since, in our society, a "housewife" is viewed as a relatively brainless and talentless creature). We even found one instance in which the author was called a "housewife" and put down for writing like one when in fact she was no such thing.

For such reviewers, when a man writes about things like doing the dishes, it's realism; when a woman does, it's an unfortunate feminine genetic limitation.

v) *Sexual compliment-put-down*
This syndrome can be summed up as follows;
She: "How do you like my (design for an airplane/mathematical formula/medical miracle)?"
He: "You sure have a nice ass."
In reviewing it usually takes the form of commenting on the cute picture of the (female) author on the cover, coupled with dismissal of her as a writer.

vi) *Panic Reaction*
When something the author writes hits too close to home, panic reaction may set in. One of our correspondents noticed this phenomenon in connection with one of her books: she felt that the content of the book threatened male reviewers, who gave it much worse reviews than did any female reviewer. Their reaction seemed to be that if a character such as she'd depicted did exist, they didn't want to know about it. In panic reaction, a reviewer is reacting to content, not to technique or craftsmanship or a book's internal coherence or faithfulness to its own assumptions. (Panic reaction can be touched off in any area, not just male-female relationships.)

B. *Interviewers and Media Stereotypes*
Associated with the reviewing problem, but distinct from it, is the problem of the interview. Reviewers are supposed to concentrate on books, interviewers on the writer as a person, human being, or, in the case of women, woman. This means that an interviewer is ostensibly trying to find out what sort of person you are. In reality, he or she may merely be trying to match you up with a stereotype of "Woman Author" that pre-exists in her/his mind; doing it that way is both easier for the interviewer, since it limits the range and slant of questions, and shorter, since the interview

can be practically written in advance. It isn't just women who get this treatment: all writers get it. But the range for male authors is somewhat wider, and usually comes from the literary tradition itself, whereas stereotypes for female authors are often borrowed from other media, since the ones provided by the tradition are limited in number.

In a bourgeois, industrial society, so the theory goes, the creative artist is supposed to act out suppressed desires and prohibited activities for the audience; thus we get certain Post-romantic male-author stereotypes, such as Potted Poe, Bleeding Byron, Doomed Dylan, Lustful Layton, Crucified Cohen, etc. Until recently the only personality stereotype of this kind was Elusive Emily, otherwise known as Recluse Rossetti: the woman writer as aberration, neurotically denying herself the delights of sex, kiddies and other fun. The Twentieth Century has added Suicidal Sylvia, a somewhat more dire version of the same thing. The point about these stereotypes is that attention is focused not on the actual achievements of the authors, but on their lives, which are distorted and romanticized; their work is then interpreted in the light of the distorted version. Stereotypes like these, even when the author cooperates in their formation and especially when the author becomes a cult object, do no service to anyone or anything, least of all the author's work. Behind all of them is the notion that authors must be more special, peculiar or weird than other people, and that their lives are more interesting than their work.

The following examples are taken from personal experience (mine, of interviewers); they indicate the range of possibilities. There are a few others, such as Earth Mother, but for those you have to be older.

i) *Happy Housewife*
This one is almost obsolete: it used to be for Woman's Page or programme. Questions were about what you liked to fix for dinner; attitude was, "Gosh, all the housework and

you're a writer too!" Writing was viewed as a hobby, like knitting, one did in one's spare time.

ii) *Ophelia*

The writer as crazy freak. Female version of Doomed Dylan, with more than a little hope on the part of the interviewer that you'll turn into Suicidal Sylvia and give them something to *really* write about. Questions like "Do you think you're in danger of going insane?" or "Are writers closer to insanity than other people?" No need to point out that most mental institutions are crammed with people who have never written a word in their life. "Say something interesting," one interviewer said to me. "Say you write all your poems on drugs."

iii)   *Miss Martyr; or, Movie Mag*

Read any movie mag on Liz Taylor and translate into writing terms and you've got the picture. The writer as someone who *suffers* more than others. Why does the writer suffer more? Because she's successful, and you all know Success Must Be Paid For. In blood and tears, if possible. If you say you're happy and enjoy your life and work, you'll be ignored.

iv)   *Miss Message*

Interviewer incapable of treating your work as what it is, i.e. poetry and/or fiction. Great attempt to get you to say something about an Issue and then make you into an exponent, spokeswoman or theorist. (The two Messages I'm most frequently saddled with are Women's Lib and Canadian Nationalism, though I belong to no formal organization devoted to either.) Interviewer unable to see that putting, for instance, a nationalist into a novel doesn't make it a nationalistic novel, any more than putting in a preacher makes it a religious novel. Interviewer incapable of handling more than one dimension at a time.

What is Hard to Find is an interviewer who regards writing as a respectable profession, not as some kind of magic, madness, trickery or evasive disguise for a Message; and who regards an author as someone engaged in a professional activity.

C. *Other Writers and Rivalry*
Regarding yourself as an "exception," part of an unspoken quota system, can have interesting results. If there are only so many available slots for your minority in the medical school/law school/literary world, of course you will feel rivalry, not only with members of the majority for whom no quota operates, but especially for members of your minority who are competing with you for the few coveted places. And you will have to be better than the average Majority member to get in at all. But we're familiar with that.

Woman-woman rivalry does occur, though it is surprisingly less severe than you'd expect; it's likely to take the form of *wanting* another woman writer to be better than she is, expecting more of her than you would of a male writer, and being exasperated with certain kinds of traditional "female" writing. One of our correspondents discussed these biases and expectations very thoroughly and with great intelligence: her letter didn't solve any problems but it did emphasize the complexities of the situation. Male-male rivalry is more extreme; we've all been treated to media-exploited examples of it.

What a woman writer is often unprepared for is the unexpected personal attack on her by a jealous male writer. The motivation is envy and competitiveness, but the form is often sexual put-down. "You may be a good writer," one older man said to a young woman writer who had just had a publishing success, "but I wouldn't want to fuck you." Another version goes more like the compliment-put-down noted under Reviewing. In either case, the ploy diverts attention from the woman's achievement as a writer—the area where the man feels threatened—to her sexuality, where either way he can score a verbal point.

Personal Statement

I've been trying to give you a picture of the arena, or that part of it where being a "woman" and "writer," as concepts, overlap. But, of course, the arena I've been talking about has to do largely with externals: reviewing, the media, relationships with other writers. This, for the writer, may affect the tangibles of her career: how she is received, how viewed, how much money she makes. But in relationship to the writing itself, this is a false arena. The real one is in her head, her real struggle the daily battle with words, the language itself. The false arena becomes valid for writing itself only insofar as it becomes part of her material and is. transformed into one of the verbal and imaginative structures she is constantly engaged in making. Writers, as writers, are not propagandists or examples of social trends or preachers or politicians. They are makers of books, and unless they can make books well they will be bad writers, no matter what the social validity of their views.

At the beginning of this article, I suggested a few reasons for the infrequent participation in the Movement of woman writers. Maybe these reasons were the wrong ones, and this is the real one: no good writer wants to be merely a transmitter of someone else's ideology, no matter how fine that ideology may be. The aim of propaganda is to convince, and to spur people to action; the aim of writing is to create a plausible and moving imaginative world, and to create it from words. Or, to put it another way, the aim of a political movement is to improve the quality of people's lives on all levels, spiritual and imaginative as well as material (and any political movement that doesn't have this aim is worth nothing). Writing, however, tends to concentrate more on life, not as it ought to be, but as it is, as the writer feels it, experiences it. Writers are eye-witnesses, I-witnesses. Political movements, once successful, have historically been intolerant of writers, even those writers who initially aided them; in any revolution, writers have been among the first to be lined up against the wall, perhaps for their intransigence, their insistence on saying what they perceive, not what, according to the ideology, ought to exist. Politicians, even revolutionary politicians, have traditionally had no more respect for writing as an activity valuable in itself, quite apart from any message or content, than has the rest of the society. And writers, even revolutionary writers, have traditionally been suspicious of anyone who tells them what they ought to write.

The woman writer, then, exists in a society that, though it may turn certain individual writers into revered cult objects, has little respect for writing as a profession, and not much respect for women either. If there were more of both, articles like this would be obsolete. I hope they become so. In the meantime, it seems to me that the proper path for a woman writer is not an all-out manning (or womaning) of the barricades, however much she may agree with the aims of the Movement. The proper path is to become better as a writer. Insofar as writers are lenses, condensers of their society, her work may include the Movement, since it is so palpably among the things that exist. The picture that she gives of it is altogether another thing, and will depend, at least partly, on the course of the Movement itself.

23
Adrienne Rich:
Poems, Selected and New

(1975)

If you still don't believe in cultural differences between Canada and the United States, you should try comparing poetry readings. You might find the same stanza forms in each country, but you'd probably find very different audiences. Unless the poet is ultra-famous, the U.S. audience would be smaller and would consist largely of students, other poets and assorted literati. In Canada it would be more varied: for some reason, Canadians read more poetry *per capita* than any other country in the English-speaking world. And the difference shows up in the way poets write in the two countries, in their assumptions about their audiences: white male American poets often write as if they think they're talking only to other white male American poets, displaying their professional bags of tricks for other connoisseurs. They have nothing to say to ordinary people, because ordinary people aren't listening. The atmosphere can get fairly rarefied.

The exceptions to this prevailing climate are, of course, the poets from the ethnic minority groups; and women. A sense of grievance, a consciousness of oppression, can often provide a force and a driving power for those who attempt to give them a voice. Such poets are less interested in displaying their verbal virtuosity than in getting something said; urgency replaces ambiguity, all seven types of it.

Adrienne Rich's selected poems is a perfect demonstration of the evolution from introspective to didactic; it's also a perfect contradiction of those who claim that politics and poetry can't be mixed. Rich is perhaps the best known living woman poet in the United States (although cultural differences of some kind showed up when a leading Canadian book review editor failed to recognize the name). Though she'd published six earlier books, it was *Diving Into the Wreck* (1973) that brought her to her current prominence. It received the National Book Award, which Rich accepted not only for herself but on behalf of the other two women who were nominated but didn't win. The jacket cover proclaims her a radical feminist, with no qualifications.

She's the kind of poet of whom an unwary critic is likely to say, "The strongest voice to emerge from the feminist movement," or some such inaccuracy. For Rich didn't emerge from the feminist movement. She's been publishing books since 1950, that's 25 years, and *Poems Selected And New* (McLeod, $9.95) is a reminder of that fact. Indeed some of these poems are strangely prophetic, anticipating many of the themes that were later hit on as fresh discoveries by the feminist movement. To read through the book is to feel, often, that others have expanded into whole books what Rich had written in a few lines, ten or fifteen years earlier.

> ... Thus wrote
> a woman, partly brave and partly good,
> who fought with what she partly understood
> hence she was labelled harpy, shrew and whore.

That's Rich on Mary Wollstonecraft in "Snapshots of a Daughter-in-Law," written, amazingly, in 1958, a poem which also quotes, for Rich's own good purposes, Dr. Johnson's quip about a female preacher being like a dog walking on its hind legs:

Not that it is done well, but
that it is done at all? Yes think
of the odds! or shrug them off forever
This luxury of the precocious child,
Time's precious chronic invalid—
would we, darlings, resign it if we could?
Our blight has been our sinecure:
mere talent was enough for us—
glitter in fragments and rough drafts.

The same poem ends with a prophecy of not the second coming, but the first; the arrival of a woman who will finally take the risks and make the leap, "be more merciless to herself than history," give up "femininity" for real achievement.

There's something of self-portraiture here, for this was the line of development Rich's own poetry took. At the beginning of the book she's just another young poet learning a craft, a craft whose terms were defined by her male contemporaries. Though her earlier poems already show a certain epigrammatic terseness of line, a clenched, somewhat unrelenting toughness of intellect, they are often abstract; it's as if the poet is talking only to herself. Even when the poems are addressed to a second person, she speaks as if she isn't really sure she will be heard.

As it develops, Adrienne Rich's poetry moves toward mercilessness, of a desirable kind. Her discovery of her own poetic voice, of what she wants to say, and of her audience, who she's saying it to, are clearly interdependent. The early poems skirt emotion or muse upon it; experiences have given rise to the poems, but we're often not too sure what, exactly, they are. In later ones emotions are not talked about but expressed or evoked, often with blunt and sometimes brutal force. The earlier poems are full of "craft;" in the later ones technique has been so thoroughly assimilated that we don't even notice it. Language is honed down, decoration trimmed off; the poet has no more use for frills, no need to demonstrate that she too is an adept. The earlier poems illustrate; the later ones state.

As the language tightens, the focus narrows and sharpens: Rich's subject becomes the struggle of woman, interpreted on almost every possible level: emotional, political, mythological, symbolic, historical. The poems become at the same time both personal and more universal: Rich is speaking, not to some nebulous listener, but to her own deepest self and to the corresponding selves of other women. For women become the audience: when she says "us," that's who she means:

> I long to create something
> that can't be used to keep us passive...

When poems are addressed to men, the tone is no longer contemplative. There are few poets who have been better able to express anger.

The intention and the result, in the last three sections of the book, is nothing less than the creation of a new history and a new mythology. A number of woman poets have been working along the same lines, but few with such success. Sometimes the poems decline into rhetoric, sometimes they become shrill, but not often. At their best they are absolutely succinct, absolutely powerful; rooted in the actual, they move into the subterranean levels where myths are alive. "Diving into the Wreck," "From a Survivor," "Trying to Talk with a Man," are Rich at her best.

The long poem at the end of the book, "From an Old House in America," is in some way Rich's most ambitious, and most definitive poem to date: compact, simple in phrasing, fiercely intellectual, uncompromising, a condensed *Leaves of Grass*, but this time from the woman's point of view:

Isolation, the dream
of the frontier woman

levelling her rifle along
the homestead fence

still snares our pride
—a suicidal leaf

laid under the burning-glass
in the sun's eye

Any woman's death diminishes me

This book is clearly a seminal one in the history of women's poetry. It's also an important landmark in the development of a remarkable individual poet. It's a necessary book: necessary for the reader, but also one feels, for the writer. There are few poems that convince you, as the best of Rich's do, that they *had* to be written.

24
Kate Millett:
Flying

(1974)

Kate Millett achieved celebrity status several years ago with her book *Sexual Politics* which discussed, almost for the first time, the anti-female bias in literature. It was a book that went out on a limb, and—in television talk shows, speeches, university seminars and public appearances of all kinds—so did its author. Her position attracted a number of people with axes and saws—what so irresistible as someone out on a limb?—who proceeded to try to cut her down, with, it appears, partial success.

Her autobiographical "documentary" *Flying* is in part a response to her experiences as airborne heroine, though *Falling* might have been a more appropriate title. The book's point of departure is the time period after the crash, after Millett has been "trashed" by the media, the women's movement, and various friends and lovers who could not deal with her success. She's picking up the pieces of her battered self, wondering if she's all right, whether she can begin again, "be someone else now. Not the one who wrote that goddam book." Initially she writes in a prose that is jerky, rambling, disconnected, as if she's just received a severe blow on the head and is suffering from shock. She follows the process of her own recuperation through its various phases and stratagems, from new work to new love affairs to travels about the countryside and from country to country, reminiscing about her past, recording her present, pausing for commentary on society (mostly American) and life (mostly hers).

If *Flying* were a novel, Millett could be praised for creating a complex, intriguing heroine, torn between an exuberant, sensual and rather selfish hedonism and the guilt, anxiety and exaggerated sense of responsibility which are the legacies of a repressive Catholic upbringing and a deserted and consequently accusing and dependent mother. "Stop being humble," a friend tells her, "drop your endless capacity for punishment. Let yourself," and we watch the heroine attempting to put this command into practice, with mixed results. We could admire, too, the way the heroine's whining—her "broken wing" stories, as she calls them—is played against the enormous demands she makes on her friends and lovers and her own capacity for using people, not from malice but simply from overabundance of energy. Most of the other characters in the book do a lot of crying, drinking, collapsing and screaming, prompted in part by the effects of this high-voltage dynamo in their midst. The only one to emerge with any serenity is the angelic husband, a Japanese sculptor who is making a wooden typewriter and who unfailingly dispenses love, peace, food and comfort when the heroine returns from her other escapades. As fiction, the book could be criticized for a swollen population of scantily-drawn minor characters and a romantic style that sometimes crosses the line into outright bathos.

But *Flying* is not fiction, it is autobiography, and the reader brings a different set of standards to bear on it. It is not the author's skill as a writer we are to praise (as she makes it clear, she is attempting to be truthful rather than skilful), but her courage. If letting it all hang out is the virtuous act it is currently supposed to be, *Flying* is certainly a virtuous book. And it is not the choice of adjectives that will be criticized, but the author's personality; all the more so because, as she notes exhaustively, she is famous.

But Millett is capable of dealing with any objection to herself or her book; in fact she makes many of them herself. She questions her own perceptions and philosophy, she apologizes constantly, and there's hardly an unpleasant thing to be said about her that she doesn't say herself. And she knows she is often tedious. As one of her friends says, "Don't leave out the banal, life is not heroical," and it's a suggestion she follows with a certain relentlessness. Reading *Flying* is like being stuck on a ten-hour bus ride beside someone who insists on telling you the story of her life, not just the highlights but all of it, with blurry snapshots of people you don't know, childhood memories only some of which are significant, information about meals, clothes and furniture (hers and other people's), parties she's been to, what X said to Y, and on and on nonstop. If you are sufficiently interested in people you will sit through it, getting over the boring parts as best you can and waiting for the insights and revelations (and Millett does provide them). Depending on your own temperament you may wonder whether you've been caught by the Ancient Mariner, who will provide a gripping narrative, lyric beauty and a moral ending in return for your captivity, or merely by the Old Man of the Sea, who won't let go. Either way, the book is compulsively written and must be compulsively read.

Nevertheless, people and social trivia and the sex lives of the famous are universally fascinating, and there's a little of the voyeur and eavesdropper in all of us. Unfortunately, some of the book takes place on the level of the Hollywood gossip column, except that the sex lives are mostly lesbian and the names dropped are mostly Women's Movement. (But perhaps this is a Canadian reaction: total personal revelation tends to be an American convention, and Canadians, caught on that bus ride, are likely to unfurl a large newspaper between themselves and the talker.) Despite her anguish and vulnerability and obvious intelligence, Millett can display just as much pettiness as those who have exercised these talents on her. But she knows this too, and reprimands herself for it.

Why write such a book? As portions of the book are about the process of writing the book, we have access to Millett's rationale. At the outset the book was therapy, an attempt to create again after the destructive experiences connected with *Sexual Politics*. It is also an attempt to redefine herself. Feeling that she has been reduced to a cardboard cut-out by the media and by fame, half-believing the feedback image of herself as an a icon, a demon or a joke, she tries to demonstrate—to herself, initially—that she is indeed a human being. *Flying* abounds with comments about the methods of media overkill, but perhaps the most succinct comes during a brilliant analysis of the Danny LaRue drag show in London: "Objectify and dismiss, objectify and applaud, objectify and slaughter." Millett's response is to refuse to be an object, to be as subjective as she knows how; *Flying* is a gigantic demonstration of her own existence as something both more and less than the colossal Women's Movement statue of herself erected by her success. She refuses both heroism and martyrdom, though both have been thrust upon her. She knows perfectly well that being a hero is dangerous, invites attack; she even shares the impulse. "How petty I am," she says, glimpsing someone "important." "How delightful it is to shit on a big shot. A name. Of course people enjoy it." She would rather be a person than a personality.

Still, a book written as therapy, as "a way of inventing the self," is essentially private, like a diary. What justifies publication, especially when the act will expose her friends and lovers to the same kind of publicity Millett herself has found so distasteful? The closest thing to Millett's answer comes in a speech she makes to a Women's Movement meeting, advocating non-violence. Having been their target, Millett distrusts ideology, rhetoric and "what is usually called politics." They dehumanize, she wants to humanize. She wishes to challenge "the traditional separation of the public and personal," to arrive at a new "politics" by beginning with an examination of the self. *Flying*, we may assume, is offered as a somewhat confused object lesson on the integration of the political and the personal.

This approach has a respectable tradition in American literature, which has long struggled with the contradiction inherent in the concept of a "democratic" hero or star: if all can be President, why isn't everyone? "How do you make everyone famous?" Millett asks, almost agreeing with the egalitarian movement for attacking her. ("Not by killing the famous," she adds.) For Whitman, the hero was Everyman, the ordinary person, and *Flying* is a modern-day, female and lesbian *Song of Myself*. It is thoroughly American in its chronicling of race hatred, street violence, media cannibalism, turmoils public and private, the edgy, frantic quality of New York life, but it's American also in its romanticism, its utopianism however qualified, its eternal conviction that new beginnings are possible, that the self is a creation and not just something you're stuck with, that salvation and love are possible. At their worst, her assumptions are naive; at their best, they give her a child-like confidence and openness.

Given the bitterness of her experiences, Millett could have slipped easily into a cynical fatalism, but there's hardly a hint of it. It is her willingness to believe, to try again, to offer herself, to be delighted, that is ultimately the most convincing thing about the *persona* in *Flying*. "The world amazes me," Millett remarks, and it is her ever-renewed capacity for amazement, at herself as well as everything else, that finally redeems the book and the sometimes dreary process of reading it.

25
The Curse of Eve—
Or, What I Learned in School

(1978)

Once upon a time, I would have not been invited to speak to you today. That time isn't really very long ago. In 1960, when I was attending university, it was widely known that the University College English department did not hire women, no matter what their qualifications. My own college did hire women, it just didn't promote them very rapidly. One of my teachers was a respected authority on Samuel Taylor Coleridge. She was a respected authority on Coleridge for a great many years before anyone saw fit to raise her from the position of Lecturer.

Luckily, I myself did not want to be an authority on Coleridge. I wanted to be a writer, but writers, as far as I could see, made even less than Lecturers, so I decided to go to graduate school. If I had had any burning academic ambitions, they would have taken a turn for the venomous when I was asked by one of my professors whether I really wanted to go to graduate school...wouldn't I rather get married? I've known a couple of men for whom marriage would have been a reasonable alternative to a career. Most, however, by force of circumstance, if not by inclination, have been like a friend of mine who is well known for never finishing anything he started.

"When I'm thirty," he said to me once, "I'll have to choose between marriage and a career."

"What do you mean?" I said.

"Well, if I get married, I'll have to have a career," he replied.

I, however, was expected to have one or the other, and this is one of the many ways in which I hope times have changed. Back then, no university in its right mind would have run a lecture series entitled "Women on Women." If it had done anything at all on the subject, it probably would have invited a distinguished psychologist, male, to talk about innate female masochism. College education for women was justified, if at all, on the grounds that it would make women into more intelligent wives and better-informed mothers. Authorities on women were usually men. They were assumed to possess that knowledge, like all other knowledge, by virtue of gender. The tables have turned and now it's women who are supposed to possess this knowledge, simply by birthright. I can only assume that's the reason I've been invited to speak to you, since I'm not an authority on women, or indeed on anything else.

I escaped from academia and bypassed journalism— which was the other career I considered, until I was told that women journalists usually ended up writing obituaries or wedding announcements for the women's page, in accordance with their ancient roles as goddesses of life and death, deckers of nuptial beds and washers of corpses. Finally I became a professional writer. I've just finished a novel, so it's as a working novelist that I'd like to approach this general area.

I'll begin with a simple question, one which confronts every novelist, male or female, at some point in the proceedings and which certainly confronts every critic.

What are novels for? What function are they supposed to perform? What good, if any, are they supposed to do the reader? Are they supposed to delight or instruct, or both, and if so, is there ever a conflict between what we find delightful and what we find instructive? Should a novel be an exploration of hypothetical possibilities, a statement of truth, or just a good yarn? Should it be about how one ought to live one's life, how one can live one's life (usually more limited), or how most people live their lives? Should it tell us something about our society? Can it avoid doing this? More specifically, suppose I am writing a novel with a woman as the central character; how much attention should I pay to any of the above questions? How much attention will I be *forced* to pay through the preconceptions of the critics? Do I want this character to be likeable, respectable, or believable? Is it possible for her to be all three? What are the assumptions of those who will do the liking, the respecting, or the believing? Does she have to be a good "role model?"

I dislike the term "role model" partly because of the context in which I first heard it. It was, of course, at university, a very male-oriented university which had a female college attached. The female college was looking for a Dean. My friend, who was a sociologist, explained that this person would have to be a good role model. "What's that?" I asked. Well, the future Dean would not just have to have high academic credentials and the ability to get along with students, she would also have to be married, with children, good-looking, well dressed, active in community work, and so forth. I decided that I was a terrible role model. But then, I did not want to be a role model, I wanted to be a writer. One obviously would not have time for both.

It may be just barely acceptable for prospective Deans to be judged as role models, but as this is also a favourite technique of critics, especially when evaluating female characters in books and sometimes when evaluating the writers themselves, it has to be looked at quite carefully. Let me cite an example: several years ago, I read a review of Marian Engel's *The Honeyman Festival*, written by a female reviewer. The heroine of this novel is Minn, a very pregnant woman who spends a lot of her time reminiscing about the past and complaining about the present. She doesn't have a job. She doesn't have much self-esteem. She's sloppy and self-indulgent and guilt-ridden and has ambiguous feelings about her children, and also about her husband, who is away most of the time. The reviewer complained about this character's lack of initiative, apparent laziness and disorganization. She wanted a more positive, more energetic character, one capable of taking her life in hand, of acting more in accordance with the ideal woman then beginning to be projected by the women's movement. Minn was not seen as an acceptable role model, and the book lost points because of this.

My own feeling is that there are a lot more Minn-like women than there are ideal women. The reviewer might have agreed, but might also have claimed that by depicting Minn and only Minn—by providing no alternative to Minn—the writer was making a statement about the nature of Woman that would merely reinforce these undesirable Minnish qualities, already too much in evidence. She wanted success stories, not failure stories, and this is indeed a problem for the writer of fiction. When writing about women, what constitutes success? Is success even plausible? Why, for instance, did George Eliot, herself a successful female writer, never compose a story with a successful female writer as the central character? Why did Maggie Tulliver have to drown for her rebelliousness? Why could Dorothea Brooke find nothing better to do with her idealism than to invest it in two men, one totally unworthy of it, the other a bit of a simp? Why did Jane Austen's characters exercise their wit and intelligence in choosing the proper man rather than in the composition of comic novels?

One possible answer is that these novelists concerned themselves with the typical, or at least with events that would fall within the range of credibility for their readers; and they felt themselves, as woman writers, to be so exceptional as to lack credibility. In those days, a woman writer was a freak, an oddity, a suspicious character. How much of that sentiment lingers on today, I will leave you to ask yourselves, while at the same time quoting a remark made to me several years ago by a distinguished male writer. "Women poets," he said, "always have a furtive look about them. They know they're invading male territory." He followed this with a statement to the effect that women, including women writers, were only good for one thing, but since this lecture is going to be printed, I will not quote this rather unprintable remark.

To return to my problem, the creation of a fictional female character . . . I'll come at it from a different angle. There's no shortage of female characters in the literary tradition, and the novelist gets her or his ideas about women from the same sources everyone else does: from the media, books, films, radios, television and newspapers, from home and school, and from the culture at large, the body of received opinion. Also, luckily, sometimes, through personal experience which contradicts all of these. But my hypothetical character would have a choice of many literary ancestresses. For example, I might say a few words about Old Crones, Delphic Oracles, the Three Fates, Evil Witches, White Witches, White Goddesses, Bitch Goddesses, Medusas with snaky heads who turn men to stone, Mermaids with no souls, Little Mermaids with no tongues, Snow Queens, Sirens with songs, Harpies with wings, Sphinxes, with and without secrets, women who turn into dragons, dragons who turn into women, Grendel's mother and why she is worse than Grendel; also about evil stepmothers, comic mothers-in-law, fairy godmothers, unnatural mothers, natural mothers, Mad Mothers, Medea who slew her own children, Lady Macbeth and her spot, Eve the mother of us all, the all-mothering sea, and Mother, what have I to do with thee? Also about Wonder Woman, Superwoman, Batgirl, Mary Marvel, Catwoman and Rider Haggard's She with her supernatural powers and electric organ, who could kill a mere mortal man by her embrace; also about Little Miss Muffet and her relationship with the spider, Little Red Riding Hood and her indiscretions with the wolf, Andromeda chained to her rock, Rapunzel and her tower, Cinderella and her sackcloth and ashes, Beauty and the Beast, the wives of Bluebeard (all but the last), Mrs Radcliffe's persecuted Maidens fleeing seduction and murder, Jane Eyre fleeing impropriety and Mr Rochester, Tess of the D'Urbervilles seduced and abandoned; also about the Angel in the House, Agnes pointing upwards, the redemptive love of a good woman, Little Nell dying to the hypocritical sobs of the whole century, Little Eva doing likewise, much to the relief of the reader, Ophelia babbling down her babbling brook, the Lady of Shalott swan-songing her way towards Camelot, Fielding's Amelia snivelling her way through hundreds of pages of gloom and peril and Thackeray's Amelia doing likewise but with less sympathy from her author. Also about the rape of Europa by the bull, the rape of Leda by the swan, the rape of Lucretia and her consequent suicide, miraculous escapes from rape on the parts of several female saints, rape fantasies and how they differ from rape realities, men's magazines featuring pictures of blondes and Nazis, sex and violence from *The Canterbury Tales* to T. S. Eliot... and I quote... "I knew a man once did a girl in. Any man might do a girl in. Any man has to, needs to, wants to, once in a lifetime do a girl in." Also about the Whore of Babylon, the whore with the heart of gold, the love of a bad woman, the whore without a heart of gold, the Scarlet Letter, the Scarlet Woman, the Red Shoes, Madame Bovary and her quest for the zipless fuck, Molly Bloom and her chamber pot and her eternal yes, Cleopatra and her friend the Asp, an association which casts a new light on Little Orphan Annie. Also about orphans, also about Salome and the head of John the Baptist, and Judith and the head of Holofernes. Also about True Romance magazines and their relationship to Calvinism. Unfortunately, I have neither the time nor the knowledge necessary to discuss all of these in the depth and breadth they deserve, and they do deserve it. All, of course, are stereotypes of women drawn from the Western European literary tradition and its Canadian and American mutations.

There are a good many more variations than those I've mentioned, and although the Western literary tradition was created largely by men, by no means all of the female figures I have mentioned were male-invented, male-transmitted or male-consumed. My point in mentioning them is to indicate not only the multiplicity of female images likely to be encountered by a reader but especially the range. Depictions of women, even by men, are by no means limited to the figure of the Solitary Weeper (that creature of helpless passivity who cannot act but only suffer), which seems to have been encouraged by the dominant philosophy about women up until the nineteenth century. There was more to women, even stereotypical women, even then.

The moral range of female stereotypes seems to me to be wider than that of male characters in literature. Heroes and villains have much in common, after all. Both are strong, both are in control of themselves, both perform actions and face the consequences. Even those supernatural male figures, God and the Devil, share a number of characteristics. Sherlock Holmes and Professor Moriarty are practically twins, and it is very difficult to tell by the costumes and activities alone which of the Marvel Comics' supermen are supposed to be bad and which good. Macbeth, although not very nice, is understandable, and besides, he never would have done it if it hadn't been for the Three Witches and Lady Macbeth. The Three Witches are a case in point. Macbeth's motive is ambition, but what are the witches' motives? They have no motives. Like stones or trees, they

simply are: the good ones purely good, the bad ones purely
bad. About the closest a male figure can come to this is Iago
or Mr Hyde, but Iago is at least partly motivated by envy
and the other half of Mr Hyde is the all-too-human Dr
Jekyll. Even the Devil wants to win, but the extreme types
of female figure do not seem to want anything at all. Sirens
eat men because that is what Sirens do. The horrible
spider-like old women in D. H. Lawrence's stories—I am
thinking especially of the grandmother in "The Virgin and
the Gypsy"—are given no motives for their horribleness
other than something Lawrence called "the female will."
Macbeth murders because he wants to be king, to gain
power, whereas the Three Witches are merely acting the way
witches act. Witches, like poems, should not mean, but be.
One may as well ask why the sun shines.

   This quality of natural force, good or bad, this quality of
thinghood, appears most frequently in stories about male
heroes, especially the travelling variety such as Odysseus. In
such stories, the female figures are events that happen to the
hero, adventures in which he is involved. The women are
static, the hero dynamic. He experiences the adventure and
moves on through a landscape that is a landscape of women
as well as one of geographical features. This kind of story is
still very much with us, as anyone who has read the James
Bond stories, Henry Miller or, closer to home, Robert
Kroetsch's *The Studhorse Man* can testify. There are few
female literary adventurers of this kind. One might call
them adventuresses, and the connotation alone indicates
how they differ from the male variety. A man who recites a
catalogue of women, such as Don Giovanni, is held to be a
rogue, perhaps, but a rather enviable one, whereas female
characters, from Moll Flanders to Isadora Wing, of Erica
Jong's *Fear of Flying*, are not allowed to do the same without a
great deal of explanation, suffering and guilt.

   I have mentioned the Solitary Weeper, that passive
female victim to whom everything gets done and whose

only activity is running away. There are male figures of a similar type but they are usually children, like Dickens's Paul Dombey, Oliver Twist and the suffering pupils of Dotheboys Hall. For the grown-up male to exhibit these characteristics—fearfulness, inability to act, feelings of extreme powerlessness, tearfulness, feelings of being trapped and helpless—he has to be crazy or a member of a minority group. Such feelings are usually viewed as a violation of his male nature, whereas the same feelings in a female character are treated as an expression of hers. Passive helpless men are aberrations; passive women within the range of the norm. But powerful, or at any rate active, heroes and villains are seen as the fulfillment of a *human* ideal; whereas powerful women, and there are many of them in literature, are usually given a supernatural aura. They are witches, Wonder Women or Grendel's mothers. They are monsters. They are not quite human. Grendel's mother is worse than Grendel because she is seen as a greater departure from the norm. Grendel, after all, is just a sort of Beowulf, only bigger and hungrier.

Suppose, however, that I want to create a female character who is not a natural force, whether good or evil; who is not a passive Solitary Weeper; who makes decisions, performs actions, causes as well as endures events, and has perhaps even some ambition, some creative power. What stories does my culture have to tell me about such women? Not very many at the public school level, which is probably the reason why I can remember nothing at all about Dick and Jane, although some vague imprints of Puff and Spot still remain. But, outside school hours, there were the comic books: Batman and Robin, Superman (and Lois Lane, the eternal dumb rescuee), the Human Torch and Zorro and many others, all male. Of course, there was Wonder Woman. Wonder Woman was an Amazon princess who lived on an island with some other Amazons but no men. She had magic bullet-deflecting bracelets, a transparent airplane, a magic lasso, and super skills and powers. She fought crime. There was only one catch—she had a boyfriend. But, if he kissed her, her superhuman strength disappeared like Samson's after a clean shave. Wonder Woman could never get married and still remain Wonder Woman.

Then there was *The Red Shoes*—not the Hans Christian Andersen fairy tale but the movie, starring Moira Shearer, with beautiful red hair. A whole generation of little girls were taken to see it as a special treat for their birthday parties. Moira Shearer was a famous dancer but alas, she fell in love with the orchestra conductor, who, for some reason totally obscure to me at the time, forbade her to dance after they got married. This prohibition made her very unhappy. She wanted the man, but she wanted to dance as well, and the conflict drove her to fling herself in front of a train. The message was clear. You could not have both your artistic career and the love of a good man as well, and if you tried, you would end up committing suicide.

Then there were Robert Graves' poetic theories, set forth in many books, especially *The White Goddess*, which I read at the age of 19. For Graves, man does, woman simply is. Man is the poet, woman is the Muse, the White Goddess herself, inspiring but ultimately destroying. What about a woman who wants to be a poet? Well, it is possible, but the woman has to somehow *become* the White Goddess, acting as her incarnation and mouthpiece, and presumably behaving just as destructively. Instead of "create and be destroyed," Graves' pattern for the female artist was "create and destroy." A little more attractive than jumping in front of a train, but not much. Of course, you could always forget the whole thing, settle down and have babies. A safer course, it would seem, and that was certainly the message of the entire culture.

The most lurid cautionary tales provided by society, however, were the lives of actual female writers themselves. Women writers could not be ignored by literary history; at least not nineteenth-century ones. Jane Austen, The Brontë sisters, George Eliot, Christina Rossetti, Emily Dickinson, and Elizabeth Barrett Browning were too important for that. But their biographies could certainly emphasize their eccentricities and weirdness, and they did. Jane Austen never got married. Neither did Emily Brontë, who also died young. Charlotte Brontë died in childbirth. George Eliot lived with a man she was not married to and never had any children. Christina Rossetti "looked at life through the wormholes in a shroud." Emily Dickinson lived behind closed doors and was probably nuts. Elizabeth Barrett Browning did manage to squeeze out a child but did not bring him up properly and indulged in seances. These women were writers, true, but they were somehow not women, or if they were women, they were not *good* women. They were bad role models, or so their biographies implied.

"I used to have a boyfriend who called me Wonder Woman," says Broom Hilda, the witch, in a recent comic strip.

"Because you are strong, courageous and true?" asks the Troll.

"No, because he wondered if I was a woman."

If you want to be good at anything, said the message, you will have to sacrifice your femininity. If you want to be female, you'll have to have your tongue removed, like the Little Mermaid.

It's true that much was made of Poe's alcoholism, Byron's incest, Keats' tuberculosis, and Shelley's immoral behaviour, but somehow these romantic rebellions made male poets not only more interesting, but more male. It was rarely suggested that the two Emilys, Jane, Christina and the rest lived as they did because it was the only way they could get the time and develop the concentration to write. The amazing thing about women writers in the nineteenth century is not that there were so few of them but that there were any at all. If you think this syndrome is dead and buried, take a look at Margaret Laurence's *The Diviners*. The central character is a successful woman writer, but it becomes obvious to her that she cannot write and retain the love of a good man. She chooses the writing and throws an ashtray at the man, and at the end of the book she is living alone. Writers, both male and female, have to be selfish just to get the time to write, but women are not trained to be selfish.

A much more extreme version of the perils of creativity is provided by the suicides of Sylvia Plath and Anne Sexton and the rather ghoulish attention paid to them. Female writers in the twentieth century are seen not just as eccentric and unfeminine, but as doomed. The temptation to act out the role of isolated or doomed female artist, either in one's life or through one's characters, is quite strong. Luckily, there are alternatives. When hard pressed, you can always contemplate the life of Mrs Gaskell, Harriet Beecher Stowe or even, say, Alice Munro or Adele Wiseman or the many other female writers who seem to have been able to combine marriage, motherhood, and writing without becoming more noticeably deformed than anyone else in this culture.

However, there is some truth to the *Red Shoes* syndrome. It *is* more difficult for a woman writer in this society than for a male writer. But not because of any innate mysterious hormonal or spiritual differences: it is more difficult because it has been made more difficult, and the stereotypes still lurk in the wings, ready to spring fully formed from the heads of critics, both male and female, and attach themselves to any unwary character or author that wanders by. Women are still expected to be better than men, morally that is, even by women, even by some branches of the women's movement; and if you are not an angel, if you happen to have human failings, as most of us do, especially if you display any kind of strength or power, creative or otherwise, then you are not merely human, you're worse than human. You are a witch, a Medusa, a destructive, powerful, scary monster. An angel with pimples and flaws is not seen as a human being but as a devil. A character who behaves with the inconsistency that most of us display most of the time is not a believable creation but a slur on the Nature of Woman or a sermon, not on human frailty, but on the special frailer-than-frail shortcomings of all Womankind. There is still a lot of social pressure on a woman to be perfect, and also a lot of resentment of her should she approach this goal in any but the most rigidly prescribed fashion.

I could easily illustrate by reading from my own clipping file: I could tell you about Margaret the Magician, Margaret the Medusa, Margaret the Man-eater, clawing her way to success over the corpses of many hapless men. Margaret the powerhungry Hitler, with her megalomaniac plans to take over the entire field of Canadian Literature. This woman must be stopped! All these mythological creatures are inventions of critics; not all of them male. (No one has yet called me an angel, but Margaret the Martyr will surely not take long to appear, especially if I die young in a car accident.)

It would be amusing to continue with these excerpts, but it would also be rather mean, considering the fact that some of the perpetrators are, if not in the audience, employed by this university. So instead of doing that, I will enter a simple plea; women, both as characters and as people, must be allowed their imperfections. If I create a female character, I would like to be able to show her having the emotions all human beings have—hate, envy, spite, lust, anger and fear, as well as love, compassion, tolerance and joy—without having her pronounced a monster, a slur, or a bad example. I would also like her to be cunning, intelligent and sly, if necessary for the plot, without having her branded as a bitch goddess or a glaring instance of the deviousness of women. For a long time, men in literature have been seen as individuals, women merely as examples of a gender; perhaps it is time to take the capital W off Woman. I myself have never known an angel, a harpy, a witch or an earth mother. I've known a number of real women, not all of whom have been nicer or more noble or more long-suffering or less self-righteous and pompous than men. Increasingly it is becoming possible to write about them, though as always it remains difficult for us to separate what we see from what we have been taught to see. Who knows? Even I may judge women more harshly than I do men; after all, they were responsible for Original Sin, or that is what I learned in school.

I will end with a quote from Agnes Macphail, who was not a writer but who was very familiar with at least one literary stereotype. "When I hear men talk about women being the angel of the home, I always, mentally at least, shrug my shoulders in doubt. I do not want to be the angel of the home. I want for myself what I want for other women: absolute equality. After that is secured, then men and women can take their turns at being angels." I myself would rephrase that: "Then men and women can take their turns at being human, with all the individuality and variety that term implies."

26
Canadian Monsters:
Some Aspects of the Supernatural in Canadian Fiction

(1977)

I first became interested in Canadian monsters, not, as you might suspect, through politics, but through my own attempts to write ghost stories and through some research I happened to be doing on Sasquatches, for a CBC "Poem for Voices."[1] My collection of other people's monsters has not been systematically acquired, and there are probably glaring omissions in it. No sooner will this article appear in print than some indignant student of the occult will, no doubt, chastise me for not having known that the central character in *I Was A Teenage Werewolf* was, like Walt Disney, a Canadian, or for some error of similar magnitude. I hasten to cover my tracks by declaring that, unlike my compatriots here assembled, I am not a professional academic, and my collecting and categorizing of monsters must be ascribed to an amateur, perverse and private eccentricity, like that of, say, a Victorian collector of ferns. (Like many writers of my generation I started to read Canadian literature in self-defence; we got tired of people telling us there wasn't any and that we should therefore not exist, or go to New York.)

But criticism, even the proliferating Canlitcrit of the last decade, hasn't had much to say about the subject, probably because magic and monsters don't usually get associated with Canadian literature. In fact, the very term "Canadian literature" would seem to exclude them, in the popular mind at least, and the popular mind is not always wrong. Supernaturalism is not typical of Canadian prose fiction; the mainstream (with those useful qualifications, *by and large* and *so far*) has been solidly social-realistic. When people in Canadian fiction die, which they do fairly often, they usually stay buried; mention of supernatural beings is as a rule confined to prayers and curses; God and the Devil appear in the third person but rarely in the first, and are not often seen onstage. The divine and demonic levels of human existence may appear through analogy or symbol, but there aren't very many apotheoses or descents to the underworld, or even white whales, scarlet letters in the sky, or *Blithedale Romance* mesmerists. Canadian fiction on the whole confines itself to ordinary life on middle-earth.[2] Recently, experimentalist Larry Garber began a story, "Susceptible to illusion as I am, I was not at all surprised when Jack (whom we had buried a few weeks previously) announced his presence at my threshold."[3] This opening ploy is meant to come as a shock to the reader, and the fact that it does indicates the extent to which it is an exception to the usual Canadian realistic conventions.

The supposed lack of otherworldly dimensions, or even worldly ones, used to be almost routinely lamented by poets and others critics. Thus Earle Birney, in his much-quoted poem, "Can.Lit.:"

> we French & English never lost
> our civil war
> endure it still
> a bloody civil bore

> the wounded sirened off
> no Whitman wanted
> it's only by our lack of ghosts
> we're haunted

And, more severely, Irving Layton, in "From Colony to Nation:"

> A dull people, without charm
> or ideas,
> settling into the clean empty look
> of a Mountie or a dairy farmer
> as into a legacy
>
> One can ignore them
> (the silences, the vast distances help)
> and suppose them at the bottom
> of one of the meaner lakes,
> their bones not even picked for souvenirs.

Fifteen years ago, this was Canada, or rather this was the image of it which everyone seemed to believe in: a dull place, devoid of romantic interest and rhetorical excesses, with not enough blood spilled on the soil to make it fertile, and above all, ghostless. Unmagical Canada, as prosaic as Mounties and dairy farmers appear to be before you actually meet some up close...

But is this a true picture of Canada or its literature, and was it ever? Over the past fifteen years a certain amount of exhumation, literary or otherwise, has been taking place, which could be viewed as archaeology, necrophilia or resurrection, depending on your viewpoint. The digging up of ancestors, calling up of ghosts, exposure of skeletons in the closet, which are so evident in many cultural areas—the novel, of course, but also history and even economics—have numerous motivations, but one of them surely is a search for reassurance. We want to be sure that the ancestors, ghosts and skeletons really are there; that as a culture we are not as flat and lacking in resonance as we were once led to believe. The Prime Minister of Canada for more than twenty years, Mackenzie King, formerly a symbol of Canada because of his supposed dullness and greyness ("He blunted us," goes the F. R. Scott poem *W.L.M.K.*, "We had no shape / Because he

never took sides, / And no sides / Because he never allowed
them to shape ...."), is enjoying new symbolic popularity as
a secret madman who communed every night with the
picture of his dead mother and believed that his dog was
inhabited by her soul. "Mackenzie King rules Canada because he is himself the embodiment of Canada—cold and
cautious on the outside ... but inside a mass of intuition
and dark intimations," says one of Robertson Davies' characters in *The Manticore*, speaking for many.

It is this talking-picture side of Canadian literature, this
area of dark intimations, which I would like to consider
briefly here. Briefly, because my own knowledge is far from
encyclopaedic; but also because Canadian fictions in which
the supernatural and the magical appear are still only
exceptions which prove what may soon no longer be the
rule.

The North, the Wilderness, has traditionally been used in
Canadian literature as a symbol for the world of the unexplored, the unconscious, the romantic, the mysterious and
the magical. There are strange things done 'neath the
midnight sun, as Robert Service puts it. (There are probably
stranger things done in Toronto, but they don't have quite
the same aura.) So it's not surprising that a large number of
Canadian monsters have their origin in native Indian and
Eskimo myths. One of the earliest uses of this kind of monster
in literary prose (I hesitate to call it "fiction," although it
probably is) is in a book called *Brown Waters and Other
Sketches* (1915), by William Blake. The narrator is fishing in
"the great barrens that lie far-stretching and desolate among
the Laurentian Mountains." He describes the landscape in
exceptionally negative terms:

> So were we too alone in one of the loneliest places this
> wide earth knows. Mile upon mile of grey moss; weathered
> granite clad in ash-coloured lichen; old *brûlé*—the trees

here fallen in windrows, there standing bleached and lifeless, making the hilltops look barer, like the sparse white hairs of age. Only in the gullies a little greenness ... dwarfed larches, gnarled birches, tiny firs a hundred years old—and always moss ... great boulders covered with it, the very quagmires mossed over so that a careless step plunges one into the sucking black ooze below.

One evening the narrator's companion tells a story concerning the disappearance of a man named Paul Duchêne, a good guide, familiar with the wilderness, who wandered off and has never been found. He then mentions the belief of the Montagnais Indians:

.... strange medley of Paganism and Christianity—that those who die insane without the blessing of a priest become wendigos—werewolves, with nothing human but their form, soulless beings of diabolic strength and cunning that wander for all time seeking only to harm whatever comes in their way.

He goes on to speak of his journey the summer before to a place called the Rivière à l'Enfer, where he camps beside a lake with black water. His guides go back for supplies, and he is left alone, whereupon he experiences an "oppression of the spirit:" "In what subtle way," he asks, "does the universe convey the knowledge that it has ceased to be friendly?" That night a tremendous storm blows up. Sitting in his tent, he hears an unearthly cry, which is "not the voice of beast or bird." He bursts from the tent and is confronted by a creature—"something in the form of a man"—which springs at him. "And what in God's name was it?" asks the narrator. The story-teller replies, "Pray Him it was not poor Duchêne in the flesh."

The juxtaposition of the oppressive landscape, the story-teller's reaction to it as hostile, and the appearance of the *wendigo* indicate that this is a tale about the Monster as Other, which represents forces outside and, in this case, opposed to the human protagonist. Duchêne, child of the wilderness, has become the wilderness as seen by the narrator—the incarnation of an unfriendly natural universe. The storm is one aspect of this landscape; the *wendigo*, soulless and destructive, is the same landscape in human form.

The *wendigo* story in *Brown Waters* is as short and simple as the folk-tale material from which it obviously derives. A more extended and much more sophisticated Monster-as-Other was created by Sheila Watson in her novel *The Double Hook* (1959). The novel begins, "In the folds of the hills, under Coyote's eye..." Coyote turns out to be a deity of sorts, part animal, part god, both below human nature and beyond it. At first, like the landscape he represents, he appears harsh and malevolent. He is Fate, he is retribution, he is Death, he is the nature of things; he is also called a "mischief-maker." But in fact he is double, like the hook of the title: "the glory and the fear," both together. His nature changes according to the vision of the perceiver, and the reader comes to know the various characters partly through their views of Coyote. "There's no big Coyote, like you think," says materialist Theophil. "There's not just one of him. He's everywhere. The government's got his number too. They've set a bounty on him at fifty cents a brush ... This is a thin mean place, men and cattle alike." By the end of the book both he and his landscape have become, if not exactly nurturing, at least more benevolent. He presides over the birth of a child, and sings, in his rather Biblical manner:

> I have set his feet on soft ground;
> I have set his feet on the sloping shoulders
> of the world.

The *wendigo* and Coyote are both landscape-and-nature creatures, nature in both cases being understood to include super-nature. Neither are human; both can act on human beings, but cannot be acted upon. They are both simply *there*, as supernatural forces in the environment and as embodiments of that environment which must be reckoned with. They are objects rather than subjects, the "Other" against which the human characters measure themselves. The environment and its monster in *Brown Waters* are so overwhelmingly negative that the best thing the protagonist can do is run away from them, which he does. The environment and its deity in *The Double Hook* also provide an ordeal for the human actors, but both environment and deity are double-natured, and the proper response to them is not simple escape but further exploration resulting in increased self-knowledge. The one character who attempts escape ends by returning, and Coyote blesses him accordingly.

It is very difficult to make a completely non-human supernatural being the protagonist in a fiction: but there are at least two Canadian novels in which the protagonist is a semi-human being. Such beings might be called "magic people" rather than "monsters." They have magical powers and otherworldly attributes, but they are nonetheless partly human and can be acted upon by ordinary human beings. A case in point is the central character in *Tay John* (1939), Howard O'Hagan's potent and disturbing novel. Tay John is a strange creature, half white man and half Indian, half mythical and half "realistic." In the first third of the book, which is written in the form of a folk tale or legend, we learn of his birth underground from the body of his dead and buried mother. He emerges and is seen wandering near the gravesite, an odd child with yellow hair, brown skin and no shadow. After he has been lured into the land of the living by the elders of the tribe and given a shadow by a wisewoman, he is marked out to be the tribe's leader and potential saviour. But first he must enter manhood by going apart to a place of his own choosing, to fast, to have a vision and to acquire a guiding spirit.

Unfortunately he picks the wrong place. It is "a valley

where no man went," and like the lake of Blake's Rivière à
l'Enfer it has black water, with similar associations:

> The water that came down from that valley was turgid,
> dark, and flowed silently, with no rapids. It was said that if
> a man drank of that water he would lose his voice and go
> from the sight of his fellows, roaming the hills at night to
> bark at the moon like a coyote. The coyote men saw by day
> was not the same they heard by night, for the coyote they
> heard by night was the voice of a man whose hands had
> become claws and whose teeth had grown long and tusk-
> like, who sat on his haunches, lifted his head to the sky and
> lamented the human speech gone from him.
>
> The spirit of that valley was cruel. Men feared that one
> night, taking the form of a great white bear, it would come
> down upon them in their sleep and leave them with a
> coyote's howl for voice and only a coyote's claws for hands,
> and each man would be for ever a stranger to his neigh-
> bour.

What the Indians fear most about the spirit of the valley is
the power it has to divide the society, to make each man a
stranger to his neighbour: "The boy says 'I'; the man says
'We'—and this word that the man speaks is the word of his
greatest magic." But Tay John chooses to say "I." The valley
of the *wendigo*-like were-coyote does present him with a sign,
but it is an ominous one: he is visited by "an old bear, with
snow-dust on his coat;" in other words, the great white bear
of the myth. He is not changed into a coyote outwardly, but
he brings back something that will have the same effect, a
bag of sand from the river. The sand contains gold, which is
not known to the Indians; but when a party of white
prospectors arrives, it is Tay John they select to guide them
to the valley, because he is the only man who has ever been
there. From this time forward he has a new name (*Tête Jaune*,
corrupted to Tay John) and is contaminated by the ego-
centric, individualistic spirit of the whites.

This trait emerges when Tay John wishes to marry. The
tribe feels that, as magic leader, he should not marry. "The

woman of Tay John is the people," they say. "He is a leader of the people and is married to their sorrows." But he will not accept this condition, and leaves the tribe to seek out the world of the white men who have given him his name.

As might be expected, the encounter is disastrous. The remaining two sections of the book consist mainly of hearsay and eyewitness reports of the doings of Tay John—his hand-to-hand combat with a grizzly, his sacrifice of his own hand to gain possession of a horse. But he doesn't fit into the white world any more easily than he did into the Indian; in both, he's an exception. His tribe wished him to be a hero and leader, but about all the whites can think of to offer him is a position as guide, or, worse, a tourist Indian, dressed up to meet the trains. He resists this tame fate and elopes into the mountains with a strange white woman, a "woman of the world" who leaves her rich protector to go off with him. Like Tay John's own mother she dies in childbirth, and Tay John is last seen pulling her corpse on a toboggan. The description reminds us of his magic origins:

> Tay John came on, more distinct now, through the curtain of swirling snow, entangled in it, wrapped in its folds, his figure appearing close, then falling back into the mists, a shoulder, a leg, a snowshoe moving on as it were of its own accord—like something spawned by the mists striving to take form before mortal eyes.
>
> "He seemed very big off there, shadowy like," Blackie said, "then again no bigger than a little boy."

When his tracks are followed, they lead nowhere:

> Blackie stared at the tracks in front of him, very faint now, a slight trough in the snow, no more. Always deeper and deeper into the snow. He turned back then. There was nothing more he could do. He had the feeling, he said, looking down at the tracks, that Tay John hadn't gone over the pass at all. He had just walked down, the toboggan behind him, under the snow and into the ground.

The semi-human hero has returned to the earth in much the same way as he emerged from it. His life, like the confused trails he makes in the snow, has been circular. Although he performs several acts beyond the range of most men and is generally regarded as singular, he has not used his gifts to benefit his people, and ultimately they do not benefit him either.

It is interesting to compare Tay John with the "magic" protagonist of a very different book, *The Sun and the Moon*[4] (1944) by P. K. Page. Kristin, born during an eclipse of the moon, is a visionary who can see things that aren't there. She can also "become" inanimate objects, seeing and feeling as they do: "She had only to sit still long enough to know the static reality of inanimate things—the still, sweet ecstasy of change in kind." As a child she likes doing this, and finds people noisy and superfluous. But when she is seventeen she meets a painter named Carl; they fall in love and become engaged, and she finds herself "stealing" his essence by "becoming" him, much as she was once able to "become" a rock or a chair. Apparently, she discovers, she can "become" things in this way only by partially absorbing them. Kristin finds that she is draining away Carl's talent and even his personality by the sheer force of her empathy with him. He himself has no idea what is going on, but finds himself losing consciousness during what her father calls her "comatose periods." He awakens feeling drained and old and shaken; and when he tries to paint her portrait, he finds that it is in fact his own he has painted. (But badly; Kristin, who has temporarily taken him over, isn't much of a painter.)

Kristin wants Carl to play sun to her moon, to "predominate," as she puts it; she feels he will be strong enough to resist her inadvertent power. But it is doubtful whether or not Carl in fact possesses enough strength to justify her faith. " 'It is as if I have surrendered my being to an alien force and it has made me less,' " he thinks, just before one of these moments of "invasion." Kristin herself says of her love and her powers of metamorphosis:

If only...I turned into trees or stones or earth when I'm
with him, it couldn't hurt him. But this way...I am like
a leech, a vampire, sucking his strength from him—the
moon eclipsing the sun...I cannot be with him without
stealing into him and erasing his own identity.

On the eve of her wedding, she finds herself faced with an
agonizing problem. She loves Carl and wants to marry him,
but she feels she must find "a solution that would protect
Carl" from her:

As we are, if I marry him, it will mean the complete
merging of two personalities. But the truth rushed to her
out of the night: it will mean the obliteration of two
personalities. That is, she thought slowly, the words like
heavy sacks that had to be carried together to form a
sentence, that is, if I have a personality of my own. For I
am a chameleon, she thought, absorbing the colours about
me and our marriage will submerge us, wipe us out as the
sun obliterates the markings of water on a stone.

The solution that she finds is worse than the problem.
During the night, she allows herself to "become" the storm-
tossed trees outside her window, projecting her soul into
their substance, except that this time she does not return to
her body. The woman Carl marries the next day is a soulless
automaton, emotionless and almost idiotic, who goes through
the motions of their life together with no joy and no pain.
The "real" Kristin has been completely absorbed by the
trees; to all intents and purposes she *is* a tree, and Carl—his
talent destroyed by this harrowing experience, and still not
knowing what has caused her to change—leaves her in
despair. The book ends, not with a description of Kristin's
reaction (for presumably she will have none), but with a
cinematic cut to the external landscape, which we must by
now presume to be the same as the inside of her head:

The sun and a small wind broke the surface of the lake to
glinting sword blades. On the far side, where the trees
marched, unchecked, right down to the water's edge, there

the lake was a shifting pattern of scarlet, vermilion and
burnt orange.

Kristin, like Tay John, has been absorbed back into the
nature that produced her.

But then, love affairs between men and the moon, or
men and trees, or mortals and faery queens, never did
work out very well, if mythology and folklore are to be
believed. It is odd to find a dryad in Canadian literature,
even though she is disguised as a rather frothy socialite,
but that is obviously what Kristin is. (All the objects she
chooses to "become" are natural ones; she does not, for
instance, ever "become" a motor car.[5]) Kristin and Tay John
are both figures of this sort, demi-gods, with unusual births
and strange attributes; like satyrs and their ilk, they are
bridges joining the human world, the natural world and
the supranatural world.

I have now mentioned four creatures, in four separate
books: two, the *wendigo* and Coyote, who are completely
non-human, gods or devils, incarnations of their respective
natural environments, and two, Tay John and Kristin, who
are semi-human but still strongly linked to nature. It would
now seem proper to examine the next rung down on the
hierarchical scale, which ought to be a priest figure if we are
using an epic analogy, or a poet or artist if we are using a
pastoral one.[6] Such a figure would be human but magical,
and in twentieth-century Canada he is likely to be a magician, for what is stage magic but ritual from which the
religion has been removed?

Two well-known Canadian authors have created magicians; they are, of course, Robertson Davies, in his Magnus
Eisengrim trilogy, and Gwendolyn MacEwen, who creates a
whole series of magicians which bear a strong generic like-
ness to one another. It would be hard to find two writers
whose approaches to prose fiction are more different; yet

their magicians have a few things in common. Both are artist figures, and both are in fact Canadian, although both disguise this plebeian origin under an assumed name. (The implication is that you can't be both Canadian and magic; or you can, but no one will believe in you if you reveal your dull grey origins.)

MacEwen specializes in magician as artist as Christ.[7] (In her first novel, *Julian the Magician*, the magician actually insists on being crucified, just to see if he can be resurrected.) Her characters are not only called magicians, they actually are; that is, they seem able actually to perform superhuman feats. Davies' Magnus Eisengrim, on the other hand, is a professional magician, the creator of a very good magic show based on the principles of illusion. But the reader is always left wondering whether MacEwen's magicians are really what they claim to be, or just clever frauds, or perhaps a little insane; whereas Davies weights the evidence in favour of the belief that Eisengrim may in fact have sold his soul to the devil.

Two of the stories in MacEwen's collection, *Noman* (1972), [8] are attempts to reconcile the Otherworld of the magical with the resolutely non-magical world of Canada, which MacEwen spells with a "K." In her earlier works these two places were always kept separate and opposed; the magic world was ancient Egypt, or the Arabian Middle East, or Greece; it contained miracles. Kanada was the place of bacon and eggs, of non-revelations, and it had to be escaped from, either mentally or physically, if you wanted any vision other than the mundane. But in "Kingsmere," which is not really a story but a description, MacEwen explores the possibilities of what she calls "Noman's land:" Mackenzie King's artificial ruins. What strikes her is the relationship between the remnants of the past (mostly European) and the landscape that frames them, or rather, that they frame:

He reassembled these broken bits of history to frame or
emphasize certain aspects of the landscape. He made
naked windows and doors for the forest and the hills.
    You stand on a terrace flanked by a row of unreal
Grecian columns. You look through a classic arch and see,
not Athens, not Rome nor even Palmyra, but the green
Gatineau hills of Kanada. You wonder if the landscape
protests these borrowed histories, these imported ruins.

For MacEwen, Kingsmere is a time-travel place, a
doorway between the past and the future:

You walk farther down, toward the interior of the
garden. Something isn't right. Into whose future are you
moving? . . . You have spotted one very large arch at the
far end of the field, and for a second you have an intense,
blinding perception of the real nature of the place. This
stone on stone, this reconstruction of a past that was never
yours, this synthetic history. Only the furtive trees are
real. Here there is a tension between past and future, a
tension so real it's almost tangible; it lives in the stone,
it crackles like electricity among the leaves.
    He tried to transplant Europe, to bring it here among
the stark trees and silent trails, but
    There, beyond the arch, is the forest.

The narrator in "Kingsmere" is afraid to pass through this
magic arch. Not so Noman, the central character in the story
of that name. Noman is the magician as Kanadian; his
name, in addition to being Ulysses' pseudonym, is probably
intended to symbolize the famous Kanadian identity crisis.
At first he pretends he cannot understand English, and his
friends construct all kinds of exotic nationalities and identities for him, "imagining a thousand possible tongues for
him, for somehow it was incongruous that he could have
worn so beautiful a coat, or danced so well in Kanada." He
finally reveals the awful truth, and his friend Kali, who has
been cooking exotic foods for him, calls him a monster and
feeds him a can of pork and beans in disgust. He shares with

Kristin the ability to become "whatever he encountered," and he seems to have worked in a carnival as a clown, an escape artist, and finally a dancer. With his thousand possible identities and his refusal to choose just one, he sets himself up (or is set up by his author) as Kanada incarnate. "Kanada," he sighs. "Papermaker. Like a great blank sheet in the world's diary. Who'll make the first entry?"

As Kanada, he sets himself the task of solving his own identity crisis, and this is where he links up with "Kingsmere." He speaks to Kali:

> "Let's possess the future as surely as we possess the past!"
>
> "But you don't *have* a past," I winked at him in the mirror.
>
> "Yes I do, damn it! I'll tell you about it later. Let's become the masters of time, let's *move into* time!"
>
> "To pave the way for our descendants?" I laughed.
>
> "No," he said, and looked at me strangely. "For our *ancestors*. They're the ones who are trapped."
>
> I didn't feel like questioning him, so I let him go on.
>
> "We've inherited this great Emptiness," he said. "An empty door that leads into the forest and the snow. No man can get through..."
>
> "Can *you?*" I asked, though I wasn't sure what he was talking about.
>
> "Yes," he said, "I think I can."

He goes about this process, which will apparently make it possible to move into the future by rediscovering and releasing the past, in three stages. First he and Kali make love, and then sit applying metaphors to their bodies;

> We sat cross-legged like children proudly comparing the maps of our bodies—the birthmarks, scars, incisions, beauty-spots, all the landmarks of our lives, those we were born with and those we'd incurred. New trails broken in the forest, old signposts no longer used, footprints of forest animals who come in the night, places of fire, places of water, portages, hill.

The metaphors, which at the beginning of the story were resolutely polyglot European, are now just as resolutely Kanadian, though they are natural rather than the canned pork-and-beans Kanadian ones we have had earlier. Next, he stages his own death, which is Kali's idea:

> "Noman, I have the answer to all your problems."
> "And what is it, Kali?"
> "You must die."
> "That's the answer to everybody's problem." he said.
> "No," I told him, "I mean you must stage a mock death, a brilliant scene in which we'll all participate. Then you can be born again, *maybe even assume a real name.*"9

Finally, after this fraudulent imitation of Christ, he and Kali go to Kingsmere, "Noman's land," and Noman peels off his clothes and makes it through the magic arch:

> He spotted an arch at one end of the terrace, like an ancient door that led into the forest, the final mystery...
> "Coming Kali?" he asked again, and when I didn't answer he went on farther into the spooky greyness....
> "Noman, what are we *doing* here?" I cried. "Whose past have we stolen? Into whose future are we moving?"
> And he (swiftly removing his clothes) called back to me—"Why, our own, of course!"
> And blithely stepped, stark naked, through the arch.

We are not told what "real name" he will assume, what the future is like on the other side of the arch, or what becomes of Noman, but by the nature of the story, and of MacEwen's Kanada itself, we can't know. It's interesting, though, that Noman's possession of himself involves an entry into the forest; in fact the end of the story is reminiscent of both O'Hagan and Page.

What we might call "the sacrificial fade-out" seems to be typical of these Canadian demi-gods and magician priests: their death or disappearance is chosen, and seems to have some element of sacrifice in it, but unlike traditional sacrifices, such as Christ's, it doesn't save or even benefit anyone else, and is more in the nature of an abdication or departure. The sacrificial fade-out is a MacEwen specialty. It's present in almost all of her magician stories, including her two novels, *Julian the Magician* and *King of Egypt, King of Dreams*; but it is most explicit, perhaps, in her short story, "The Second Coming of Julian the Magician," a serio-comic treatment of the dilemma of a real magic man in a non-magical age and country. Julian materializes on Christmas Day, 1970, at noon, at the top of a ferris wheel in "a second-rate carnival." The magic signs of his birth are "three white balloons" in his left hand and "an inverted crucifix made out of red and green tinsel paper" in the middle of his forehead. The left-handedness and the inversion are significant, as is the tinsel paper: Julian is a tacky upside-down Christ, fated to be tacky and upside-down by the lack of faith of his potential believers. He realizes that in this incarnation he has a choice of performing in carnivals or in "cheap burlesque halls," and that his iconography is contained only in comic books and people's dreams:

> In the comic books my cloak is red, green or yellow; there are little wings on my boots, little wings on my head, lightning bolts or sacred hammers in my fists. Only the children worship me now.

He is "Atman, his identity hidden only by a 'B' at the beginning of his name."

But even when he walks on walls or makes it rain or creates black fire, his audiences are bored or uneasy, since they believe "it's all done with mirrors," his magic mere trickery. And a lot of it is. He's a student of Houdini and Blackstone, although he insists that even tricks and illusions are real magic as long as they are believed: "the Master of Illusions doesn't make you believe what he wishes, but what you wish." His failure is the failure of the audience:

> During my acts no-one swooned; no-one approached me afterwards with nervous diseases for me to cure. (How

very different from my last life when the peasants regarded me as holy man, a healer. But then this is North
America. Could Christ have taught in Rome?)

He quickly realizes that his "enemy" is the Twentieth
Century itself, the Dr. Zero of the comics, the Power House
of the city, the Machine. He had a terrible nightmare, in
which a Fat Woman named Reality ("But you can call me
Reali for short") grabs his magic wand and chases him with
it. Reality and the city and the machine are one, and he
refuses to be "tricked into reality." He decides to destroy the
electrical city by blowing up the Power House where he has
a job as night watchman, and he accomplishes this, in fact or
fantasy. Then, observed only by the children who are his
sole congregation, he performs an apotheosis, disappearing
from the top of the ferris wheel in the same way he appeared.
His encounter with reality has not been a pleasant one.

"Yet still I wave this wand like a sarcastic tongue at the
universe... know myself to be both icon and iconoclast,"
says Julian, a speech that could have been made as well by
Robertson Davies' Magnus Eisengrim. He would have
phrased it differently, however. For MacEwen, the magician
is a poet, concerned with the transforming power of the
Word; for Davies he is clearly a novelist, concerned with
illusions produced by hard work and a meticulous attention
to detail. MacEwen's magicians want to control the universe,
but Davies' contents himself with controlling the minds of
the audience. Julian creates real birds out of mud, and
nobody cares because nobody can believe he's really done it.
Eisengrim gives them fake snow on a stage, but does it so
well that it looks real. This is his magic: he's applauded, not
for what he does—nobody *really* thinks he's magic—but for
his consummate skill in doing it. Perhaps this is why he's
a professional success and Julian is a failure.

Like "Noman," "Eisengrim" is a pseudonym.[10] Davies'
magician started life in a "Kanadian" small town of the pork
and beans variety, narrow, puritanical, judgmental; his real

name is plain Paul Dempster. His hatred of Canada stems from his persecution at the hands of this town, and its efforts to stifle his childish interest in magic. He is kidnapped by a figure paralleling MacEwen's Fat Lady Reality, a cheap conjuror who abuses him sexually while subjecting him to a bitter apprenticeship in a carnival that is not just second-rate but third-rate. Here he learns a view of magic that is equivalent to the underbelly of God: cynicism, fraud and trickery, cunning as well as conjuring, exploitation, the audience as dupe. From these humble beginnings he works his way up in the world of international magic as, among other things, an escape artist and mechanical genius, with a stopover in the legitimate theatre as a "double," and is finally able to create a distinguished magic show that brings him worldwide fame.

Although he is a consummate artist, he is also, curiously, a kind of non-person, a Noman figure who is no-one because he has the capacity to be everyone, as well as to be invisible. His first job in "Wanless' World of Wonders" is to crouch inside a mechanical monster named Abdullah, who is supposed to be a card-playing automaton but is really a trick worked from inside to defraud the customers. Of this period in his life he says:

> ...when I was in Abdullah, I was Nobody. I was an extension and magnification of Willard; I was an opponent and a baffling mystery to the Rube; I was something to be gawped at, but quickly forgotten, by the spectators. But as Paul Dempster I did not exist. I had found my place in life, and it was as Nobody.

He lives under several pseudonyms from this time on; as the "double" of a famous actor, he takes the curious name of "Mungo Fetch," "fetch" being a Scottish word for an unlucky vision of yourself you see before you die. When he finally creates his own show, its *pièce de résistance* is a much more sophisticated version of Abdullah, a Golem-like oracular brazen head, which utters disturbing truths about members of the audience. Like Abdullah it's a fraud, though like Abdullah its effects on the audience are real and sometimes disastrous; Eisengrim's relationship to it is that of the invisible power. With both Abdullah and the brazen head, however, is some question as to whether Eisengrim is their master or their slave, controlled by the monsters he thinks he is directing and creating.

Eisengrim is "wolvish," a quality which has suggested his last assumed name. It's made clear that this ruthless quality is a result of his hideous early experiences and is responsible for his having survived them. It's also responsible for his success as a magician. Both he and the other characters in the book insist that he's both an artist and a genius, as well as a glorified trickster and fraud, a Master of Illusions. His "wolvishness" is linked to "an intensity of imagination and vision," and to what another character, quoting Spengler, calls "the Magian World View:"

> It was a sense of the unfathomable wonder of the invisible world that existed side by side with a hard recognition of the roughness and cruelty and day-to-day demands of the tangible world. It was a readiness to see demons where nowadays we see neuroses, and to see the hand of a guardian angel in what we are apt to shrug off ungratefully as a stroke of luck. It was religion, but a religion with a thousand gods, none of them all-powerful and most of them ambiguous in their attitude toward man. It was poetry and wonder which might reveal themselves in the dunghill, and it was an understanding of the dunghill that lurks in poetry and wonder.... Wonder is marvellous but it is also cruel, cruel, cruel.

And Eisengrim partakes of the cruelty as well as the magic. On one level Davies' trilogy is about spiritual vampirism, the exercise of sinister, devouring power over others. Eisengrim has been the victim in such a relationship, but he later becomes the devourer. On another level the novels are about retaliation, the justice rather than the mercy of the universe; and such justice is unpleasant, if not sinister. One of Eisengrim's friends says:

> ... the Devil is the setter of prices, and a usurer, as well. You buy from him at an agreed price, but the payments are all on time, and the interest is charged on the whole of the principal, right up to the last payment.

To which Eisengrim replies, "Do you think you can study evil without living it?" He implies that he has lived it, and this is certainly true. Eisengrim's public personality is a deliberate creation; he is, in a way, his own monster, with his own ego incarnate in the brazen head. The last word in the trilogy is "egoist," and it's an open question whether the religion for which Eisengrim acts as magician-priest is really a religion of wonder, as he sometimes claims, or merely a religion of himself, a form of devil-worship.

And this brings us to the last category of magician or monster I'll discuss here. I began with Blake's *wendigo*, a monster representing a destructive external environment, so it's fitting to end with the *wabeno*, a monster representing a destructive internal one. The *wabeno* appears in Wayland Drew's *The Wabeno Feast* (1973), a novel which cuts between two time-streams: a not-so-distant future in which Canada is dissolving into chaos, and the eighteenth-century past, at the peak of the Hudson Bay Company's power. The episodes from the past are told through the journal of a would-be factor, one MacKay, who journeys into the wilderness with his sinister double, Elborn. Early in the voyage, Elborn encourages the *voyageurs* to tell "tales of death and terror:"

> They tell of the wendigo, a mythical creature of Indian lore, and each elaborates on the other's imagining until in his fantasy Elborn beholds a creature thirty feet in height, a naked, hissing demon whose frog-like eyes search out unwary travellers and roll in blood with craving to consume them! Another whispers that the creature lacks lips to cover its shattered teeth, and a third describes its feet

like scabrous canoes on which it rocks howling through the swamps at evening.

MacKay refuses to pay heed to these stories. He is an eighteenth-century man, determined to be practical and rational and to make money; we learn that he has already renounced love and religion.

MacKay does not meet the wendigo, the monster from without. Instead he encounters the wabeno, and in company with Elborn is privileged to witness the singular ceremony staged by the wabeno and his followers on a nearby island. The wabeno is "the most powerful" of the Indian shamans, the translator tells them:

> ...whether his influence be curative or pernicious he knew not, although he thought the latter. The wabeno, he said, would use any means to cure disease or to quench an unrequited love, and those who placed themselves in his influence and used his potions on themselves or on others must submit entirely their will to his, for the remedies might grow extreme... It was good, he added, that the power of the wabeno had declined, and that such sorceries as he practised so as to conjure an overturn of nature grew less common as the Company's influence spread.

The wabeno and his followers differ from other Indians in their height, the "military precision" of their tents, and their white garments. Their skins also are a peculiar shade of white.

The wabeno feast itself is an orgy which begins with murder and cannibalism, continues as a frenzied dance in which the performers leap through fire so that their sexual organs are burned away, and ends with the wabeno setting fire to the entire island. The wabeno and his band vanish, although no-one knows whether or not they have died in the fire:

> Elborn maintained that they had fled, and that they would spread their dementia like a plague until the last had been

run to earth; but for my own part I believe that we had heard the dawn crying of the loons, and that the shaman and his band had found that morning the death which they had sought so eagerly.

Although the wabeno makes only one appearance in the novel, he is its organizing symbol. The translator opposes the wabeno to the Company, but in fact they stand for the same things: the desire for power through the destruction of others, which in the end is the same as self-destruction. MacKay, who dedicates himself to the Company's goals of accumulating beaver skins by debauching the Indians so they will want trade goods, is insane by the end of the book. In fact he was probably insane at its beginning; his mocker and shadow, Elborn, appears to exist in his own mind only, and when he kills Elborn he is, like Poe's William Wilson, killing himself. MacKay's story counterpoints the twentieth-century half of the book; here we see the spirit of the wabeno infecting the whole of society. It is of course significant that the wabeno and his band are white; the only Indians in the book who are able to live in dignity and self-sufficiency, without drunkenness, murder and disease, are those who have made a vow not to mingle with the white traders or use any of their goods,[11] just as the only twentieth-century characters who escape the destruction of society, both physical and spiritual, are those who choose to make a canoe journey alone into the wilderness.

It is usual for a critic to present some general conclusions at the end of an effusion such as this. I'm not sure that I have any to offer; as I noted, I'm a mere collector of Canadian monsters, and I present them so that their rarity and exotic beauty may be admired, not necessarily in order to interpret them. There are many more phenomena of a similar kind; ghosts, witches, talismans, time travellers, premonitory dreams, poltergeists and affairs with bears (this latter seems to be a peculiary Canadian interest, as I've collected three). But I've surely dredged up enough specimens to indicate that there is indeed "a mass of dark intimations" in the Canadian literary soul.

I have also arranged my specimens in a rough paradigm, which, curiously, corresponds to the order in which their respective books were written. The wendigo and Coyote, which we may call "environmental forces" or Monsters as Other, come from quite early books,[12] as do the two demigods or "magic people" I've mentioned. The magicians, on the other hand, are creatures of the sixties and seventies, and seem rather more concerned, symbolically, with man's relationship to his society and to himself, as opposed to his relationship with the natural environment. The final example, the wabeno, combines both concerns in a rather allegorical and very contemporary fashion. In the tradition of the horror movie, I've begun with a terrifying thunderstorm and ended with a man-made conflagration; that is, I've begun with a story which plays upon man's fear of natural power and ended with one illustrating the dangers inherent in his own lust for power. The connection between this pattern and the changes in Canadian society and outlook over the last sixty years is perhaps too obvious to be mentioned. In any case, such a critical pattern exists in the mind of the critic rather than in the external world. Perhaps the critic is himself a kind of magician, for, as Julian the Magician says, in his incantation for making an egg disappear:

> ... *like everything else in the universe its existence depends on your seeing it — that alone — and its existence is the gift of your inner eye.*

And, in the face of this, who will say there are no wendigos, or that the picture of Mackenzie King's mother does not actually talk? There is more to Kanada than meets the eye . . .

NOTES

1 "Oratorio for Sasquatch, Man and Two Androids" in *Poem for Voices*, Canadian Broadcasting Corporation, 1970. The first eleven lines are not mine.

2 I could suggest two reasons for this, neither of which have anything to do with innate lack of *panache* on the part of Canadian fiction writers. The first is that the Canadian fiction tradition developed largely in the twentieth century, not the romantic nineteenth. The second is that in a cultural colony a lot of effort must go into simply naming and describing observed realities, into making the visible real even for those who actually live there. Not much energy is left over for exploring other, invisible realms.

3 "Visions Before Midnight," *Circuit*, 1970.

4 *The Sun and the Moon* was first published under the pseudonym Judith Cape.

5 She does "become" a chair, but only on the level of its molecules.

6 Epic: gods, semi-divine heroes, priests and oracles. Pastoral: Nature, satyrs etc., singing shepherds.

7 See her early poem, "The Magician as Christ."

8 See also "The Return of Julian the Magician" in the same collection.

9 The italics are mine.

10 See Robertson Davies, *Fifth Business* (1970), and *The Manticore* (1972), but with special reference to *World of Wonders* (1975).

11 Compare also the story of Kakumee and the Tornak in Farley Mowat's *People of the Deer*. Here also the spirit of the "whites" is seen as a demon and its influence on the native people is entirely destructive.

12 Sheila Watson's *The Double Hook*, although published in 1959, was actually written a decade earlier.

27
Adrienne Rich:
Of Woman Born

(1976)

Adrienne Rich is not just one of America's best feminist poets or one of America's best woman poets, she is one of America's best poets. Her most exemplary poems are read not because they are supposed to be good for us, but because they are good, and in some cases (which is all any poet can ask for) they are very good. This is not to deny the feminist content of her poems, or their sometimes overtly polemical intent. At her best, Rich pulls off what few poets with the courage of their convictions can ever manage: she is eloquent, she convinces and inspires. She is a serious writer and an important one, and her prose book on the institution of motherhood is a serious and important book.

"Motherhood?" The very word evokes the trivial. "It's a motherhood issue," we say, meaning that no one could be against it. "American as Mom and apple pie," we say, meaning banal, but comforting, permanent, healthy, a *given*. But it's the unexamined assumptions behind phrases like this that Rich is writing about. Such assumptions, she says, are unwarranted; in fact, *all* assumptions about "motherhood" are unwarranted, because it is something we really know very little about. Science would back her up: even among young primates, such as baboons, "mothering" is not an instinct. It is a learned process, and female primates isolated in youth from models of "mothering" reject their offspring. What then do we learn about mothering, what are we taught? The sum of these things and their hidden rationales constitute motherhood as an "institution;" the way they shape how women live their lives, and the conflicts between what women are taught they should be feeling and doing and what they actually feel and do, constitute motherhood as "experience."

Rich is writing about pernicious myths. One of the most pernicious, of course, is that mothering is an instinct, that it simply wells up in all "real" women who give birth to children (and according to the same myth, a woman who does not give birth to children is not a "real" woman; she is a cipher). Once a biological mother, you will automatically become a Madonna, a virtuous model of self-sacrifice and devotion. This myth is pernicious because it leaves many women feeling inadequate, baffled or even evil if the promised happiness and fulfillment fail to materialize. It also means that few wish to teach motherhood or even discuss it: why teach an "instinct?" The very suggestion that mothering is not an instinct opens up a number of worm-cans that not only most men but most women prefer to keep tightly closed. To question the institution at all—that set of beliefs which requires mothers to be at once both superhuman and sub-human—is to evoke the most primal and deeply threatening fears going around, fear of rejection by one's own mother. Yet, as Rich says, we all have mothers; every adult in this society was raised by a person who was expected to be a "mother," to take primary and largely single responsibility for her children, who felt thwarted by this and projected her resentment onto her children to a greater or lesser degree. Many did not choose motherhood; it was thrust upon them by a society unwilling to provide either contraception or recognized and dignified opportunities for any other occupation but "housewife." If we learn mothering from our mothers, would it not be better to replace the present institution with one with less built-in resentment?

This seems to me the question at the core of the book, though Rich touches ground elsewhere. There are interesting chapters on historical motherhood, bits of information on such diverse but pertinent subjects as the development of obstetrical forceps, the takeover of midwifery by male doctors, puerperal fever (often caused because the attending physician had come straight from the dissection of corpses without washing his hands), the rise of the factory system and its effects on home life, the segregation of women and children from fathers by the institutions of "work" and "the home." There are reflections on the paucity of female-centered mythologies, with the Core-Persephone myth cited as a meaningful exception. Rich is most moving on the subject of her own life as a mother. It would be nice to be able to say that her experiences of the fifties—the drugged childbirths, the hostile hospitals, the incredible pressures from relatives, the isolation, the consequent guilt and rage—are things of the past, but notwithstanding the advent of more human obstetrical practices and definitions of "motherhood" that allow more freedom, her experiences are probably still typical for a large part of the female population.

This is an important book, but it is not flawless. One could quibble about many points. Some will question the historical and anthropological material, others the theoretical underpinnings. Some are bound to find the book too harsh on men: if women are objecting to being lumped together as Woman, cannot men be given credit for their individualities too? Aren't there any *nice* men? Don't some men love their children, too? I myself would question the rather sensationalistic last chapter, which takes off from the case of a woman who chopped up her two youngest children on the front lawn of her suburban house and goes on to suggest that such emotions and such actions are possible for all mothers under "the system." The work of Mary Van Stolk on battered children indicates that this is simply not so, any more than child-battering is a possibility for everyone. (It isn't, says Van Stolk; only for those who have learned it, often by being battered themselves. But the axioms of our society encourage it, just as they encourage rage in mothers.)

This is a book that can be quarelled with, but it cannot be ignored, or dismissed because of this or that fine point, this or that emphasis. To write a flawless book on this subject would be impossible; to write a popular one would be equally impossible, because Rich is saying a number of things many would rather not hear. However, it was not Rich's intention to write a flawless book or a popular one; rather, she wished to open a dialogue, a dialogue which must be pursued. There is really nothing less at stake than the future of the human race. If "mothering" is learned, then ways of mothering can be changed; if "mothering" is learned, so is "fathering." And so are violence, cruelty, aggression, punishment, and war. These things are learned by children, absorbed by them before school age; under the current system, young children are "taught" almost exclusively by isolated, guilty, squashed, trapped, tired, bored and thwarted women, who are taught to believe that they themselves are second-rate failures and children are at once their punishment, their vindication and their fate. How much better if children could be *chosen*, and loved for what they are, not viewed as an inadequate substitute for a "career" or some kind of parasitic burden?

Rich's final view is not against mothering. On the contrary:

> The mother's battle for her child—with sickness, with poverty, with war, with all the forces of exploitation and callousness that cheapen human life—needs to become a common human battle, waged in love and in the passion for survival. But for this to happen, the institution of motherhood must be destroyed...
>
> To destroy the institution is not to abolish motherhood. It is to release the creation and sustenance of life into the same realm of decision, struggle, surprise, imagination, and conscious intelligence, as any other difficult, but freely chosen work.

This book is about "why." "How" is another question.

28

Marie-Claire Blais:

St. Lawrence Blues

(1976)

Marie-Claire Blais is undoubtedly the Quebec writer best-known outside Quebec. In fact, it is perhaps through her work, especially the much-praised *A Season in the Life of Emmanuel* and *The Manuscripts of Pauline Archange*, that Quebec itself is best-known outside Quebec, at least as a country of the imagination. She is almost unique among Quebec writers in that her work has been translated into twelve languages. She has won France's most coveted literary prize, the Prix Medicis, as well as several other awards, and she's drawn the attention of numerous critics, most importantly the late Edmund Wilson, who singled her out for special praise in his book *O Canada*.

Her reputation has been fairly earned. The dozen or so novels, the several volumes of poetry, the seven plays for stage or radio she's written during her brief but incandescent career display an astonishing range of style and subject, from the experimental and dream-like to the grimly realistic, from the bleak lives of impoverished children on Quebec's back streets to the convoluted philosophical musings of Baudelarian social outcasts who choose crime or suicide as their only means of protest. Although sometimes intimidated by the uncompromising nature of her books, critics have always been dazzled by their brilliance of execution.

This brilliance was apparent early. Blais made her literary debut in 1959 at the age of nineteen, with *La Belle Bête (Mad Shadows)*, an hallucinatory tale of jealousy, hatred, mutilation and incest set in a lurid and only semi-real rural Quebec. The contrast between her age and her subject matter was sensational, and she was treated as a "discovery," both in Quebec and in English Canada. Much was made of her background of comparative poverty, her shoeboxes full of novels, her lack of formal education—she'd dropped out of school at fifteen and taken secretarial jobs in order to support herself—and the precocious intensity of her writing. Some critics saw her as a young genius, others as a child prodigy who would burn out early. It took her several years and as many novels to recover from her initial notoriety and prove herself as a serious writer.

It's paradoxical that a writer whose name has been so closely associated with the Quebec cultural renaissance, the "quiet revolution" of the early sixties, one who was recognized abroad as its major and sometimes as its only literary voice, should have spent these important years outside the country. But her exile was not intentional. She went where her fortunes took her: first to Paris on a Canada Council grant, where she underwent the painful experience of being treated as a hopeless provincial in the city regarded at that time as the French cultural Mecca; then to New England, where she mingled with the Cape Cod artistic community and taught herself English by reading the novels of Jane Austen; later to Brittany, where she lived and wrote on a communal seven-acre farm. But although she was not physically present in Quebec, she was certainly there in spirit, and no one who has read the work of Jacques Ferron, Roch Carrier or Réjean Ducharme, to name a few, can doubt her right to membership in the Quebec literary community. In the past fifteen years,

Quebec has evolved a manner as well as a matter which is unique and unmistakable, and Marie-Claire Blais has been central to that evolution.

She has recently moved back to Quebec, where she is currently re-establishing her roots and becoming acquainted with the new Quebec which came into being during her absence. For her there are two Quebecs. The old one was characterized by brutality, suffering and repression, symbolized by those sadistic nuns and slightly mad priests, those hulking, child-beating farmers and the tubercular urban poor that haunt her books. This was, at least in part, the Quebec of her own convent-educated childhood. For her it was a society that specialized in judging, condemning and punishing, and, although as a novelist she might be expected to feel some regret at the disappearance of a society that has provided so much of her own subject matter, she is not sorry to see it go. The new Quebec, she thinks, is a far different place: vibrant, alive, with a new confidence and freedom. But although she is enthusiastic about the changes, she is less certain about the intense political activity and awareness that brought at least some of them into being. Writers, she feels, should observe and record; they cross the line into political involvement at their own peril: "A writer is a *temoin*, a witness," she has said. "Dogmatism closes a writer off."

In some ways, *St. Lawrence Blues* is the first book in which Blais has attempted to bridge the gap between the old Quebec and the new one, to show representatives of both encountering each other, disputing, reacting. As such it's a very ambitious work, wide in scope, swarming with characters, aiming for breadth as well as depth. Blais has done many detailed studies of single characters, but *St. Lawrence Blues* is populous and many-faceted.

It's a fresh departure for her in other ways as well. She has always been amazingly versatile, switching with ease from romantic fantasy to novels of ideas to psychological studies to carefully-drawn social chronicles. But *St. Lawrence Blues* is

none of these. The predominant note is satire. It's not a totally
new element for Blais, as her previous work has often
contained satirical and even humorous interludes; but these
were asides, whereas in *St. Lawrence Blues* the tone is
constant.

The book takes the reader on a tour through the seamy
layers of present-day Quebec. The narrator is a Quebecois
Everyman, an amiable minor rascal and self-proclaimed
nonentity nicknamed Ti-Pit, "little nobody." Ti-Pit is an
orphan who feels he belongs nowhere. Earlier in his life he's
been put through one of these repressive nun-run orphanages
so familiar to the readers of Blais; later, he's been hired out to
a brutal farmer. Now he's a drifter, living in roominghouses,
working at degrading jobs until he can no longer stand them,
getting by however he can. Everything interests him but he
trusts nobody; consequently he is close-mouthed with his
friends and associates, but carries on a constant silent
conversation with himself. *St. Lawrence Blues* is the trans-
cription of this oral diary, and it's evident from its verbal
richness, astute commentary and improvised fantasies that
despite his stunting and dehumanizing background Ti-Pit
has somehow been able to retain both his mother-wit and
his humanity.

Through his shrewd yet innocent eyes we are allowed to
view a wide assortment of Quebecois, some sinister, some
grotesque, some pathetic: Baptiste, an old-style working class
drudge who is finally rewarded for his years of slavery at the
Rubber Company by being fired so the boss won't have to
give him a pension; his son Ti-Guy, an incurable addict,
despised and neglected by his conservative father just as
the father has been despised by society; Vincent, the
worker-priest, constantly defrauded by those he tries to help;
Mère Fontaine, the motherly, sentimental owner of Ti-Pit's
boardinghouse, who steeps herself in police and murder literature and lives vicariously through her tenants, which include
Mimi, a babyfaced female impersonator, Lison, a pregnant

nymphomaniac, and two fifteen-year-old lesbian prostitutes, Josée and Monique. Through a chance encounter in a tavern, Ti-Pit is introduced to a side of Quebec life new to him: he meets Papillon, a verbose, self-aggrandizing poet who wants Ti-Pit to teach him *joual*, the language of the people, so he can use it to further his own literary ambitions. Papillon's friends include a shady lawyer from Quebec City who is writing a pornographic novel, Corneille the publisher, and Papineau, named ironically for a nineteenth century Quebec patriot, a phoney Marxist ascetic who demonstrates his own ideological purity by attacking that of his friends, and forces his wife to live on rice while he himself is having a secret affair with a lush rich-living Westmount matron. Papillon's wife is involved in a peculiar brand of Quebec feminism: she and her friends storm the *Men Only* section of Ti-Pit's tavern, disrupting a few old alcoholics and proclaiming their right to drink Molson's on an equal footing. Papillon himself is annoyed by this because he feels she's stolen his own political cause by becoming even more *joualonese* than he himself has been able to. The bourgeoise intelligentsia in *St. Lawrence Blues* treat political ideas as if they are dog bones, squabbling over sole possession; a situation familiar to anyone who has watched the ultra-nationalist fringes in the rest of Canada during the past few years.

These people are all diversions for Ti-Pit: fascinating and amusing, but not central to his real life. His own past reappears in the form of Ti-Cul, his best friend from orphanage days. Whereas Ti-Pit has adjusted to his half-life by trying to stay out of trouble, Ti-Cul is a savage pessimist who has embraced it. He writes violent, bitter letters to Ti-Pit from prison, and when he gets out he butchers the farmer who once victimized them both. Instead of applauding, Ti-Pit finds the crime sickening and rejects Ti-Cul's efforts to involve him. He too has hated the farmer for his brutality, but he does not see greater brutality as the proper response. He is not interested in the role of the romantic rebel, or indeed in any of the roles being played out by those around him.

Blais brings all the elements of her broad social canvas together at the end of the book in a giant demonstration against social injustice, which is supposed to be heroic but instead turns into a combination of farce and tragedy. The groups of demonstrators, including nuns, prostitutes, students, fishermen, homosexuals, and even some disgruntled policemen who feel the public is not grateful enough, wallow about in the ever-present snow, exchange insults, scuffle and shout each other down until the police break up the march with needless viciousness, killing a student in the process. Only then can the bewildered and injured treat each other with anything resembling kindness and humanity. For Blais, ideology separates, suffering unites.

Reading *St. Lawrence Blues* is like listening to the many voices of Quebec arguing among themselves. It's a domestic argument, and as such, parts of it are not totally comprehensible to an outsider. There are private grudges, puns on names and titles, snide references, innuendos and complicated in-group jokes. But like all domestic arguments, it provides more intimate and in many ways more accurate insights into the personalities of those concerned than their polished official facades would ever give away. This is the book of a culture laughing at itself; though as befits a colonized culture, the laughter is not totally lighthearted, not without bitterness and a characteristic Quebecois sense of macabre irony.

It's important to remember that *St. Lawrence Blues* was originally called *Un Joualonais, Sa Joualonie*, a title whose virtual untranslatability underlines not only the courage of the translator but the nature of the special situation the book deals with. Ti-Pit's kingdom, his *"joualonie,"* is a colony within a colony within a colony: the lower classes oppressed by the rich French within Quebec and by the English who control both of them, oppressed in their turn by their economic position *vis-à-vis* the United States. "Maitres Chez Nous," the rallying-cry of the early Separatist Movement, indicates what was lacking; a sense of control over one's own cultural and economic destiny. *Joual* is the language spoken by the "joualonie" (the term comes from a dialect form of the French word "cheval"), the language of the man on the street, the "little guy," the "assholes" who demonstrate at the end of the book.

And here there's a joke within a joke, for Blais herself has been criticized by certain ultra-*joualonist* Quebec literary figures for her early work and its lack of purity according to their standards. For them *joual* is a shibboleth: those who speak it pass, those who don't fail. But in *St. Lawrence Blues* Blais out-*jouals* the most ardent *joualonists*, thereby proving that she can do it too, while at the same time jumping these pretensions through hoops of her own construction.

Every character in the book is defined by his or her relationship to this language. Ti-Pit himself is a natural inhabitant of "joualonie," and its logical product. Papillon the poet, on the other hand, has had to learn it—his own language would have been a more Parisian middle-class French—and like all converts he overdoes it: he speaks it self-consciously, proclaiming its virtues at every turn and sprinkling his conversation with oaths such as "holy pyx" and "bleeding veronica" in a way that makes the strictly-trained Ti-Pit blink. Papillon is a linguistic purist; at one point he picks a fight over an English-language restaurant, declaring, "Revolution, the dignity of our people, is a matter of details, of bacon and eggs." He longs to be accepted as one of the people and writes in what he considers to be "pure" *joual*; yet he is constantly being attacked by those further to the left. One of his most crushing humiliations comes when he has an affair with a Parisienne, who has trouble understanding his accent, calls him a "noble savage," and patronizes him in much the same way that he himself patronizes Ti-Pit.

The irony of the Quebec situation as depicted in *St. Lawrence Blues* is that the real *joualonese*, the natives, don't care about their language. If they think about it at all, it's as a sign of their lack of education, their oppression, their inability to make themselves understood. The most poignant example of this is Ti-Foin ("little hay" or "hayseed"), a poor farmer's son who has come to Montreal because he couldn't stand the wretchedness of life at home. "I want to talk to you like a man," he says; then he bursts into tears, declaring that he has no words because nobody has given him any. It is only the *petit-intelligentsia* who idealize *joual*, while at the same time using it to score points against one another and exploiting it for their own ideological or artistic ends. Their world is permeated with an inverse snobbery which Ti-Pit himself cannot understand. He admires the big cars and plush apartments of the intelligentsia, as well as the contents of their overstocked refrigerators, but he has little use for their slogans.

However, *St Lawrence Blues* is far from being simply a political allegory. Ti-Pit is a fully developed character in his own right, and it's against his very human personality that the frivolity, viciousness and bloodless idealism of the others are measured. His motives are simple: he wants to be happy, to get as much as he can from life, despite its limited prospects. Behind his protective cynicism and his taciturn exterior, he has a love of words and of what they can describe, and a practical charity most of the other characters lack. As he is a bastard and an orphan himself, he sympathizes with underdogs of all kinds; he even defends Ti-Cul the murderer. He dislikes the death, violence and squalor which surround him, and resists the despair of Ti-Guy, the hatred and destructiveness of Ti-Cul and the nihilism of his co-worker the ambulance-driver, for whom all human life is worthless and expendable. Despite much evidence that would refute him, he believes that "life is better than limbo."

The novel's loosely-constructed, frenetic and sometimes wandering narrative is held together by one single thread: Ti-Pit's search for a sense of self-worth, for an identity. His real name is not Ti-Pit at all: it is Abraham Lemieux, and someone calls him by this name for the first time in his life at the beginning of the novel. "Ti-Pit" means "nobody;" Abraham

Lemieux, however, has quite a different connotation. Abraham was the father of a people, and "Lemieux" means "the best." "Come to think of it," Ti-Pit remarks, "Lemieux has a noble, cheerful ring...." Throughout his wanderings and encounters, Ti-Pit is looking for some element in his society which will recognize him, and implicitly all those like him, as something more than a bastard and orphan, something more than a nobody. But those of his own class are too helpless, too twisted by cruelty, or too hard-pressed by practical necessities, and the bourgeoise intelligentsia are presented as clowns or absurdities who have lost touch with human realities in their worship of abstractions. Perhaps, Blais may be suggesting, it is Abraham Lemieux and the qualities he represents—hard-won experience, charity, practical wisdom and a tolerant love of life—who will "father" the emerging society of Quebec. But it's a vague and tenuous hope. At the end of the book, Ti-Pit dreams of meeting Papillon, as he did in the opening chapter. Papillon calls him by his *joual* nickname, and Ti-Pit replies, "Ti-Pit, never heard of him ... my name is Abraham, Abraham Lemieux." But as Ti-Pit himself remarks, it is only a dream.

Blais may be hinting that *joual* and the impoverished kingdom of *joualonie* will have to be changed, renounced, even obliterated, before its inhabitants can attain the human dignity for which they seek. But that event is a long way off, even in imagination, for men like Ti-Pit, who must experience the social conditions which have formed *joualonie*, who can react to them as one reacts to a kick, but who, lacking credible leaders, do not have the power to change them. On this level, *St. Lawrence Blues* is more than an amusing satire. Hidden beneath its surface, as Abraham Lemieux is hidden beneath the surface of Ti-Pit, is the threat of revolution.

29
Audrey Thomas:
Ten Green Bottles, Ladies and Escorts

(1977)

This year marks the tenth anniversary of Audrey Thomas' debut as a writer. *Ten Green Bottles* was first published in the States in 1967. It was out of print for many years, but Oberon has now re-published it, and offers a new book, *Ladies & Escorts*, as a "companion piece." In a way, everything Thomas writes is a companion piece to everything else. More than most writers, she is constantly weaving and re-weaving, cross-referencing, overlapping, even repeating her materials. Both these books are collections of short stories; but, though Thomas' novels threaten to fragment, to splinter into their component images, the experience of reading these books together is much like reading a novel. The stories reinforce and echo each other, even across that ten-year space.

Thomas once said that she writes about "the terrible gap between men and women," and the phrasing is an indication of her even-handed approach. For though her women are usually bewildered, afraid of not being loved, unable to cope and dependent on men though resentful of them, her men are far from being the potent, capable figures these women suppose them to be. When she writes from the point of view of a male character, we are likely to discover a man who feels smothered by such clinging vines, or who feels literally crushed—as in "Aquarius"—by a woman's flaunted sexuality. Men, in their turn, visualize their women as all-powerful goddesses who mock and diminish them. Neither side is able to imagine its own power, only that of the other. It is typical of a Thomas heroine that she should long for a simple domestic life, with husband and children, something pastoral, with a wood stove and home-spun yarn, only to find she is hopeless at lighting fires and afraid of everything outside the door, and that her husband is up to something with the next-door neighbour, while she herself is attracted by the young Indian fishermen down at the fishing dock.

The distance between men and women is only one of the "terrible gaps" Thomas writes about. Her characters often exist in a state of prolonged culture shock. Men against women, reality against arcadia, Europe against America, and, even more starkly, the white West against some country further south, Africa or Mexico—these are the collisions whose psychic contusions she traces. When Thomas' heroines aren't locking themselves in alien bathrooms for fear of snakes, they sometimes have a somnambulistic courage. The white woman dream-walking through a foreign culture, aware of its dangers but not of what they are, unable to understand her surroundings but sure some important truth is hidden there, is a recurrent figure in the Thomas landscape. Isobel of the accomplished novel *Blown Figures* appears again in *Ladies & Escorts*, but the prize sleepwalker here is the hippychild Caroline of "Rapunsel," wandering alone through Africa doing a little vibe-collecting and sketching and keeping a journal in one of Thomas' favourite languages, mirror-writing. Africa finally manifests itself to her not as the friendly nuns and colourful market figures, but as a man she may or may not have dreamed, whose face she never

sees. "Why did you come here?" he asks, before threatening
to rape or kill her. It is incorrect to say, as the Oberon
catalogue does, that for Thomas "the heart of darkness is not
in the interior of Africa ... but in the salons of America."
Her heroines are terrified of Africa because it is terrifying,
and because—like sexual love—they can neither understand
nor control it. Part of the darkness is in them, but, if we are
to believe Thomas' work at all, part of it is really there, just
as in her Mexican stories the grotesque lives of her characters find their counterparts in the actual images supplied to
them by Mexico itself. Thomas didn't need to invent "The
More Little Mummy in the World," a mummified baby on
public display which gives her a fitting reflection of her
heroine's abortion. (This, by the way, is yet another appearance of the lost unborn child, a central image in Thomas'
work from the beginning.)

Thomas is a writers' writer, which shouldn't prevent her
from being a readers' writer as well. She has enormous
verbal skills: a passion for words—words as games, words as
magic or refrain, words as puzzle or multi-leveled pun—a
wonderful ear for dialogue and dialect, a flexible style.
Her fascination with language for its own sake accounts for
much of the sheer panache of her writing, though it occasionally leads her into less successful excesses (as in "Fear
Here," where the outflow of words is not balanced by the
final jugular chop of the story.) She is at her best when her
stylistic gifts and her obsession with language are reflected
by her material. Her finest stories not only demonstrate
language, they are about language: the impossibility, and
the necessity, of using it for true communication.

Her best stories, too, are about the difficulty of doing
whatever it is that she does as a writer. She is not at heart a
"story-teller," that is, a constructor of plots which will carry
in themselves the weight of her meaning. In fact, she is at her
least convincing with her most "finished" plots. Instead she
is a fictionalizer. "Writers are terrible liars," she begins one
story. She then confesses that the story before it was an

inflated distortion of an actual event, and proceeds to tell another story which we are tempted to believe is more "true," until we come to the end and discover the author and the principle character giggling over what names they will have in the story and even what name the story will have. The story, even if "true," is revealed as an artefact. This device—the story told, re-told in a different way, exposed, told again—occurs throughout Thomas' writing. Take the curious case of the African cook-steward. This man appears in two of Thomas' novels, *Mrs Blood* and *Blown Figures*. In these his name is Joseph, and it is Joseph also in one story from *Ten Green Bottles*. In another story a figure clearly based on the same man is called Samuel. He is back again in *Ladies & Escorts*, but this time we are given an entirely different version of where he came from and what happened to him. Is the author just "using material" in one story but telling the truth in the other? We will never know.

Thomas' work is not like a mystery story, where a series of hidden clues add up finally to the one, the inevitable truth. Rather it is—as a whole, and also in its parts—more like a folk-tale collected in several variant forms. No one story is the true story, but the sum of the stories is. A reader will either love this approach for its richness and its surreal echo effects or be very frustrated by it. Those who insist on the cut and dried should probably avoid Thomas.

It's amazing that Audrey Thomas has managed to write as much as she has in the last ten years: three novels, two novellas, and two books of stories. Despite her output and its ambition, range and quality, she has not yet received the kind of recognition such a body of work merits, perhaps because she is that cultural hybrid, an early-transplanted American. Of course her work has flaws; everyone's does. She can be sentimental, repetitious, and sometimes merely gossipy. But page for page, she is one of the country's best writers.

30
Marge Piercy:
Woman on the Edge of Time,
Living in the Open

(1976)

Marge Piercy now has eight books to her credit, four novels and four books of poetry. Her work has always had the courage both of her convictions and of its own (the difference between the two has occasionally been one of her problems), and the present books are no exception. She is a serious writer who deserves the sort of considered attention which, too often, she does not get.

For instance, none of the reviews of *Woman on the Edge of Time* I've read to date seems even to have acknowledged its genre. Most have assumed that the book is intended as a realistic novel, for that is certainly how it starts out. It appears to be the slice-of-life story of a 37-year-old Chicana welfare recipient named Consuelo, whose past history we are given in the first few pages of the book. Consuelo had a child, was deserted by her husband, and subsequently took up with a black, blind pickpocket whose death drove her into a depression in which she accidently broke her daughter's wrist. For this offence she was committed to a mental institution and has had her child taken away from her. The only person left for her to love is her doped-up prostitute niece Dolly, but in defending Dolly she breaks the nose of Dolly's pimp and is recommitted by him. The rest of the book takes place "inside" (with one escape and one visit to the outside) and the descriptions of institutional life are enough to make the reader believe that Connie will be driven mad by sadistic doctors and indifferent attendants. This part of the book is rendered in excruciating, grotty, Zolaesque detail, pill by deadening pill, meal by cardboard meal, ordeal by ordeal, and as a rendition of what life in a New York bin is like for those without money or influence it is totally convincing and depressing.

However, even before Connie is recommitted she has been having visits from a strange creature named Luciente. Luciente turns out to be a visitor from the future; Connie thinks the visitor is a young man and is surprised when she is revealed as a woman. By making contact with Connie's mind, Luciente can help Connie project herself into the world of the future, Luciente's world. Connie travels there extensively, and needless to say the reader goes with her.

Some reviewers treated this part of the book as a regrettable daydream or even a hallucination caused by Connie's madness. Such an interpretation undercuts the entire book. If Connie is insane, her struggles to escape from the institution must be viewed in an entirely different light from that in which the author puts them, and the doctors, the pimp and the indifferent family are somewhat justified in their callous treatment. Other reviewers did not see Connie as insane but took Luciente and her troupe to be a pointless exercise in "science fiction," an exercise which should have no place in a piece of social realism. But Piercy is not that stupid. If she had intended a realistic novel she would have written one. *Woman on the Edge of Time* is a utopia, with all the virtues and shortcomings of the form, and many of the things reviewers found irksome are indigenous to the genre rather than the author.

By *utopia*, I mean books such as Morris's *News from Nowhere*, Bellamy's *Looking Backward*, Hudson's *A Crystal Age*, or even Wyndham's *Consider Her Ways*. These differ greatly from plot-centred otherworld fantasies such as Tolkien's, and though they may share some elements with "science fiction," this category is too broad for them. The books I've mentioned all send an emissary from an oppressive contemporary society into the future as a sort of tourist-journalist, to check out improved conditions and report back. Such books are not really about the hero's adventures, though a love affair of some sort is usually thrown in to sweeten the didactic pill. The real hero is the future society; the reader is intended to comparison-shop in company with the time-traveller, questioning the invariably polite inhabitants and grumbling over disconcerting details. The moral intent of such fables is to point out to us that our own undesirable conditions are not necessary: if things can be imagined differently, they can be done differently.

Hence the inevitable long-winded conversations in which traveller and tour guide, in this case, Connie and Luciente, plod through the day-to-day workings of their societies. What about sewage disposal? birth control? ecology? education? Books of this sort *always* contain conversations like this, and it is to Piercy's credit that she has given us a very human and rather grouchy traveller and a guide who sometimes loses her temper. The world of the future depicted here is closest in spirit perhaps to Morris's. It's a village economy, with each village preserving the ethnic flavour of some worthy present-day minority: American Indian, American Black, European Jewish (suburban WASP is not represented). It is, however, racially mixed, sexually equal, and ecologically balanced. Women have "given up" childbirth in order that men won't regret having given up power, and children are educated more or less communally, with a modified apprentice system. There's quite a lot of advanced bio-feedback, and instant communication through "kenners," which is uncomfortably reminiscent of silliness such as Dick Tracy's two-way wristwatch radios. But they do have communal "fooders," and, I'm happy to note, dishwashers.

Reading utopias is addictive—I found myself skipping through some perfectly acceptable passages about electric shock treatments and visiting hours at the asylum to find out what the inhabitants of Mattapoisett do about breast-feeding (both sexes indulge; men get hormone shots), about motherhood (bottle babies, elective "mothers," production in balance with nature's capacity to support it, adolescent separation rituals), about criminals (if incorrigible they're executed, because no one wants to be a prison guard), even about what they use to mulch cabbages. Writing utopias is addictive too, and Piercy expends a good deal of energy trying to get every last detail *in*, to get it *right*, and to make rather too sure we get the point.

Numerous dangers await the author of a utopia. For one thing, inhabitants of utopias somehow cannot help coming across as slightly sanctimonious and preachy; they've been like that since Thomas More. And in addition all utopias suffer from the reader's secret conviction that a perfect world would be dull, so Piercy is careful to liven things up with festivals, ceremonies, nice clothes, and a hopeful description of untrammeled sexual interchange. There are problems, of course, but we are allowed to see the inhabitants working them out through council meetings and "wormings," a wonderful name for a session at which you accuse and complain. Some of these projections are a bit much: it's especially hard to write about communication between cats and humans in any way that isn't whimsical; and utopian children have difficulty being anything but cute or bratty. But the language Piercy has devised for her utopians has unexpected felicities as well as its leaden moments; some of the utopian passages even manage to be oddly moving. The poignancy comes in part from Connie's hunger for human contact and love, in part from the resemblances she sees between the utopians and her lost child, lover, and friends. The outer virtues of Mattapoisett are overshadowed by an inner one: it is the only place where Connie is loved.

However, several issues are dodged. The utopians refuse to fill Connie in on history, so we never find out much about how it all happened. They're engaged in a war with an enemy, but we don't learn much about this, either. And they tell Connie they are not "the" future, but only a possible future, and that they need her help in the present to avoid "winking out." (I wish this didn't sound so much like the resuscitation of Tinker Bell in *Peter Pan*.) At one point Connie stumbles into *another* future—presumably what will happen if we don't all put our shoulders to the wheel—in which women are termitelike objects, and the air is so polluted you can't see the sky.

The Mattapoisett call to action only bewilders poor Connie, whose scope is of necessity limited. She ends by bumping off a few of the evil asylum shrinks, and because of the ambiguity of the last sections we're left with the uneasy feeling that Mattapoisett may have been a paranoid fantasy after all. The only evidence against this interpretation is that Connie isn't educated enough to have such a utopian vision.

This is a genre more at home in 19th-century England than the America of the 1970s, where moral earnestness seems to have gone out of fashion. It's a daring thing for Piercy to have attempted, and it's entirely in keeping with her previous literary production that she should have done so. *Woman on the Edge of Time* is like a long inner dialogue in which Piercy answers her own questions about how a revised American society would work. The curious thing about serious utopias, as opposed to the satirical or entertainment variety, is that their authors never seem to write more than one of them; perhaps because they are products, finally, of the moral rather than the literary sense.

To turn from Piercy's utopia to her poetry is to turn from an imagined world to an imagination, from a sense to a sensibility. The poetry investigates the values which Mattapoisett assumes as axioms, and for this reason— although utopias intrigue me—I find the poetry more convincing. Piercy is committed to the search for honesty, however painful; to action, however futile; to getting it said and getting it done, however awkward the result may be. She's a feminist and a radical, but her poetry fleshes out these concepts in complex and sometimes startling ways, and she's no simpleminded sloganeer. "I ram on," she says of herself and her poetry; "I must make from this soft body some useful thing." And, most succinctly,

> Like the common blackbird I sit in the wind
> scrapping for my food, my place, my kind
> sometimes shrieking and sometimes singing.

Her poetry is "unfashionable," in that it is not flattish, understated, careful or bland. It reads as if she's never been in a creative writing class. The words crowd, lavish and lush; metaphors logjam, polemic rages, similes breed similes and sometimes unconscious puns, and it's all part of Piercy's earthy aesthetic:

> Better, I thought, for me in my rough being
> to force makeshift connections,
> patches, encounters, rows,
> better to swim in trouble like a muddy river rising
> than to become at last all thesis
> correct, consistent but hollow
> the finished ghost
> of my own struggle.

And it *is* better, because out of all the surge and flux, the sometimes dutiful rhetoric, Piercy can build moments and sometimes whole poems that she would not have achieved with careful elegance. "People of the Shell," for instance, is superb, and it is not alone. Lines and aphorisms surface, flash and sink, poems transform themselves, words swirl. The literary ancestor here is not Dickinson but Whitman, and the vision is finally, despite the small ironies, a romantic one.

Like Whitman, Piercy must be read in chunks, not sips, and appreciated for her courage, gut energy and verbal fecundity, not for laconic polish. Dancing is hard and you may fall down, her poetry implies, but she is going to dance anyway. She rams on, and the reader can only applaud.

PART III
1977-1982

PART III
1977-1982

It's more difficult for me to characterize this period, since I'm still in it.

Obviously some of my earlier concerns stayed with me, and though I was still asked to review women writers, it stopped being exclusive, partly at my insistence. Knee-jerk responses have always bothered me, partly of course when directed at me, but having had so many knees jerked in my direction I think I know one when I see one and the attitude, coming from certain sectors, that no man has a valid "subject" or can produce anything of value is certainly a knee and a half. Female critics have to be willing to give writing by men the same kind of serious attention they themselves want from men for women's writing. And why leave all the reviewing of men's books to men? I'm still amazed though at the amount of male paranoia that's running around out there, and the forms it takes. When men express surprise that you're wearing a dress you know they must have a strangely distorted idea of what constitutes a feminist. The Movement is no longer small and concentrated, but diffuse and grassroots; in fact, it's the editorials in *Homemakers' Magazine*, which may account for certain frightened attempts by certain frightened men to pigeonhole and stigmatize "feminists" as the female equivalent of rapists. My awareness of these attitudes engendered speeches such as "Writing The Male Character."

I have always seen Canadian nationalism and the concern for women's rights as part of a larger, non-exclusive picture. We sometimes forget, in our obsession with colonialism and imperialism, that Canada itself has been guilty of these stances towards others, both inside the country and outside it; and our concern about sexism, men's mistreatment of women, can blind us to the fact that men can be just as disgusting, and statistically more so, towards other men, and that women as members of certain national groups, although relatively powerless members, are not exempt from the temptation to profit at the expense of others. Looking back over this period, I see that I was writing and talking a little less about the Canadian scene and a little more about the global one.

31
A Harvest Yet to Reap:
A History of Prairie Women

(1977)

When I was growing up in the 1950s, everyone who had heard of it at all "knew" that the "Suffragist" movement was composed of a bunch of eccentric old spinsters. Similarly, we "knew" that the WCTU and the Ladies' Aid and Missionary Society and any organizations with similar names were populated by steel-jawed, steel-corseted biddies with dead foxes around their necks. Nellie McClung was remembered, as she is on the recent stamp commemorating her, as a rather ugly, abrasive middle-aged battleaxe. I'm not sure who circulated these ideas, but, as the editors of this book (who also grew up in the 1950s) point out, it was the age of "Mom and Debbie Reynolds singing 'French Heeled Shoes'."

A Harvest Yet To Reap is a book that shatters, both by its beautifully chosen text and its resonant pictures, all the above stereotypes. (The WCTU was *young*! Nellie McClung was not only pretty, she was *funny*!) Though its slant is feminist, its appeal is general. It has a scrapbook format, with excerpts from letters, speeches, government propaganda, newspaper articles, and books arranged to provide an insightful history of Prairie women from the

point of view of those who actually lived the experience. The
period covered is roughly 1885 to 1925, and some of the
excerpts are from interviews with women who are still alive.
Though the sepia tones and period costumes give the
material the flavour of ancient times, this is recent history.

The book is a grab-bag and a gold-mine. It achieves
some of its best effects through juxtaposition and contrast.
The Government of Canada leaflets designed to lure women
to the Prairies, where they were badly needed—as everyone
agreed, you couldn't run a family farm without a family—
picture a life of light labour, with flower-hatted maidens in
genteel frilled dresses marketing their eggs in the afternoons
and spending the evenings in music and "book-lore" to
"keep up the tone of the men." But not much tone could be
kept up in the sod shacks of early Prairie reality pictured
a few pages later, where eight people were often crammed
into a single leaking room and women had to do field-
labour as well as all the gardening, poultry-keeping, nursing,
food preparation, child-bearing, and whatever cleaning was
possible. In the hard work, the isolation, and the absence of
women friends, the lives of these women were similar to
those of Ontario pioneer women of 100 years earlier, though
the Prairies were even colder and the distances between
neighbours greater; but their heads were cluttered up with
60 years of velvet-covered Victorian poop about dependency
and fragility. Catherine Parr Traill, whatever else con-
cened her, did not have to worry about being ethereal while
she milked the cows.

And the laws were worse. In the 1880s, "dower right"
had been confiscated, and a Prairie wife could not inherit by
right any of the farm she might have spent her life working
on. Fathers were the sole legal parents of children; they
could even put them up for adoption without the consent of
the mother. Men could get a quarter-section of free land;
women—unlike their counterparts in the U.S.—could not.
However, if a man sold his farm and absconded with the

money, leaving his wife with the children, it was she who became responsible for their support. Laws like this explain something of the missionary fervour behind the WCTU: if a man spent all his money on drink, his wife couldn't stop him, and the children really *did* starve. There was no welfare.

Women put up with this state of affairs at first because they were told it was divinely ordained. Also, as Nellie McClung says, because they had no time to protest; they were working too hard. But when the land was more widely settled and they had a little time, they did protest. They were, on the whole, better organized and more energetic than their sisters in the East, partly because the conditions against which they were fighting were not only unfair but also inhumane. Some of the most telling bits in this section of the book come from their opponents, but it's to the credit of the Prairies that much of the support came from male-run newspapers and grain growers' organizations. One of the questions the book raises but does not answer is the reason for the collapse of these movements after the vote was finally won.

The book is suggestive rather than exhaustive. It abounds with fascinating snippets, asides, things you never knew, things you would like to follow up. Birth control, for instance, was a taboo subject, but friends passed their secret recipes back and forth. (These included cocoa butter and sponges soaked in soapsuds.) There are popular songs, newspaper verses, cartoons, advice columns, and a report of the famous Mock Parliament put on by Nellie McClung and cohorts, in which women debated the pros and cons of giving the vote to men. There are pictures of women from all walks of life—farm women, soldiers, prostitutes, factory women— and of all ages, including several grotesque photos of little girls dressed as people thought they should be—and many nationalities. As the editors say, the book is heavy on English-speaking white women because neither Indian women nor

European women left many records, but the Central European wedding portraits, with the fanatic-eyed husbands and their cowed, unsmiling wives, are among the most haunting in the book.

There are a few minor shortcomings. The index is not as reliable as it might be, and there are some details that could have been explained. (What is a "barrowcoat"?) On the whole, though, the book is a fine rediscovery, an excavation. That the history and the women it salutes should have been buried so deep, so quickly, is one of the puzzles that prompted the editors to create it: "How did it happen, we wondered, that their lives had been so completely forgotten?"

32
Anne Sexton:
A Self-Portrait in Letters

(1977)

Anne Sexton was one of the most important American poets of her generation. She was both praised and condemned by critics for the intense "confessional" quality of her poetry. At first, it would have been easy to dismiss her, as the fifties often dismissed budding young female writers as just another stir-crazy neurotic housewife who wanted to write. But it was not easy to do so for long. She was a housewife and she was also neurotic—she is emphatic, in her letters, about both—but she had energy, talent and ambition. Although she did not start to write seriously until she was twenty-nine, by the end of her eighteen-year poetic career she had published nine books and had whatever worldly success poetry can bestow. She had won a Pulitzer Prize, had appeared at international poetry festivals, had held down a university teaching position although she had never gone to university, and had attracted a wide readership. In 1974, for no immediate reason, she killed herself at her home in Weston, Mass.

Before doing so, she had willed this book of letters into existence. She had appointed both a literary executor and an official biographer, and for her entire adult life she had been a hoarder, saving everything—pressed flowers, dance cards, postcards and snapshots. She also saved carbon copies of her letters, and the editors of this book had to read their way through 50,000 assorted papers before making this relatively small selection. One's immediate reaction is to rush to the incinerator, not with this book, but with one's own scrap heaps. Do any of us, really, want strangers reading our mash notes to highschool boyfriends, our petty gossip and our private love letters after we are dead? For some reason perhaps not unconnected with her final act, Anne Sexton did. Her carefully preserved correspondence was part of the monument to her dead self she had been building for much of her life. If you can stop time with yourself inside it, no unknown monster from the future can get at you. And Anne Sexton had a profound fear of the future.

The letters of poets are not necessarily any more interesting than the letters of bank managers, but Anne Sexton was an exceptional writer of letters. Although, as her editors make painfully clear, she was often difficult and at times impossible to live with, she kept the best of herself for her relationships-by-mail. It is probable that she found it easier to deal with people at this distance. In any case, her letters—even to people we are told she disliked—are charming, inventive, immediate and alive, though sometimes overly eager to please, even fawning. Of course, many of them are to fellow-writers, and they swarm with literary asides and details of the kind that delight historians, but it is not this that holds the reader's attention. Rather it is the sinuous, mercurial and engaging voice of the letters themselves.

But it is not the voice of Anne Sexton; it is only one of her voices. She herself was in the habit of splitting herself in two—"good Anne" and "bad Anne"—and the letters are written by "good Anne." A much bleaker voice authored her poems, and yet another was responsible for the rages and episodes of paranoia, breakdown, shameless manipulation and alcoholism that marked her life. She was demanding of her friends, insatiably hungry for attention and especially for approval and love. She was a flamboyant romantic, capable of extreme joy and extreme depression almost in the same minute. But we learn about this side of her from her tough-minded editors—one of them her daughter—who are to be congratulated for resisting the doubtless strong temptation to turn out a pious cosmetic job. In their hands, Sexton emerges as neither a heroine nor a victim but as an angular, complex, often loving and at times rather insufferable human being.

The letters themselves, however, are not exactly a "self-portrait." Like the letters of Sylvia Plath, Sexton's letters read like a sort of cover, a blithe mask. Plath's breathless and often glassy epistolary style seems to have almost nothing to do with the person who wrote her extraordinary poems. Sexton's letters and poems are closer to each other, but there is still an enormous gulf between the two. Even when she is describing her own suicide attempts, Sexton's letters do not read like the letters of someone who wanted to die. They are very much those of a woman who wished, passionately, to live, and who wished to live passionately.

This wish and her eventual suicide were not, to her mind, incompatible. Although she says at one point that suicide is the opposite of poetry, she was also capable of speculating on suicide as a way of acquiring "a certain power . . . . . I guess I see it as a way of cheating death." (It is typical of her that she descends to earth rapidly, adding, "Killing yourself is merely a way to avoid pain despite all my interesting ideas about it.")

A suicide is both a rebuke to the living and a puzzle that defies them to solve it. Like a poem, suicide is finished and refuses to answer questions as to its final cause. The unfortunate effect of such acts is to obscure the lives of their authors, leaving only the riddle of their deaths.

It would be a shame if this happened in the case of Anne Sexton. These letters should be read, not just for the clues to her suicide which they certainly contain, but for their exuberance and affirmation: not for their death but for their life.

33
Timothy Findley:
The Wars

(1977)

For at least three reasons, the publication of Timothy Findley's novel *The Wars* is a major literary event. The first reason has to do with the state of the publishing industry in Canada. The book is published by Clarke, Irwin, which until recently existed primarily as a textbook publisher. When Clarke, Irwin did fiction, it was usually discreet fiction, and they did not promote it lavishly: their fruit-juice cocktail parties were a mild industry joke. Although their list contained such distinguished authors as Alden Nowlan, they were not the publishers that sprang to mind when you were recommending a fiction house. Yet here is Findley's book—which is hardly discreet, containing as it does several unorthodox sexual incidents, including a homosexual gang rape—coming out with the sort of fanfare usually associated with McClelland & Stewart: posters, high praise from literary heavies, a promotional dinner at Toronto's Park Plaza Hotel, and a cross-country tour for the author (who, with Findleyesque eccentricity, refuses to fly in airplanes; he's going by car). The message is clear: Clarke, Irwin is making a bid for McClelland & Stewart territory, and they're making it with fiction. The Canadian textbook industry, dealt a heavy blow by the phasing out of the required curricula, was given a finishing chop by the recent American drive into Canadian schools; and Canadian fiction, once published for prestige only, is in healthier financial shape than ever before. For Clarke, Irwin, Findley is both a gamble and an investment.

For writers, there's another message here. *The Wars* is not Findley's first novel, but very few Canadians have read the other two. Once, not so long ago, it was received wisdom that the proper way to publish a Canadian novel was to do it with an American house, whose agency would distribute it in Canada. But this was changing about the time Findley published his first book, *The Last of the Crazy People.* "Timothy Findley lives near Ontario, Canada," the dust-jacket proclaimed, demonstrating an endearingly vague knowledge of Canadian geography. Although Findley's second novel, *The Butterfly Plague,* did well enough in the States to be bought as a paperback, Findley remained virtually unknown in his own country. His books were simply not promoted, and they were not noticed by reviewers, who by that time were reviewing both major foreign books and books by Canadians published by Canadian houses. Books by Canadians published by foreign houses fell between two stools. The message again is clear: the most sensible way to publish a Canadian novel is to choose a Canadian publisher in Canada, an American one in the States, and an English one in England. Selling world rights to an American house does not work well for Canadians.

The second reson for the importance of *The Wars* is the light it casts on the state of reviewing in this country. Once—and this could surely be said, for instance, of the late Nathan Cohen—many reviewers were better than most of the Canadian material available to them for review. We were thus often treated to the spectacle of energetic and intelligent minds striving to make emperor's clothes out of sows' ears, or, conversely, turning themselves into irritable papershredders out of sheer frustration. Now the situation may have reversed itself. The newspaper most widely respected for its literary opinions is, without a doubt, *The Globe and Mail*; it is felt, perhaps erroneously, that, like *The New York Times*, its pronouncements can make or break a book financially. Yet some joker handing out the book reviews at the *Globe* thought it would be a ripping idea to get Donald Jack to review *The Wars*, presumably because both *The Wars* and Jack's Bartholomew Bandy trilogy use The First World War as background for their stories. There's nothing wrong with Jack—you can get many a wheezy chuckle from his accounts of complicated English bathrooms and harebrained pilots buzzing garden parties—but Jack is a humorist and *The Wars* is a tragic novel. Choosing this reviewer was like choosing Red Buttons to review *Hamlet*. Jack found *The Wars* "an unacceptable distortion," presumably because so many men got killed in it and the author did not laugh. Some books judge their reviewers and this is a case in point. If this is the best our major literary newspaper can do, we need another major literary newspaper.

The third reason for the importance of *The Wars* is, of course, the thing itself. It's an accomplished novel by a literary type that is fast becoming a rarity in Canada's expanding book trade: a totally serious writer. At one time here you had to be a totally serious writer to be a writer at all, because you weren't going to make any money anyway. Now there's room for writers of all kinds, with suppliers of junk books making great headway. I'm not against this; if we're going to have junk, and we are, it might as well be indigenous junk. But a distinction must be made between the writers of books and the writers of what Jack McClelland once called "koobs." Timothy Findley writes books.

There's a fallacy that "koobs" are entertaining and books are not. *The Wars*, among its other merits, is gripping reading. Findley has been an actor, a playright and a television script-writer (he worked on *The National Dream*, for instance), and this shows in the tightness, the drama and the visual quality of his writing. The story he is telling is perfect for Findley's talents. It concerns Robert Ross, a young Canadian officer in the war, and a mysterious act he committed which crippled and blinded him and about which almost everyone who knows about it is unwilling to talk. Findley pieces his narrative together almost like a good television documentary, using vignettes, descriptions of old photographs, interviews with survivors now almost at the point of death themselves, objective commentary, and guess-work. He cuts the novel like a film, so that one taut scene follows another, with little filling or rumination.

What holds this pastiche together is a character Findley calls "you," a researcher who is attempting to reconstruct Ross's action and to unravel its meaning. "You" might be the author, but it might be the reader as well; for, although the ostensible *genre* of *The Wars* is the war story, its method is that of the detective story. We are given clues, fragments out of which we must attempt to make a coherent whole. "People can only be found in what they do," Findley says, and the reader must ponder and guess as the author moves from one quick glimpse to another.

Some reviewers have found the researcher, this so-called "device" of Findley's, to be an extraneous gimmick. Some have also commented on the curious opaqueness of the central character. Robert Ross *does*, but he almost never *says*, and the things he does say are as banal as everyone's letters home. None of them comes close to explaining how his extraordinary final act emerged from the personality of this quiet, self-effacing young man. In fact, Ross and the researcher are two halves of the same process. Ross is the thing observed, the researcher is the observer; and, by the end of the book, we feel that neither can fully exist without the other. The researcher, too, becomes multiple as he roams hospitals, interviews soldiers and old women, and scrabbles through piles of photographs that have all the awkwardness, familiarity and mystery of old snapshots. What do the war and Robert Ross *mean*, now they are finished and buried? Among other things, *The Wars* is about the function of memory and our persistence in time. The researcher is haunted and Robert Ross is the ghost, fixed in the mind at the moment of his fiery sacrifice and self-destruction.

Ross seems to me to be an essentially Canadian hero. Critics have compared *The Wars* to the work of Wilfred Owen and Robert Graves, but surely a better comparison would be with Colin McDougall's fine Canadian war novel, *Execution*. Ross is neither bloodthirsty nor much of a patriot. He gets sucked into the huge sinkhole of the trenches partly through a romantic image of death and glory and partly because he is running away from his stifling and suddenly insupportable family. His sister, a hydrocephalic, falls from her wheelchair and dies, and Robert's mother insists that he shoot her pet rabbits. Because he can't bear to kill the rabbits, Robert puts himself into a situation in which he has to kill horses, Germans, and, finally, some of his fellow soldiers. When he commits his last heroic act, no one can decide whether or not it is really heroic; and because this act is a protest against the death-force of the war, not an endorsement of it, he is court-martialled *in absentia*. Like those other recently-adopted Canadian heroes, Louis Riel and Norman Bethune, Ross is scorned and vilified by the society that produced him. Findley makes it clear that Ross is to the army what animals are to men, victims of a destructive and evil will to power.

Perhaps I shouldn't have used the word "Canadian," as it is now fashionable to identify literary productions by region rather than by nation. It is often assumed that every region but Ontario has an authentic voice, just as it is assumed that every group but the Celts and Anglo-Saxons have loveable ethnic peculiarities and every city but Toronto has a soul. I sometimes wonder about Toronto, but there can be no doubt about the existence of a Southern

Ontario literature, and *The Wars* is a distinguished addition to it. Although it is set, for the most part, in Europe, its sensibility is Southern Ontario Gothic, Rosedale variation. Findley is one of the few Canadian writers (Robertson Davies is another) who can write about the upper class of Upper Canada without making its members look like fatuous twerps. Although Ross's ingrown-toenail family is grotesque, it is, in Findley's hands, believable. As in his other books, he is especially good with female characters of the wisewoman-madwoman variety. Here, it is Mrs Ross, who keeps a flask in her muff when she goes to church, hates her relatives, and dominates her family through fits and scenes. The relationship between Mrs Ross and Robert is pathological, but it is the pathology of a society that is under scrutiny. "Control yourself," Robert is told. Finally, he does.

The difference between a book and a koob may finally be that a koob is self-evident and a book is not. Although *The Wars* has an obvious appeal for those interested in the First World War—Findley did a lot of research on clothing styles, methods of shipping men and horses, trench warfare, gas attacks, firearms and the like—its ambiguities, hints and correspondences invite the sort of pattern-making that delights chronic readers. Few books are flawless, and Findley's Achilles heel is a tendency to creep along the edge of sentimentality when it comes to our furry and feathered friends. But the starkness and power of its story overwhelms these weaker moments, and justifies, for once, the hyperbole on the jacket. This is a book that deserves and should get both a literary audience and a wide popular one.

34
Diary Down Under

(1978)

Day One: Brisbane Airport.

A huge Coca-Cola sign. A billboard, advertising jeans, shows a woman with her hands over her breasts, with the slogan: "Every Guy Should Have A Pair."

When we entered Australia, at Darwin, in the middle of the night, we were sprayed for bugs: two tanned Qantas men, spray-can in either hand, striding down the aisles of the plane. "Bugless we are," proclaims Australia, "and bugless we will remain." So you can eat with confidence the lettuce in your sandwiches of rubber cheese.

Brisbane has hibiscus in bloom, humidity, tropical palms, and flying foxes, which swoop about in the dusk, attacking the fruit trees. People here don't find them picturesque. The houses are raised bungalows, with tin roofs and open, lattice-walled areas underneath. Downtown Brisbane is seedy in a 1930s Graham Greene way. The people we talk to tell us that Queensland politics are incredible: public demonstrations are banned, and the police do whatever the premier tells them to. They never thought it could happen.

Strikes are frequent, productivity is low, and there's been a major drought; so the farmers all over Australia are in trouble. Someone blew up three people outside the Sydney

Hilton, but no one knows who. The government talks of "stringent measures." In West Australia, there's a movement to break away and form a separate country. Not everything here is foreign.

Day Two: The Flight to Adelaide.

Wrinkled hills, some dry-looking squares of farm; sinuous, dragony rivers, and a few lakes or ponds ringed with white. Mars-red hills, then the scrub forest of the South Australian coast. I realize I know almost nothing about the geology (my good intentions about reading up beforehand came to nothing). Who did what to the land, when? I know there were convicts, but where and so what? Australians seem to know more about Canada than we know about them. They had the Commonwealth drilled into them, they tell me.

We arrive at the Adelaide airport to find that our one piece of luggage, along with Galway Kinnell's and that of an entire string quartet, has disappeared. We aren't worried; there aren't many places it can go. At the hotel, which also has a Graham Greene air, I settle down to read the Adelaide Festival literature and try to figure out what I'm supposed to be doing here. The festival has a modern Festival Hall with several theatres in it, and auxiliary space all over town. It imports operas, orchestras, musical comedies, plays, quartets, ballets, from America, England, Japan, Europe; the Kabuki Theatre is here, and *For Coloured Girls Who Have Considered Suicide When the Rainbow is Enuf*.

Then there's Writers Week. It's supposed to start tomorrow, but you can tell from the coloured brochures that it doesn't loom too large in the minds of the festival organizers. There's a small separate programme, though, which promises various delights: The Orlando Winery Luncheon, sundry doings at the Writers' Pavilion, various readings and book launchings, and some papers on current

Australian writing. The logo on the front of the programme shows a line of heads, each with a pencil behind the ear, mouths wide open as though devouring the words "WRITERS' WEEK."

Day Three: A Side Trip.

The Orlando Winery Luncheon. Winery luncheons are a regular Writers' Week feature. We wait for our buses at the Parade Grounds near the Writers' Pavilion, which is a large red-striped open tent. The men are in casual summer shirts, the women in sundresses and hats. Jennifer Rankin, an Australian poet we met earlier in London, says she can tell the male overseas writers at first glance. I thought it might be the white-rat pallor, but no, she says, it's their feet. We looked hard at all the available feet, including Galway Kinnell's (USA) and Richard Murphy's (Ireland), and yes, she's right, though you can't put your finger on it.

We pass up the first two buses, which look full, only to be told that the third one is indefinitely delayed because the Australian Literary Council hasn't arrived. We stew on the tarmac till they turn up, wearing little green hats, like gnomes. (Should the Canada Council be given such hats? It makes identification easier.)

When the Council have settled themselves, we move off through the parklands and rivers that surround Adelaide's city core, then past some older houses with white scrollwork balconies and into the suburbs: Kentucky Fried Chicken, neat bungalows, well-watered gardens. Outside the city, however, the land is parched. The leaves of the trees are still green, but the ground is dry and brown.

After an hour and a half, we reach the Barossa Valley, a wine-producing area settled by Germans. Miniature Rhineland castles, Lutheran churches, taverns with barrel signs. The buses stop at Orlando's, and the writers disgorge onto Orlando's green lawn, dotted with upended kegs, each bearing an umbrella, a plate of German sausage, and three bottles of wine. We scuttle from umbrella to umbrella, avoiding the scorching sun.

The premier of South Australia, Don Dunstan, is here to open Writers' Week. He used to be an actor, and he makes a very classy speech about the importance of literature. He sounds as if he means it, and probably does; the Chief Justice here writes poetry. South Australia, we are told, is a far cry from Queensland. Here the government is both Labour and liberal, and the arts flourish. (I try to imagine Bill Davis making an equally passionate speech on this subject; fail.)

After the speech the food comes out and we crouch under an umbrella eating magnificent pears and plums, discussing past and current trends in Australian poetry. The search for the "genuinely Australian," the pull of "international" literature, the definition of the Outback (where almost nobody lives) as the "real" Australia, the shift towards "urban poetry." Australians have more ties with England than we do, but the God of many Australian painters is New York. There's a heavy post-Creeley clique in Sydney, apparently, among whom avoiding capital letters is mandatory. "Rationalizing English," they call it.

We end up talking, as writers tend to, about publishing. It's been flourishing here since about 1965, but I'm still not clear what "flourishing" means. Then we move on to critics. There's a good deal of resentment if you go to England and make good, but at least they'll take you seriously then. On the other hand, they don't like it if you get too big, and Patrick White has been trounced rather nastily. As one writer put it, "They cut tall poppies here."

Wheels within wheels, literary operators, tiny animosities, crab-like jostlings for position; cultural politics played out with veiled compliments and sneers; groups, anti-groups, loners. Paranoia thriving like suburban roses.

We arrive back feeling dizzy and wizened. Despite our precautions we are sunburned. Think about convicts: no

hats or umbrellas. Think about sunstroke and feel I have it.
The sun really *can* kill you, they say. The aborigines think
the whites are crazy to oil and fry their skins the way they do.
They themselves sit under trees.

Day Four: Friendly Street.

Tonight I go to my first reading, held in the Pavilion;
it's given by the Friendly Street Poets, an Adelaide "group."
This term is used loosely: styles range from tight lyric to pop
mod. There are two audiences: those who sit inside the tent
and can hear, those who sit outside and can't. The ones
who can't hear make use of the cash bar, which is in
operation just behind the tent. It's fashionable with some
of these to shout things at the readers. I ask who the
shouters are and am told they are from Melbourne, as if this
explained everything.

The last reader is a woman, and they give her a
particularly hard time: whistles, catcalls, cries of "We love
you." It's a kind of music-hall atmosphere, which she's able
to handle for a while by flipping remarks back at the jeerers.
At the end of the reading there's a scuffle over the mike.
Some of the young sprouts want to seize it; much shouting,
cries of "Shuttup" and "Now you'll hear some *good* poetry."
The audience drifts away. The definitive thing about a tent
is that you can't throw anyone out. Richard Murphy, the
Irish poet, even more white-faced than usual, says he hopes
they won't be at *his* reading. Consider taking some dead mice
and old cabbages to my reading, to hurl in self-defence. Am
told the performance this evening is not all that typical; am
also told foreigners didn't understand the genuine Okker
bluff-bloke style.

Day Five: AusLit.

In the Writers' Pavilion, a survey of current Australian
literature: fiction, the media, non-fiction in the morning;

children's literature, drama, poetry in the afternoon. I can't go in the afternoon because it's my turn to baby-sit Jess, but I sit under the red canvas in the morning, scribbling down names and bits of commentary. The fiction commentator feels they've had enough of something called "the kitchen sink school" and approves of recent "international," "experimental" trends. This seems to mean that fantasy and discontinuous form are in, and Brautigan, Pynchon and Vonnegut are causing ripples, if not waves. The aboriginal culture has not made much impact on the more recent Australians, though the reviewer feels that interest in things aboriginal is on the increase. (Reading the papers and literary magazines: there are a few aboriginal writers writing in English, and some small native-rights groups which have adapted the rhetoric of American blacks. But the aboriginals are even more outnumbered in Australia than the Indians in Canada, and they've made much less headway.)

The media paper is by a newspaperwoman, so much of the commentary concerns the state of journalism. Tom Wolfe is news here. Radio is given good marks, television bad ones. Television is American-dominated, and indigenous TV drama declining.

The good news is the film industry. This, we are told, is in the midst of a revival; in fact, there are several Australian feature films playing to good audiences right here in Adelaide. One Australian tells me, "Look, we just said to the Americans, 'We love your films but we can't let you control distribution any more.'"

In the afternoon, while Jess sleeps in the bedroom, I sit in the bathroom—of necessity our writing place during this tour—writing my paper for the next day. I squeeze out three pages of notes on the usual Canadian obsessions. I'm supposed to be talking about Influence and Independence, with emphasis on *Survival*, which has somehow penetrated here.

In the evening we get a baby-sitter and go off to see an indigenous Australian film. (Actually we went off to see some Polish experimental theatre, but it was sold out.) We choose the nearest movie, *The Mango Tree*, starring Geraldine Fitzgerald. A pleasant film set in a small town at the turn of the century. ("All Australian films are about the past," someone told me.) A boy with a strong mother and a dead father has perceptions, sees death through an episode with a sadistic religious fanatic, has an affair with his French teacher, leaves the town after his mother dies. It's shot slowly, with considerable attention to detail. (Like many Canadian films, it seems to be saying, "Look at this, you don't see this much in the movies," or: "This may look like a frontier Western town, but please note that it's an *Australian* frontier Western town.") The pacing and even the subject-matter are more reminiscent of, say, *Why Shoot the Teacher* and *Who Has Seen The Wind* than of American films.

After that, we run across town (it's a small city; you can indeed run across it) to see an Australian group called Back to Bourke Street. Bourke Street is a street in Melbourne where live music-hall variety shows once flourished, and Back to Bourke Street is a celebration and send-up of the original Australian popular songs that were sung there. Four talented actor-singers caper through songs with such titles as "Kangaroo Hop," "My Home Down Under," and "I'm An Aussie Through & Through." At last we feel we've found the real Australia.

(Wherever I was, and whatever I was looking at, there was always some Australian around to tell me that this wasn't the *real* Australia—I had to go to Perth, or Melbourne, or Sydney, or somewhere else. Which reminded me of Canada. Margaret Whitlam, the enormous, hearty wife of Gough, who has been a folk hero ever since being deposed, had the last word to say on the real Australian syndrome. "We're all real here," she growled, "and we're all bastards." Which also reminded me of Canada.)

Return to the hotel, having memorized the chorus to "Is He an Aussie, Is He, Lizzie, Is He an Aussie, Is He, Ay?" Feel I have achieved Cultural Insight. The Australians have their own landscape, their own songs, and their own language. What more do they need?

From this time on I become fascinated with Australian slang, which is as vigorous, distinctive and rich as any. It was developed by the main (though unwilling) settlers, Cockney English and Irish, both great wordsmiths. Much of it is unprintable. Of the more printable phrases, I like *jellyblubber* (for jellyfish), *dickhead* (for fool), *Ozzie, mozzie* and *cozzie* (for Australian, mosquito, and bathing costume, respectively).

Day Six: Influence and Independence.

Today, after I burble about the real Australian film I've seen, I'm told by everyone that this was a lemon, a melon, and every other derogatory fruit imaginable. Commercial junk, they say; not the real Australia. I *should* have gone to see *Picnic at Hanging Rock*.

In the morning I'm part of a panel on "Influence and Independence," during which representatives of five other colonial cultures also state their views. I regurgitate statistics on Canadian publishing and paraphrase *Survival*. Alistair Campbell from New Zealand says they used to resent Australia but can't be bothered any more. Ee Tiang Hong, from Malaysia, is a surprise. "I learned the English language the hard way," he says. "I began by saying 'I am, I am, I am,' and went on to say, 'I am a man, I am a man.' So I owe both my existence and my gender to the English language." In his view, English in ex-colonies is not always the language of oppression; at the moment, since its use is almost forbidden by an extremely nationalistic government, it is practically a language of political protest.

Jayanta Mahaptra from India says that in his country there are sixteen languages, with English being the seventeenth. His primary concern is not "Influence and Independence," but hunger. So he reads some poems on hunger, putting down all of us who have dutifully addressed the topic proposed. Norman MacCaig of Scotland begins by saying that it's one of the most unpleasant facts a man has to face that there are ten times as many Englishmen as Scotsmen; he goes on from there.

Fay Zwicky from Western Australia speaks last. She begins by referring to D. H. Lawrence's *Kangaroo*, in which he said that Australians had great dead empty hearts, like the continent, despite their outward boisterous amiability. She then wonders when Australia is going to write *Moby Dick*, laments its provincialism, asks when it's going to stop nosing around for its identity and get down to it, and affirms its potential. This is all painfully familiar. Canada is lucky D. H. Lawrence never wrote a book called *Beaver*. If he had, he'd doubtless have commented on that rodent's fabled habit of biting off its own testicles, thus defining us forever.

The audience is polite to us foreigners, but lights into Fay Zwicky with an energy that demonstrates she's hit home. It's pleasant for me to sit back and watch other people worrying an identity crisis, for a change.

Several astonishing questions posed by the Australians:

—Don't I think it's fortunate Canada is right beside the United States, and can benefit from the continual tension of having to define itself?

—Isn't it wonderful to have winter? (The Australians are fascinated by the idea of snow. What is it like, they ask? Styrofoam, I tell them, only cold.) In Australia, they say, the weather is either so nice that you don't want to write, or so hot that you can't. They have a charming picture of Canadian writers holed up during blizzards with little oil lamps, writing masterpieces.

—How exciting to have the French. It must give such variety and richness to the culture. (I can see their point. Australia does tend to be rather uniform.)

—Aren't Canadians tickled pink that they've produced a critic of world stature such as Northrop Frye? (They are upset when I tell them that it's become almost an academic social knee-jerk to sneer at Frye. "We cut tall poppies," I tell them.) Australians are just as worried about not having produced a Northrop Frye as they are about not having produced a *Moby Dick*. It's strange to find oneself viewed as the possessor of a coveted cultural property.

I have to admit I've never before seen any of these questions from this point of view, exactly. I begin to feel euphoric about being Canadian.

But in the evening we go again to the Polish theatre and get in this time, and I come out cursing fate that I wasn't born a Pole. The group is Cricot II and they performed a piece called *The Dead Class*, which is indescribable. I wonder why we spent the morning talking about what we talked about.

Day Seven: Another Crack at the Real Australia.

Today we skip classes and go to the beach, driven by Kate Jennings, a well-known feminist poet, and accompanied by Richard Murphy from Ireland, who is feeling quite ground down by it all.

We park the car in a deserted lot near a river filled with pelicans and cormorants, and climb dunes covered with unfamiliar grasses. Kate is jumpy about poisonous snakes—fear of reptiles is one of the first things a child learns in Queensland, where she's from—so we avoid the stumpy, tail-less lizards. The beach is misty and deserted, with huge breakers rolling along it for miles and miles. Richard Murphy immediately sprints away and disappears; the rest of us scatter, as if by common consent that we've had too many words and need a rest. If this isn't the real Australia, it's at least part of it.

This was the end of Writers' Week for me. I left with a list of names, a certain amount of guilt (why didn't I know more?), and a feeling of having seen a surface which I'd barely scratched. After this we went to Sydney, where we found:

— a lingerie store called Boobtique.

— one of the best restaurants I've ever been in, Tony's Berowra Waters, for which you have to book four months ahead. It's worth it.

— a group of matriarchal feminists, many from the Anglican Church, who told me about the beleaguered state of feminism in Australia and presented me with a book called *Dammed Whores and God's Police*, which sums it up.

— a men's hairdressing establishment called The Stallions' Stable.

— aboriginal rock carvings, explained lovingly by a park ranger. "Some people say, 'Oh, is that all?' " he said, disapprovingly.

— stunning beaches.

— the best fish & chips in the world, now that England's have gone downhill.

— a billboard at the airport, showing a man on a motorcycle, with the wheel bulging out from his legs toward the viewer. A woman sits behind him, her hands reaching around to his crotch. The slogan: "Unsnap a Stud." Advertising a soft drink called "Stud."

It's all the real Australia.

35
Last Testaments:
Pat Lowther and John Thompson

(1978)

It is very difficult to review the work of those recently dead. Less so when the writer has come to the natural end of, as we say, a long and distinguished career; but when the writer is young and has died violently, how should we respond? The first impulse is to ignore the fact in an attempt to avoid morbidity and necrophilia, and to treat such writers as if they were still alive. We should be able, we feel, to evaluate the poetry objectively, treat it as an artifact to be considered apart from the life in which it was embedded.

But the deaths remain. What dead poets have in common is simply this: they will write no more poems. We cannot use the word "promising" or condescendingly hope for better from them next time. All we have from them is all there will ever be. A review of a living poet cannot help being written with one eye on the poet: she will read it, whether it's a good review or not, and she will judge us. But reviewing a dead poet pressures the reviewer into declaiming like Brutus over Caesar's corpse. The poet cannot answer back. Tribute, we feel, must be paid, and justice must be done now or it never will be. The pull towards elegy is strong.

So I'll say at the outset that both the poets I'm reviewing here are dead and both were young. Both had been called "promising," and both were considerably more. Pat Lowther was murdered. Her husband has been convicted but is currently appealing. John Thompson's death was one of those Marilyn Monroe puzzles that balance on the thin line between accident and impulsive suicide. I knew both poets and had worked with both, and I will try not to let that fact or my sorrow at these premature deaths influence what I have to say about the poetry. In this I will of course be unsuccessful, but the reader is warned.

A Stone Diary is Pat Lowther's fourth book of poetry and the first to be published by an established Canadian publisher as opposed to a small press. It appeared posthumously after considerable delay caused by the fact that no one knew who legally owned the manuscript, since at the time of her death Lowther had not yet answered the letter informing her of the book's acceptance. Some critics, naturally enough, picked out for special comment such poems as "Kitchen murder," "Suicides," and "To a woman who died of 34 stab wounds." Lowther, we were told, was preoccupied with violence. The implication was that she was either inviting her own death or had some kind of eerie foreknowledge of it. But Lowther was no more preoccupied with violence than are most serious poets of the twentieth century. The violence is there, Lowther would have said, in personal life as well as in the public life we cannot help being a part of; the poetry merely acknowledges its presence. If any facet of Lowther's work can be linked to the manner of her death, it would surely be, not any undue fascination with violence, but her lyric optimism, that quality that drove her again and again to attempt a positive universal view that would transcend the negative facts the social observer in her could see so clearly. It is, after all, optimism rather than fatalism that tempts us to ignore threats to ourselves.

Like that of Milton Acorn, an older Canadian poet and her friend, Lowther's poetry was constantly pushing towards the integration of her socialist politics with a personal vision on one side and a biological and cosmological one on the other. Thus the dead Pablo Neruda, in the impressive series of poems addressed to him, becomes in turn mineral, animal, and finally vegetable, "a seed patient as time." In "Chacabuco, the pit," a poem on the death-camp set up in Chile after the destruction of the Allende government, Lowther finally achieved the kind of statement that she'd been working towards in her previous books: a poem which is at once fully political, factually horrifying, and ultimately hopeful, which encompasses both the atrocities which humanity can perpetrate and the possibilities for human dignity and grace. The last poem in the book, "In the silences between," shows humankind moving towards its own fuller humanity; though, significantly, the eyes are only *"like /* the eyes of humans."

Lowther's earlier work was someimes faulted for its stylistic eclecticism and its tendency towards vagueness. It was as if she had so much to say, wished to include so much in her poetic universe, that she would seize the nearest verbal tools, leaving work sometimes half-articulated to start on the next new poem. She was never lacking in passionate intensity; only, sometimes, in the techniques she used to express it. And, like many woman poets initially unsure of themselves, she would occasionally cover her tracks with that kind of nervous whimsy that proclaims, "Don't hit me, I'm only joking." But in *A Stone Diary* the poetry is tighter, terser, more incisive. There had been many fine Lowther poems before it. *A Stone Diary* is her first thoroughly fine book.

Lowther's death is especially sad because she was obviously just coming into her own. Techniques mastered, vision clarifying, she was on the verge of writing more deeply and with greater range than she had ever done. Reading John Thompson's *Stilt Jack*, on the other hand, you feel you've come to a terminal book. The sort of thing that it is could not have been improved on in the future. Had he

lived, Thompson would have had to stop writing altogether
or turn in an entirely new direction. *Stilt Jack* takes one
particular tendency in his earlier work (his only other
published book is *At The Edge of the Chopping There Are No
Secrets*) and pushes it to the verge and over. It's an accomplished book in the same sense that a play is accomplished
once the curtain falls. One of the meanings is "finished."

In his Introduction, Thompson explains that he's using
an ancient couplet form, the Persian *ghazal*. The couplets,
Thompson says, "have no necessary logical, progressive,
narrative, thematic (or whatever) connection. The ghazal is
immediately distinguishable from the classical, architectural,
rhetorically and logically shaped English sonnet . . . its order
is clandestine . . . The ghazal allows the imagination to move
by its own nature: discovering an alien design, illogical and
without sense—a chart of the disorderly, against false reason
and the tacking together of poor narratives. It is the poem of
contrasts, dreams, astonishing leaps . . . . "

I've quoted at such length from the Introduction, not
only because it's the first thing to hit the reader upon
opening the book, but because I think it's something of a red
herring. Thompson leads us to believe that he's practising,
sort of for the exercise, like those late-nineteenth-century
sestina writers, an alien though conventional poetic form. He
uses phrases like "interest in the form," "careful construction" and "controlled imaginative progression." He
emphasises "escape from brief lyrical 'unity,'" disjunction,
"breaks." Then, having armoured himself and convinced us
that he's a craftsman and a sane fellow, that he's deliberate
and controlled, that his disunity is fully intended and
perhaps the slightest bit pretentious, he proceeds to kick us
into the pit.

Stilt Jack is not in fact the rather academic exercise
that the Introduction suckers us into expecting. It's a
cross between a moan and a beautifully modulated howl;
a profoundly anguished and despairing book. The poet

for comparison is not Adrienne Rich, whom Thompson mentions in the Introduction, somewhat bafflingly, as being a practitioner of *ghazals*. Try John Berryman without the coyness and with a lot less self-pity. Nor is the book the disjointed creature Thompson describes. Although the individual poems do make the leaps Thompson promises, the book as a whole presents an overwhelmingly unified vision.

There are only a few things it makes any sense at all to do. You can go fishing. You can get drunk. You can eat, though this activity is, when examined further, likely to prove faintly disgusting. In fact, being human is essentially disgusting: "Give up words," the poet says in many ways. Lowther's impulse towards the cosmos is to incorporate it somehow into the human body, the body of being human. But when Thompson says he would rather be a stone or the Great Bear, he wants escape from the human body and in particular from the human head. Purity is a fish on a hook, a knife. Images of iron, of metal and cutting edges, occur again and again. The voice of these poems would like to want honesty, simplicity, happiness and love, but cannot quite believe in their possibility. Nor can he believe he does in fact want them. "I'm in touch with the gods I've invented," he says. "Lord, save me from them."

The book is a long meditation on whether or not it's worthwhile to remain alive, and if so, what for. There's some romantic posturing here, and a good deal of contempt for the homelier comforts. ("If one more damn fool talks to me about sweetness and light . . . .") The poet tells us a few too many times that darkness is his element, that he's "mad," and there's more than one rhythmic echo of Lear's storm scene. But *Stilt Jack* nevertheless continues to startle and even charm, when the muttering and pained ruminating of its voice resolves itself into moments of clear seeing, clear statement, or simple truth. "Eat, let the blade / be surprised by joy."

Set against the self-torturing of the speaking voice is the occasional luminescence of the seeing eye. "The world is full of the grandeur," says the second-last poem, "and it is." It is not the world of things—animals, fish, potatoes, stones—that is flawed, but the human consciousness inhabiting that world. (Women, incidentally, are sometimes classed with things, and therefore innocent. When they're perceived as having brains, they're more likely to be sinister.) I will quote one poem in full, not because it's the best but because it so perfectly illustrates both Thompson's techniques and his vision:

A pineapple tree has grown in this kitchen
two years, on well water. Right here

a man went to set a fire in the stove
and the blade froze on the match.

Those winds: in summer turn the head rancid, in winter
drive a cold nail through the heart down to the
      hardwood floor.

Daisies, paintbrush, bellflower, mustard, swamp iris;
hackmatack, crowns driven northeast: they're there.

Pigs fattened on boiled potatoes; horses mooning in hay;
in the woodshed he blew his head off with a shotgun.

Stilt Jack is a "finished" book without, curiously, being a completed one. It ends too abruptly, and I suspect that Thompson, had he lived to see the book through its editorial stages, would not only have altered some of the spelling and punctuation but would have seen fit to flesh out the last quarter of the book. Nevertheless, it's a most impressive act. The inside cover flap calls it "the last testament of a major poet at the pinnacle of his craft." "Major" depends on your frame of reference; certainly for readers of Canadian poetry in the 1970's this is an essential book. "Pinnacle?" Unfortunately, we'll never know.

36
Tillie Olsen:
Silences

(1978)

Tillie Olsen's is a unique voice. Few writers have gained such wide respect based on such a small body of published works: one book of short stories, *Tell Me A Riddle*, and the unfinished novel, *Yonnondio: From The Thirties*. Among women writers in the United States, "respect" is too pale a word: "reverence" is more like it. This is presumably because women writers, even more than their male counterparts, recognize what a heroic feat it is to have held down a job, raised four children, and still somehow managed to become and to remain a writer. The exactions of this multiple identity cost Tillie Olsen twenty years of her writing life. The applause that greets her is not only for the quality of her artistic performance but, as at a gruelling obstacle race, for the near-miracle of her survival.

Tillie Olsen's third book, *Silences*, is about this obstacle course, this ordeal, not only as she herself experienced it but as many writers have experienced it, in many forms. It begins with an account, first drafted in 1962, of her own long circumstantially-enforced silence. She did not write for a very simple reason: a day has twenty-four hours. For twenty years she had no time, no energy and none of the money that would have bought both. It may be comforting to believe that garrets are good for geniuses, that artists are made in Heaven and God will take care of them; but if you believe, as

313

Tillie Olsen does, that writers are nurtured on Earth and nobody necessarily takes care of them, society cannot be absolved from the responsibility for what it produces or fails to produce in the way of literature.

Though Tillie Olsen begins with her own experience, she rapidly proceeds to that of others. The second part of the book is a grab-bag of excerpts from the diaries, journals, letters, and concealed autobiographical work of a wide range of writers, past and present, male and female. They are used to demonstrate, first, the ideal conditions for creation as perceived by the writers themselves, and second, almost every imaginable impediment to that creation. The financial and cultural pressures that gagged Melville, the religious agonies of Hopkins, the bitterness of Thomas Hardy after the vicious reception of *Jude the Obscure*, Willa Cather's feeling of nullity in face of the suave eastern establishment; political, cultural, sexist and sexual censorship; the denial of a voice to a race, a class, a sex, by the denial of its access to literature; breakdowns, abdications, addictions; all are cited. Reading this section may be hazardous if you are actually writing a book. It's like walking along a sidewalk only to be shown suddenly that your sidewalk isn't a sidewalk but a tightrope over Niagara Falls. How have you managed to do it at all? "Chancy luck," Tillie Olsen replies, and in view of the evidence she musters, she's probably—for all writers not white, male, rich, and from a dominant culture—quite right.

Tillie Olsen's special concern is with how her general observations on silencings apply, more heavily and with additions, to women. Here, the obstacles may seem to be internal: the crippling effects of upbringing, the burdens of motherhood, the lack of confidence that may prevent women from writing at all; and, if they do write, their own male-determined view of women, the fear of competing, the fear of success. We've heard a lot of this before, but it's invigorating to see its first expressions by women coming new to the problems: Virginia Woolf worrying about her childlessness, Katherine Mansfield having to cope with all the domestic arrangements while John Middleton Murray nagged her about tea. And, in contrast, quotations from men whose wives dedicated their lives to sharpening pencils and filling the inkwell for them. As Tillie Olsen points out, almost all of the women in the nineteenth century who wrote were childless and/or had servants. Her study of Rebecca Harding Davies, author of the remarkable *Life In The Iron Mills*, is a telling example of what happened to one writer who made the switch from solitude to biological fecundity.

In construction, *Silences* is a scrapbook, a patchwork quilt: bits and pieces joined to form a powerful whole. And, despite the condensed and fragmentary quality of this book, the whole is powerful. Even the stylistic breathlessness—the elliptical prose, the footnotes blooming on every page as if the author, reading her own manuscript, belatedly thought of a dozen other things too important to leave out—is reminiscent of a Biblical messenger, sole survivor of a relentless and obliterating catastrophe, a witness: "I only am escaped alone to tell thee." The tone is right: the catastrophes do occur, daily, though they may not be seen as such. What Tillie Olsen has to say about them is of primary importance both to those who want to understand how art is generated or subverted and to those trying to create it themselves.

The true measure of a book's success, for the reader, is the number of people she wants to give it to. My own list is already long.

37

Sylvia Plath:

Johnny Panic and the Bible of Dreams

(1979)

When a major work by a major writer is published post-humously, no one bats an eye. Minor works by minor writers presumably don't get published until the author has been dead long enough to have become quaint. *Johnny Panic and the Bible of Dreams* is a minor work by a major writer, and it's the contrast that causes niggling. Whom does such a publication benefit? Not the author, and not the author's reputation, which is doing very well without it. Not the general reader hitherto innocent of the Plath opus and myth who may stumble upon it and wonder what all the shouting is about. I suppose the answer is "the student," if by "student" is meant any reader already sympathetic enough to Plath's work to have read most of it already and to be interested in foreshadowings, cross-references, influences and insights. And this is the kind of audience *Johnny Panic* assumes. It's a prose catch-all, composed of short stories, short prose essays and journal entries, and as such it ought to round out one's knowledge of the writer and perhaps offer some surprises. Luckily it does both.

I have to admit at the outset that this kind of publication makes me uneasy almost by definition, hinting as it does of rummagings in bureau drawers that the author, had she lived, would doubtless have kept firmly locked. What writer of sane mind would willingly give to the world her under-graduate short stories, her disgruntled jottings on the doings of unpleasant neighbours, her embarrassing attempts to write formula magazine fiction? But I must also admit that I read *Johnny Panic* with considerable absorption and, at moments, fascination. It was a shock akin to seeing the Queen in a bikini to learn that Sylvia Plath, an incandescent poet of drastic seriousness, had two burning ambitions: to be a highly-paid travel journalist, and to be a widely published writer of magazine fiction, either of the *New Yorker* or—can it be?—of the *Ladies' Home Journal* variety. To this end she slogged away in the utmost self-doubt and agony, composing over seventy stories, most of which were never published, and filling notebooks with the details of what she thought of as real life: styles of clothing and interior decoration, mannerisms and acquaintances, sketches of the physical world which she believed she had no talent for observing. (Poetry she considered a mere escape, a self-indulgence, an indulgence in self; and as such unreal, since she was not totally convinced of her own worth or even of her own existence.)

It's easy to sneer at such ambitions, and the editor does not altogether resist the temptation, though his disapproval is gentle and underlined by a statement of crushing valid-ity: Sylvia Plath's genuine medium was poetry. Of course this is true; but her desire for journalistic success, which seems so incongruous in view of the final excellence of her achievement, must be placed in context. Sylvia Plath became famous only after she was dead. These pieces were written by a young unknown writer who had gone almost straight from the status of student into another subordinate position, as the wife of a poet already hailed as a rising star. Her desperate attempts to write publishable magazine pieces and to make money were also attempts to assert herself as a real person, an adult worthy of consideration, in a world which had so far failed to acknowledge her.

On one level *Johnny Panic* is the record of an apprentice-ship. It should bury forever the romantic notion of genius blossoming forth like flowers. Few writers of major stature can have worked so hard, for so long, with so little visible result. The breakthrough, when it came, had been laboriously earned many times over. But there's more to *Johnny Panic* than juvenilia. The writing varies widely in quality and interest, or rather in the quality of the interest; for although the young Sylvia Plath squeezed out some fairly dismal stories, as most young writers do, all the pieces presented here are revealing. Some things stand brilliantly on their own: two short later essays, "America! America!," and "A Comparison," several of the notebook entries, the title story, which foreshadows *The Bell Jar*, and "Tongues of Stone." Two pairs—notebook entry, short story—demonstrate the transformation from observed real life to fiction; in both cases the notebook entries have a spontaneity that the stories, in their desire to be literary, almost lose. There are some straight formula pieces, most notably, "Day of Success," which is about a young wife and mother who keeps her dashing playwright husband by being domestic. At first sight these stories are merely no more deplorable than other such fifties set pieces, but on second reading they cause pricking of the thumbs. Even when she was trying to be trite, Sylvia Plath could not conceal the disconcerting insights into her own emotional mainsprings that characterize her poetry. The unevenness of the stories is often the result of a clash between the chosen formula and the hidden message that forces its way through, seemingly despite the writer. "What visions were to be had came under thumbscrews, not in the mortal comfort of a hot-water-bottle and cozy cot," thinks Dody Ventura in "Stone Boy With Dolphin." Though she deplored it and tried to deny it, so did Sylvia Plath.

The author has been well served, both by her publisher—the cover is both handsome and appropriate, the presentation lowkey—and by her editor, though it's a slight tease to tell the reader that Sylvia Plath wrote "vivid, cruel" things about people and then refused to print them. The stories are arranged chronologically but in reverse order. This creates an archeological effect: the reader is made to dig backwards in time, downwards into a remarkable mind, so that the last, earliest story, "Among the Bumblebees," emerges like the final gold-crowned skeleton at the bottom of the tomb, the king all those other bodies were killed to protect. Which it is.

38
Valgardsonland:
Red Dust

(1979)

This is the third book of short stories by W. D. Valgardson. The first book is *Bloodflowers*, the second *God Is Not a Fish Inspector*. All are published by Oberon Press and all are worth having.

I'll begin by getting a minor quibble out of the way. In the cover blurbs on the second and third books, Oberon makes a point of telling us how well the previous books have sold, what a large audience they have, or how many times they've been reprinted. If, say, Jack McClelland were to do this to an author, it would come across as decidedly crass, an attempt to make us feel we should purchase a book because other people have. And it's a disservice to Valgardson. It makes him sound like a writer who's deliberately pandering to some kind of cheesy popular taste, though in reality nothing could be further from the truth. "Uncompromising" means nothing if not Valgardson. "Unrelenting" might be even more accurate.

The blurb on *Red Dust* claims it's "an even better book than its predecessors," which is also a disservice. But a writer cannot be faulted for the understandable puff-mindedness of his publishers. *Red Dust* is equal to, not better than. Valgardson is one of those writers who seems to have sprung fully-formed from his own head, with, in his very first book, a well-developed view of his own universe and all the skills necessary to articulate it. If you place "Bloodflowers," the first story in the first book, beside "Red Dust," the last story in the latest book, who could choose between them? Both, in their realization of what they set out to do, are flawless.

It's a critical fallacy of our times, derived perhaps from psychology or optimistic self-help books, that a writer should "grow," "change," or "develop." This fallacy causes us to demand the same kind of behaviour from writers that we expect from children or radishes: "grow," or there's something wrong with you. But writers are not radishes. If you look at what most writers actually do, it resembles a theme with variations more than it does the popular notion of growth. Writers' universes may become more elaborate, but they do not necessarily become essentially different. Popular culture, based on the marketing of novelties, teaches us that change is desirable in and for itself. Valgardson is its antithesis.

In Valgardsonland, which is an identifiable locale with its own weather and its own limited set of possibilities, the universe does not change. It hasn't changed from the first book to the third, and why should it? It is not Valgardson's prerogative to change it; he cannot change Fate, the heavy hand of which is everywhere at work. Valgardson does not appear to manipulate his characters or situations, though of course every author is doing that all the time. The illusion he creates is that of a meticulous chronicler of an implacably hostile and nasty world.

In Valgardsonland, as in the moral universe envisaged by John Stuart Mill, evil is widespread and powerful. Good exists in limited quantities, but in any clash between the two it will probably lose. The conditions existing between human beings are much like those pictured by E. J. Pratt under the sea: a mute struggle, a constant rending and tearing, a desperate and stubborn battle to survive and keep eating. In Valgardsonland, when it isn't snowing—"snowing" is too soft a word for what it does there—it's dusty and broiling. The physical surface over which characters move is pocked with traps: sandpits, snowdrifts, sinkholes, oceans, treacherous ice. Its animal life takes the form of things you shoot at, or, less agreeably, bears that tear out your guts and half-wild husky dogs. Domestic dogs, when they appear, are likely to have distemper or get hit by cars. This world is harsh even by the standards of Canadian fiction, which abounds in such unpleasantnesses, but in itself it is morally neutral. Though it looks a lot like Milton's Hell, it isn't out to get you, exactly, nor will you be able to avoid it if you're good. Such a world does not demand goodness as the price of survival, merely knowledge, vigilance, and luck; and for some even these aren't enough.

I don't find this view unduly pessimistic. Though dramatic, and possibly influenced by Valgardson's own Icelandic background, both cultural and literary, it's accurate enough for people without much money who live in a harsh climate, and these are the kind of people Valgardson is best at writing about. The climate exposes them to danger, the lack of money removes the possibility of escape, which is probably why most of Valgardson's characters behave like cornered rats. Like Alice Munro, Valgardson has totally discarded the pious Victorian concept of ennobling poverty. This is why, too, the most frequent deadly sin in Valgardson's stories is not pride but greed: everyone's hungry. In "Celebration," in which a man locks a woman out in the snow to freeze and later causes the deaths of his two children, the initial fight is over a plate of fried potatoes. Compassion, insight, kindness, and what is usually thought of as love, are luxuries, Valgardson seems to say. His characters for the most part cannot afford them.

Middle-class characters, when Valgardson deals with them at all, are contrasted with his poorer types (one hesitates to say "working class, " since a lot of Valgardson's characters are below even this line: they don't work). They're shown up as ignorant of the forces that shape the lives of others, and because of this and their ability to effect change through money, destructive. They're given to moralizing and abstraction, and beside the other characters, who are busy falling into the ocean, hanging themselves, or getting pregnant by unknown men, are made to seem weak and silly. They also have inner monologues, which the others don't.

For instance, the first story in *Red Dust*, "Beyond Normal Requirements," is about an English teacher who's driving an Indian boy back to the reservation from boarding school to attend the funeral of his suicide brother. The teacher can't understand the suicide, but wants to, and keeps digging away at the Indian: "his joy was to ferret out the motive." The boy, on the other hand, isn't interested in reasons, explanations, motives. He merely accepts facts. Indeed, many of Valgardson's characters seem to act without anything identifiable as a "motive" at all. They do things because these are the sorts of things they do, and they don't subsequently reflect. There's the danger of a Rousseauesque sentimentality in this approach: the poor, the foreign, the native, as more elemental and basic and therefore more virtuous than other people. But Valgardson is so deft you hardly notice it, and his elementals are simply too unpleasant to slip very far over the brink into sentimentality.

There's another motif which occurs often enough in Valgardson's stories to deserve mention: the sacrifice. Sometimes the sacrifice is a death, or an assumed death; sometimes it's something else, such as a rape. Most of the time the sacrifice is unintended by the victim: in "Bloodflowers," a young man is kept prisoner by islanders who hope he'll make the third in a superstitious cycle of three deaths; in "The Curse," a woman is stoned by her community in the mistaken belief that she's a witch who has caused a child's illness; in "Red Dust," a man allows his feebleminded niece to be brutally raped in exchange for a hunting dog he wants. Very occasionally, as in the story in which a farmer with an incurable illness kills himself so his wife won't be left bankrupted by medical expenses, the sacrifice is deliberate, and this is about as close as Valgardson gets to any kind of redemptive human act.

Valgardson's world is easy enough to label part by part, but harder to convey. Finally it is made with language. The technique—laconic, flat, but with breathtaking twists and plummets and sudden dark gaps in understanding that open like crevasses—is hard to fault. It does what it should. One could argue that there are other things to be done, and of course there are; but not, I suspect, by Valgardson. He's staked out his territory, and now it exists.

39
E. L. Doctorow:
Loon Lake

(1980)

What happens to a writer such as E. L. Doctorow when a
novel such as *Ragtime* sells 220,000 copies in hardback, gets
translated into twenty languages, and wins the National
Book Critics Circle Award for fiction? A writer of a certain
kind would merely try to duplicate these lush results as
quickly as possible. A writer who is more serious must
risk or perish. Everything about Doctorow's career to date
indicates that he considers the novel a vehicle for social and
moral commentary as well as an art form which should
stretch the author's resources to their limits. But success on
the *Ragtime* scale in America almost automatically makes it
more difficult for a writer to take himself seriously, partly
because other, less successful writers begin to discount him.
Post-romantic inverse snobbery attached to sales figures is
still with us. Does 220,000 hardback copies really mean
you're a schlock artist? Then there are all those critics
gunning from the shrubberies. You've walked Niagara Falls
on a tightrope once, but can you do it again?

This is not a metaphysical problem. It's one of the facts of life and writing in America today, and it has demoralized more than one good writer. Doctorow is not one to shirk it: you can almost hear the gritting of his teeth as he charges it head-on. It's no accident that *Loon Lake* has odd punctuation, excerpts of freeish verse written by one of the characters, and passages jump-cut so that the reader has to figure out who's talking and what the time-frame is. It's no accident, in other words, that *Loon Lake* would be regarded as "experimental" if it weren't by the author of *Ragtime*. It's a sad commentary on the state of publishing, as well, that if it weren't by the author of *Ragtime* most commercial publishers would have rejected it as too literary. That Doctorow's verbal acrobatics by no means exclude involvement suggests that the line between "literature" and "entertainment" is one drawn by publishers rather than writers.

It's also no accident that one of the central motifs of *Loon Lake* is the fascination of success for those who aren't successful and the corrosive, dehumanizing effects of it on those who are. The central character is a young man who calls himself Joe Paterson, because the name he inherited from his sad-sack, hunky father is unpronounceable. In any case he's dismissed his working-class parents—poor, dispirited, "all dried up"—and is looking for better ones. He's another Jay Gatsby or Ishmael, name-change and all, that perennial willed orphan by which American fiction is so heavily populated, running away in search of his fate, an elusive woman, and America, which in this tradition are usually the same thing. He goes by boxcar rather than ship, as *Loon Lake* is set for the most part during the Depression. Captain Ahab is played by a captain of industry named Bennett, who owns almost everything anybody in the book works for, walks on or comes in contact with, including a piece of organized crime and a number of souls. The zanies and prophets are rolled into one, failed poet Warren Penfield, who sets out to kill Bennett but ends up living at his Loon Lake Adirondacks estate as a drunken kept fool. (So much for the arts in

America, owned and emasculated by capitalism, we suppose.) The White Whale has dwindled into a half-witted animalistic carnival Fat Lady, who is rented out sexually after hours. Instead of being harpooned she is raped to death by a mob, for money, of course. Like Nature, she's undiscriminating; she accepts all comers, as it were, and for this Joe Paterson rather applauds her than otherwise.

A comparison with *Moby Dick* may seem excessive, but that's the league Doctorow is playing in. *Loon Lake* can also be seen as an odd cross between the *The Great Gatsby* (there's even a moonbeam-coloured, visionary Daisy Fay, though from the wrong side of the tracks) and *The Grapes of Wrath* (there's even a Roseasharn). It's the point at which wealth and poverty, privilege and servility, ambition and economic necessity, social prestige and the criminal underbelly of America intersect that fascinates Doctorow. Who's in bed with whom concerns him, both literally and figuratively, and the sexual encounters carry more than romantic weight. You can't take off your social class with your clothes, and "possession," for Doctorow, is more than a figure of speech. The only woman in the book who isn't a victim never sleeps with anyone. Instead she's a famous aviatrix, and rich enough to be able to afford indifference. Preferable, it seems, as the sexually functional women in the book don't seem to get a lot out of it. Men fall in love with them, true, but as wispy symbols rather than people. They in turn use their sexuality to *get* things and are therefore useable. If this makes you uncomfortable, you can always choose to view it as period realism, which it probably is.

Joe Paterson has energy, ambition, and a vision of himself that demands success. Billionaire Bennett and poetic Penfield are his spiritual fathers; on some level, the thuggish, calculating immigrant survival-artist, the sloppy romantic visionary, and the man who runs America by squeezing blood out of everyone else are closely related. At first Paterson doesn't know where to put or how to use his potential: shall he side with the workers, from whom he springs, against Bennett, whom he envies and hates? Or would that mean defeat, a life of no more than grim endurance, like that of his parents? Paterson's moral dilemma is America's, and the options are limited. You can be oppressed, like the mine and factory workers Doctorow renders so tellingly, dupes of company finks, criminals and uncaring capital; you can be a moonstruck escapist, like Penfield; or you can be Bennett. "I had expected not to like F. W. Bennett," Joe muses. "But he was insane. How could I resist that? There was this manic energy of his, a mad light in his eye. He was free! That was what free men were like, they shone their freedom over everyone."

There are many brilliant parts in *Loon Lake*; it's one verbally dazzling solo performance after another. The period detail is lovingly done and the physical presence of both people and places is evocative and solid. I have a quibble about the loons, which are made to do things no loon I've been familiar with has ever done (loons are not cormorants or seagulls), but apart from that I willingly suspended disbelief. Until the end of the book, that is. The publisher's blurb says that the ending "resolves the mystery of Joe's life and snaps the earlier sequences into perfect, inevitable order." Well, not quite. Doctorow's reach just slightly exceeds his grasp. He's one of the most courageous and interesting writers around, and it's hard to imagine him writing anything lacking in courage and interest. But though his eye is on the big picture, the reader has to deal with the somewhat maddening sensation of scrabbling around for a few pieces of the jigsaw puzzle lost down the back of the sofa. *Loon Lake* anatomizes America with insight, passion and inventiveness, but it leaves us with a small nagging doubt as to whether it really is more than the sum of its parts.

40
Witches

(1980)

When I was walking through the rain in Cambridge today, lugging a heavy bag of books, having been sent to the wrong place, it was hard for me to believe that almost 20 years had passed since I first walked through Cambridge in the rain, lugging a heavy bag of books, with the deep suspicion that I had been sent to the wrong place. I had ostensibly come to Radcliffe to study Victorian literature, and that part of it was all right, since one of my fellow Canadians was teaching it here. But underneath my Victorian exterior I fancied myself a poet, a fancy that—as anyone who has ever been a graduate studentess in English will know—it was death to admit. And all the modern poetry, as well as the devices for listening thereto, were locked in Lamont Library, which was restricted to students and banned to studentesses. Getting out a book of modern poetry required somewhat the same procedures as those needed to extract a book of pornography from the X section of the Widener Library, and, being of a retiring nature, I didn't want anyone to see me doing the former under the mistaken impression that I was doing the latter. To this fact I owe my ignorance of modern American poetry, as well as my Canadian nationalism—for the Canadian poetry was not kept with the *real* poetry, but was down with Canadiana in the bowels of the Widener, underneath Ethnology and Folklore, and freely accessible to students and studentesses alike.

Walking around Cambridge today, trying to find out what I was supposed to be doing—a continuation of a lifelong endeavour—I was reminded of many happy afternoons spent in the bathtub on the third floor of 6 Appian Way (which is, alas, no more), reading Charles Dickens, scribbling dismal poems, and listening to the rain and the pitter-patter of sexual perverts as they scampered up and down the fire escape. I was also reminded of those many nights when I sat up until dawn, popping No-Nods and trying to get my term papers finished on time—for I have to confess that I actually wrote this speech this afternoon in the Greenhouse Restaurant, over a Frogurt and a cup of Sanka. It is to my habits of procrastination in things academic that I owe my success as a writer, for if I had done scholarship true justice, how would I ever have had time to write? (I did, however, learn an important distinction in graduate school: a speculation about who had syphilis when is gossip if it's about your friends, a plot element if it's about a character in a novel, and scholarship if it's about John Keats.)

It was at Radcliffe, too, that I first heard about role models. The position of dean, or was it don, was open, and there was much discussion about who should fill it. "We need a good role model," someone said. "What's that?" I asked, being from Canada. It was explained to me that, for role-modelhood, even at a university, scholarship was not the only requirement. One also had to be punctual, clean behind the ears, a good mother, well dressed, and socially presentable.

I'm afraid I'm a bad role model, but then, I long ago decided that I could be either a good role model or a writer, and for better or worse I chose writing.

Which brings me to the title of my address, a title I plucked from the air when presented with the need for one, without having the least idea of what I was going to say. I did feel, however, that it was appropriate to talk of witches here in New England, for obvious reasons, but also because this is the land of my ancestors, and one of my ancestors was a witch. Her name was Mary Webster, she lived in Connecticut, and she was hanged for "causing an old man to become extremely valetudinarious." Luckily, they had not yet invented the drop: in those days they just sort of strung you up. When they cut Mary Webster down the next day, she was, to everyone's surprise, not dead. Because of the law of double jeopardy, under which you could not be executed twice for the same offence, Mary Webster went free. I expect that if everyone thought she had occult powers before the hanging, they were even more convinced of it afterwards. She is my favourite ancestor, more dear to my heart even than the privateers and the massacred French Protestants, and if there's one thing I hope I've inherited from her, it's her neck.

One needs a neck like that if one is determined to be a writer, especially a woman writer, and especially if you are good at it. After 10 years of the Women's Movement we like to think that some of the old stereotypes are fading, but 10 years is not a very long time in the history of the world, and I can tell you from experience that the old familiar images, the old icons, have merely gone underground, and not far at that. We still think of a powerful woman as an anomaly, a potentially dangerous anomaly; there is something subversive about such women, even when they take care to be good role models. They cannot have come by their power naturally, it is felt. They must have *got it from somewhere*. Women writers are particularly subject to such projections, for writing itself is uncanny: it uses words for evocation rather than for denotation; it is spell-making. A man who is good at it is a craftsman. A woman who is good at it is a dubious proposition. A man's work is reviewed for its style and ideas, but all too often a woman's is reviewed for the supposed personality of the author as based on the jacket photograph. When a man is attacked in print, it's usually for saying what he says; when a woman is attacked in print, it's often for being who she is.

Which brings me to the next unforunate aspect of witches. Witches were consulted in private, but their only public role was to be persecuted; or, as we say, "hunted." And here, with brief mention of the fact that in the current wave of book banning taking place in Canada, all the most prominently publicized banned writers have been women, I'd like to switch from women writers—who, after all, have it rather soft in this century, on this continent, and whose necks are strong enough to survive a little name-calling whenever they stick them out—to a larger and more alarming picture.

Witch-hunting was probably always political in nature, an attempt by the powerful to control the potentially subversive, and it still is. The difference between witch-hunting and more conventional forms of justice and punishment is that in the latter you're supposedly being punished for what you've done, but in the former it's enough to be who you are. I'm a member of Amnesty International, and I read their monthly bulletins, which I would like to give *gratis*, a year's subscription, to the next literary critic who accuses my work of being unduly pessimistic. Political witch-hunting is now a worldwide epidemic. Torture for the purposes of extracting a confession, which will in turn justify the torture, is not a thing of the past. It did not end with racks, stakes, and Grand Inquisitors, or with Cotton Mather. It's here with us now, and growing. One of the few remedies for it is free human speech, which is why writers are always among the first to be lined up against the wall by any totalitarian regime, left or right. How many poets are there in El Salvador? The answer is none. They have all been shot or exiled. The true distinction in the world today is not between the so-called left and the so-called right. It's between governments that do such things as a matter of policy, or that wink at them when they are done, and those that do not. It would be simple stupidity to suppose that North America is by nature exempt. We've had witch-hunts before, and there is every indication that we're on the verge of having them again. When times are tough, when the Black Plague strikes or the economy falters and people get restless, those in authority start looking around for someone to burn.

When you are a fiction writer, you're confronted every day with the question that confronted, among others, George Eliot and Dostoevsky: what kind of world shall you describe for your readers? The one you can see around you, or the better one you can imagine? If only the latter, you'll be unrealistic; if only the former, despairing. But it is by the better world we can imagine that we judge the world we have. If we cease to judge this world, we may find ourselves, very quickly, in one which is infinitely worse.

41
An End to Audience?

(1980)

I have been asked here presumably because I am story-teller
and you wish to know something about the state of story-
telling, either in this country or in this decade or both. So I
don't see how I can do worse than by beginning with a few
stories.

Here we find ourselves immediately at the heart of the
problem; for how am I to know what kind of stories you wish
to hear? Do you wish to hear stories about John and
Mary, two perfectly well-adjusted people who have a mature
relationship, a nice house, two and a half children, a dog and
some hobbies that they share? Or do you wish to hear stories
about John and Mary being devoured by a great white
shark? Perhaps you would like to know about the day John
wakes up and notices that Mary has turned into a great white
shark, in which case we will quickly realize that we are in the
middle of a modern psychological novel and change the
subject at once. Or perhaps you would rather hear, in a
liberationist mode, about the day Mary wakes up and notices
that John has *always* been a great white shark and she'd better
make some speedy decisions about her own priorities. But I
would insult your intelligences by supposing that you all
want to hear the same kinds of stories, and this is the clue to

the marketing problems facing almost all publishers today. As a story-teller then, all I can do is to tell the kinds of stories I wish to tell or think I ought to tell and hope that someone or other will want to listen to them, which is, and has been for some time, the plight of the writer in a post-romantic society.

You will notice that I'm calling myself a story-teller rather than a novelist. This notion got put into my head by an interviewer who recently asked me, How do you distinguish between story-telling and literary art? I don't, I said. Literary art is simply the means by which the story-teller feels he or she can most efficiently tell a particular story. By story-telling, we obviously don't mean just the plot. Think of a simple joke; now think of the same joke told, first well and then badly. It's the timing, isn't it? And the gestures, the embellishments, the tangents, the occasion, the expression on the face of the teller, and whether you like him or not. Literary critics talking about fiction may call these things style, voice and narrative technique and so forth, but you can trace them all back to that moment when the tribe or the family is sitting around the fire or the dinner table and the story-teller decides to add something, leave something out or vary the order of telling in order to make the story a little better. Writing on the page is after all just a notation, and all literature, like all music, is oral by nature.

Neither of my parents are writers, but both of them are very good story-tellers; and since they're both from Nova Scotia, I'd like to illustrate one kind of story by giving you a couple of samples of the kind of thing I used to hear around the dinner table when I was growing up. Anyone from rural Nova Scotia is well-steeped in what we now call the oral tradition but which they didn't call anything of the sort. Sometimes they called these stories "yarns;" sometimes they didn't call them anything. They were just things that had once happened.

For instance, there was the ingenious man who lived down around the South Shore and built a circular barn for his cows. The cows spent the night facing outwards, with their rear ends all facing inwards towards the centre of the circle, which made mucking out the barn more efficient. Each cow had its own door, and the doors, equidistant around the perimeter of the circle, were worked by a central pulley. Every morning people would gather from miles around to watch the cows being let out of the barn. At the sound of a horn, the doors would all fly upwards at once, and the cows, urged on by little boys with switches, would squirt out of the barn like drops from a lemon. Or so my father said. As for my mother, one of the most memorable events in her life was the day the hellfire-and-brimstone preacher at the Woodville United Church got too carried away. During one especially thunderous phrase his false teeth shot from his mouth; but he reached up with his hand, caught them, re-inserted them and continued on without missing a beat. "The pew shook," said my mother, stressing the fact that my grandfather was very strict about behaviour in church: to laugh would be certain death.

These are true stories and there are many more like them; everyone knows stories like that, and they are one point of beginning for a novelist. Another point of beginning would go something like this:

On his way home from the war with Troy, Odysseus made a side trip to the land of the dead. Near a grove sacred to Persephone, he dug a trench, as he had been instructed to do, and let it fill with blood from a sacrificed ram and a black ewe. Attracted by the smell of the blood, many ghosts crowded around the trench, including those of Odysseus' own mother and several of his friends. But he would not let them drink until the ghost he had been waiting for appeared, the ghost of Teiresias, who had been both man and woman and was thus very wise and able to foretell the future. He drank from the trench and instructed Odysseus;

after that many of the ghosts drank, and the blood made them substantial and gave them voices, so that Odysseus was able to converse with them.

Anyone listening to these stories can tell at once that they are of quite different sorts. We think of the first kind as "real" or "true," and of the second kind as "imaginary," "fabulous" or "mythological." Yet you have only my word for it that the first stories are true, and no proof at all that the second one is not. Put both kinds together and you have, for instance, James Joyce.

Why do people tell stories, "real" stories or "made up" stories, and why do people listen to them? Nobody knows, but it seems to be something that the human race has always done. At this point we could all hug ourselves and conclude that therefore the human race will always do it, and we need not bother our heads any more about the matter. But my central message to you tonight is that authorship as we know it, literature as we know it, is in serious danger of becoming extinct. If this is so, and I will present my evidence in due time, we had better start wondering whether we think authors and stories, poetry and fiction, are a good thing or a bad thing. And if they are a good thing, what are they good *for?*

Let me proceed in an oblique way by telling you a few more stories.

I was recently at a University in the United States, on one of those jaunts that includes a poetry reading, lunch with everyone who teaches Women's Studies, and a few hours spent with Creative Writing classes in poetry. I have nothing against universities or creative writing classes; I have attended the former and taught the latter. But something odd was going on. The creative writing class was pervaded by an unnatural calm. A student would read his poem, which had been Xeroxed and passed around in advance. There would be a few ruminative noises. Then the other members of the class would speak, hushed and reverent, in tones that recalled a Quaker prayer meeting. They said things like this: "I think you could do without that colon." "Maybe you could break that line after the word 'language.'" "I like it, it works for me." "It works for me too, except for the place where he rhymes 'spastic' with 'plastic.'"

Finally I could stand it no longer. "Why am I here?" I said. "What do you want me to talk to you about? What do you want to ask me? This is just a roundabout way of saying, Why are *you* here? What kind of activity do you think writing poetry is, and why do you do it? Where do you see yourselves going with it after you've finished with this class? Who's out there listening to you, and where are you going to publish? Do you see your audience as other poets who will admire the placement of your colons, or do you envisage a more general readership? Talking of reading, what do you read? Do you care enough about poetry to say, ever, that you think someone's poem is *terrible?*"

Well, it quickly became evident that I had stepped way over the line that separates decorum from bad taste in creative writing classes such as these. One was not, it appears, supposed to question the *raison d'être* of such classes. One was not supposed to discourage the students. One was supposed to radiate the air of genteel encouragement appropriate to, say, physiotherapists, or people who teach recreational ceramics. The role of the poet in her society was not to be examined. The goal of the class was to keep its enrolled and fee-paying students from quitting in despair, to give them all passing grades so as not to discourage next year's crop, and, with luck, to teach the student to turn out poems publishable in the kinds of little magazines favoured by the instructor. None of this was said. It was all implicit. I had done a bad thing, I had fiddled with the underpinnings of a delicately balanced structure, and the students, although mute during official time, were eager to talk afterwards. I spent an uneasy night at the Holiday Inn, plagued by dreams of a time in the future when all writing would be done by creative writing students, for creative writing students; though my waking self has been aware for some time that between the activity known as creative writing and writing itself there is no necessary connection.

That was a story about confusion and uncertainty—loss of nerve, we might call it—on the part of a body of potential writers. Here is one about confusion and uncertainty on the part of a body of potential readers.

This summer, I returned to the summer camp where, twenty years before, I had taught Nature Study, Campcraft and something called Tripping, which at that time meant only going out on canoe trips. The occasion was the camp's twenty-fifth anniversary, and the camp director was importing former members who had since become what the world thinks of as successful, presumably as an inspiration of some sort. It was pleasant to revisit the place where I had once skulked through the woods, gathering funguses and collecting snakes and caterpillars and revolving my plans to become a great writer. But as I told my young audience, none of whom were over 18, I was clearly insane at the time, as there was no visible evidence in 1959 that any Canadian, let alone me, could ever become a great writer. One might as well have been thinking of flight, without aircraft or wings. Looking back, I can see that my delusions must have come from reading too many Mary Marvel comic books, because they certainly didn't come from anywhere else in the culture that surrounded me.

I then went on to discuss the changes that have taken place in book publishing in this country since 1959. I spoke of the establishment of the small literary and/or nationalist presses in the mid-sixties, the sudden explosion of creativity, first in poetry and then, beginning in about 1969, in the novel, the creation of an audience for new Canadian work where once there had been none, the increased media coverage, and the fact that it was now possible for Canadian writers—not all but at least some—to make their livings practising their art.

My young audience was puzzled. "But you're talking about *money*," they said. It seemed they were still living with the post-romantic version of the artist that's been with us ever since Keats died of consumption and Shelley drowned. They wanted me to be starving in a garret or spending a few hours a week with my head in the oven. Such sufferings would somehow make me authentic

Their attitude was a good example of the inverse snobbery that is still very much alive when it's a question of writers and money, even and especially among writers. A writer who makes money is assumed to have sold out. The fact is that there is no necessary relation between the quality of an author's writing and financial success. Chaucer didn't write for money, Shakespeare did. James Joyce was poor all his life, Charles Dickens made a fortune. Melville tried to make a fortune, but failed at it. On the other hand, he wrote *Moby Dick*, which flopped in his lifetime, but seems to have done quite well since.

"Why do you have the odd notion," I said, "that artists should not be paid for their work?"

"Because they enjoy it," they said.

"Would you want to employ a doctor who did not enjoy being a doctor?" said I.

"No," said they.

"Do you think doctors should be paid?" said I.

They did. "What is the difference between a doctor and a writer?" I asked them. They didn't know, but there is one. If you don't believe me, try the following exercise:

Imagine yourself at a party. You meet a young man. You ask him what he wants to be. "I want to be a doctor," he says. Imagine your reaction. Now pretend he says, "I want to be a writer." What do you feel now?

Is it not true that you regarded the first young man as maybe a little dull but a sane, stable, worthy member of society? As for the second, you probably gave, admit it, an internal shrug. Pretentious, you thought. Neurotic. Maybe a fruit-cake or even a nut-cake. He'll never do it anyway.

You get points in this society for wanting to be a doctor, not just because everyone knows what doctors are for, but because we all know they make money. It's even marginally more acceptable for a woman in this society to want to be a writer than it is for a man, because we don't really take the activity seriously. If a woman wants to do flower painting or crewel work or writing in her spare time, that's all right with us; you can do it at home, in between taking care of your family, as long as it doesn't interfere with the serious business of life, which is your husband's. We are willing to give a certain amount of attention to writers who have, as we say, made it, not necessarily because we admire the work they do, but because we feel that if they sell that many copies there must be something to it. It's not the writing but the making it we'll applaud. In fact, the television talk-show host—who must be, in some way at least, a representative of his society—is much more likely to approve of you if you say you're only in it for the bucks and that your biggest ambition is to sell a million copies. Watch him cross his legs and wince, though, if you say you want to make good art. That puts you at once into the category of those creeps our members of Parliament object to from time to time, the ones jumping around in long underwear or painting pictures that look like someone spilled the ketchup.

A friend of mine told me once that when she'd been in France a man, upon hearing she was a writer, commented, "It is an honourable profession." In Canada we don't—even now—think of writing as an honourable profession. We don't think of it as a profession at all. We think of it, still, as something called "expressing yourself." I'm sure you've all heard the one about the writer and the brain surgeon who met at a cocktail party. "So you write," said the brain surgeon. "Isn't that interesting. I've always wanted to write. When I retire and have the time I'm going to be a writer." "What a coincidence," said the writer, "because when I retire I'm going to be a brain surgeon."

Deep down inside, most people think that writing is sosmething anyone can do, really, because after all it's only expressing yourself. Well, it's probably true that anyone can write. Anyone can play the piano too, but doing it well is another thing. If writing is merely and only self-expression, then all the philistine reactions to it I've been caricaturing above would be, in my opinion, quite justified.

Readers and critics both are still addicted to the concept of self-expression, the writer as a kind of spider, spinning out his entire work from within. This view depends on a solopsism, the idea that we are all self-enclosed monads, with an inside and an outside, and that nothing from the outside ever gets in. It goes hand in hand with that garland of clichés, the one with which women writers in particular are frequently decorated, the notion that everything you write *must* be based on personal experience. *Must*, because those making this assumption have no belief in the imagination, and are such literalists that they will not invest interest in anything they do not suppose to be "true." Of course all writing is based on personal experience, but personal experience is experience—wherever it comes from —that you identify with, *imagine* if you like, so that it becomes personal to you. If your mother dies and you don't feel a thing, is this death a personal experience? "If a clod be washed away by the sea, Europe is the less," said John Donne; or, to paraphrase him as Adrienne Rich does, "Every woman's death diminishes me."

We like to think of writing as merely personal, merely self-expression, and hopefully neurotic, because it lets us off the hook. If that's all it is, if it is not a true view of the world or, Heaven forefend, of a human nature of which we ourselves partake, we don't have to pay any serious attention to it. I happen to believe that at its best writing is considerably more and other than mere self-expression. But what more, what other?

Earlier this summer I was with another group of apprentice writers. They were taking a summer course and many of them were quite earnest and advanced. "Why do you want to write?" I asked them, being by this time very curious about the answers. The first man, an ex-policeman, said he wrote in order to entertain people and to leave a record of himself behind. I did not question why one would want to do either of these things. There were some versions of the self-expression motif, elaborated in the direction of Jungian depth therapy; one does encounter, from time to time, the view that writing is somehow good for the writer, like vitamin pills or primal screaming. One man hinted that writing might have what he called a "political" function.

"What about," said I, "the desire for revenge and the wish to be important?" Blushes all around. Again, I had mentioned something you weren't supposed to. But if one is answering the question, "Why do you want to be a writer?" rather than the one I asked, then such petty motivations cannot be overlooked, because there's a little of that in every young writer when he envisages himself as a future, successful writer.

The question I actually asked was, "Why do you want to write?" and I believe the two questions are quite different. To think of *being a writer* is to imagine oneself as a noun, a thing called a writer; it is to imagine oneself playing a certain kind of role, being treated in a certain kind of way by society. It is to see one's body in a special dress, relating to other bodies as a social entity. *Being a writer* is signing your name in bookstores and making a horse's ass of yourself on TV talk shows and giving speeches like this one. It is concerned with versions of the self; it is *self* centred, and it has nothing much to do with writing, except insofar as it provides you with material.

To think of writing, on the other hand, is to think of a verb. Writing itself is a process, an activity which moves in time and through time, and it is self-less. I don't mean that it thereby makes the writer unselfish; on the contrary, a writer these days has to be selfish to the point of ruthlessness, if only—at the lowest level—to be able to seize the time necessary to write from all those who are clamouring for it. But writing is self-less in the same way that skiing is, or making love. How can you take part intensely in such an involving polyaesthetic activity and still be thinking about yourself? In writing, your attention is focused not on the self but on the thing being made, the thing being seen, and let us not forget that *poet* means *maker* and *seer* means *one who sees*.

The writer has about the same relation to the thing written, once that thing is finished, as fossilized dinosaur footprints have to the beast who made them. The footprints are a record both of the animal's existence and of the fact that once upon a time he walked, fast or slowly, through this particular stretch of mud. While she is writing, the writer is to the thing being written as the pianist is to the music being played and recorded, provided it's an improvisation. Once she's finished, the primary relationship is not between the thing written and the writer but between the thing written and the reader. The thing written may bear traces of the process that created it, and indeed it's fashionable these days to *write in* such traces; or it may not. In either case the piece of writing exists now in the world, as does a piece of bread. Like a piece of bread, it can be measured and run through a computer. If you eat the piece of bread, it will evoke certain sensations in you according to your sense of taste, your allergies, your state of mind and how hungry you are. Meanwhile, the process that created the piece which is now causing you either to long for more or to run for the bathroom has been lost in time. The person who wrote the poem I seem to remember composing yesterday no longer exists, and it's merely out of courtesy to librarians that we put everything with the word *Shakespeare* on the title page into the card file together.

Or it would be merely out of courtesy, were it not for the fact that each piece of writing changes the writer. The verb changes the noun, the verb changes future verbs. Shakespeare, whoever he was, was also the only creature who went through the experience of writing those plays, one after another after another.

Reading is also a process and it also changes you. You aren't the same person after you've read a particular book as you were before, and you will read the next book, unless both are Harlequin Romances, in a slightly different way. When you read a book, it matters how old you are and when you read it and whether you are male or female, or from Canada or India. There is no such thing as a truly universal literature, partly because there are no truly universal readers. It is my contention that the process of reading is part of the process of writing, the necessary completion without which writing can hardly be said to exist.

"If the earth were destroyed, and you were left alone on the moon, would you still write?" I asked the summer students. Opinion was divided. This was of course just a version of the question I have often been asked myself: "Who do you write for?" What the asker usually assumes is that I have some particular kind of audience in mind— women, say, or Canadians—and that I am trying to slant what I say to appeal to such an audience, so they will buy more of my books. This is not the case, I say. "Then are you only writing for yourself?" they say. This also is not the case. It is hard, apparently, to grasp the idea that the writer may be writing *for* other people in the sense of assuming a common language and a human brain at the other end of his activity, but not *for* in the sense of trying to ingratiate, flatter, harangue or manipulate. One may have no image in one's mind of what one's ideal reader looks like, but one does have expectations of what such a being *is* like. The ideal reader, for a serious writer, is intelligent, capable of feeling, possessed of a moral sense, a lover of language, and very demanding. By *demanding*, I don't mean picky. Above all, such a reader will know what kind of book you are writing and will not expect you, as so many critics do, to be writing the book she would write if she were you; nor will the ideal reader expect a romance to be a satire, or a tragedy to be a comedy. There was a noticeable decline in the level of hockey-playing when the league was expanded to include audiences uneducated enough in the sport to think it was cute to throw rolls of toilet paper onto the ice.

"Well," I said to the summer students, "you've said some things I wouldn't disagree with, but I'll go a little farther. Here is what I believe about what you all say you want to do. I believe that poetry is the heart of the language, the activity through which langauge is renewed and kept alive. I believe that fiction writing is the guardian of the moral and ethical sense of the community. Especially now that organized religion is scattered and in disarray, and politicians have, Lord knows, lost their credibility, fiction is one of the few forms left through which we may examine our society not in its particular but in its typical aspects; through which we can see ourselves and the ways in which we behave towards each other, through which we can see others and judge them and ourselves."

Writing is a craft, true, and discussions of the position of colons and the rhyming of *plastic* and *spastic* have some place in it. You cannot be a concert pianist without having first learned the scales, you cannot throw a porcelain vase without having put in a good number of hours at the wheel. But writing is also a vocation. By *vocation* I mean a lifetime pursuit to which you feel called. There is a big difference between a doctor who goes into medicine because he wants to cure people and one who goes into it because that's where he thinks the money is. They may both be able to fix your broken leg, technically just as well; but there is a difference.

Under the right conditions, the first may turn into Norman Bethune. The second never will. If you want to be a writer, you should go into the largest library you can find and stand there contemplating the books that have been written. Then you should ask yourself, "Do I really have anything to add?" If you have the arrogance or the humility to say yes, you will know you have the vocation.

Writing is also a profession, and, at its best, an honourable one. It has been made honourable by those who have already been members of it. Whether you like it or not, every time you set pen to paper you're staring at the same blank space that confronted Milton, Melville, Emily Brontë, Dostoevsky and George Eliot, George Orwell and William Faulkner and Virginia Woolf and William Carlos Williams, not to mention the latest hero, Gabriel Garcia Marquez. Imitation is not emulation; nobody expects you to write the books of these writers over again. But unless you're trying to do as well, unless you're trying to do as well as you can, you are not worthy of the profession. There's a certain amount of cynicism among writers, just as there is among doctors. But if all doctors were hacking off legs with septic instruments in barber shops and losing sponges inside people's lungs because they're drunk during the operation, we would not think of medicine as an honourable profession but as a game played for money by charlatans and quacks, and doctors would still quite rightly be known as leeches.

Writing can also be an art, and one of the reasons that so many writers dodge this on television talk shows is that art is hard to define or describe. Money is easier to talk about, so we talk about money. Nevertheless, art happens. It happens when you have the craft and the vocation and are waiting for something else, something extra, or maybe not waiting; in any case it happens. It's the extra rabbit coming out of the hat, the one you didn't put there. It's Odysseus standing by the blood-filled trench, except that the blood is his own. It is bringing the dead to life and giving voices to those who lack them so that they may speak for themselves. It is not "expressing yourself." It is opening yourself, discarding your *self*, so that the language and the world may be evoked through you. *Evocation* is quite different from *expression*. Because we are so fixated on the latter, we forget that writing also does the former. Maybe the writer *expresses*; but *evocation*, calling up, is what writing does for the reader. Writing is also a kind of sooth-saying, a truth-telling. It is a naming of the world, a reverse incarnation: the flesh becoming word. It's also a witnessing. *Come with me*, the writer is saying to the reader. *There is a story I have to tell you, there is something you need to know*. The writer is both an eye-witness and an I-witness, the one to whom personal experience happens and the one who makes experience personal for others. The writer *bears witness*. Bearing witness is not the same as self-expression.

There's something complusive about the act of writing. All writers play Ancient Mariner at times to the reader's Wedding Guest, hoping that they are holding the reader with their glittering eye, at least long enough so he'll turn the next page. The tale the Mariner tells is partly about himself, true, but it's partly about the universe and partly about something the Wedding Guest needs to know; or at least, that's what the story tells us.

Jacob, so one of the stories goes, wrestled with an angel all night, neither prevailing against the other; and he would not let go until the angel blessed him. *What is your name?* said the angel, unable to give the blessing until the name was spoken. When the angel gave the blessing, it was not for Jacob alone but for his people. There is not a writer alive who would fail to interpret this story as a parable of his own relationship with his art. The encounter with language is a struggle in which each side is equally active, for what writer has not felt the language taking him over at times, blocking him at others? We all hope for the blessing; we all hope finally to be able to speak our names. And, we hope that if we receive the blessing it will not be for ourselves alone.

I notice that I've just used the word "hope" three times, which may surprise some of you, since I doubt that there's a writer in Canada who is asked more often, "Why are you so pessimistic?" I will dodge the question of whether or not the media bunnies (both male and female, and not to be confused with serious journalists) who ask this question lead lives that can be called real in most senses of the word. What I usually say to them is, *What you think is pessimistic depends very largely on what you believe is out there in the world.* I myself think that compared to reality I'm a reincarnation of Anne of Green Gables, but that's beside the point. I think that the world consists of Hell, Purgatory, Middle Earth, Limbo, Paradise and Heaven. Most of them are here with us in this room tonight. It is the duty of the writer not to turn down a visit to any of them if it's offered. Some people only live in a couple of these places but nobody lives in just one. I suspect that the people who ask the question want books to transport them to Paradise, as some compensation for being stuck in Purgatory or Limbo: the band-aid theory of literature. But back to hope. Writing, no matter what its subject, is an act of faith; the primary faith being that someone out there will read the results. I believe it's also an act of hope, the hope that things can be better than they are. If the writer is very lucky and manages to live long enough, I think it can also be an act of charity. It takes a lot to see what is there, both without flinching or turning away and without bitterness. The world exsists; the writer testifies. She cannot deny anything human.

So, I said to the summer students. Are you up to it?

Time will tell whether they are or not, but even if they are, they still may not become writers; or if they do, they may become writers of quite another kind. I said earlier that literature as we know it is in serious danger of becoming extinct, and now that I've told you all the good things it does I will frighten you by telling you why.

Writer and audience are Siamese twins. Kill one and you run the risk of killing the other. Try to separate them, and you may simply have two dead half-people. By "audience," I don't necessarily mean a mass audience. People still write in Russia; many of them write the forbidden. It has always been one function of the artist to speak the forbidden, to speak out, especially in times of political repression. People risk imprisonment and torture because they know there are other people who are hungry for what they have to say. Inhabitants of concentration camps during the second world war jeopardized their already slim chances of survival by keeping diaries; why? Because there was a story that they felt impelled to tell, that they felt the rest of us *had* to know. Amnesty International today works the same way: all it does is tell stories. It makes *the story* known. Such stories have a moral force, a moral authority which is undeniable. The book of Job begins with a series of catastrophes, but for each there is a survivor. Story-telling at its most drastic is the story of the disaster which is the world; it is done by Job's messengers, whom God saved alive because someone had to tell the story. *I only am escaped alone to tell thee:* When a story, "true" or not, begins like this, we must listen.

But such stories are being silenced all over the world. The countries with the most writers in jail are Russia and Argentina. That doesn't mean that these countries treat writers the worst. At least the writers are in jail. In some other countries they are merely dead. El Salvador no longer possesses any poets not in exile. The rest have been murdered.

In any totalitarian takeover, whether from the left or the right, writers, singers and journalists are the first to be suppressed. After that come the union leaders and the lawyers and judges. The aim of all such suppression is to silence *the voice*, abolish the word, so that the only voices and words left are those of the ones in power. Elsewhere, the word itself is thought to have power; that's why so much trouble is taken to silence it.

Nothing to worry about here, you say. We live in a free society. Anyone can say anything. The word is not an issue here; you don't get killed for social and political criticism, and anyway novels and poetry are just a few artists *expressing themselves.* Nobody takes them seriously. It won't happen here.

Well, perhaps. But there's more than one way to skin a cat. Let us take a brief look at what's happening to publishing in this country, in fact in the entire Western world, at this very moment.

First, we are witnessing a fragmentation of the audience on an unprecedented scale. The fragmentation of the audience has to do partly with changes in publishing. Huge popular bestsellers are being bought for enormous sums, and the paperback rights sold for even more enormous sums. This means that vast amounts of money are invested in such books, and vast amounts must be used to promote them; otherwise the investors will not make their money back. Less money is available for other purposes, and the middle-range serious work of fiction is being squeezed right out of the market. Difficult and "experimental" works have already found a place with small literary presses; but the readership for such books is tiny.

In addition, chain bookstores are controlling more and more of the book business. In the States it's forty percent, in Canada I believe it approaches sixty. If the trend continues, the smaller independent bookstores, who have traditionally supported serious fiction and poetry, are going to go belly-up in increasing numbers. The result will be that the chains will have a virtual monopoly on what gets published. In fact, it's likely that publishers will have to have a guarantee from the chains that they'll carry a book before even agreeing to publish it. What that means for prospective authors is that they'll either have to write *Jaws* or it'll be back to the mimeo machine in the cellar, which is where we all started out in this country twenty years ago.

Should this happen, the concept of "authorship" as we've come to know it may very well become obsolete. Already, south of the border, books are increasingly thought of, not as books, but as "entertainment packages." Someone gets an idea and a team is hired to put it together: movie, paperback, foreign sales, t-shirts, the works. The author is not called an author but an "element." Well, what's so bad about that, you may ask? Isn't that how the mediaeval mystery plays were written, and won't such team-created articles give us a more typical, a truer version of society than one made by just a single writer? Isn't that maybe more *collective?*

After all, the individual "author" has been with us only for a few hundred years. Before that, art was made by the community. Maybe we should view these entertainment packages, in which the writer is only "an element," as sort of like primitive folk art? Maybe, but in the days of the oral tradition, poetry and story-telling were used not only for entertainment. They were used to preserve the history of the tribe, to impart wisdom, to summon and propitiate the gods. I am not sure that *Princess Daisy* does very many of those things.

Then there's the problem of distribution. The serious reading audience may still exist, though if it can't get the kind of books it wants it may simply fade out as we enter the post-literate age. In the competition for larger and larger amounts of money, the literate audience too will suffer.

This aspect of the problem has special application to Canada, for the following reason. Much bookstore ordering is now done through computer terminals, all of which are located in the United States. It takes eight weeks for a store in the Canadian West to receive an ordered book through the current, non-computerized Canadian system. It takes only a few days to get one by computer. If you were a bookstore owner, wouldn't you opt for a high turnover of easily-ordered books, rather than going to a lot of trouble for Canadian books that arrive well after the time you could

have used them? Unless Canadians find a way of keying into
or circumventing this system, *all* Canadian books will soon
be back in the cellar with the mimeo machine. The only way
you'll be able to buy them is by mail order.

And even then, you may find them limited in scope. I've
implied that the writer functions in his or her society as a
kind of soothsayer, a truth teller; that writing is not mere
self-expression but a view of society and the world at large,
and that the novel is a moral instrument. *Moral* implies
political, and traditionally the novel has been used not only
as a vehicle for social commentary but as a vehicle for
political commentary as well. The novelist, at any rate, still
sees a connection between politics and the moral sense, even
if politicians gave that up some time ago. By "political" I
mean having to do with power: who's got it, who wants it,
how it operates; in a word, who's allowed to do what to
whom, who gets what from whom, who gets away with it and
how.

But we're facing these days an increasing pressure on
the novel. I'll be careful when I use the word "censorship,"
because real censorship stops a book before it's even been
published. Let us say "suppression." The suppression is of
two kinds. One has do with the yanking of books out of
schools and libraries, and is usually motivated by religious
objections to depictions of sexual activity. I happen to
find this stance pornographic, for the following reason.
Pornography is a presentation of sex in isolation from
the matrix which surrounds it in real life; it is therefore
exaggerated, distorted and untrue. To select the sexual bits
from a novel like *The Diviners* and to discard the rest is
simply to duplicate what pornographers themselves are
doing. It would take a very salacious mind indeed to find
The Diviners, or indeed the works by Alice Munro, myself
and others which have been put through this particular
centrifuge, unduly arousing. You have to wade through too
much other stuff. Literary writers are easy targets; they

don't shoot off your kneecaps. It's a lot safer to villify them
than it is to take on the real pornographers.

(The Bible, of course, contains blasphemy, torture,
rape, sodomy, orgies, murder, lying and lots of other unpleasant things. It also contains the Sermon on the Mount,
which would mean a lot less without its setting. Its setting is
the world as it is, human nature as it is. Christ consorted with
publicans and sinners, not just because they were more of a
challenge but because there were more of them; he didn't
have too much use for holier-than-thous. Incidentally, the
Bible itself has more than once appeared on lists of banned
books.)

Nevertheless, I don't think writers can scream very
hard about their books being removed from schools. The
students should do the screaming if they want the books,
and a system in which parents were not allowed to protest
about what their children are being taught would be a fascist
dictatorship. The only way to fight this trend is by counter-
protest, and it remains to be seen whether enough people
feel strongly enough about the corollary to free speech, free
reading, to make this effective. But libraries are another
matter. Libraries are for adults, and no one has the right to
remove anything from them without the consent of the
community at large.

The other kind of suppression is semi-political and is,
in my view, more dangerous. There are two cases before
the courts right now on which I can't comment. Suffice it
to say that if the plaintiffs win them the effect will be to
scare publishers away from anything with serious political
comment. In fact these cases, although they have not yet
been decided, are already having this effect. The novel
takes as its province the whole of life. Removal of the
right to comment on politics will gut it.

If you think Canada is really a country dedicated to
democracy and the principle of free speech, remember the
War Measures Act. Remember the letters to the editor.

Remember how few people spoke out. We are a timorous country, and we do tend to believe that what those in authority do *must*, somehow, be justified.

What we're facing, then, is a literary world split between the huge entertainment-package blockbusters written by "elements" and deemed both money-making and politically innocuous by the powers that be, and a kind of publishing underground to which the rest of us will be banished. The literary audience, which has never been a mass one, will either content itself with the literary equivalent of Muzak— writing to suck your thumb by—or it will stop reading altogether. Some bright soul will put together a mail-order operation, perhaps. As for the writers, they will either become "elements" or they will fulfill my nightmares about the creative writing students. They will stop writing for readers *out there* and write only for readers *in here*, cosy members of an in-group composed largely of other writers and split into factions or "schools" depending on who your friends are and whether you spell I with a capital I or a small one. This tendency will merely support the average serious reader's impression that such writing has nothing to say to *him*. This is already happening to poetry, though in Canada, which as we all know is a cultural backwater, it hasn't happened quite as thoroughly yet.

You may have thought I was going to say something about Canadian novels, and how we all ought to read them because, although nasty-tasting, they are good for us because they tell us about ourselves. I didn't do that because I think the problem is far larger than Canada; although the trends I've outlined will be reflected in Canada too, if they continue unchecked. Of course in entertainment packages it doesn't matter a hoot whether the "element" is Canadian or not, and the citizenship of great white sharks is irrelevant. But in serious literature there is always a voice, and there is no such thing as a voice without a language and without an accent. All true namings have an accent, and accents are local. This does not make the naming of their world less true, however, but more true. Those who have maintained over the years that "Canadian" and "universal" are mutually exclusive may soon find themselves proved right, because the only universal things around are going to be entertainment packages, and you can bet your bottom dollar they won't be Canadian.

If you doubt what I say, take a look at the current state of criticism, both in this country and elsewhere in the Western world. The critic is that curious creature, a reader-writer, and he reflects trends even more accurately than *Toronto Life*. In his popular form he's supposed to function as a kind of stand-in for the average, intelligent reader, or so I was told at school. He's supposed to keep us informed about what's going on in writing, what writers are producing, and what effect these productions had on him as a reasonably experienced reader. Once upon a time in Canada, criticism was either non-existent or serious, because there were very few Canadian books and very few people read them, and those who did and cared enough to take the time to write about them were dedicated souls. In fact, twenty years ago it would not have been an exaggeration to say that the level of criticism was quite far above the level of what was being criticized. Now we have both popular and academic critics. Popular book criticism takes place in the back rows of something called the entertainment section. Too frequently, entertainment editors try to match books up with reviewers who are guaranteed to hate them, because a peevish view filled with witticisms at the writers' expense is thought to amuse the readership and increase circulation. Snide gossip and tittle-tattle have become regular features of such entertainment sections. As for the academic community, that segment of it that concerns itself with Canadian writing, it's heavily into metonomy and synecdoche, but they don't have a lot to do with what writing is about, unless you stop at the craft and don't bother at all with the vocation or the art.

A country or a community which does not take serious literature seriously will lose it. *So what?* say the Members of Parliament, the same ones who object to the creeps in long underwear. *All we want is a good read. A murder mystery, a spy thriller, something that keeps you turning the pages. I don't have the time to read anyway.*

Well, try this. It could well be argued that the advent of the printed word coincided with the advent of democracy as we know it; that the book is the only form that allows the reader not only to participate but to review, to re-view what's being presented. With a book you can turn back the pages. You can't do that with a television set. Can democracy function at all without a literate public, one with a moral sense and well-developed critical faculties? Can democracy run on entertainment packages alone?

And in whose interest is it that participatory democracy continue to function anyway, even in the imperfect way that it does? Not that of governments, which would like to see a combination of bureaucracy and oligarchy, with the emphasis on the bureaucracy. Not that of big business, which would like a quiescent labour market stuffed to senility with entertainment packages. Canada could easily pass legislation that would protect the book industry we now so tenuously have. Quotas on paperback racks, like the radio quotas that have done so well for the record industry; a system of accredited bookstores, like the ones in, dare I mention it, Quebec. It wouldn't be difficult, but who cares enough to make it happen?

I will leave such questions with you, since you are, after all, the audience. It will not be by the writers, who are too few in number to have any influence at the polls, but by the audience itself that such questions will ultimately be answered.

42
Midnight Birds:
Stories of Contemporary
Black Women Writers

(1981)

Midnight Birds is a collection of fifteen recent pieces of short fiction, all of them by women who are also Black and American. There's an excellent preface by Mary Ellen Washington, and each writer also introduces herself in a short preliminary piece, an arrangement that makes the book handy for teaching.

It's of note that the book's subtitle mentions "women," "contemporary" and "Black," but doesn't bother with "American." (Black women do exist elsewhere.) It's also of note that this book is being reviewed in an issue of this magazine devoted to "Third World" writing. And it's also of note, given these contexts, that I myself am female, but neither Black nor American. I am in fact Canadian, a citizen of a country which was until recently dominated by one imperial power and is now dominated by another. Could it be that the editors of *The Harvard Educational Review* perceived that I have something in common with the writers in this collection? Could they be right?

The writers themselves have no doubts about their identity as Americans, nor should they. Their prose is American, their settings are American; even their assumption, shared by the editor and most of the writers, that things can be improved almost by sheer faith, is at its core profoundly American. These women are not writing about genital mutilation or polygamy or purdah, which luckily are not problems they have to deal with directly. These women are writing, these women *can* write, which makes them different at once from most Third World women. They are as American as jazz and lynching. By what strange squint—the same one, presumably, that sees white male American writers as the norm and everyone else as the exception—have they been relegated to the "Third World" category?

It certainly cannot be a reflection on the quality of the writing. This is American writing at its finest, by turns earthy, sinuous, thoughtful, and full of power. *Midnight Birds* includes such well-known names as Alice Walker, Toni Morrison, Toni Cade Bambera and Ntozake Shange, as well as names not quite so well-known but which deserve to be: Alexis Deveaux, Paulette Childress White, Frenchy Hodges, Gayle Jones and Sherley Anne Williams. Prose techniques range from the window-pane clarity of Alice Walker to the verbal improvisations of Alexis Deveaux and Ntozake Shange. The writers as a whole are concerned with the need to forge or re-discover a language of their own, since the mainstream white male language they were taught they ought to think in has served them so badly. As pieces of writing, there's not a dud in the lot. It's no disparagement of writers like Achebe, but simple curiosity to wonder why this book has been placed on the "Third World" shelf. Isn't Harlem in New York? Is it perhaps that white Americans would rather not see the visions of these women as visions of their own society, but as visions of somewhere else, somewhere foreign and other? But there are many more worlds than three, even in America, and some of them overlap.

I once met an academic who specialized in Commonwealth Literature. When I asked him why he had chosen to do that, he said that he found it much easier to trace the patterns of relationship between writer and audience, to investigate the social function of literature, at the periphery rather than at the centre. If you are a member of an imperial culture, a Roman rather than a Gaul, you can take things for granted, to the point of ignorance or amnesia, in a way that the Gauls cannot. Black American women are, paradoxically, both Gauls and Romans, but these writers identify most of the time with the Gauls.

Which makes a difference in their own attitudes towards what they are doing. For instance, if you were to ask a white American male writer who he's writing for, you would probably get a somewhat abstract answer, unless he's a member of an ethnic minority. But the writers in *Midnight Birds* know exactly who they're writing for. They're writing for other Black American women, and they believe in the power of their words. They see themselves as giving a voice to the voiceless. They perceive writing as the forging of saving myths, the naming of forgotten pasts, the telling of truths. They do not want their books to be admired merely for their aesthetic qualities. They want them to be taken back into the society from which they have sprung and to change things there.

These writers think it's important that a people be able to see its own reflection in the mirror of art, and they see art very much as a mirror, when they aren't seeing it as some even more practical tool such as a shovel. Almost every writer talks about the extent to which she has written out of her own experience and derived the power to do so from her own community. Alexis Deveaux stands for many:

> Writing helps me unravel the images and forces at work in my own life, and therefore, by extension, in the lives of Black women and Black people around me. I hope to communicate something not just about my life, but about

our life. It's all one life—isn't it? And I'm very concerned about the images of Black women in literature because whatever is written down becomes the word, and stays. . . . I want to say something about the Black woman as a three-dimensional human being. So often we've seen her depicted as . . . ugly and useless. I want to change that. In the most radical and revolutionary ways possible.

(p. 15)

Both the writers' attitudes and the readers' anticipated responses depend on factors which we're used to thinking of as extra-literary; which should probably lead us to re-examine what we mean by this term. Can art and the world really be separated? Perhaps art for art's sake is a luxury, one you can afford only when you're well-fed. Despite their private successes, these women are still very close to hunger.

As in early feminist theory, there's still some confusion between the desire to create heroic figures and the pull towards truth-telling. Gayle Jones, for instance, has been criticized for not making her characters more admirable. The editor comments:

Diane Johnson said in *The New York Review of Books* that a white reader, like herself, could not relate to such de-humanized pictures of black life and lamented that all of Jones' women characters were brutalized and dull. . . . One wishes for the heroic voice, for the healing of the past; but it is presumptuous to demand that these things appear before their time.

(p. 127)

There will always be a conflict between those who want writers to create good role-models and the kind of writer who feels that a picture of life that leaves out the rock bottom would be profoundly untrue. For the most part, these writers resolve the conflict in that most American of ways: by seeing the ordinary as heroic.

White American feminists might have some trouble, too, with the way men are dealt with here, though nobody from a colony would. In a colony, both men and women are oppressed, the women doubly so, though the men feel emasculated by having their decision-making powers taken away from them. The writers in *Midnight Birds* display a tenderness, a pity, towards their Black male characters which it would be hard to match among contemporary white American feminists. The men are often dying, of dope, bullet wounds and other forms of violence slow and swift, and the woman characters, although often badly treated by them, cannot turn their backs on them. One of the most harrowing scenes in the book is from Toni Morrison's *Sula*, in which a woman burns her own son to death because he has become a hopeless addict; yet even this act is rendered as profoundly maternal.

In a recent discussion about writing, someone described to me a cartoon in *The New Yorker*: a small girl is hunched over a book, in tears, and her mother is warning the returning father, "Shh! Beth is dying!" The girl's capacity to be moved is seen as comic. But isn't that moment what the act of writing is supposed to aim for? Not sentimentality, to be sure—and these writers are rarely sentimental—but empathy on the part of the reader. These writers have no doubts about that. They want to involve the reader, they want to move her, and, at their best, they succeed. "Universal" literature is not literature that ignores the local, the particular. On the contrary, it is literature that renders the particular so concretely that even readers from outside the constituency can be moved. It's not the Third World that these women are writing about, but it is a world very different from the one most people who read books in America inhabit. Or rather its the same world; though it is seen, with honesty, passion and painful clarity, through different windows.

43
Nadine Gordimer:
July's People

(1981)

July's People is the latest novel by the astonishing South
African writer Nadine Gordimer, and it's one of her best to
date. It's set in a future that could be tomorrow: the blacks of
South Africa have finally staged a general uprising and the
country is in a state of civil war, with predictable foreign
participation: Cuba and Mozambique on one side, the United
States on the other, the outcome in doubt.

The war itself and the rights and wrongs of the partic-
ipants do not form Gordimer's primary subject, however.
Rather she focusses on its effects at the private and human
level. "July's People" are Bam and Maureen Smales and
their three small children, a white, middle-class, self-
consciously liberal family for whom their black manservant,
July, has worked with apparent devotion for the past fifteen
years. When it's become obvious that the rioting and killing
are out of control and that the Smales have left flight too
late, July rescues them by guiding them to his own family
village hundreds of miles away in the middle of the African
bush. They take with them only what they have remembered
to snatch up at a moment's notice. For everything else, they
realize, they are now dependent upon their former depend-
ant.

In less skilled hands this could have become a self-righteous and potentially malicious cautionary tale, of the "Look what's going to happen to you" variety. But Gordimer handles the nuances of the relationships involved with exquisite dexterity. The Smales in their pre-revolutionary suburban colonial setting were not *bad* whites. They were not bigots, they told themselves, they favoured more self-determination for blacks, they went jogging. They are not depicted as angels, however; only as typical of their kind. July is no angel. His rescue of them is motivated more by habit and the desire to maintain a status quo in which he has a relatively favoured place than by charity.

Now that they think he's no longer their servant, the Smales desperately want July to turn out to be a person much like themselves. Just as desperately, July clings to his role, because the only way he can see these people is as rich masters whose position and therefore his own will soon be restored. Each side makes a fetish of the other, while the subtle shifts in power and status make such fantasies increasingly impossible. The Smales owe their lives to July. Nevertheless, they can't really stand it when he starts learning, without their permission, to drive their car.

The culture-shock for the Smales is massive. Uprooted, deprived of material objects, existing on tea and boiled grain, they can hardly maintain any coherent image of their own identities. Only gradually do they come to experience concretely, by the observation of details that would have been merely picturesque to them before—a chief dressed in cast-off whites' clothing, the rusting bits of white junk scattered around the village—the fact that this kind of culture-shock has been going on for black South Africans for hundreds of years.

July has other "people" in addition to the Smales: the wife he has seen only at two-year intervals, during his leaves of absence; the children conceived by her, also at two-year intervals; the extended family of which he is the head and for which he provides; and, beyond the village, the larger "country" to which he belongs, headed by a chief who wants to fight the revolutionaries rather than joining them because he simply cannot imagine the end of white power. For these people the Smales are at first a marvel, then a curiosity, and increasingly a burden, since they must be fed and sheltered out of the already marginal resources of the village. "They have nothing," Maureen Smales notes with wonder.

July's People delivers its characters over to the reader with a chilling precision and a degree of understanding which would not ordinarily be called compassionate. Yet compassionate it is, for Gordimer is not accusing. *July's People* is not concerned with villains and heroes but with the depiction of a next-to-impossible situation. Novels about the future, as Ursula Le Guin has said, are really about the present. The situation in South Africa is already impossible on any human level, Gordimer is saying, not only for the blacks but for the whites. The blacks at least have a sense of belonging. The whites, if the Smales are any example, don't even have that.

This is a densely yet concisely-written book, beautifully shaped, powerful in its impact. It should gain for its author the wide audience she deserves.

44
Ann Beattie:
Falling in Place

(1980)

Ann Beattie is already well known for her three previous works of fiction: a novel, *Chilly Scenes of Winter*, and two volumes of short stories, *Distortions* and *Secrets and Surprises*. Readers of her earlier books will not be disappointed in *Falling in Place*, her second novel. Neither will they be particularly amazed. It's similar territory, seen, if possible, with an even sharper vision, a more mordant sense of humour.

To say that Ann Beattie is a good writer would be an understatement. Her ear for the banalities and the petty verbal cruelties of the late '70s middle-American domestic idiom is faultless, her eye for the telling detail as ruthless as a hawk's. She knows her characters inside out, down to the very last nastiness and snivelling sentiment, and she spares us nothing. The characters themselves are representative rather than exceptional: both halves of a splitting marriage, the husband enraged because he feels he married the wrong woman and had the wrong children, the wife obsessed, for lack of anything better, by her dead dog; their children, whose mutual hatred mirrors that of their parents, the boy fat and unhappy, the girl despising everything except Peter Frampton; the husband's young lover, the lover's ex-lover; the ex-lover's lover. There are loose connections among them, but part of Beattie's point is the looseness of the connections.

All could be illustrations for Christopher Lasch's *The Culture of Narcissism*, demanding love and commitment from those around them but unwilling to give it. They feel that their lives are entirely out of control, that they lack power and cannot be expected to take responsibility for the consequences of their actions. Their dominant moods are anger and self-pity, and we find their triviality enraging until we come to see them not as minor sadists but as drowning people clutching each other's throats out of sheer panic. Adrift in a world of seemingly pointless events, bombarded with endless media flotsam, trapped in a junkyard of unsatisfactory objects, plugged into the monologues of others who appear to be deaf to their own, these characters cry out for meaning and coherence, but their world hands them nothing more resonant than popular song titles and T-shirt slogans.

Despite it all they remain yearning romantics. What they want from each other is nothing less than salvation, and Beattie's vision is ultimately a religious one. With religion having been designated as uncool, however, they're stuck in Middle Earth. Heaven is being in love, and stoned too if you can manage it, and Hell is a family barbecue. In fact, not just Hell but the entire cosmology is other people. "Save me," says Cynthia, as she falls into the arms of her just-returned lover Spangle. We know he can't.

The only answer for these glutted but spiritually famished people would be God or magic. God appears only as a T-shirt slogan — "God Is Coming And She Is Pissed" — and magic is represented by a third-rate party magician who gets a crush on Cynthia in a laundromat. He's a fraud, but he does represent magic of a kind: his love for Cynthia, unrequited though it is, is the only bit of disinterested altruism in the book. He doesn't want to possess her, he wants to wish her well, and it is through his magic binoculars that Cynthia sees her vanished lover as he finally appears again. It isn't much, but in view of the odds, it's a tiny miracle.

The society Beattie depicts is chaotic and random. Things happen to these characters, they change, but there is no plot in the traditional sense of the term. The major event, the shooting of the husband's daughter by his 10-year-old son, is an accident, and the general reaction to it is stunned disbelief. "Things just fall into place," says one character, commenting on *Vanity Fair*. "Maybe things just fell quickly because of gravity," thinks another, "and when they stopped, you said they were in place." Which is a comment also on Beattie's particular art. Sometimes the reader feels caught in an out-of-control short story, sometimes in a locked train compartment filled with salesman's samples and colossally boring egomaniacs, but most of the time, thanks to Beattie's skill, her novel not only convinces but entrances. The details are small, but the picture of our lives and times built up from them is devastating.

45
An Introduction to
The Edible Woman

(1981)

I wrote *The Edible Woman* in the spring and summer of 1965, on empty examination booklets filched from the University of British Columbia, where I had been teaching freshman English for the previous eight months. The title scene dates from a year earlier; I'd thought it up while gazing, as I recall, at a confectioner's display window full of marzipan pigs. It may have been a Woolworth's window full of Mickey Mouse cakes, but in any case I'd been speculating for some time about symbolic cannibalism. Wedding cakes with sugar brides and grooms were at that time of particular interest to me. *The Edible Woman*, then, was conceived by a twenty-three-year-old, and written by a twenty-four-year-old, and its more self-indulgent grotesqueries are perhaps attributable to the youth of the author, though I would prefer to think that they derive instead from the society by which she found herself surrounded.

(*The Edible Woman* was not my first novel. The first one had been composed in a rentable broom closet in Toronto, but it had been rejected by all three of the then-existent Canadian publishers for being too gloomy. It ended with the

heroine deciding whether or not to push the male protagonist off a roof, a conclusion that was well ahead of its time in
1963 and probably too indecisive now.)

I finished *The Edible Woman* in November of 1965 and
sent it to a publisher who'd displayed some interest in my
previous book. After an initial positive letter, I heard
nothing. I was too busy worrying about my PhD Orals to
follow up at that point, but after a year and a half I began
probing and discovered that the publisher had lost the
manuscript. By this time I was marginally visible, having
won an award for poetry, so the publisher took me out to
lunch. "We'll publish your book," he said, not looking me in
the eye. "Have you read it?" I said. "No, but I'm going to,"
he said. It was probably not the first book he'd published out
of sheer embarrassment.

The Edible Woman appeared finally in 1969, four years
after it was written and just in time to coincide with the rise
of feminism in North America. Some immediately assumed
that it was a product of the movement. I myself see the book
as protofeminist rather than feminist: there was no women's
movement in sight when I was composing the book in 1965,
and I'm not gifted with clairvoyance, though like many at
the time I'd read Betty Friedan and Simone de Beauvoir
behind locked doors. It's noteworthy that my heroine's
choices remain much the same at the end of the book as
they are at the beginning: a career going nowhere, or
marriage as an exit from it. But these were the options for
a young woman, even a young educated woman, in Canada
in the early sixties. It would be a mistake to assume that
everything has changed. In fact, the tone of the book seems
more contemporary now than it did in, say, 1971, when it
was believed that society could change itself a good deal
faster than presently appears likely. The goals of the
feminist movement have not been achieved, and those who
claim we're living in a post-feminist era are either sadly
mistaken or tired of thinking about the whole subject.

46
Canadian-American Relations:
Surviving The Eighties

(1981)

I am always pleased to be able to return to the scene of my youthful debaucheries—which were of course purely intellectual in nature—especially since it is also the land of my ancestors. My ancestors would have been pleased to return to it as well, I suspect, once they'd found out what Canada was really like, but there had been a slight disagreement over who should rule this country—divinely constituted law and order in the person of George III or a lot of upstart revolutionaries—and my ancestors had departed for the north in search of some place where you could still get a decent cup of tea, thus becoming part of the brain drain; a drain, according to my father, from which the States has never entirely recovered. Canadian-American relations were a frequent topic of conversation in my grandmother's house. There were the Canadian relations and then there were the American relations, who lived mostly in Boston. That's what makes Canadian-American relations somewhat touchy at times: they *are* relatives. There's nothing that rankles more than a cousin, especially one with a Rolls-Royce.

I'll preface this speech by saying that if you really feel you have to bring me all the way down from the frozen north to tell you how all of us are going to make it through the next ten years, you're in deep trouble. The fact is that nobody knows, least of all me. What you are about to hear is merely the fruit of idle speculation.

I have two things to say in defence of idle speculation. First, it's what universities are for. Where else could one devote three months of one's life to an investigation of whether John Keats did or did not have syphilis? Second, I'm a novelist, and idle speculation is what novelists do. How odd to spend one's life trying to pretend that non-existent people are real: though no odder, I suppose, than what government bureaucrats do, which is trying to pretend that real people are non-existent. However, when you invite a novelist to speak to you, what you get is a novelization.

I'll warn you right at the beginning that although this is a slightly mean speech, I do know the difference between an individual and a foreign policy. Americans as individuals can be enthusiastic, generous and optimistic in ways undreamt of by your average Canadian. How could I think otherwise when the Americans so consistently give me better reviews than do my begrudging, dour and suspicious fellow countrymen? Americans worship success; Canadians find it in slightly bad taste. In fact, Canadians find Canadians in slightly bad taste, which is probably why Texas is currently cornering the market on Canadian studies. This does not startle the Canadians: they always knew Texans had bad taste. (They'll collect *anything*).

No Canadian ever made a speech in the United States without beginning with an apology, and that was mine. Having now fulfilled the obligations which politeness and protocol demand, I'll proceed to the speech proper, which is supposed to be about Canadian-American relations, and what the future holds for them.

Canadian-American relations sounds like a dull subject, and it is, unless you've ever tried explaining them to an American. What you get in return is usually a version of "You're so cute when you're mad, honey." Americans don't usually *have* to think about Canadian-American relations, or, as they would put it, American-Canadian relations. Why think about something which you believe affects you so little? We, on the other hand, have to think about you whether we like it or not.

Last month, during a poetry reading I was giving, I tried out a short prose poem called "How To Like Men." It began by suggesting that one might profitably start with the feet and work up, the toes being an innocuous enough part of the body, one would think. Unfortunately the question of jackboots soon arose, and things went on from there. After the reading I had a conversation with a distressed young man who thought I was being unfair to men. He wanted men to be liked, not just from the soles to the knees, but totally, and not just as individuals but as a group. He found it negative and inegalitarian of me to have alluded to war and rape. In vain did I point out to him that as far as any of us knew these were two activities not widely engaged in by women, the first perhaps from lack of opportunity, the second for what we might delicately call lack of interest. He was still upset. "But we're both in this together," he protested. I had to admit that this was so; but could he, maybe, see that our relative positions might be a little different?

This is the kind of roadblock one runs into with Americans, when one has been unable to prevent the dinner-table conversation from veering around to Canadian-American relations. Americans are quite happy to claim that we're both in this together when it comes to a discussion of continental energy resources; in fact, they sometimes talk as if they'd be more than willing to share the benefits of the American system with us, by having us join them. A Texan once put this proposition to Pierre Berton, one of our larger writers. Berton retorted that he thought this would be a dandy idea. The Americans could get back the Queen, whom they've always coveted, and revert to constitutional monarchy, and do away with the FBI and receive the much more colourful Royal Canadian Mounted Police in return, and change to a three-party system and become officially bilingual. Well, that wasn't exactly what the Texan had in mind.

Such unconscious imperialism is not confined to Texas. During an early '70s feminist "international" conference being held in Toronto, the Canadian sisters ended up locking themselves in the john because they felt that the American sisters were being culturally imperialistic. They claimed to be speaking for Woman, capital W, universal, but as far as the Canadian sisters could tell they thought Woman, capital W, was not only white and middle-class but American as well. Then there's the history of the Canadian labour movement, which was annexed to the American labour movement in the thirties in the name of the United Front. Then, too, Canadians succumbed to that most seductive of slogans, "We're all in this together," and they've been finding ever since that their fellow workers have been quite happy to collect their dues but not all that interested in hearing about such boring items as wage parity and the alarming tendency of American companies to close down their Canadian branch plants whenever there's a slump in trade. The discussion has a tendency to break down into a version of afternoon soap-opera, those scenes in which the puzzled man says "What are you trying to tell me?" and the woman, wringing her hands, says, "You haven't been listening! You don't understand!" One could sum up the respective stances by saying that the typical American one is unthinkingly and breezily aggressive and the Canadian one peevishly and hesitantly defensive, and there's even some accuracy in such a generalization, but that doesn't help us much if we want to know why.

Why and how are often closely related, and how in this case is historical. I won't go back to the war of 1812 and the Fenian raids, as it is bad manners to remind one's hosts of their failure to invade and conquer one's country by military means. ("We won't do that again," an American once said to a friend of mine. "We don't need to, we own it anyway.") I'll skip the two World Wars as well, merely pointing out in passing that if Americans thought Canadians were sitting back and sucking their thumbs and watching it all on television during the Vietnam years, meanwhile benefitting from arms manufacture, it was a mere nothing to what happened between 1939 and Pearl Harbour. I'll go to the postwar years, when I began to have a memory, and trace for you my own progress from wild colonial girl to the person who gives these kinds of speeches, because I think that progress is typical of my generation, the generation of 1960's literary nationalism.

I was born in 1939, which means that I was ten in 1949 and twenty in 1959. I spent a large part of my childhood in northern Quebec, surrounded by many trees and few people. My attitude towards Americans was formed by this environment. Alas, the Americans we encountered were usually pictures of ineptitude. We once met two of them dragging a heaving metal boat, plus the motor, across a portage from one lake to another because they did not want to paddle. Typically American, we thought, as they ricocheted off yet another tree. Americans hooked other people when they tried to cast, got lost in the woods and didn't burn their garbage. Of course, many Canadians behaved this way too; but somehow not *as* many. And there were some Americans, friends of my father, who could shoot a rapids without splintering their canoe and who could chop down a tree without taking off a foot in the process. But these were not classed as Americans, not *real* Americans. They were from Upper Michigan State or Maine or places like that, and were classed, I blush to admit, not as Americans but as honourary Canadians. I recognize that particular cross-filing system, that particular way of approving of people you as a rule don't approve of, every time a man tells me I think like a man; a sentence I've always felt had an invisible comma after the word *think*. I've since recognized that it's no compliment to be told you are not who you are, but as children we generalized, cheerfully and shamelessly. The truth, from our limited experience, was clear: Americans were wimps who had a lot of money but did not know what they were doing.

That was the rural part of my experience. The urban part was somewhat different. In the city I went to school, and in the early years at any rate the schools I went to were still bastions of the British Empire. In school we learned the Kings of England and how to draw the Union Jack and sing Rule Britannia, and poems with refrains like, "Little Indian, Sioux or Cree, Don't you wish that you were me?" Our imaginations were still haunted by the war, a war that we pictured as having been fought between us, that is, the British, and the Germans. There wasn't much room in our minds for the Americans and the Japanese. Winston Churchill was a familiar figure to us; Theodore Roosevelt was not.

In public school we did not learn much about Americans, or Canadians either, for that matter. Canadian history was the explorers and was mostly brown and green, for all those trees. British history was kings and queens, and much more exciting, since you could use the silver and gold coloured pencils for it.

That era of Canadian colonialism was rapidly disappearing, however. One explanation for the reason it practically vanished during the postwar decade—1946 to 1957, say, the year I graduated from high school—is an economic one. The Canadians, so the theory goes, over-extended themselves so severely through the war effort that they created a capital vacuum in Canada. Nature and entrepreneurs hate a vacuum, so money flowed up from the United States to fill it, and when Canadians woke up in the sixties and started to take stock, they discovered they'd sold their birthright for a mess. This revelation was an even greater shock for me; not only was my country owned, but it was owned by the kind of people who carried tin boats across portages and didn't burn their garbage. One doubted their competence.

Looking back on this decade, I can see that the change-over from British cultural colony to American cultural colony was symbolized by what happened after school as opposed to in it. I know it's hard to believe in view of my youthful appearance, but when I was a child there was no television. There were, however, comic books, and these were monolithically American. We didn't much notice, except when we got to the ads at the back, where Popsicle Pete reigned supreme. Popsicle Pete would give you the earth in exchange for a few sticky wrappers, but his promises always had a little asterisk attached: "Offer good only in the United States." International world cynics may be forgiven for thinking that the same little asterisk is present invisibly in the Constitution and the Declaration of Independence and the Bill of Rights, not to mention the public statements of prominent Americans on such subjects as democracy, human dignity and freedom, and civil liberties. Maybe it all goes back to Popsicle Pete. We may all be in this together, but some of us are asterisked.

Such thoughts did not trouble our heads a great deal. When you were finished with Donald Duck and Mickey Mouse (and Walt Disney was, by the way, a closet Canadian), you could always go on to Superman (whose creator was also one of ours). After that it would be time for Sunday night radio, with Jack Benny and Our Miss Brooks. We knew they talked funny, but we didn't mind. Then of course there were movies, none of which were Canadian, but we didn't mind that either. Everyone knew that was what the world was like. Nobody knew there had once been a Canadian film industry.

After that I went to high school, where people listened to American pop music after school instead of reading comic books. During school hours we studied, among other things, history and literature. Literature was still the British tradition: Shakespeare, Eliot, Austen, Thomas Hardy, Keats and Wordsworth and Shelley and Byron; not experiences anyone should miss, but it did tend to give the impression that all literature was written by dead Englishmen, and—this is important—by dead English*women*. By this time I wanted to be a writer, and you can see it would be a dilemma: being female was no hindrance, but how could one be a writer and somehow manage to avoid having to become British and dead? The generation before mine compromised; they settled for the British part and emigrated to England, taking their chances on the death. My generation, in ways I'll come to in a minute, took another road.

In history it was much the same story. We started with Ancient Egypt and worked our way through Greece, Rome and mediaeval Europe, then the Renaissance and the birth of the modern era, the invention of the steam engine, the American revolution, the French revolution, the Civil War and other stirring events, every single one of which had taken place outside Canada.

Finally, in the very last year, by which time many future citizens had dropped out anyway, we got a blue book called *Canada In The World Today*. It was about who grew the wheat, how happy the French were, how well the parliamentary system worked for everybody and how nice it was that the Indians had given us all their land in exchange for the amenities of civilization. The country we lived in was presented to us in our schools as colourless, dull and without much historical conflict to speak of, except for a few massacres, and nobody did *that* any more. Even the British war of conquest was a dud, since both of the generals died. It was like a hockey game in which both teams lost.

As for Canada in the World Today, its role, we were assured, was an important one. It was the upper northwest corner of a triangle consisting of Canada, the United States and Britain, and its position was not one to be sneezed at: Canada, having somehow become an expert at compromise, was the mediator. It was not to be parochial and inward-looking any more but was to be international in outlook. Although in retrospect the role of mediator may shrink somewhat—one cannot quite dispel the image of Canada trotting back and forth across the Atlantic with sealed envelopes, like a glorified errand boy—there's a little truth to be squeezed from this lemon. Canadians, oddly enough, *are* more international in outlook than Americans are; not through any virtue on their part but because they've had to be. If you're a Canadian travelling in the United States, one of the first things you notice is the relative absence of international news coverage. In Canada, one of the most popular news programmes ever devised has two radio commentators phoning up just about anyone they can get on the line, anywhere in the world. Canadians live in a small house, which may be why they have their noses so firmly pressed to the windows, looking out.

I remember *Canada In The World Today* with modified loathing—"Canada comes of age," it trumpeted, not bothering to mention that what happened to you when you came of age was that you got pimples or a job or both—and still not a year passes without some politician announcing that Canada has finally grown up. Still, the title is significant. Canada sees itself as part of the world; a small sinking Titanic squashed between two icebergs, perhaps, but still inevitably a part. The States, on the other hand, has always had a little trouble with games like chess. Situational strategy is difficult if all you can see is your own borders, and beyond that some wispy brownish fuzz that is barely worth considering. The Canadian experience was a circumference with no centre, the American one a centre which was mistaken for the whole thing.

A few years ago I was in India and had occasion to visit both the Canadian and American enclaves in New Delhi. The Canadian there lived in a house decorated with Indian things and served us a meal of Indian food and told us all about India. One reason for going into the foreign service, in Canada anyway, is to get out of Canada, and Canadians are good at fitting in, partly because they can't afford to do otherwise. They could not afford, for instance, to have the

kind of walled compound the Americans had. We were let in
to do some shopping at the supermarket there, and once the
gate had closed you were in Syracuse, N.Y. Hot dogs,
hamburgers, cokes and rock music surrounded you.
Americans enter the outside world the way they landed on
the moon, with their own oxygen tanks of American air
strapped to their backs and their protective spacesuits firmly
in place. If they can't stay in America they take it with them.
Not for them the fish-in-the-water techniques of the modern
urban guerilla. Those draft dodgers of the sixties who made
it as far as Canada nearly died of culture shock: they
thought it was going to be like home.

It's not their fault, though. It's merely that they've been
oddly educated. Canadians and Americans may look alike,
but the contents of their heads are quite different. Americans
experience themselves, individually, as small toads in the
biggest and most powerful puddle in the world. Their sense
of power comes from identifying with the puddle. Canadians
as individuals may have more power within the puddle,
since there are fewer toads in it; it's the puddle that's seen as
powerless. One of our politicians recently gave a speech
entitled, "In the Footsteps of the Giant." The United States
of course was the giant and Canada was in its footsteps,
though some joker wondered whether Canada was in the
footstep just before or just after the foot had descended. One
of Canada's problems is that it's always comparing itself to
the wrong thing. If you stand beside a giant, of course you
tend to feel a little stunted. When we stand beside Australia,
say, or the ex-British West Indies, we feel more normal. I
had lunch recently with two publishers from Poland. "Do
Canadians realize," they said, "that they live in one of the
most peaceful, happy and prosperous countries on earth?"
"No," I said.

Back to my life story. We've reached 1960. I was at
University, in the City of Toronto—which had not yet

become the Paris of the Northeast, the place where people from Buffalo go for the weekend, clean, safe, glitzy, filled with restaurants of high quality, and up to its eyeballs in narcissism. Instead it was known as Hogtown; it was a synonym for essence of boredom, and the usual joke about it was, "I spent a week in Toronto last night." Very funny if you didn't want to be a writer, but what if you did? Some of us did, and there we were, living in a city in which there was one theatre, no ballet, one art gallery and no literature that a serious person would take seriously, or so we thought. Being young snobs, we declined to know much about it. Although we wanted to become writers, we certainly didn't want to become *Canadian* writers. It was the period of late existentialism, and we wore long black stockings (those of us who were female) and no makeup (male and female alike) and read Sartre and Beckett. Canadian writers were associated in our minds with the damp unromantic vestibules of United Churches in March, smelling of damp wool. "Canadian writer" for us was an oxymoron.

And no wonder. For statistics fans, here's a batch: all the novels and books of poetry by Canadians, published in Canada, in the year 1961, could be and were reviewed in part of one issue of the *University of Toronto Quarterly*. I think there were about five novels and under twenty books of poetry, but that included the mimeo jobs and the flatbed press numbers which were not yet dignified by being called "little press books." Poets of my generation published their own work because nobody else would. It was not an activity born of heroism or the desire to appear artistic. Our publishing activities, tiny and futile as they were, were motivated by one thing: desperation. Even the "established" writers were doing well if they sold 200 copies of a book of poetry, country-wide. A novel that sold a thousand was a raving best-seller. Needless to say, you could hardly expect us to make a living at it, and anything resembling the American notion of literary success was out of the question. Canadian books were routinely not taught in schools and universities. I myself have never taken a course on Canadian literature.

The reason for this deplorable state of affairs was not that Canadians didn't read books. They just didn't read *Canadian* books. Colonies breed something called "the colonial mentality," and if you have the colonial mentality you believe that the great good place is always somewhere else. In those days you could walk into a bookstore, any bookstore, and find it (not surprisingly) full of books; but they would all be *imported* books. Down at the back there would be a shelf labelled *Canadiana*, and there would be the Canadian novels, along with the Canadian cookbooks and the coffee-table books entitled *Our Magnificent North.* No self-respecting young writer wanted to end up as *Canadiana*.

So some of us went to England, which was where I was headed, intending to work as a waitress and write great literature in garrets in my spare time. I was intercepted however by a Woodrow Wilson Fellowship, back in the days when there were any, and found myself at Harvard.

One of the exciting things that happened to me at Harvard was that I helped to corner a lurking sexual pervert upon the roof of the graduate women's dormitory. The other exciting thing, some might say entirely unrelated, was that I was requested at the beginning of my first year by the graduate advisor to fill in my gaps. As it turned out, I had only one gap, the others having been adequately filled in by the University of Toronto. My gap was American literature, and so, to my bemusement, I found myself reading my way through excerpts from Puritan sermons, political treatises of the time of the American revolution, and anguished essays of the early nineteenth century, bemoaning the inferiority not only of American literary offerings but of American dress design, and wondering when the great American genius would come along. It sounded familiar. Nobody pretended that any of this was superb literature. All they pretended was that it was necessary for an understanding of the United States of America, and it was. As we huddled in the front parlour of Founders' House on the Appian Way, in the fall of '62, just after President Kennedy had announced the Cuban Missile crisis, drinking tea and wondering whether the human condition was about to become rapidly obsolete, it was possible to look back through three hundred years of boring documents and see the road that had led us to this nasty impasse. The founding Puritans had wanted their society to be a theocratic utopia, a city upon a hill, to be a model and a shining example to all nations. The split between the dream and the reality is an old one and it has not gone away.

Canada suffers from no such split, since it was founded not by idealists but by people who'd been kicked out of other places. Canada was not a city upon a hill, it was what you had to put up with. Americans think anything can be changed, torn down and re-built, re-written. Canadians tend to think nothing can. Both are wrong, of course. Americans get discouraged when they can't get instant results; they vacillate between romantic idealism and black humour, its opposite. Canadians on the other hand think any change will probably be for the worse. Consequently they are less easily stampeded, less extreme in their trends. Americans have riots; Canadians have panel discussions on riots. Which may be why they won't invest in things like the telephone. Alexander Graham Bell was one of ours, once.

But I digress. There I was, at one of the greatest universities in the world, studying third-rate poems and dreary journals and the diaries of Cotton Mather, and why? Not because they were great world literature, but because they could tell me something about the society that produced them. Believe it or not, this was an amazing and dangerous insight. If old American laundry lists were of interest at Harvard, why should not old Canadian laundry lists be of interest in Toronto, where they so blatantly weren't? Everyone who was anyone in Toronto dismissed Canadian literature as second-rate and therefore not worth studying; but here before my very eyes were reams and reams of second-rate, and I had to write exams on it in order to fill my gap.

It was at Harvard then that I first began to think seriously about Canada. Even the idea of thinking seriously about Canada had something shocking about it: seriousness and Canada just didn't seem to go together. It was almost revolutionary. Unknown to me, other members of my generation were beginning to do the same thing. Then, as a generation, we did something very odd: instead of staying where we were and becoming part of the brain drain, we went back to Canada. Then we did something even odder. Instead of trying to publish in New York or London, or Paris (for this movement back to the indigenous was occurring at an even greater speed in the province of Quebec) we started thinking in terms of Canadian publication for a Canadian audience. Because the few established publishers were reluctant to publish work that was too experimental or too nationalist—the two were, strangely enough, sometimes equated—writers became involved in setting up their own publishing companies. Nobody expected the results. The growth of both audience and industry between 1965 and 1970 was phenomenal. To our surprise, people, even Canadian people, wanted to read what we wanted to write. Most of us were apolitical art-for-art's-sakers when we set out, but the lesson was clear. American branch plants and our own conservatives wouldn't publish us. If we wanted to be heard, we had to create the means of production and maintain control over it.

One of the things that quickly became apparent to us was that Canadians were remarkably ignorant about their own history and literature. For the most part they didn't know they had any, and lots of them were resistant to hearing anything about it. They'd been trained to think of themselves as international, and for them that term meant not national. It did not occur to them that in order to have international relationships you have to have nations first, just as in order to have interpersonal relationships you have to have persons.

About this time it became fashionable to talk about the absence of a Canadian identity. The absence of a Canadian identity has always seemed nonsense to me, and the search for it a case of the dog chasing its own tail. What people usually mean by a national identity is an advertising gimmick. Everything has an identity. A stone has an identity, it just doesn't have a voice. A man who's forgotten who he is has an identity, he's merely suffering from amnesia, which was the case with the Canadians. They'd forgotten. They'd had their ears pressed to the wall for so long, listening in on the neighbours, who *were* rather loud, that they'd forgotten how to speak and what to say. They'd become addicted to the one-way mirror of the Canadian-American border—we can see you, you can't see us—and had neglected that other mirror, their own culture. The States is an escape fantasy for Canadians. Their own culture shows them what they really look like, and that's always a little hard to take.

The cultural nationalism of the early '70s was not aggressive in nature. It was a simple statement: we exist. Such movements become militant only when the other side replies, in effect, No you don't. Witness feminism.

In 1972, I wrote and published a book about Canadian Literature. It was called *Survival*, and was an introductory guide to the subject, for the average reader. One of the reasons I wrote it was that nobody else had. Within it, the revolutionary seed planted at Harvard many years before burst into full flower, producing, in the minds of some, a large crop of thistles. Canadian critics felt it owed much to the noxious influence of Northrop Frye, under whom I'd studied up there, but they overlooked the noxious influence of Harvard's own Perry Miller, under whom I studied down here. Canadians tend to be touchy about imported noxious

influences: they want all noxious influences to be their very
own. They feel the same way for instance about acid rain. If
we want our lakes killed we'd rather do it ourselves; not
that you folks aren't doing a good job.

As far as I could see, *Survival* merely belaboured the
obvious. Everyone, surely, would agree that the literature
produced by a society has some connection with the society.
It follows that by reading the literature you can get a bearing
on the society. After a quick scan of classic Canadian
literature—that is, anything written before 1970—I concluded that Canadian literature had certain *leitmotifs* running
through it. Victims abound; the philosophy is survivalism,
the typical narrative a sequence of dire events which the
hero escapes from (if he does escape) not with triumph or
honour or riches but merely with his life. I talked about the
difference between being a genuine victim and being one by
choice. I drew certain conclusions relating to Canada in the
World Today, and I prefaced the whole thing with a few
reasons why people should read their own literature and not
just everybody else's. Worst of all, I said that Canada was a
cultural colony and an economic one as well.

Some people thought these were the most important
words set down since Moses went up the mountain. Others
thought no such thing. Canadian nationalism is by no means
homogeneous in nature or even thickly spread. The ultra
left thought I was being petit bourgeois. The merely left
thought I hadn't put in enough about the songs of the
people. Another branch of the left (whom I hesitate to call
national socialists because it gives entirely the wrong idea)
thought I was showing an historical perspective and was
being dialectical. In case you're unsure, that was good. The
paranoid ethnic centre thought I was being national socialist.
The conservative right thought I had written a book on
something that didn't exist at all, like a mediaeval theolo-
gian debating how many angels could dance on the head of a
pin. The feminists took the five basic victim positions I'd

outlined—something like the five basic positions of ballet—
and applied them to women. Critics fast on their feet said the
book was an interesting expression of my artistic sensibility.
Eighty thousand ordinary Canadians bought the book; a
large market penetration, as they say in the trade. The
Americans however did not publish it; as my editor in New
York said, "Listen sweetie, Canada is *death* down here."

Having an identity is one thing, having a negative
one is another. Some objected to the victim motif; others
said that people died all over world literature, not just in
Canada. Survivalism, of course, is not the same as tragedy or
existential despair or even pessimism about the human
condition. It's being stuck in a blizzard with one match; a
kind of minimalism, fine, but if you get that fire lit it's a
triumphant event, considering the odds. Nor is the stance
purely negative. In a world where there seems to be increasingly less and less of more and more, it may be a more useful
as well as a more ethical attitude towards the world than the
American belief that there is always another horizon, a new
frontier, that when you've used up what's in sight you only
have to keep moving.

Survival was part of the English-Canadian cultural
nationalism that peaked in about 1975. Meanwhile, the
Liberal economic nationalists under Walter Gordon had
been defeated and so had the NDP ones under the Waffle:
the government was against nationalism; continentalism was
their favoured phrase. The writers and artists, having made
certain gains, wandered off to their private cabbage patches
or settled down to the dogwork of such organizations as the
newly formed Writers' Union, and newspaper headlines
turned their attention elsewhere. One could be forgiven for
thinking that fighting the nationalist fight was like rolling a
big stone up a hill time after time, only to have it kicked
down again by one's very own government.

On both cultural and economic fronts, regionalism
replaced nationalism as something to feel self-righteous

about. To the jaundiced viewer, regionalism was merely the thesis of *Survival* writ small, with Ottawa replacing the States as the overbearing giant and the provinces competing with each other for the position of chief victim. There seemed to be a contest going on as to which one could outwhine the others. "Centralist thinking" became a bad word.

Then, out of the blue, what to our wondering eyes should appear but the National Energy Policy? Canada, it seems, was going to get back its own oil. It would have cost less if they'd done it earlier or never sold it in the first place, but why quibble? "Canada comes of age," someone predictably announced, and the United States reacted as though someone had just seduced its sister.

Which is where we are now.

The United States does not think of its own nationalism as being anything out of the ordinary, but it has never cherished warm feelings for other peoples'. Reaction to the current Canadian wave has ranged from anger, to squeeze plays of the If-you-don't-let-us-buy-you, We-won't-let-you-buy-us variety, to jocular condescension. I give you an example of the latter from the Toronto Star, June 20, 1981. The headline reads, *U.S. Patronizes Us With Nelson Eddy Tag*, and the copy explains:

> George Ball, ex-diplomat and ambassador and now a New York investment banker, said yesterday: "At the moment the current (Ottawa) government is going through one of those spasms of nationalism such as happened in the 1960's when Walter Gordon was finance minister. I think they'll get over it. It's a political issue. It comes and goes."
>
> That patronizing assessment was nothing compared with a day earlier, when witnesses at a merchant marine committee hearing were slashing Canada for winning away too much seaport business. "I like to think of Canada as a Nelson Eddy," remarked Democrat Barbara Mikulski,

recalling the American actor who played a Mountie in the 1936 movie *Rose Marie*. "What we need here is a legislative Jeanette Macdonald," she added; presumably to lure Canada away from its ardent pursuit of trade.

"No, No," said committee chairman Mario Biaggio, "Canada can be Jeanette Macdonald because in the movies Eddy always gets the girl."

I guess a little verbal castration is better than getting a bomb dropped on you, but let us remember there has always been more than one way of getting the girl. Are we talking about a proposal of marriage, in which case the States would proclaim, "with all my worldly goods I thee endow" in exchange for Canada's adopting the missionary position? Are we talking about proposition, in which case Canada is to assume the same position in exchange for a few roses and a box of chocs? It doesn't sound like a love affair, somehow. There's a fourth alternative which is not mentioned in polite company—every girl's got her price, say the cynics, and Canada has always been a cheap lay—and even a fifth, in which Nelson Eddy gets the same thing without having to pay anything at all, justifying his actions by believing that Canada was behaving provocatively and secretly loves it anyway. You'll notice that in each case Canada gets screwed; we've just been haggling a little about the out-of-pocket expenses. What it all goes to show, I suppose, is the danger of metaphors. In any case, it looks as if Canada doesn't want to play the female lead, not at the moment and maybe not any more. Someone once said that Canada is ruled by men with crystal balls, referring to Mackenzie King's habit of consulting his mother's spirit before deciding what not to do. Perhaps the fellows in Ottawa are changing to a more reliable method of decision-making.

Ah, say the futurists. But surely the nation state is obsolete. Even national governments are fast-fading archaisms; it's really international big business that's running things, and by the 21st century it's going to be one world, one way or another. Think of fibre optics and the imminent demise of the postal system; think of satellite transmission, ready and able to beam anything anywhere any time. National borders, those little moats countries build around themselves, their ability to determine what will be seen and heard within and what will stay without, will have become ineffectual in a few decades. Let's not try to turn back the clock. Open it up and let everything slosh back and forth from brain to brain, and then we won't have any nasty little pockets of nationalists who want to retain their own language and customs and blow up mailboxes or each other to prove it.

But of course it won't be a question of back and forth. It will only be forth, an expansion outward of the boundaries of whomever controls the technology for information transmission. I hate to say it, but it probably won't be Canada. The fight over who gets a pay TV licence, going on in Canada right now, is only the tip of the tip of the iceberg. Control what goes into people's heads and you control what comes out.

If you think that's unduly pessimistic, listen to this one. You hear the most amazing things on the Canadian Broadcasting Corporation; just the other day there was a programme on new weapons technology. The neutron bomb is already old-fashioned. The Russians, apparently, are working on something involving ultra-sound. They send a sort of amplified disco overhead in rockets, and it frazzes out the brain cells of everyone who hears it and turns them into smiling docile idiots. It doesn't damage property or genetic material, just your ability to think and therefore to protest. The ever-present satirist among us commented that it probably wouldn't make that much difference to the Canadians anyway, as they are already smiling docile idiots, but that was a little unfair. If the neutron bomb is the ultimate capitalist weapon, anti-personnel without being anti-real-estate, ultra-sound is the ultimate totalitarian one. The lumpen proletariat will become truly lumpen at last.

I've just given you two ways in which nationalism can be transcended. Neither sounds very attractive, but maybe I'm just being a little Luddite about it and docile idiocy of one kind or another is the wave of the future. Both suggest that there may be things to worry about that are more important than who gets to be Nelson Eddy.

There's a third way to transcend nationalism, and for that I'll go back for a moment to 1962. Perry Miller, in his lectures on American Romanticism, suggested that there was not one America but two: the America of Thoreau and Lincoln, the articulators of human dignity and human values and true democracy, and the other America which is opposed to them. I suggest that there are not only two Americas but two Canadas as well, and two Englands and two Russias; that, in fact, no country has a monopoly on any human characteristic, good or evil. The most lethal weapon on earth is the human mind; but on the other hand it is only the mind that is capable of envisioning what is humanly desirable and what is not. Totalitarian control of any kind is not. The world is rapidly abandoning the nineteenth-century division into capitalist and socialist. The new camps are those countries that perform or tolerate political repression, torture and mass murder and those that do not. Terrorism of the hijacking and assassination variety is now international; so is the kind practised by governments against their own citizens. The most important field of study at the moment is not Canadian literature or even old American laundry lists, delightful as these may be. It's the study of human aggression. I seem to recall that a revolution was once fought on the slogan, "No taxation without representation." For 1981 there's a more appropriate slogan: "No annihilation without representation." The only drawback is the lack of any one mad king to rebel against, and I expect the sense of futility felt by many Americans in face of the sick and gargantuan and apparently uncontrollable power struggle that's going on makes them in a way honourary Canadians. I say apparently uncontrollable because I am, after all, an optimist. Power corrupts, but it has never managed to corrupt everybody.

Americans and Canadians are not the same; they are the products of two very different histories, two very different situations. Put simply, south of you you have Mexico and south of us we have you.

But we *are* all in this together, not just as citizens of our respective nation states but more importantly as inhabitants of this quickly shrinking and increasingly threatened earth. There are boundaries and borders, spiritual as well as physical, and good fences make good neighbours. But there are values beyond national ones. Nobody owns the air; we all breathe it.

47

Amnesty International:
An Address

(1981)

The subject we have come together to address is one which increases in importance as the giants of this world move closer and closer to violent and fatal confrontation. Broadly put, it is: what is the writer's responsibility, if any, to the society in which he or she lives? The question is not a new one; it's been with us at least since the time of Plato; but more and more the answers of the world's governments have taken the form of amputation: of the tongue, of the soul, of the head.

We in Canada are ill-equipped to come to grips even with the problem, let alone the solution. We live in a society in which the main consensus seems to be that the artist's duty is to entertain and divert, nothing more. Occasionally our critics get a little heavy and start talking about the human condition, but on the whole the audience prefers art not to be a mirror held up to life but a Disneyland of the soul, containing Romanceland, Spyland, Pornoland and all the other Escapelands which are so much more agreeable than the complex truth. When we take an author seriously, we prefer to believe that her vision derives from her individual and subjective and neurotic tortured soul—we like artists to have tortured souls—not from the world she is looking at. Sometimes our artists believe this version too, and the ego takes over. *I, me* and *mine* are our favourite pronouns; *we, us* and *ours* are low on the list. The artist is not seen as a lens for focussing the world but as a solipsism. We are good at measuring an author's production in terms of his craft. We are not good at analyzing it in terms of his politics, and by and large we do not do so.

By "politics" I do not mean how you voted in the last election, although that is included. I mean who is entitled to do what to whom, with impunity; who profits by it; and who therefore eats what. Such material enters a writer's work not because the writer is or is not consciously political but because a writer is an observer, a witness, and such observations are the air he breathes. They are the air all of us breathe; the only difference is that the author looks, and then writes down what he sees. What he sees will depend on how closely he looks and at what, but look he must.

In some countries, an author is censored not only for what he says but for how he says it, and an unconventional style is therefore a declaration of artistic freedom. Here we are eclectic; we don't mind experimental styles, in fact we devote learned journals to their analysis; but our critics sneer somewhat at anything they consider "heavy social commentary" or—a worse word—"message." Stylistic heavy guns are dandy, as long as they aren't pointed anywhere in particular. We like the human condition as long as it is seen as personal and individual. Placing politics and poetics in two watertight compartments is a luxury, just as specialization of any kind is a luxury, and it is possible only in a society where luxuries abound. Most countries in the world cannot afford such luxuries, and this North American way of thinking is alien to them. It was even alien in North America, not long ago. We've already forgotten that in the 1950's many artists, both in the United States and here, were persecuted solely on the grounds of their presumed politics. Which leads us to another mistaken Canadian belief: the belief that it can't happen here.

It has happened here, many times. Although our country is one of the most peaceful and prosperous on earth, although we do not shoot artists here, although we do not execute political opponents and although this is one of the few remaining countries in which we can have a gathering like this without expecting to be arrested or blown up, we should not overlook the fact that Canada's record on civil rights issues is less than pristine. Our treatment of our native peoples has been shameful. This is the country in which citizens of Japanese origin were interned during the Second World War and had their property stolen (when a government steals property it is called "confiscation"); it is also the country in which thousands of citizens were arrested, jailed and held without warrant or explanation, during the time of the War Measures Act, a scant eleven years ago. There was no general outcry in either case. Worse things have not happened not because we are genetically exempt but because we lead pampered lives.

Our methods of controlling artists are not violent, but they do exist. We control through the marketplace and through critical opinion. We are also controlled by the economics of culture, which in Canada still happen to be those of a colonial branch-plant. In 1960 the number of Canadian books published here was minute, and the numbers sold pathetic. Things have changed very much in twenty years, but Canadian books still account for a mere 25 percent of the overall book trade and paperback books for under 5 percent. Talking about this situation is still considered nationalistic chauvinism. Nevertheless, looked at in the context of the wider picture, I suppose we are lucky to have any percent at all; they haven't yet sent in the Marines and if they do it won't be over books, but over oil.

We in this country should use our privileged position not as a shelter from the world's realities but as a platform from which to speak. Many are denied their voices; we are not. A voice is a gift; it should be cherished and used, to utter fully human speech if possible. Powerlessness and silence go together; one of the first efforts made in any totalitarian takeover is to suppress the writers, the singers, the journalists, those who are the collective voice. Get rid of the union leaders and pervert the legal system and what you are left with is a reign of terror.

As we read the newspapers, we learn we are existing right now in a state of war. The individual wars may not be large and they are being fought far from here, but there is really only one war, that between those who would like the future to be, in the words of George Orwell, a boot grinding forever into a human face, and those who would like it to be a state of something we still dream of as freedom. The battle shifts according to the ground occupied by the enemy. Greek myth tells of a man called Procrustes, who was a great equalizer. He had a system for making all human beings the same size: if they were too small he stretched them, if they were too tall he cut off their feet or their heads. The Procrustes today are international operators, not confined to any one ideology or religion. The world is full of perversions of the notion of equality, just as it is full of perversions of the notion of freedom. True freedom is not being able to do whatever you like to whomever you want to do it to. Freedom that exists as a result of the servitude of others is not true freedom.

The most lethal weapon in the world's arsenals is not the neutron bomb or chemical warfare; but the human mind that devises such things and puts them to use. But it is the human mind also that can summon up the power to resist, that can imagine a better world than the one before it, that can retain memory and courage in the face of unspeakable suffering. Oppression involves a failure of the imagination: the failure to imagine the full humanity of other human beings. If the imagination were a negligible thing and the act of writing a mere frill, as many in this society would like to believe, regimes all over the world would not be at such pains to exterminate them. The ultimate desire of Procrustes is a population of lobotomized zombies. The writer, unless he is a mere word processor, retains three attributes that power-mad regimes cannot tolerate: a human imagination, in the many forms it may take; the power to communicate; and hope. It may seem odd for me to speak of hope in the midst of what many of my fellow Canadians will call a bleak vision, but as the American writer Flannery O'Connor once said, people without hope do not write novels.

48
Northrop Frye Observed

(1981)

This is not Frye objectified, but Frye subjectified, a mini-memoir, if you like, by one of his former students whose ambition it was to become a writer.

And a strange ambition it was, too, at Leaside High School in 1956. It was a sudden one. Up to 1956, I'd thought I was going to be a botanist, or, at the very least, a Home Economist, though by then I knew that this latter was unlikely: people with snarls on the insides of their zippers were not so destined. There was nothing at Leaside High School to indicate to me that writing was even a possibility for a young person in Canada in the twentieth century. We did study authors, it's true, but they were neither Canadian nor alive. However, the spirit bloweth where it listeth, and after a short period of looking over my shoulder to see if it really meant to be blowing on somebody else I resigned myself to fate and tried to figure out how to go about the thing. I contemplated journalism school; but women, I was told, were not allowed to write anything but obituaries and the ladies' page; and although some of my critics seem to be under the impression that this is what I ended up writing anyway, I felt that something broader was in order. University, in short, where I might at least learn to spell.

Luckily I had a sympathetic English teacher named Miss Billings. She did not tell me how awful my poetry was (it did rhyme, however), but instead led me to understand that Victoria College at the University of Toronto was where I ought to be. There was someone there called Northrop Frye, she said. I had never heard of him, but then I had never heard of almost everything. I took her word.

I entered Victoria College in 1957, the year that Frye published *Anatomy of Criticism,* but I didn't know that then. Frye was only a blur on the horizon, something I would have to deal with in third year, when I took Milton. Meanwhile I was agonizing over the fact that I'd spent the summer trying to read *The Waste Land* and hadn't understood a word of it. I wondered if it was too late for Botany after all, and began writing poems that didn't rhyme and had coffee cups in them, which may have had something to do with Eliot or something to do with the fact that I was killing far too much time in the coffee shop; where Frye, incidentally, never went. For undergraduates, Frye was a kind of rumour. You heard things about him, but you rarely saw him. Occasionally you could hear him typing.

In third year, having struggled through Anglo-Saxon and Chaucer, I actually got to take a course from him. In those days you were either in something called the General Course, which lasted three years, or you were in a four-year Honours course, which made you specialized. In Honours English, life was chronological and Milton came in the third year. Northrop Frye taught Milton. "Taught" isn't exactly the word. Frye said, "Let there be Milton," and lo, there was. It was done like this. He stood at the front of the room. He took one step forward, put his left hand on the table, took another step forward, put his right hand on the table, took a step back, removed his left hand, another step back, removed his right hand, and repeated the pattern. While he was doing this, pure prose, in real sentences and paragraphs, issued from his mouth. He didn't say "um," as most of us did, or leave sentences unfinished, or correct himself. I had never heard anyone do this before. It was like seeing a magician producing birds from a hat. You kept wanting to go around behind Frye or look under the table to see how he did it.

Which brings us to the delicate question of "influence." There are those who, upon hearing that I was once a student of Northrop Frye's, need to have their fingers pried loose from the hem of my garment. Conversely, there are those who start circling to the left, hoping to catch a glimpse of the Mark of the Vampire which they are sure must lurk somewhere, if not on my neck, at least in my work. Those who have never occupied that blissful position, "a student of Frye's," assume that he exerted some odd Svengali-like influence on young writers, taking their putty-like minds and running them through the Play-Doh machine of his "system" until they came out molded. If such an asumption had any truth to it, Canada ought to have filled up with a lot of zonked-out Trilbys, all "students of Frye," all warbling Frye's tune. Why didn't it?

Possibly because any genuine writer is "influenced" only by sources with which he already has some affinity. Writers are pilferers, as Eliot has remarked; the caddis-fly larvae of the literary world. Or possibly because Frye wasn't interested in "influencing" anyone, especially young writers. His approach to creation was not prescriptive. The last thing he ever would have done to his students would have been to tell them what or how to write, and nothing would embarrass him more than to be credited with producing a sort of poetic backup section. Or possibly because, if Frye is right, and poets are influenced by other poets, novelists by other novelists, the only thing Frye would be able to influence would be other critics. This he has certainly done; but poets? I've read somewhere the expression, "a Northrop Frye poet," but I'm not sure what it means. A view of poetry so comprehensive as Frye's surely subsumes just about everything. In any case, as he himself has said, poets are ornery, especially in the face of critical systems. Try to confine them in one and they'll react by doing something quite other. The critic's job is not to tell poets what to do, but to tell readers what they have done. The writer's job is to write. This was an arrangement that seemed appropriate to me, and still does.

Back in 1960, Frye came and went, distantly but benevolently enough. Occasionally he would murmur something indicative of the fact that he had actually read one's tawdry effusion in this or that campus literary journal, but he offered neither criticism nor guidance, merely a general attentiveness, a sort of literary phototropism. It was rather like being watched by a sunflower. He was not what you would call intrusive. At that stage of my life I was a good deal more upset by Robert Graves than I was by Frye. *The White Goddess* gave me the cold sweats: I wanted to be a poet, true, but not at the price of cannibalizing my fellow creatures, as Graves seemed to think I was honour-bound to do. Women could only be poets, he said, if they were willing to *be* the White Goddess, a prime example of whom was Coleridge's Nightmare Life-In-Death. I had no particular wish to thick men's blood with cold — I preferred a nice game of bridge, any day — and although some of my work seems to have had that effect on certain Canadian critics, it was inadvertent. How reassuring to turn instead to Frye's essay on Emily Dickinson, which presents her neither as the White Goddess, despite her manner of dressing, nor as a feeble neurotic, but as a skilled professional who knew exactly what she was doing. It was, somehow, a more positive role-model.

So although Frye was not an "influence" in the sense that people usually mean the word, that is, a manufacturer of plaster castings, he was an influence in another and greater respect. He was a counterbalance not only to Mr. Graves and his oddly arachnoid theories of poetic creation, but also to the Canadian *milieu* of the late fifties. At this time

Toronto was not the multi-restauranted glitter city it is today, entranced by its own trendy reflection, but Hogtown, the place Montrealers made jokes about. It had one repertory theatre, no ballet company, and hardly any decent brie. Canadian authors were invisible to the general public, ghettoized in the *Canadiana* section by booksellers, along with the cookbooks on 101 Things To Do With Maple Sugar, and considered oxymorons by snobbish young would-be writers like myself, who thought we had to run away to England in order to let our genius fully flower. On the average, there were about five novels by Canadians published in Canada per year, and sales were doing very well if they reached a thousand copies. There were two advantages to this state of affairs. The first was that if you published anything of a serious literary nature, anything at all, you would get reviewed somewhere, and you would be read by the hard-core Canadian Literature audience, which had a shifting population of about two hundred. The second was that women were not discriminated against. To announce that you wanted to be a writer did not produce a gender-specific response. Nobody said, "You can't do that because you're a girl." They did not tell you you were up against Shakespeare and Melville. Instead they said, "A what? "

Even at the university level, your fellow seekers after wisdom were likely to think you pretentious or deluded. But then there was Frye, who possessed that most necessary of qualifications for credibility in Canada, an international reputation. Frye appeared to take writing for granted. He seemed to view it not as something done by the emotionally brain-damaged but as an essential human activity. He took our ambitions seriously. In Toronto, in 1959, this was more than encouraging.

The same people who clutch my hem at parties also want to know whether I didn't find being a student of Frye's awfully, well, intimidating. Usually I say Yes or No, as occasion seems to require. A full explanation would take longer. The curious fact remains that it's possible to be very impressed by a mind without necessarily being intimidated by a person. I was more intimidated by the Philosophy professor who lectured with his eyes closed and could always tell when an extra person was in the room. It was hard, though, to be completely intimidated by anyone as easily embarrassed as Frye. It's also hard to be intimidated by someone who's trying so hard not to be intimidating. Frye, when he'd had the bad luck to come face to face with one of his students outside the lecture hall, would lapse from perfectly-punctuated prose into a kind of reassuring and inarticulate mumble. "They're just as frightened of you as you are of them," my parents used to say about things like bumblebees. The same could be said of Frye. So lacking in intimidation was I, I recall, that I wrote and published a literary parody in which I applied archetypal criticism to the Ajax commercial, the eternal battle of the recurrent figure of the Housewife against the dark and menacing figure of The Dirt. Undergraduate, but then, what's the use of being an undergraduate if you can't be undergraduate? The point is that I did not fear retaliation. I expected Frye to find it almost as funny as I did, which may or may not have happened. Possibly he thought I was just getting it right.

It's quite possible though that my version of Frye is subjectively coloured by the fact that my parents were from Nova Scotia. The things that intimidated other people did not intimidate me. The deadpan delivery, the irony, the monotone, and the concealed jokes, may have seemed odd to those from Ontario, but to me they were more than familiar. In the Maritimes they're the norm. Puritanism takes odd shapes there, some brilliant, most eccentric, and no Maritimer could ever mistake a lack of flamboyance for a lack of commitment, engagement, courage or passion. Light dawned when I found out Frye had originated in New Brunswick. Not quite the same as Nova Scotia, where my relatives all lived, but close enough. A Nova Scotian joke of the 1930s had been that Nova Scotia's main export was brains. Frye was an export.

When I visited Australia, the Australians were constantly asking, "Why is there no Australian Northrop Frye?", much as Canadians of my generation used to ask why there is no Canadian *Moby Dick* and Americans of 1840 used to ask why there was no American Walter Scott. It's a good question, but there's an even better one: why is there a *Canadian* Northrop Frye? Or, to particularize, how did such a creature ever survive having been born in Moncton, New Brunswick, and having grown up in Sherbrooke, Quebec, in the first part of this century?

To those who do not know these places it's difficult to explain my amazement. Let us say only that a soul waiting to be reincarnated as a major literary critic would have chosen another location and time, on the supposition that there are easier ways of doing it. Canada, from the literary point of view, was a bit of a void. There was a tradition, it's true, but it had the curious habit of vanishing and having to be re-discovered by each successive generation. There's always been a certain amount of dredging involved. Canadian nationalists of the kind whose eyes whirl around a lot (as distinguished from lumpish and stolid ones like me) have, in recent years, accused Frye of all sorts of things vis à vis Canada: continentalism, internationalism, ignoring them, and so forth. But it seems to me that almost every seminal idea in the newly watered fields of Canlit, including the currently fashionable "regionalism," sprang, if not fully formed, at least in some form, from the forehead of Northrop Frye, back in the days when he was dutifully reviewing Canadian poetry for *The Canadian Forum* and other slender journals, a task which may have contributed to Frye's formulations of the connection between the imagination and the society it finds itself surrounded by. Frye is of course a social thinker whose efforts have always been directed towards the evaluation not only of the writer but of the reader.

What better field for an educator than a country in which almost nobody knows how — in the broader sense — to read?

There were, however, poets of considerable range and skill buried down there in the Canlit substrata, and Frye did his best with them, E. J. Pratt in particular. But what about their influence on him, or their shared view of the universe? Parts of Frye read as if they could have been written by A. M. Klein, had he been a critic; there is something of the same Adam-naming-the-beasts motif about both of them. Some have referred to Frye's labelling of literary genera and species as "dead taxonomy," which only means among other things that they have never seen two taxonomists having an argument. They have never reflected either on the fact that a kangaroo is just as alive whether you call it by its Latin name or by no name. But Frye's push towards *naming*, towards an interconnected system, seems to me a Canadian reaction to a Canadian situation. Stranded in the midst of a vast space which nobody has made sense out of for you, you settle down to map-making, charting the territory, the discovery of where things are in relation to each other, the extraction of meaning. The poets were doing it with their own times and spaces, Frye was doing it with literature as a whole, but the motive — which is that too of Innes and McLuhan, those other megasystem thinkers of the University of Toronto — is *au fond* the same. Frye's central metaphor is spatial and it is very large. An American or English critic of this time would not have even thought of anything like this. The English were doing their usual social classification, handing out the nuances and assigning rungs on the ladder, and the Americans were deep in the motors of their chosen poems, figuring out which little gizmos got pressed to make the thing work. Metonymy and synecdoche are the newest items, I'm told; but the days when I would have had to find out what they meant are long past.

Which brings me back to my starting point. It's twenty-odd years later and tomorrow I have to get on the plane for Winnipeg, where people will ask me about page-turnability and bad images of men. If I were an American I wouldn't have to do this; if I were English I could do it all in London, and the questions would be different; but this is Canada, which was, is and remains a whole different hockey game. That, however, is another story. My next rhetorical question is, What have I to do with Frye, now that I'm no longer a student? Has anything, as it were, rubbed off? And if so, is it of much use to a writer, trapped in the practical, struggling from plot to plot, character to character, book-signing to book-signing, T.V. station to T.V. station, and every Fall brought face to face with waving acres of low demotic?

Well, being a former student of Frye's does help out with the answers. When someone asks you, live, on air, how come you're such a pessimist and why you don't have happier endings, you can think to yourself, "Because I'm writing in the ironic mode, thickhead." You can't say it too loud, of course—Frye's dream of a language of common literary discourse hasn't made it to the heavy rock stations yet—but at least, in the silence of the night, as you toss and turn in your Holiday Inn bed, having failed to discover how to lower the room temperature, haunted by the smart replies you did not think of at the time—at least you can whisper it to yourself.

And when things are at their nadir and the reasons for which you wrote your book appear to have come completely unbuckled from the result, which seems to be a long line of people wanting you to write things in the fronts of their copies—things such as, "Happy Birthday with love from Annie"—in vain do you remonstrate that you are not Annie—you can always tell yourself that the pursuit of literature is a significant human activity.

Believing it is sometimes an act of faith. But then, Northrop Frye believes it, and he *knows*.

49
Jay Macpherson:
Poems Twice Told

(1982)

When I was young, poetry reviewing in Canada was very ingrown. Poets reviewed the work of their friends and enemies then, partly because few others were interested in reviewing poetry at all, partly because the poetry world was so small that everyone in it was either a friend or an enemy. However, it was understood that anyone likely to read the review would know which was which.

Writers still occasionally review their friends and enemies, but it can no longer be assumed that the average reader knows it. So I feel it necessary to state by way of prelude that Jay Macpherson not only taught me Victorian literature back in 1960—like all good teachers, she behaved as if it mattered, thus converting my surly contempt for the subject into fascinated admiration—but is one of my oldest and most appreciated friends. Having said that, I will retreat to the middle distance, from which the reviewer's voice should issue impartial as God's (though it rarely does) and try to deal with the subject at hand.

Impossible, of course. Re-reading *The Boatman*, the first of the two books included in this volume, makes me remember Jay Macpherson as I first knew her. I was enormously impressed, not just by the fact that here in front of me was a real poet, and a woman at that, who had actually had a book published—no mean feat in the Canada of those days—but by her wardrobe. She always wore clothes that were by no means "fashionable," clothes in fact that nobody else could get away with, but which seemed exactly right for *her*.

It's the same with the poetry. No one else writes like this. In fact, looking back, it seems that no one else ever did, and that all the fuss about a "mythopoeic school" of poetry was simply misguided criticism. If "mythopoeic" means that the poet lets on she knows about mythologies, the most unlikely among us would have to accept the label. (Daphne Marlatt, George Bowering and Frank Davey, for example.) Although a critic intent on the usual version of this theory might make a case for *The Boatman* and its involvement with the shapes of traditional stories, *Welcoming Disaster* would probably defeat him. Its personal and indeed sometimes notably eccentric voice carries the reader far beyond any notions of "school." Macpherson's poetry is one-of-a-kind, not in defiance of current convention so much as apart from it. It's a world unto itself, and from *The Boatman's* poem called "Egg" comes the best advice for approaching it: "Let be, or else consume me quite."

The Boatman has been much written about, but for the sake of those who may not be familiar with it I'll say a little about it. It appears to be a "sequence" of very short, condensed lyric poems. (I say "appears," because it was not planned that way; Macpherson is not a programmatic writer, and her work, when it falls into sequences, does so because her imagination is working with a certain body of material, not because she thinks she needs a poem of a certain kind to fill a gap and then composes it.) They are not all of the same kind: some are straight-faced lyrics, some are sinister or comic parodies on the same subjects (*pace* Blake's two sets of *Songs*) and some are puzzle-poems, or riddles. I tend to get on a little better with the straight lyrics. The others are adroit and clever, though they seem to me to exist, as many kinds of jokes do, for the purpose of defusing a profound uneasiness.

The central voice of *The Boatman* is one of a complex and powerful grief, and its central symbols revolve around separation and loss. Like all hermetic poetry, *The Boatman* offers the reader multiple choices about its true "subject." Is it "about" the relationship between two lovers, the relationship between Creator and fallen world, the relationship between author, book and reader, or dreamer and dream, or man and his imaginative world? Why not all? The most potent poems in the book, for me, are those in the small sequence-within-a-sequence, "The Ark," eight eight-line lyrics that are astonishing for their simplicity and grace, and for the amount of emotional force they can pack into sixty-four lines. They are "about" all of the above, and after more than twenty years of reading them I still find them devastating.

One of Macpherson's most exquisite poems is in the small section entitled "Other Poems" — post-*Boatman*, pre-*Disaster*. It's called "The Beauty of Job's Daughters," and I won't quote from it because you need to read the whole thing, but it's an excellent example of what an outwardly-formal, flexibly-handled lyricism can do. It also epitomizes one of the main themes of *The Boatman*: the "real" world, that of the imagination, is inward.

Between *The Boatman* and "Other Poems," and *Welcoming Disaster*, came a long pause. Macpherson's total output has been minute compared with that of most other Canadian poets of her stature, and she's about the farthest thing from a "professional" poet you could imagine. A young novelist said to me recently, "Poetry isn't an art, it's a circuit." For Macpherson, never a circuit-rider, poetry isn't a "profession" but a gift, which is either there or not there but can't be made to be there by exercise of will. In fact, the first poems in *Welcoming Disaster* are about the loss or absence of the imaginative world so beautifully evoked in "Job's Daughters," the failure of inspiration, and the futility of trying to conjure it up. As well as its redemptive qualities:

"Breathing too is a simple trick, and most of us learn it. / Still, to lose it is bad, though no-one regrets it long." When the Muse finally shows up, what she reveals this time is not paradise regained.

If *The Boatman* is "classical" (which, in purity of line, simplicity of rhythms, and choice of myths and symbols, it is), then *Welcoming Disaster* is, by the same lights, "romantic:" more personal, more convoluted, darker and more grotesque, its rhythms more complex, its main symbol-groupings drawn not only from Classical and Biblical mythology but from all kinds of odd corners: nineteenth-century Gothic novels (and their twentieth-century avatars, such as *Nosferatu* and Karloff movies), the Grimms' Goose Girl story ("What Falada Said"), Babylonian mythology ("First and Last Things"), lore of magicians, ghouls, mazes and crossroads. The main movement of the book concerns a descent to the underworld; and, as everyone knows, the most successful recipes for this include a plan for getting not only there but back, usually by means of the advice or actual company of a sybil, spirit guide or boatman. (The boatman in *The Boatman* is mainly Noah; in *Welcoming Disaster* it's his upside-down counterpart, Charon, who takes you not to the world renewed but to the world dead.) In this case the fetish-cum-spirit guide-cum-God-cum-sinister ferryman is a teddy bear, which—again— only Macpherson could get away with.

What's in the underworld? In Egyptian mythology it's the place where the soul is weighed; for Orpheus, it's the place where the lost love is finally lost; in Jackson Knight's book on Virgil (cited in Macpherson's notes) the underground maze leads to the king and queen of the dead, especially the queen: it's a place of lost mothers. There are echoes too of all those nineteenth-century ghosts, from Catherine Earnshaw on down, who come to the window at night, of vampiristic or sinister-double relationships which recall Blake's Shadow and Emanation figures; of Faustian pacts with darkness. Jungians will revel in this book, though it is hardly orthodox Jungianism. But the important thing is that in the process some poems emerge that would more than satisfy Houseman: they do make the hair stand up on the back of your neck. "They Return," for instance, or "Hecate Trivia," or "Some Ghosts and Some Ghouls."

Welcoming Disaster, like *The Boatman*, has its more playful moments, but on the whole its tone ranges between the eerie and the ruthless: poems of invocation or rigorous and sometimes bloody-minded self-analysis. Macpherson was never much of a meditative Wordsworthian, if such labels apply. She's much more like Coleridge: inner magic, not outer-world description or social comment, is her *forte*.

When I was asked to write this review it was suggested that I include an "appreciation" of Macpherson's "career." But what do we mean by a poet's "career," apart from the poems? Do poets even have "careers?" Some do, but it's a word that seems more appropriate when applied to politicians: something pursued, worked at, having to do with leverage and personal advancement and the media-created persona. Jay Macpherson is simply not career-minded in this way. There's nowhere she wants to get, in the sense of "getting somewhere." She reminds us that poetry is not a career but a vocation, something to which one is called, or not, as the case may be. She's still the best example I know of someone who lives as if literature, and especially the writing of poetry, were to be served, not used.

50
Writing The Male Character

(1982)

I'm more than delighted that you've invited a token woman to give the Hagey lectures this year, and though you might have chosen one more respectable than myself, I realize that the supply is limited.

My lack of respectability I have on good authority: the authority, in fact, of the male academics at the University of Victoria, in British Columbia, where I was being interviewed on radio not long ago. "I did a little survey," said the rather pleasant male interviewer, "among the professors here. I asked them what they thought of your work. The women were all very positive, but the men said that they weren't sure whether or not you were respectable." So I'm giving you advance warning that everything you are about to hear is not academically respectable. The point of view I'm presenting is that of a practising novelist, inhabitant of New Grub Street for many years, not that of the Victorianist I spent four years at Harvard learning to be; though the Victorianism does creep in, as you can already see. So I will not even mention metonymy and synecdoche, except right now, just to impress you and let you know that I know they exist.

All of the above, of course, is by way of letting the male members of the audience know that, despite the title of this lecture, they don't need to feel threatened. I believe we have now reached, as a culture, the point at which we need a little positive reinforcement for men. I'm starting my own private project along these lines tonight. I have with me some gold stars, some silver stars and some blue stars, fictional ones of course. You get a blue star, if you want one, just for being unthreatened enough to have actually turned up tonight. You get a silver star if you are unthreatened enough to laugh at the jokes, and you get a gold star if you don't feel threatened at all. On the other hand, you get a black mark if you say, "My *wife* just *loves* your books." You get two black marks if you say, as a male CBC producer said to me not long ago, "A number of us are upset because we feel women are taking over the Canadian literary scene."

"Why do men feel threatened by women?" I asked a male friend of mine. (I love that wonderful rhetorical device, "a male friend of mine." It's often used by female journalists when they want to say something particularly bitchy but don't want to be held responsible for it themselves. It also lets people know that you *do* have male friends, that you aren't one of those fire-breathing mythical monsters, The Radical Feminists, who walk around with little pairs of scissors and kick men in the shins if they open doors for you. "A male friend of mine" also gives—let us admit it—a certain weight to the opinions expressed.) So this male friend of mine, who does by the way exist, conveniently entered into the following dialogue. "I mean," I said, "men are bigger, most of the time, they can run faster, strangle better, and they have on the average a lot more money and power." "They're afraid women will laugh at them," he said. "Undercut their world view." Then I asked some women students in a quickie poetry seminar I was giving, "Why do women feel threatened by men?" "They're afraid of being killed," they said.

From this I concluded that men and women are
indeed different, if only in the range and scope of their
threatenability. A man is not just a woman in funny clothes
and a jock strap. *They don't think the same*, except about
things like higher math. But neither are they an alien or
inferior form of life. From the point of view of the novelist,
this discovery has wide-ranging implications; and you can
see that we are approaching this evening's topic, albeit in a
crabwise. scuttling, devious and feminine manner; nevertheless, approaching. But first, a small disgression, partly to
demonstrate that when people ask you if you hate men, the
proper reply is "which ones?"— because, of course, the other
big revelation of the evening is that *not all men are the same*..
Some of them have beards. Apart from that, I have never
been among those who would speak slightingly of men by
lumping them all in together; I would never say, for
instance—as some have—"Put a paper bag over their bodies
and they're all the same." I give you Albert Schweitzer in
one corner, Hitler in another.

But think of what civilization would be today without
the contributions of men. No electric floor polishers, no
neutron bomb, no Freudian psychology, no heavy metal
rock groups, no pornography, no repatriated Canadian
Constitution ... the list could go on and on. And they're fun
to play Scrabble with and handy for eating up the leftovers. I
have heard some rather tired women express the opinion
that the only good man is a dead man, but this is far from
correct. They may be hard to find, but think of it this way:
like diamonds, in the rough or not, their rarity makes them
all the more appreciated. Treat them like human beings!
This may surprise them at first, but sooner or later their
good qualities will emerge, most of the time. Well, in view of
the statistics ... some of the time.

That wasn't the digression ... this is the digression. I
grew up in a family of scientists. My father was a forest
entomologist and fond of children, and incidentally not

threatened by women, and many were the happy hours we spent listening to his explanations of the ways of the wood-boring beetle, or picking forest tent caterpillars out of the soup because he had forgotten to feed them and they had gone crawling all over the house in search of leaves. One of the results of my upbringing was that I had a big advantage in the schoolyard when little boys tried to frighten me with worms, snakes and the like; the other was that I developed, slightly later, an affection for the writings of the great nineteenth century naturalist and father of modern entomology, Henri Fabre. Fabre was, like Charles Darwin, one of those gifted and obsessive amateur naturalists which the nineteenth century produced in such abundance. He pursued his investigations for the love of the subject, and unlike many biologists today, whose language tends to be composed of numbers rather than words, he was an enthusiastic and delightful writer. I read with pleasure his account of the life of the spider, and of his experiments with ant-lions, by which he tried to prove that they could reason. But it was not only Fabre's subject matter that intrigued me; it was the character of the man himself, so full of energy, so pleased with everything, so resourceful, so willing to follow his line of study wherever it might lead. Received opinion he would take into account, but would believe nothing until he had put it to the test himself. It pleases me to think of him, spade in hand, setting forth to a field full of sheep droppings, in search of the Sacred Dung Beetle and the secrets of her egg-laying ritual. "I am all eyes," he exclaimed, as he brought to light a little object, not round like the Sacred Beetle's usual edible dung-ball, but cunningly pear-shaped! "Oh blessed joys of truth suddenly shining forth," he wrote. "What others are there to compare with you!"

And it is in this spirit, it seems to me, that we should approach all subjects. If a dung-beetle is worthy of it, why not that somewhat more complex object, the human male? Admittedly the analogy has certain drawbacks. For instance, one dung-beetle is much like another, whereas, as we've noted, there's quite a range in men. Also, we are supposed to be talking about novels here, and, to belabour the obvious, a novel is not a scientific treatise; that is, it can make no claim to present the kind of factual truth which can be demonstrated by repeatable experiments. Although the novelist presents observations and reaches conclusions, they are not of the same order as the observations of Fabre on the behaviour of the mating practices of the female scorpion, although some critics react as though they are.

Note that we have landed in the middle of a swamp, that is, at the crux of the problem: if a novel is not a scientific treatise, what is it? Our evaluation of the role of the male character within the novel will of course depend on what kind of beast we think we're dealing with. I'm sure you've all heard the one about the four blind philosophers and the elephant. Substitute "critics" for "philosophers" and "Novel" for "elephant" and you'll have the picture. One critic gets hold of the novelist's life and decides that novels are disguised spiritual autobiographies, or disguised personal sexual phobias, or something of the kind. Another gets hold of the *Zeitgeist* (or Spirit of the Times, for those unlucky enough never to have had to pass a PhD language exam in German) and writes about the Restoration Novel or the Novel of Sensibility or The Rise of the Political Novel or The Novel of Twentieth Century Alienation; another figures out that the limitations of the language have something to do with what can be said, or that certain pieces of writing display similar patterns, and the air fills with mythopoeia, structuralism and similar delights; another goes to Harvard and gets hold of the Human Condition, a favourite of mine, and very handy to fall back on when you can't think of anything else to say. The elephant however remains an elephant, and sooner or later gets tired of having the blind philosophers feeling its parts, whereupon it stretches itself, rises to its feet and ambles away in another direction altogether. This is not to say that critical exercises are futile or trivial. From what I have said about dung-beetles—which also preserve their innermost secrets—you will know that I think the description of elephants is a worthwhile activity. But describing an elephant and giving birth to one are two different things, and the novelist and the critic approach the novel with quite different sets of preconceptions, problems and emotions.

"Whence comest thou?" says a well-known male character in a multi-faceted prose narrative with which I am sure you are all familiar. "From going to and fro in the earth, and from walking up and down in it," answers his adversary. Thus the novelist. One would of course not want to continue with this analogy—a critic is not God, contrary to some opinions, and a novelist is not the Devil, although one could remark, with Blake, that creative energies are more likely to emerge from the underworld than from the upper world of rational order. Let us say only that the going to and fro and the walking up and down in the earth are things that all novelists seem to have done in some way or another, and that the novel proper, as distinguished from the romance and its variants, is one of the points in human civilization at which the human world as it is collides with language and imagination. This is not to limit the novel to a Zola-like naturalism (though Zola himself was not a narrow Zola-like naturalist, as anyone who has read the triumphant final passage of *Germinal* will testify); but it is to state that some of the things that get into novels get into them because they are there in the world. There would have been no flogging scene in *Moby Dick* if there had been none on nineteenth century whaling ships, and its inclusion is not mere sado-masochism on the part of Melville. However, if the book consisted of nothing but, one might have cause to wonder.

Thus one must conclude that the less than commendable behaviour of male characters in certain novels by women is not necessarily due to a warped view of the opposite sex on behalf of the authors. Could it be . . . I say it hesitantly, in a whisper, since like most women I cringe at the very thought of being called — how can I even say it — a *man-hater* . . . could it be that the behaviour of some men in what we are fond of considering real life . . . could it be that not every man always behaves well? Could it be that some emperors have no clothes on?

This may seem to you an obvious point to make. But not so. Among the going to and fro that novelists do these days is the going to and fro across Canada during the McClelland & Stewart Wreck-an-Author tour, talking to media denizens, and some of the walking up and down they do happens after reading the reviews of their books. Let's pretend for the sake of argument that media denizens and newspaper critics bear at least some relation, if not to the average reader, at least to the officially promoted climate of opinion; that is, what it is considered, at the moment, fashionable and therefore safe to state publicly. If so, the officially promoted climate of opinion these days shows a noteworthy shift towards male whining.

Let me take you back a few years, to the days of Kate Millett's *Sexual Politics*, which was preceded ancestrally by Leslie Fiedler's *Love and Death in the American Novel*. Both were criticisms based on an analysis of the relations, within novels, of men and women, and both gave black marks to certain male authors for simplistic and stereotyped negative depictions of women. Well, that was interesting, but the worm has turned. Now we're handing out black marks for what male critics (and, to be fair, some female ones) consider to be unfavourable depictions of men by female authors. I base this conclusion mainly on reviews of my own books, naturally, since that's what I see most of, but I've noted it elsewhere too.

Now, we know there's no such thing as value-free novel writing. Creation does not happen in a vacuum, and a

novelist is either depicting or exposing some of the values of
the society in which he or she lives. Novelists from Defoe
through Dickens and Faulkner have always done that. But it
sometimes escapes us that the same is true of criticism. We
are all organisms within environments, and we interpret
what we read in the light of how we live and how we would
like to live, which are almost never the same thing, at least
for most novel readers. I think that political interpretations
of novels have a place in the body of criticism, as long as we
recognize them for what they are; but total polarization can
only be a disservice to literature. For instance, a male friend
of mine—just to let you know I have more than one—wrote a
novel which has a scene in it in which men are depicted
urinating outdoors standing up. Now, so far as I know, this is
something men have been doing for many years, and they
are still doing it, judging from the handwriting in the snow;
it is merely one of those things that happens. But a female
poet took my friend to task in print. She found this piece of
writing not only unforgivably Central Canadian—you can
tell she was from British Columbia—she also found it
unforgivably *macho*. I'm not sure what novelistic solution
she had in mind. Possibly she wanted my friend to leave
out the subject of urination altogether, thus avoiding the
upsetting problem of physiological differences; maybe she
wanted the men to demonstrate equality of attitude by
sitting on toilets to perform this function. Or maybe she
wanted them to urinate outdoors standing up but also to feel
guilty about it. Or maybe it would have been all right if they
had been urinating into the Pacific Ocean, regionalism
being what it is today. You may think this kind of criticism is
silly, but it happens all the time on New Grub Street, which
is where I live.

For the female novelist, it means that certain men will
find it objectionable if she depicts men behaving the way
they do behave a lot of the time. Not enough that she may
avoid making them rapists and murderers, child molesters,

warmongers, sadists, power hungry, callous, domineering, pompous, foolish or immoral, though I'm sure we will all agree that such men do exist. Even if she makes them sensitive and kind she's open to the charge of having depicted them as "weak". What this kind of critic wants is Captain Marvel, without the Billy Batson *alter ego*; nothing less will do.

Excuse me for underlining the obvious, but it seems to me that a good, that is, a successfully-written, character in a novel is not at all the same as a "good," that is, a morally good, character in real life. In fact, a character in a book who is consistently well-behaved probably spells disaster for the book. There's a lot of public pressure on the novelist to write such characters, however, and it isn't new. I take you back to Samuel Richardson, author of such running-away-from-rape classics as *Pamela* and *Clarissa*. Both contain relatively virtuous women and relatively lecherous and nasty-minded men, who also happen to be English gentlemen. No one accused Richardson of being mean to men, but some English gentlemen felt that dirt had been done to them; in other words, the insecurities were primarily class ones rather than sex ones. Obligingly, Richardson came up with *Sir Charles Grandison*, a novel in which he set out to do right by the image of the English gentleman. It starts out promisingly enough, with an abduction with intent to rape by a villain after that priceless pot of gold, the heroine's virginity. Unfortunately Sir Charles Grandison enters the picture, saves the heroine from a fate worse than death, and invites her to his country residence; after which most readers kiss the novel goodbye. I however always sit to the end, even of bad movies, and since I'm the only person I've ever met who has actually made it through to page 900 of this novel I can tell you what happens. Sir Charles Grandison displays his virtues; the heroine admires them. That's it. Oh, and then there's a proposal. Feel like reading it? You bet you don't, and neither do all those male critics who complain about the image of men in books by women. A friend of mine—not a male one this time, but a perceptive reader and critic—says that her essential criterion for evaluating literature is, "Does it live or does it die?" A novel based on other people's needs for having their egos stroked, their images shored up, or their sensitivities pandered to is unlikely to live.

Let us take a brief look at what literature has actually done. Is *Hamlet*, for instance, a slur on men? Is *Macbeth*? Is *Faust*, in any version? How about the behaviour of the men in *Moll Flanders*? Or *Tom Jones*? Is *A Sentimental Journey* about the quintessential wimp? Because Dickens created Orlick, Gradgrind, Dotheboys Hall, Fagin, Uriah Heep, Steerforth, and Bill Sykes, must we conclude that he's a man-hater? Meredith was unrelentingly critical of men and quite admiring of women in such novels as *Richard Feverel* and *The Egoist*. Does that mean he's the equivalent of a class traitor? How about the fascinating Isabel Archer's failure to match herself with a man who's up to her, in James' *Portrait Of A Lady*? Then there's *Tess of the D'Urbervilles*, with sweet gentle victimized Tess, and the two male protagonists, one of whom is a cad, the other a prig. I give you *Anna Karenina* and *Madame Bovary*, just to do a little culture-hopping; and while we're at it, we might mention that Captain Ahab, although a forceful literary creation, is hardly anybody's idea of an acceptable role model. Please note that all these characters and novels were the creations of men, not women; but nobody, to my knowledge, has accused these male authors of being mean to men, although they've been accused of all sorts of other things. Possibly the principle involved is the same one involved in the telling of ethnic jokes: it's all right within the group, but coming from the outside it's racism, though the joke may be exactly the same. If a man depicts a male character unfavourably, it's The Human Condition; if a woman does it, she's being mean to men. I think you can to a certain extent reverse this and apply it to women's reactions to books by women. I, for instance, was expecting to be denounced by at least a few feminists for having written my characters Elizabeth and Auntie Muriel in *Life Before Man*, both of whom would be less than desirable as roommates. But not a bit of it. By the time the book appeared, even feminist critics had tired somewhat of their own expectations; they no longer required all female protagonists to be warm but tough, wise and experienced but sensitive and open, competent, earth-motherly and passionate but chock full of dignity and integrity; they were willing to admit that women too might have blemishes, and that universal sisterhood, though desirable, had not yet been fully instituted upon this earth. Nevertheless, women have traditionally been harder on women's image issues in connection with books by women than men have. Maybe it's time to do away with judgement by role-model and bring back The Human Condition, this time acknowledging that there may in fact be more than one of them.

Incidentally, you could make a case—if you wanted to—for concluding that women authors have historically been easier on men in their books than male authors have. Nowhere in major English novels by women do we find anything approaching that fallen angel and monster of depravity, Mister Kurtz, of *Heart of Darkness* fame; about the closest you could come, I think, would be the infamous Simon Legree (but I said *major* novels). The norm is more likely to range between Heathcliff and Mr Darcy, both of them flawed but sympathetically depicted; or, to invoke the greatest single English novel of the nineteenth century, George Eliot's *Middlemarch*, between dried-up envious Mr Casaubon and idealistic but misguided Dr Lydgate. The wonder of this book is that George Eliot can make us understand not only how awful it is to be married to Mr Casaubon, but how awful it is to *be* Mr Casaubon. This seems to me a worthy model to emulate. George Orwell said that every man's life viewed from within is a failure. If I said it, would it be sexist?

The Victorians, of course, had certain advantages that we lack. For one thing, they were not as self-conscious about the kind of thing we're discussing this evening as we have been forced to become. Though under constant pressure from the Mr and Mrs Grundies of their world never to write a line that might bring a blush to the cheek of a maiden of eighteen, which would in fact give you quite a lot of latitude today, they were not hesitant about depicting evil and calling it evil, or parading in front of their readers whole menageries of comic and grotesque figures, without worrying that such portraits might be interpreted as a slur upon one sex or the other. Female Victorian novelists had a couple of other advantages. Sex was out, so if they were creating a male character they could get away without trying to depict what sex felt like from a male point of view. Not only that, novels were assumed to be female-oriented, which meant that it took them a while to be viewed as a serious art form. Some of the first English novels were by women, the readership was preponderantly female, and even male novelists slanted their work accordingly. There are of course lots of exceptions, but on the whole we can say that the novel for almost two centuries had a decidedly female bias, which may account for the fact that many more male writers depicted female characters as central protagonists than the other way around. The advantage to the female novelist (as opposed to the Walter Scott romancer) was obvious. If novels were aimed at women, women had inside information.

The novel as a form has changed and expanded a good deal since then. Still, one of the questions people have been asking me most frequently is, "Do you write women's novels?" You have to watch this question, since, like many other questions, its meaning varies according to who's asking it and of whom. "Women's novels" can mean pop *genre* novels, such as the kind with nurses and doctors on the covers or the kind with rolling-eyed heroines in period costumes and windblown hair in front of gothic castles or Southern mansions or other locales where villainy may threaten and Heathcliff is still lurking around in the Spanish moss. Or it may mean novels for whom the main audience is assumed to be women, which would take in quite a lot, since the main audience for novels of all kinds, with the exception of Louis L'amour western romances and certain kinds of porn, is also women. Or it can mean feminist propaganda novels. Or it can mean novels depicting male-female relationships, which again covers quite a lot of ground. Is *War and Peace* a women's novel? Is *Gone With The Wind*, even though it's got a war in it? Is *Middlemarch*, even though it's got The Human Condition in it? Could it be that women aren't afraid to be caught reading books that might be considered "men's novels," whereas men still think something they need will fall off them if they look too hard at certain supposedly malevolent combinations of words put together by women? Judging from my recent walking to and fro in the earth and going up and down in bookstores for the purpose of signing my name on a lot of fly-leafs, I can tell you that this attitude is on the fade. More and more men are willing to stand in the line and *be seen*; fewer and fewer of them say, "It's for my wife's birthday."

But I almost put the boots to my old friend and cohort, the redoubtable Pierre Berton, when he asked me on television why all the men in my recent book *Bodily Harm* were wimps. Displaying the celebrated female compassion, not to be confused with feeble-mindedness, I merely dribbled aimlessly for a few minutes. "Pierre," I should have said, "who do you think is likely to have had more experience of men in sexual relationships: you, or me?" This is not quite so mean as it sounds, and there's even something to it. Women as people have a relatively large pool of experiences from which to draw. They have their own experiences with men, of course, but they also have their friends', since, yes, girls do discuss men more than men — beyond the dirty anecdote syndrome — discuss women.

Women are willing to talk about their weaknesses and fears to other women; men are not willing to talk about theirs to men, since it's still a dog-eat-dog world out there for them and no man wants to reveal his underbelly to a pack of fang-toothed potential rivals. If men are going to talk about their problems with women to anybody, it's usually either to a shrink or—guess what? to another woman. In both reading and writing, women are likely to know more about how men actually behave with women than men are; so that what a man finds a slur on his self-image, a woman may find merely realistic or indeed unduly soft.

But to go back to Pierre Berton's assertion. I thought quite carefully about my male characters in *Bodily Harm*. There are three of them with whom the heroine actually sleeps, and the fourth main male character with whom she doesn't. A female novelist and critic noted that there is one good man in the book and no good women, and she's quite right. The other men are not "bad"—in fact they are quite nice and attractive as male characters in literature go, a sight better than Mr Kurtz and Iago—but the *good* man is *black*, which is perhaps why the "mean-to-menners" overlooked him. When playing the role-model game, you have to read carefully; otherwise you may be caught in an embarrassing position, like that one.

Now, back to the practical concerns of New Grub Street. Let us suppose that I am writing a novel. First: how many points of view will this novel have? If it has only one point of view, will it be that of a man, a woman or a seagull? Let us suppose that my novel will have one point of view and that the eyes through which we see the world of the novel unfolding will be those of a woman. Immediately it follows that the perceptions of all male characters in the book will have to pass through the perceiving apparatus of this central character. Nor will the central character necessarily be accurate or just. It also follows that all the other characters will be, of necessity, secondary. If I'm skilful I will be able to bounce another set of perceptions off those of the central character, through dialogue and between-the-lines innuendo, but there will be a strong bias toward A as truth-teller and we will never get to hear what Characters B and C really think when they're by themselves, urinating outdoors perhaps or doing other male things. However, the picture changes if I use a multiple point of view. Now I can have Characters B and C think for themselves, and what they think won't always be what Character A thinks of *them*. If I like, I can add in yet another point of view, that of the omniscient author (who is of course not "me," the same me that had bran muffins for breakfast this morning and is right now giving this speech) but yet another voice within the novel. The omniscient author can claim to know things about the characters that even they don't know, thus letting the reader know these things as well.

The next thing I have to decide is what tone I'm taking, what mode I'm writing in. A careful study of *Wuthering Heights* will reveal that Heathcliff is never to be observed picking his nose, or indeed even blowing it, and you can search through Walter Scott in vain for any mention of bathrooms. Leopold Bloom on the other hand is preoccupied with the mundane wants of the body on almost every page, and we find him sympathetic, yes, and comic and also pathetic, but he is not exactly love's young dream. Leopold Bloom climbing in through Cathy's window would probably slip. Which is the more accurate portrayal of Man with a capital M? Or, like Walter Mitty, does each man contain within him both an ordinary, limited and trivial self and a heroic concept, and if so, which should we be writing about? I carry no brief for either, except to remark that serious novelists in the twentieth century usually opt for Leopold, and poor Heathcliff has been relegated to the Gothic romance. If a given serious novelist of the twentieth century is female, she too will probably go for Leopold, with all his habits, daydreams and wants. This doesn't mean she hates men; merely that she's interested in what they look like without the cloak.

All right. Suppose I've chosen to have in my novel at least one male character as a narrator or protagonist (not necessarily the same thing). I do not want to make my male character unnaturally evil, like Mr Hyde; instead I'm trying for Dr Jekyll, an essentially good man with certain flaws. That's a problem right there; because, as Stevenson knew, evil is a lot easier to write about and make interesting than goodness. What, these days, is a believable notion of a good man? Let us suppose that I'm talking about a man who is merely unbad; that is, one who obeys the major laws, pays his bills, helps with the dishes, doesn't beat up his wife or molest his kids, and so forth. Let's suppose that I want him to have some actual good qualities, good in the active, positive sense. What is he to do? And how can I make him—unlike Sir Charles Grandison—interesting in a novel?

This I suspect is the point at which the concerns of the novelist coincide with those of society. Once upon a time, when we defined people—much more than we do now—by how far they lived up or failed to live up to certain pre-defined sexual role models, it was a lot easier to tell what was meant by "a good man" or "a good woman." "A good woman" was one that fulfilled our notions of what a woman should be and how she should behave. Likewise "a good man." There were certain concepts about what constituted manliness and how you got it—most authorities agreed that you weren't just born with it, you somehow had to earn, acquire or be initiated into it; acts of courage and heroism counted for something, ability to endure pain without flinching, or drink a lot without passing out, or whatever. In any case there were rules, and you could cross a line that separated the men from the boys.

It's true that the male sexual role model had a lot of drawbacks, even for men—not everybody could be Superman, many were stuck with Clark Kent—but there were certain positive and, at that time, useful features. What have we replaced this package with? We know that women have been in a state of upheaval and ferment for some time now, and movement generates energy; many things can be said by women now that were once not possible, many things can be thought that were once unthinkable. But what are we offering men? Their territory, though still large, is shrinking. The confusion and desperation and anger and conflicts that we find in male characters in novels don't exist only in novels. They're out there in the real world. "Be a person, my son," doesn't yet have the same ring to it as "Be a man," though it is indeed a worthy goal. The novelist *qua* novelist, as opposed to the utopian romancer, takes *what is there* as a point of departure. What is there, when we're talking about men, is a state of change, new attitudes overlapping with old ones, no simple rules any more. Some exciting form of life may emerge from all this.

Meanwhile, I think women have to take the concerns of men as seriously as they expect men to take theirs, both as novelists and as inhabitants of this earth. One encounters, too often, the attitude that only the pain felt by persons of the female sex is real pain, that only female fears are real fears. That for me is the equivalent of the notion that only working-class people are real, that middle-class people are not, and so forth. Of course there's a distinction between earned pain and mere childish self-pity, and yes, women's fear of being killed by men is grounded in authenticity, not to mention statistics, to a greater extent than men's fear of being laughed at. Damage to one's self-image is not quite the same as damage to one's neck, though not to be underestimated: men have been known to murder and kill themselves because of it.

I'm not advocating a return to door-mat status for women, or even to the arrangement whereby women prop up and nurture and stroke and feed the egos of men without having men do at least some of the same for them. To understand is not necessarily to condone; and it could be pointed out that women have been "understanding" men for centuries, partly because it was necessary for survival. If the other fellow has the heavy artillery, it's best to be able to anticipate his probable moves. Women, like guerrilla fighters, developed infiltration rather than frontal attack as their favoured strategy. But "understanding" as a manipulative tool—which is really a form of contempt for the thing understood—isn't the kind I would like to see. However, some women are not in the mood to dish out any more understanding, of any kind; they're feeling a lot like René Lévesque: the time for that is over, they want power instead. But one cannot deprive any part of humanity of the definition "human" without grievous risk to one's own soul. And for women to define themselves as powerless and men as all-powerful is to fall into an ancient trap, to shirk responsibility as well as to warp reality. The opposite also is true; to depict a world in which women are already equal to men, in power, opportunities and freedom of movement, is a similar abdication.

I know I haven't given any specific directions for writing the male character; how can I? They're all different, remember. All I've given are a few warnings, an indication of what you're up against from the real world and from critics. But just because it's difficult is no reason not to try.

When I was young and reading a lot of comic books and fairy tales, I used to wish for two things: the cloak of invisibility, so I could follow people around and listen to what they were saying when I wasn't there, and the ability to teleport my mind into somebody else's mind, still retaining my own perceptions and memory. You can see that I was cut out to be a novelist, because these are the two fantasies novelists act out every time they write a page. Throwing your mind is easier to do if you're throwing it into a character who has a few things in common with you,

which may be why I've written more pages from a female
character's point of view than from a male's. But male
characters are more of a challenge, and now that I'm
middle-aged and less lazy I'll undoubtedly try a few more
of them. If writing novels—and reading them—have any
redeeming social value, it's probably that they force you
to imagine what it's like to be somebody else.

Which, increasingly, is something we all need to know.

Acknowledgements

Index

Acknowledgements

We would like to thank the following for their kind permission to reprint the work contained in this volume:

1. Some Sun for this Winter. Review of *Winter Sun* by Margaret Avison. *Acta Victoriana*, 85 (Jan. 1961), pp. 18-19. Reprinted by permission of the publisher.
2. Narcissus: Double Entendre. Review of *Alphabet*, No. 1 and *Mad Shadows* by Marie-Claire Blais. *Acta Victoriana*, 83, (Feb. 1961), pp. 14-16. Reprinted by permission of the publisher.
3. Apocalyptic Squawk from a Splendid Auk. Review of *The Cruising Auk* by George Johnston. *Acta Victoriana*, 84, no. 1 (Dec. 1959), pp. 25-26. Reprinted by permission of the publisher.
4. Kangaroo and Beaver. Review of *Tradition in Exile* by J. P. Matthews. *Alphabet*, No. 5 (Dec. 1962), pp. 78-79. Reprinted by permission of the publisher.
5. F. D. Reeve. Review of *Aleksandr Blok: Between Image and Idea* by F. D. Reeve. *Alphabet*, No. 6 (June 1963), pp. 70-71. Reprinted by permission of the publisher.
6. Superwoman Drawn and Quartered: The Early Forms of *She*. *Alphabet*, No. 10 (July 1965), pp. 65-82. Reprinted by permission of the publisher.
7. Four Poets from Canada. Review of *Phrases from Orpheus* by D. G. Jones; *The Absolute Smile* by George Jonas; *An Idiot Joy* by Eli Mandel; and *North of Summer* and *Wild Grape Wine* by Al Purdy. *Poetry*, 114, No. 3 (June 1969), pp. 202-207. Copyright 1969 by The Modern Poetry Association. Reprinted by permission of the Editor of *Poetry*.
8. Some Old, Some *New*, Some Boring, Some *Blew*, and Some Picture Books. *Alphabet*, No. 17 (Dec. 1966), pp. 61-64. Reprinted by permission of the publisher.
9. MacEwen's Muse. *Canadian Literature*, No. 45 (Summer 1970), pp. 24-32. Reprinted by permission of the publisher.
10. The Messianic Stance. Review of *West Coast Seen*, ed. Jim Brown and David Phillips. *Canadian Literature*, No. 47 (Winter 1971), pp. 75-77. Reprinted by permission of the publisher.
11. Nationalism, Limbo and the Canadian Club. *Saturday Night*, 86, (Jan. 1971), pp. 75-77. Reprinted by permission of the publisher.

12. Eleven Years of *Alphabet. Canadian Literature*, No. 49 (Summer 1971), pp. 60-64. Reprinted by permission of the publisher.
13. Love is Ambiguous...Sex Is a Bully. Review article of *Love in a Burning Building* by A. W. Purdy. *Canadian Literature*, No. 49 (Summer 1971), pp. 71-75. Reprinted by permission of the publisher.
14. Travels Back. *Maclean's*, 86 (Jan. 1973), pp. 28, 31, 48. Reprinted by permission of the author.
15. How Do I Get Out of Here: The Poetry of John Newlove. *Open Letter*, 2nd Series, No. 4 (Spring 1973), pp. 59-70. Reprinted by permission of the publisher.
16. Mathews and Misrepresentation. *This Magazine*, 7, No. 1 (May-June 1973), pp. 29-33. Reprinted by permission of the publisher.
17. Reaney Collected. *Canadian Literature*, No. 57 (Summer 1973), pp. 113-17. Reprinted by permission of the publisher.
18. Diving into the Wreck. Review of *Poems 1971-1972* by Adrienne Rich. *New York Times Book Review*, 30 December 1973, pp. 1-2. © 1973 by The New York Times Company. Reprinted by permission.
19. Review of *Blown Figures* by Audrey Thomas. *New York Times Book Review*, 1 February 1976. © 1976 by The New York Times Company. Reprinted by permission.
20. Review of *Half-Lives* by Erica Jong. *Parnassus: Poetry in Review*, 2, No. 2 (Spring/Summer 1974), pp. 98-104. Reprinted by permission of the publisher.
21. What's So Funny? Notes on Canadian Humour. *This Magazine*, 8, No. 3 (Aug.-Sept. 1974), pp. 24-27. Reprinted by permission of the publisher.
22. Paradoxes and Dilemmas: The Woman as Writer. From *Women in the Canadian Mosaic*, ed. Gwen Matheson (Toronto: Peter Martin Associates Limited, 1976), pp. 256-73. Reprinted by permission of the publisher.
23. Review of *Poems, Selected and New* by Adrienne Rich. *The Globe and Mail*, 6 December 1975, p. 35. Reprinted by permission of the author.
24. Review of *Flying* by Kate Millett. *The Globe and Mail*, 27 July 1974, p. 30. Reprinted by permission of the author.
25. The Curse of Eve—Or, What I Learned in School. From *Women on Women*, ed. Ann B. Shteir. (Toronto: York University, Gerstein Lecture Series, 1978), pp. 13-26. Reprinted by permission of York University.

26. Canadian Monsters: Some Aspects of the Supernatural in Canadian Fiction. From *The Canadian Imagination: Dimensions of a Literary Culture*, ed. David Staines. (Cambridge and London: Harvard University Press, 1977), pp. 97-122. Copyright ©1977 by the President and Fellows of Harvard College. Reprinted by permission of the publisher.

27. Review of *Of Woman Born: Motherhood as Experience and Institution* by Adrienne Rich. *The Globe and Mail*, 11 November 1976, p. 41. Reprinted by permission of the author.

28. Introduction to *St. Lawrence Blues* by Marie-Claire Blais. (Toronto: Bantam Books, 1976), pp. vii-xvi. Reprinted by permission of the author.

29. Review of *Ten Green Bottles* and *Ladies & Escorts* by Audrey Thomas. *The Globe and Mail*, 16 April 1977, p. 25. Reprinted by permission of the author.

30. Review of *Woman on the Edge of Time* and *Living in the Open* by Marge Piercy. *The Nation*, 4 December 1976, pp. 601-2. Copyright 1976 *The Nation* Magazine. Reprinted by permission of The Nation Associates, Inc.

31. Review of *A Harvest Yet To Reap: A History of Prairie Women*, ed. Linda Rasmussen and others. *Books in Canada*, 6, No. 2 (Feb. 1977), pp. 9-10. Reprinted by permisssion of the author.

32. Review of *Anne Sexton: A Self-Portrait in Letters. New York Times Book Review*, 6 November 1977, p. 15. ©1977 by The New York Times Company. Reprinted by permission.

33. Review of *The Wars* by Timothy Findley. *The Financial Post*, 12 November 1977, p. 6. Reprinted by permission.

34. Diary Down Under, published as "Atwood Among the Ozzies." *Saturday Night*, 93, No. 5 (June 1978), pp. 45-47, 49-51. Reprinted by permission of the publisher.

35. Last Testaments. Reviews of *A Stone Diary* by Pat Lowther and *Stilt Jack* by John Thompson. *Parnassus: Poetry in Review*, (Spring/Summer), 1978, pp. 192-96. Reprinted by permission of the publisher.

36. Review of *Silences* by Tillie Olsen. *New York Times Book Review*, 30 July 1978, pp. 1, 27. ©1978 by The New York Times Company. Reprinted by permission.

37. Review of *Johnny Panic and the Bible of Dreams* by Sylvia Plath. *New York Times Book Review*, 28 January 1979, pp. 10, 31. ©1979 by The New York Times Company. Reprinted by permission.

38. Valgardsonland. Review of *Red Dust* by W. D. Valgardson. *Essays on Canadian Writing*, No. 16 (Winter 1979-80), pp. 187-190. Reprinted by permission of the publisher.
39. Review of *Loon Lake* by E. L. Doctorow. *The Washington Post Book World*, 28 Sept. 1980, pp. 1-2, 10. ©*The Washington Post Book World*. Reprinted by permission.
40. Witches. An address delivered upon receiving the Radcliffe Alumnae Medal, Spring 1980. Reprinted in *Radcliffe Quarterly*, Vol. 66, No. 3 (Sept. 1980), pp. 4-6. © 1980 Radcliffe College. Reprinted with permission of the *Radcliffe Quarterly*.
41. An End To Audience? An address delivered in the Dorothy J. Killam Lecture Series, Dalhousie University, 8 October 1980. Reprinted in *Dalhousie Review*, Vol. 60, No. 3 (Autumn 1980), pp. 415-433. Reprinted by permission of the publisher.
42. Review of *Midnight Birds: Stories of Contemporary Black Women Writers*, ed. Mary Helen Washington. *Harvard Educational Review*, 51, No. 1 (February 1981), pp. 221-23. Reprinted by permission of the publisher.
43. Review of *July's People* by Nadine Gordimer. *The Chicago Sun-Times Book Week*, 31 May 1981, p. 26. © *Chicago Sun-Times*, 1981. Reprinted by permission.
44. Review of *Falling in Place* by Ann Beattie. *The Washington Post Book World*, 25 May 1980, pp. 1, 9. ©The Washington Post. Reprinted by permission.
45. Introduction to the Virago Modern Classic Edition of *The Edible Woman*, 1981. Reprinted by permission of the publisher, Virago Press, London, England.
46. Canadian-American Relations: Surviving the Eighties. An address delivered to The Harvard Consortium in Inter-American Relations, Fall 1981. Reprinted by permission of the author.
47. An address delivered during a world meeting of Amnesty International in Toronto, Fall 1981.
48. Northrop Frye Observed. Previously unpublished.
49. Review of *Poems Twice Told* by Jay Macpherson. *Books in Canada*, Vol. 11, No. 4 (April 1982), pp. 14-15. Reprinted by permission of the author.
50. Writing the Male Character. A somewhat different version of this paper was delivered as a Hagey Lecture at Waterloo University, February 1982. This version printed in *This Magazine*, Vol. 16, No. 4 (Sept. 1982), pp. 4-10. Reprinted by permission of the publisher.

Index

Absolute Smile, The 57f
Achebe, Chinua 359
Acorn, Milton 65, 141, 176, 309
Acta Victoriana 19
Allan Quatermain 36, 50ff, 52
Alger, Horatio 142f
Alphabet 20, 24f, 90-96, 143
Anatomy of Criticism 94, 399
Anna Karenina 421
Aquin, Hubert 136
As For Me and My House 132
*At The Edge of the Chopping
    There Are No Secrets* 310
Atwood, Jess 301
Austen, Jane 178, 218f, 225,
    260, 377f
Avison, Margaret 21ff, 65,
    86, 142
Ayesha; or The Return of She 53f
Aylward, David 66

Baird, Irene 147
Bambera, Toni Cade 359
Beattie, Ann 366ff
Beckett, Samuel 381
Belford, Ken 81
Bell, Alexander Graham 383
Bell Jar, The 318
Bellamy, Edward 274
Belyi, Andrei 34
Berryman, John 311
Berton, Pierre 373f, 424f
Best of Leacock, The 185
Bethune, Norman 294
Bible, The 156, 354, 410
Bird in the House, A 176
Birney, Earle 136
Bissett, Bill 64f, 81, 92, 140

Black and Secret Man 59
Black Night Window 115
Blais, Marie-Claire 19, 25,
    259-67
Blake, William 159, 232-36,
    249, 408, 410, 417
Blasted Pine, The 132, 183
Blew Ointment 65
Blithedale Romance 230
Blok, Aleksandr 33f
Bloodflowers 320f
Blown Figures 164ff, 271
Boatman, The 407-11
Bodily Harm 424f
Bowering, George 80, 136, 408
Boys' Own Paper 185
Brautigan, Richard 301
Brave New World 143
Breakfast for Barbarians, A 69-77
Brontë, Charlotte 225
Brontë, Emily 225f, 347
Brontë sisters, the 194, 225
Brown, Jim 79, 81
*Brown Waters and Other
    Sketches* 232-36
Browning, Elizabeth Barrett
    225
Buckler, Ernest 133, 136
Burroughs, Edgar Rice 36
Butler, Samuel 54
Butterfly Plague, The 291
Byron, Lord 86, 98, 200, 225,
    377

Call My People Home 141
Callaghan, Barry 131
Callaghan, Morley 146
Canada First 79

Canada In The World Today 378f
Canadian Forum 86, 404
Canterbury Tales, The 220
Carrier, Roch 136, 260
Carter, Dyson 147
Cather, Willa 314
Cave, The 115
Chaucer, Geoffrey 143, 177f,
    340
Chilly Scenes of Winter 366
Churchill, Sir Winston 85,
    95, 376
Circuit 132
Civil Elegies 140
Clarissa 420
Cocksure 132, 183, 185
Cohen, Leonard 136, 200
Cohen, Nathan 291
Coleridge, Samuel Taylor 50,
    159, 215, 401, 411
Collected Poems 141
Consider Her Ways 274
Copperfield 64f
Coupey, Pierre 82
Creeley, Robert 299
Cruising Auk, The 27ff
Crystal Age, A 36, 274
Culture of Narcissism, The 367
Curnoe, Greg 94f

Dali, Salvador 172f
*Damned Whores and God's
    Police* 306
*Dance of Death in London
    Ontario, The* 152
Darwin, Charles 415
Davey, Frank 408
Davies, Rebecca Harding 315
Davies, Robertson 232, 240f,
    246-49, 295

Dawn 42-46, 49f, 52
de Beauvoir, Simone 370
Defoe, Daniel 419
Delta 86
Devaux, Alexis 359ff
Dewdney, Keewatin 66
Dickens, Charles 53, 143, 178,
    223, 330, 340, 419, 421
Dickinson, Emily 200, 225, 278
    401
Disney, Walt 229, 377
Distortions 366
Diviners, The 226, 353
Diving Into the Wreck 160-63,
    206
Doctorow, E. L. 325-28
Donne, John 342
Dostoevsky, Feodor 333, 347
Double Hook, The 234f
Drew, Wayland 249ff
Ducharme, Réjean 260
Dudek, Louis 31
Dunstan, Don 299

Eddy, Nelson 388f
Edible Woman, The 369f
Egoist, The 421
Eliot, George 94, 178, 194, 218,
    225, 333, 347, 377, 422
Eliot, T. S. 28, 90, 220, 399
Engel, Marian 218
Englishness of English Art, The
    143
Execution, 32, 294

Fabre, Henri 415
Faerie Queene, The 37
Falling in Place 366ff
Far Point, The 63f
Fatherless Sons 147

Faulkner, William 179, 347, 419
Fear of Flying 222
Ferguson, Max 132
Ferron, Jacques 136, 260
Fiddlehead 86
Fiedler, Leslie 418
Fielding, Henry 220
Fifth Business 132
Findley, Timothy 12, 290-95
Fitzgerald, F. Scott 142
Flying 210-14
*For Coloured Girls Who Have
    Considered Suicide When the
    Rainbow is Enuf* 297
Franklin, Benjamin 142
Freud, Sigmund 68, 195
Friedan, Betty 370
Fruits & Vegetables 167ff
Frum, Barbara 13
Frye, Northrop 19, 93, 136, 152
    156, 305, 398-406
Fulford, Robert 83f, 89
Fuseli Poems 59

Games People Play 58
Garber, Lawrence 132, 230
Garneau, St Denys 136
Gaskell, Elizabeth 226
Germinal 418
Glassco, John 137
Globe and Mail, The 13, 292
God Is Not a Fish Inspector 320
Godfrey, David 140
Golden Bowl, The 142
Gone With The Wind 424
Gordimer, Nadine 363ff
Gordon, Walter 387
Gotlieb, Phyllis 65
Grant, George 136, 146
Grapes of Wrath, The 327

Graves, Robert 45, 68, 224, 294
    401
Great Gatsby, The 142, 327
Greene, Graham 296f
grOnk 65f
Grove, Frederick Philip 142
Gutenberg Galaxy, The 94

Haggard, Rider 35-54, 75, 220
Half-Lives 167-74
Haliburton, Thomas 140f, 146
Hamlet 421
Hard Times 132
Hardy, Thomas 314, 377
*Harvard Educational Review,
    The* 358
Harvest Yet to Reap, A 283-86
Hawthorne, Nathaniel 53
Heart of Darkness 422
Hébert, Ann 136
Heine, Heinrich 181
Hemingway, Ernest 36
Hiebert, Paul 180, 187f
Hine, Daryl 20, 24
Hitler, Adolph 85, 158, 414
Hodges, Frenchy 359
Homemakers' Magazine 281
Honeyman Festival, The 218
Hopkins, Gerard Manley 314
Huckleberry Finn 179
Hudson, W. H. 36, 274
Hulcoop, John 79f
Huxley, Aldous 143
Hyphid 64

Incomparable Atuk, The 132,
    180, 183f
Innes, Harold 405
Intercourse 64
Is It the Sun, Philibert? 136
Ivanhoe 51

Jack, Donald 292
James, Henry 26, 142, 421
Jaws 351
Jess 51ff
Johnny Panic and the Bible of Dreams 316-319
Johnson, Samuel 206f
Johnston, George 27ff
Jonas, George 57f, 142
Jones, D. G. 55ff, 59, 136
Jones, Gayle 359, 361
Jong, Erica 167-74, 222
Joshua Doane 147
Journals of Susanna Moodie, The 20
Journeyings and the Return 66
Joyce, James 337, 340
Jude the Obscure 314
July's People 363ff
Julian the Magician 74, 241, 245
Jung, Carl 68, 410
Jungic, Zoran 79f, 82

Kangaroo 304
Kearns, Lionel 80
Keats, John 225, 330, 372, 377
Kennedy, John F. 383
Kildeer, The 157
King of Egypt, King of Dreams 245
King, William Lyon Mackenzie 231f, 252, 389
Kinnell, Galway 297f
Kipling, Rudyard 29, 35f, 64
Klein, A. M. 86, 176, 405
Knight, Jackson 410
Kroetsch, Robert 222

Ladies and Escorts 268-71
Lady Oracle 14

Lampman, Archibald 31, 140, 146
Lane, Patrick 81
LaRue, Danny 213
Lasch, Christopher 367
Last of the Crazy People, The 291
Laughing Stalks 132
Laurence, Margaret 136, 176, 226
Lawrence, D. H. 222, 304
Layton, Irving 19, 24, 31, 64, 136, 200, 231
Leacock, Stephen 140, 146, 180 186ff
Leaves of Grass 208f
Lee, Dennis 36, 140
Lee, Hope Arnott 24
Le Guin, Ursula 365
Le Pan, Douglas 136
Lies 115
Life 85
Life Before Man 422
Life In The Iron Mills 315
Ligeia 53
Lilith 36
Lincoln, Abraham 391
Literary Lapses 186
Livesay, Dorothy 135, 140, 146
Living in the Open 272-78
Longfellow, Henry Wadsworth 82
Looking Backward 274
Loon Lake 325-28
Love and Death in the American Novel 143, 418
Love in a Burning Building 97-102
Lowry, Malcolm 142
Lowther, Pat 82, 307ff

MacArthur, Peter 147
Macbeth 421
MacCaig, Norman 304
Macdonald, George 36
MacEwen, Gwendolyn 58, 67-78, 132, 136, 159, 240-46
Mackenzie, William Lyon 85
MacLennan, Hugh 141, 146
MacPhail, Agnes 228
Macpherson, Jay 24, 86, 407-11
Mad Shadows (La Belle Bête) 25f, 260
Madame Bovary 421
Mahaptra, Jayanta 303f
Maltese Cross Movement, The 66
Mandel, Eli 58ff, 86, 136
Mango Tree, The 302
Mansfield, Katherine 315
Manticore, The 232, 246-49
Manuscripts of Pauline Archange, The 259
Marlatt, Daphne 80, 408
Marquez, Gabriel Garcia 347
Marriott, Anne 140, 146
Mather, Cotton 332, 383
Mathews, Robin 129-50
Matthews, J. P. 30ff
Mayne, Seymour 81
McCarthy, Joseph 85
McClelland, Jack 111, 292, 320
McClung Nellie 135, 283, 285
McDougall, Colin 132, 294
McIntyre, James 92
McKinnon, Barry 81
McLuhan, Marshall 59, 66, 405
Medvedev, Pavel N. 34
Melville, Herman 53, 314, 340, 347, 402, 417
Meredith, George 53, 421
Middlemarch 422, 424

Midnight Birds 358-62
Mill, J. S. 13, 321
Miller, Henry 36, 222
Miller, Perry 391
Millett, Kate 210-14, 418
Milton, John 347, 399
Mitchell, W. O. 140, 146
Moby Dick 304f, 327, 340, 404
Modest Proposal, A 183
Moll Flanders 421
Montcalm, Louis Joseph Marquis de 85
Moore, Brian 142
More Poems for People 141
More, Thomas 275
Morris, William 274
Morrison, Toni 359, 362
Moving In Alone 115
Mrs Blood 164, 271
Ms Magazine 195
Munro, Alice 136, 226, 322
Murphy, Richard 298, 300, 305
Murray, John Middleton 315

National Dream, The 292
National Lampoon 188
Neruda, Pablo 309
New: American and Canadian Poetry 64
New York Times, The 292
New Yorker, The 317, 362
Newlove, John 64, 81, 114-28, 136
News from Nowhere 274
nichol, bp 66
Night-Blooming Cereus 157
Nihilist Spasm Band 92
Nin, Anais 153
Nobody Owns Th Earth 140
Noman 132, 241-47

Nonsense Novels 186
North of Summer 60f
Northern Blights 132
Nosferatu 410
Nowlan, Alden 64, 136, 290

O Canada 259
O'Connor, Flannery 179, 397
Of Woman Born 254-58
O'Hagan, Howard 235-38, 244
Olsen, Tillie 313-15
Olson, Sig 65
Ondaatje, Michael 142
Orwell, George 347, 396, 422
Owen, Wilfred 294
Ozick, Cynthia 195

Page, P. K. 96, 238ff, 244
Pamela 420
Parker, Gilbert 147
Pater, Walter 36
Peter, John 24
Peter Pan 276
Phillips, David 79, 81
Phrases from Orpheus 55
Pickering, Joseph 65
Picnic at Hanging Rock 303
Piercy, Marge 272-78
Pierre 53
Plath, Sylvia 200f, 226, 289,
    316-19
Playboy 64
Plink Savoir, The 144
Poe, Edgar Allen 36, 53, 200,
    225, 251
Poems 151
Poems, Selected and New 205-9
Poems Twice Told 407-11
Poetry 20
Pogo 121

Poor Richard's Almanac 142
Portrait of a Lady 421
Power Politics 20
Pratt, E. J. 86, 133, 136, 321, 405
Praz, Mario 36
Préfontaine, Yves 136
Princess Daisy 352
Prochaine Episode 136
Punch 176ff
Purdy, Al 60ff, 64, 97-102, 136,
    154
Pygmalion 178
Pynchon, Thomas 301

Queen's Quarterly 86
Quiller-Couch, Sir Arthur 197

Radcliffe, Ann 220
Ragtime 325f
Rankin, Jennifer 298
Reaney, James 20, 24f, 86, 90-
    95, 135f, 143, 151-59
Red Dust 320f, 323f
Red Heart, The 152f
Red Shoes, The 224, 226f
Reeve, F. D. 33f
Reid, Jamie 80
Rich, Adrienne 12, 160-63,
    205-9, 254-58, 311, 342
Richard Feverel 421
Richardson, John 137-40, 146
Richardson, Samuel 420f
Richler, Mordecai 84, 180,
    183-6
Riel, Louis 85, 294
Rising Fire, The 70, 77
Roberts, Charles G. D. 136
Romantic Agony, The 36
Roosevelt, F. D. 86
Roosevelt, Theodore 376

Ross, Sinclair 133, 136
Rossetti, Christina 200, 225
Ruskin, John 143

St Lawrence Blues (Un Joualonais, Sa Joualanie) 259-67
Sarah Binks 132, 180-83
Sartre, Jean-Paul 381
Saturday Night 83
Schroeder, Andreas 82
Scobie, Stephen 81
Scott, Duncan Campbell 140, 143
Scott, F. R. 135, 140, 176, 183, 232
Scott, Sir Walter 51, 404, 423, 426
Season in the Life of Emmanuel, A 259
Second Sex, The 143
Secrets and Surprises 366
Selah 68f, 72
Self-Portrait in Letters, A 287ff
Sentimental Journey, A 421
Separations 81
Service, Robert W. 29, 31, 232
Seton, E. T. 136
Sexton, Anne 226, 287ff
Sexual Politics 210, 213, 418
Shadow Maker, The 70, 73, 75ff
Shakespeare, William 98, 143, 178, 340, 377
Shange, Ntozake 359
Shaw, George Bernard 178
She 35-54
Shearer, Moira 224
Shelley, Percy Bysshe 98, 225, 377
Silences 313-15
Sir Charles Grandison 420f

Smith, A. J. M. 32, 183
Song of Myself 214
Songs My Mother Taught Me 164
Souster, Raymond 31, 86, 159
Spenser, Edmund 178
Stevenson, Robert Louis 35, 427
Stilt Jack 309-12
Stone Diary, A 308f
Story of O, The 185
Stowe, Harriet Beecher 226
Studhorse Man, The 222
Suit of Nettles, A 152
Sula 262
Sun and the Moon, The 157, 238-40
Sun is Axeman, The 55
Sunshine Sketches of a Little Town 132, 180, 186f
Surfacing 20, 105f
Survival 14, 19, 106, 129-50
Swift, Jonathan 183
Swinburne, Algernon 36

Tamarack Review 86
Tay John 235-38
Tell Me A Riddle 313
Ten Green Bottles 268-71
Tennyson, Alfred Lord 54, 177
Tess of the D'Urbervilles 421
Thackeray, William M. 178, 220
This Magazine 129, 140
Thomas, Audrey 164ff, 268-71
Thomas, Dylan 200f
Thompson, John 308-12
Thoreau, Henry David 391
Time Magazine 83, 184
Tish Magazine 79

T.Q. Now 79
Tolkien, J. R. R. 274
Tom Jones 421
Toronto Life 356
Toronto Star, The 84, 388
Tradition in Exile 32, 143
Traill, Catharine Parr 284
Tristram Shandy 153
Twain, Mark 178
Twelve Letters to a Small Town 152
Typescapes 66

University of Toronto Quarterly 381

Valgardson, W. D. 320-24
Van Stolk, Mary 257
Vanity Fair 368
Virginian, The 179
Vonnegut, Kurt 301

Wabeno Feast, The 249ff
Wacousta 137ff
Walker, Alice 359
Wallace, Joe 147
War and Peace 424
Warkentin, Germaine 91, 159
Wars, The 12, 290-95
Washington, Mary Ellen 358
Waste Land, The 399
Watson, Sheila 234f
Welcoming Disaster 408ff
West Coast Seen 79-82
West, Nathaniel 142
White Goddess, The 68, 224, 401
White, Patrick 299
White, Paulette Childress 359
Whitlam, Gough 302
Whitlam, Margaret 302

Whitman, Walt 214, 278
Who Has Seen the Wind 302
Why Shoot the Teacher 302
Wild Grape Wine 61f
Williams, Sherley Anne 359
Williams, William Carlos 347
Wilson, Edmund 259
Wind Our Enemy, The 141
Winter Sun 21ff
Wiseman, Adele 226
Wister, Owen 179
Witches' Head, The 46-54
Wodehouse, P. G. 143, 178
Wolfe, General James 85
Wolfe, Tom 301
Woodcock, George 20
Woolf, Virginia 314, 347
Woman on the Edge of Time 272-76
Words 79
Wordsworth, William 92, 159, 377, 411
Wuthering Heights 180f, 426
Wyndham, John 274

Yates, J. Michael 79
Yeats, W. B. 34
Yonnondio: From the Thirties 313

Zola, Emile 417
Zwicky, Fay 304

Margaret Atwood has earned international recognition as one of today's most gifted and important writers. Her works include five novels—among them *The Edible Woman, Surfacing,* and *Life Before Man*—eight books of poetry, a short-story collection, children's books, and *Survival,* a much-acclaimed study of Canadian literature. She has won the Canadian Governor-General's Award, the Radcliffe Alumnae Medal, and the Molson Prize, among others, and her books have been translated into fourteen languages.

She lives on a farm near Alliston, Ontario, with novelist Graeme Gibson and their daughter, Jess.